FAE
Taxation 3 (RoI)
2022–2023

Published in 2022 by
Chartered Accountants Ireland
Chartered Accountants House
47–49 Pearse Street
Dublin 2
www.charteredaccountants.ie

ISBN: 978-1-913975-28-9

Typeset by Deanta Global Publishing Services
Printed by eprint books limited, Dublin

Contents

Trading as a Sole Trader

Learning Objectives

By the end of this chapter you will be able to:

- Analyse the potential tax implications for a business trading as an unincorporated entity, with particular reference to the:
  - definition of a trade;
  - commencement rules;
  - optimum use of losses in the start-up years;
  - advantages and disadvantages of operating as a sole trader; and
  - cessation rules and terminal loss relief.
- Understand the restriction on tax reliefs for high-income individuals.

1.1 Life Cycle of a Business

A business will always have a life cycle. This cycle may last for many generations of owners, and in other cases may be significantly shorter. The typical life cycle of a business can be separated into the following phases:

- start-up;
- growth;
- maturity; and
- decline/sale/handover.

The challenges faced by the owners and management of a business will differ with each stage of the life cycle, as will the tax issues which can arise. The tax advice required by owners/management will therefore depend on where the business is in its life cycle. A business should be built on a sound foundation, so tax advice in the early stages will often be crucial to how the business manages its tax affairs.

A business can typically be operated through a limited liability company, i.e. an incorporated entity, or as a sole trade, i.e. an unincorporated entity. Sole traders are usually small business operations as often there is no particular commercial or tax benefit for them to operate as a limited company. As a sole trade grows and expands there are likely to be both commercial and tax reasons for the business to trade more successfully and efficiently as a limited company. The tax implications of operating under either structure must be considered separately. The decision to transfer an unincorporated business to a limited company, to incorporate, is dealt with in **Chapter 2**. In this chapter we focus on sole traders and the associated tax implications.

1.2 What is a "Trade"?

In most cases, Irish businesses operate either through limited liability companies or as sole traders. Sole trade businesses are typically small business operations, primarily because, as a trade grows and expands, the likelihood that a trade would be transferred to a limited company becomes more probable. This is generally for commercial reasons, and not just tax reasons. Often in the early years, however, there are no particular commercial or tax requirements to operate a trade through a limited company and, in such cases, traders will operate as sole traders. While this chapter focuses on the tax issues for sole traders only, students should be aware that the commentary in **Sections 1.3, 1.5** and **1.6** are equally applicable to companies.

The question "Does a trade exist?" may often arise. The answer can often impact significantly on the subsequent tax implications. You will have already addressed this in your earlier studies and should revise the key points. A brief outline of the issues to be considered is set out below.

Over the years, this 'trade' question has given rise to a significant body of case law. In general, the rate of income tax is much higher than, for example, the rate of capital gains tax (CGT). Consider the following questions:

- Is an isolated transaction that gives rise to a profit to the vendor a trade for tax purposes, or indeed liable to tax at all?
- Is the disposal of a refurbished house by a part-time builder liable to income tax or capital gains tax?

The Taxes Consolidation Act 1997 (TCA 1997) contains all relevant tax legislation in respect of income tax, corporation tax and CGT. Section 3(1) TCA 1997 describes a trade as including "every trade, manufacture, adventure or concern in the nature of a trade". It can often be difficult to establish if a particular activity constitutes trading, taking into account the above legislative definition of a trade. Guidance as to what constitutes a trade must also therefore be taken from case law. A trade will typically take on the generally accepted meaning. More specific and practical guidance can be found in the UK Royal Commission *Badges of Trade Rules*. The 'badges of trade' concept has been covered as part of your CA Proficiency 1 studies and students should be familiar with these trading criteria.

Key Issue

Students should revise the badges of trade rules. These rules can be critical in understanding whether or not a trade exists for tax purposes. In summary, the badges of trade factors to be taken into account in determining if a trade exists consist of the following:

- subject matter realised;
- length of the period of ownership;
- frequency of the number of transactions;
- supplementary work on or in conjunction with the property realised;
- circumstances giving rise to the realisation of property; and
- motive for the transaction.

Students will not be expected to know all relevant case law. A review of applicable case law could, however, assist your understanding of what a trade is for tax purposes.

If a taxpayer were to operate on the mistaken basis that a trade did not exist, the implications of such a position being challenged could lead to significant tax liabilities.

1.3   When does the Trade Commence?

The date on which a trade commences is a question of fact, being the set of circumstances applicable to that particular trade/activity. There is a significant body of case law in this area that can be used as the basis for establishing when a trade commences. For example, in the UK case *Birmingham and District Cattle By-Products Ltd v. IRC* (1919), it was held that the trade commenced when the company first received raw materials for processing. The activities undertaken by the company prior to receipt of its stock, in this case being a significant outlay in respect of machinery/infrastructure, was held not to constitute the commencement of a trade.

It is worth noting that sales do not have to have been made for a trade to have commenced. In certain cases, therefore, the date on which the trade commences is not always clear and will require consideration.

1.4   Commencement Rules: Basis of Assessment for Income Tax Purposes

The commencement rules will determine the income tax liability of profits in the first three years of a new trade. It is assumed that the student is familiar with the commencement rules, but in summary, they are as follows:

- **Year 1 (First Year)** In the first year of trading, the Case I profits liable to income tax will be those taken from the date of commencement to 31 December of that year.
- **Year 2 (Second Year)** In the second year of trading, the Case I profits liable to income tax will be computed by reference to the following criteria:
  - if there is a 12-month period of accounts ending in the second year, which is the only accounting period in that year, the profits liable to income tax will be the profits of that 12-month accounting period; **or**
  - if there is an accounting period ending in the second year of trading, and the period is **less** than 12 months and is the only accounting period ending in that second year, the profits liable to income tax will be for a 12-month period ending on that accounting date; **or**
  - if there are two or more accounting periods ending in the second year of trading, the profits liable to income tax will be for the 12-month period ending on the latest accounting date; **or**
  - where none of the above apply, the taxable accounting period in the second year of trading will be from 1 January to 31 December.
- **Year 3 (Third Year)** In the third year of trading, the profits liable to income tax will be the profits of the 12-month accounting period ending in that third year. The third-year profits liable to income tax may be reduced if a second-year "excess" arises. This excess is the amount of profits liable to income tax in the second year less the actual profits that arose. Put simply, actual profits are profits that arise between January and December.

Example 1.1

John Ryan commenced his sole trade printing business on 1 May 2021. He has prepared his first set of accounts up to 30 April 2022, being his first 12 months of trading.

John's taxable profit in his first year is €120,000 and he plans to change his accounting date to November, and confidently predicts profits of €200,000 in the short period ending 30 November 2022. Year 3 profits for the 12-month period up to 30 November 2023 are projected to be €220,000.

John's accountant has told him that his commencement profits liable to tax will be computed (using the projected figures provided) as follows:

Year 1 – 2021

  1 May 2021 to 31 December 2021: €120,000 × 8/12   €80,000

continued overleaf

Year 2 – 2022
There are two accounting period ends in 2022. The Year 2 rules state that, where there are two accounting periods ending in the year, the taxable profits will be based on the 12-month period ending on the later accounting period end.

	€
April 2022 y/e €120,000 × 5/12	50,000
1 May 2022 to 30 November 2022	200,000
Total profits liable to tax in 2022	250,000

Year 3 – 2023
The profits liable to income tax in the third year of commencement will be the profits arising in the 12-month period up to 30 November 2023, i.e. €220,000 from 1 December 2022 to 30 November 2023.

There is, however, provision that the third-year assessable profits can be reduced by the second-year excess. The second year excess is computed as follows:

	€	€
Profits assessed in Year 2 vs actual profit (Jan to Dec)		250,000
1 January 2022 to 30 April 2022	40,000	
1 May 2022 to 30 Nov 2022	200,000	
1 December 2022 to 31 December 2022: €220,000 × 1/12	18,333	258,333
Year 2 excess		N/a

As the actual profits in the second year are higher than the profits assessed, there is no second-year excess and therefore no adjustment. If the actual profits arising in 2022 were less than €250,000, then the excess would be deducted from the 2023 taxable profits in Year 3.

In the vast majority of cases a sole trader will not have a high expectation of profits in the early years of trading, the likelihood being that trading losses will be incurred. The commencement rules therefore compute the Case I losses arising from the trade. The critical issue is that, if the individual has any other income, the losses arising in the trade can be utilised to reduce the individual's total taxable income. This issue will be discussed in **Section 1.7**.

1.5   Pre-trading Expenditure

As mentioned above (**Section 1.3**) the actual date on which a trade commences is not always clear. The basis of assessment for the commencement rules also needs to be considered.

> **Key Issue**
> Students should ensure that they are familiar with all computational rules and, if required, be in a position to prepare a tax computation.

Expenditure incurred in the period prior to commencement may not always be considered deductible for tax purposes. Section 82 TCA 1997 considers the possible tax deductions for pre-trading expenditure incurred by a trader. Expenditure that is revenue in nature (i.e. not capital, such as buildings, plant, etc.) incurred within three years prior to commencement of trading may be deductible for tax purposes (despite the fact that the expenditure may not be reflected in the profit and loss account of the period).

For pre-trading expenditure relief to apply:

▣ the expense must be allowable as a deductible expense, and it would not be otherwise considered as not being deductible. It must also be related to that trade/activity; and

▣ the expense can only be set-off against the income of that trade or profession, i.e. it cannot be set-off against any other income of the trader.

Example 1.2

Carrying on from **Example 1.1**, John Ryan incurred the following costs before trading commenced on 1 May 2021:

▣ He spent €5,000 on a feasibility study carried out by a printing industry expert in March 2018.
▣ He spent €3,000 in total on attending a printing industry conference held every June in Killarney, which he attended in June 2018, 2019 and 2020.
▣ He spent €2,000 on a laptop in September 2019. Before trading commenced, he only used it for material in relation to his printing business. He still uses it.

In regard to these costs you advise:

▣ The feasibility study expense is not deductible – the expenditure was incurred more than three years before he started to trade.
▣ The conference costs are all allowable under the wholly and exclusively test.
▣ The cost of the laptop is not allowable as a Case I deduction as it is capital expenditure.
▣ He can, however, claim normal wear and tear allowances on this item of plant and machinery.

In summary, he can claim an additional €3,000 as a trading deduction for the period ended 30 April 2022, as well as additional capital allowances of €250.

1.6   Arriving at the Tax-adjusted Profit or Loss of the Trade

A company's financial statements are drawn up to show a true and fair view of its financial position. However, the results shown in the profit and loss account do not necessarily correspond to the amount assessable to corporation tax. This means that a process is required to prepare corporation tax computations from the financial statements, which takes the form of a number of 'add backs' and deductions as required under tax law. The 'profit before tax' figure in the financial statements is the starting point and is subject to adjustments, i.e. the add back and deductions, to arrive at the corporation tax liability.

1.6.1   Expenditure not Deductible for Income Tax Purposes

The following expenditure, while often included in the profit and loss for accounting purposes, is specifically not deductible for the purposes of the tax computation (i.e. it is added back):

▣ any expenses not incurred wholly and exclusively for the purposes of the trade;
▣ any expenses laid out for non-business use (e.g. for domestic or personal use);
▣ any drawings from the trade;
▣ capital expenditure (but capital allowances may be available on plant and equipment, etc.);
▣ entertainment expenditure;
▣ political donations;
▣ non-specific provisions in respect of bad debts;
▣ donations below a specific threshold amount;

- certain motor expenses (e.g. the cost of leasing a high-value passenger vehicle may be restricted for tax purposes);
- amounts otherwise to be considered as charges (e.g. certain interest or annual payments); and
- depreciation of assets.

The above expenditure must be identified and excluded when computing profits that are liable to tax for an accounting period. The sole trader will be required to make the required adjustments to the reported accounting net profit/loss for amounts not deductible for tax purposes.

Example 1.3: Non-deductible expenditure

In preparing his accounts for the period ended 30 April 2022, John Ryan advises you of the following:

- He claimed a deduction for €250 he gave to election campaign of a local politician.
- He has also claimed a deduction for the costs of a trip to Manchester with his son to see a Champions League game on the basis that it was only an add-on to the real reason for going – to look at a second-hand printing machine he wanted to buy. The total cost of the trip was €1,000.
- He made a provision for bad debts of €5,000 on the basis that "some customers are bound not to pay me". He also claimed a deduction for this.

You point out to him that he needs to adjust his profit for tax purposes as follows:

- The €250 in donations needs to be added back. Political donations are not allowable.
- John must isolate that costs of the trip to Manchester which are wholly and exclusively for the purposes of his printing trade and the cost of the trip which is not for the purposes of the trade must be added back.
- The bad debt provision is a general provision and needs to be added back.

If a sole trader's spouse or other member of their family work in the business, it is important that this is recognised formally, i.e. that they take a wage or salary from the business, which will ensure that the married persons standard rate band for income tax purposes can be maximised. However, the wage/salary payment must be for actual services rendered wholly and exclusively to the business and should be reasonable and commensurate to the duties performed. This is an area of particular interest to Revenue when undertaking tax audits (see Revenue's *Tax and Duty Manual*, Part 04-06-23). In the case of a married couple, opportunities to maximise the married persons standard rate band for income tax purposes should always be considered.

1.6.2 Revenue versus Capital

A sole trader is liable to income tax on the full amount of "profits or gains" in their trade or profession. Income tax, however, will not be assessed on the capital profits of a trader. Typically, an item is regarded as revenue in nature if it is an item of stock for resale, whereas capital items would be more permanent in nature and held for use in the trade (as opposed to being for immediate resale). In certain circumstances, however, it may be difficult to establish whether a receipt is to be regarded as capital or revenue.

A capital receipt of a trader may be taxable for CGT purposes, whereas a revenue receipt is subject to income tax as a trading receipt. The difference in tax rates between the two tax heads is significant (i.e. a CGT rate of 33% or 10% versus an income tax rate of up to 40% plus PRSI/USC).

The following issues are relevant to the revenue versus capital analysis:

- A conclusion has to be determined from the relevant circumstances of the case.
- A receipt that relates to an asset forming part of the capital business assets (e.g. sale of goodwill) of a business should, on general principles, be considered to be a capital receipt.
- A receipt that relates to a permanent capital asset used as a means of producing goods/services for resale (i.e. used to produce goods for sale) is considered a capital receipt.
- An asset acquired in the normal course of the trade and subsequently sold, or combined into goods, is most likely a revenue receipt.

■ Compensation payments received in respect of a trader's capital assets are considered as capital receipts.

■ Payments in respect of a trader's stock are revenue in nature.

Example 1.4

In preparing his accounts for the period ended 30 April 2022, John also advises you of the following:

■ In March 2022, he sold a second-hand machine that the business had been using for €10,000 and "put it through the P&L". He had bought it for €8,000 in June 2021, so he had included the €2,000 profit in the accounts.

■ He also sold three large rolls of paper for €5,000 each. He had bought the three of them for €10,000 in total.

■ He had meant to use them over the next two years or so, but got an offer he couldn't refuse and took the money. He had included the €5,000 profit in the accounts.

You point out to him that he needs to adjust his profit for tax purposes as follows:

■ The profit on the sale of the machine is liable to CGT, not income tax. As he bought and sold it within the same accounting period, neither depreciation nor capital allowance issues arise.

■ This is a "bulk" disposal of trading stock, so an income tax treatment is appropriate.

1.7   Case I Loss Relief for an Ongoing Sole Trade Business

Often a sole trader may be operating at a loss, for both accounting and tax purposes. This could either be due to a decline in market demand/conditions, or due to costs exceeding revenue in starting up or expanding the trade.

The key loss relief provisions for trading losses arising to a sole trader are set out below. These rules are covered in detail CA Proficiency 1.

Loss relief	Use	Claim or automatic?	Effect on tax liability
Section 381 TCA 1997	Set against statutory total income for year of loss.	Claim must be made to Revenue not later than two years after the end of the tax year in which the loss occurred.	Reduces current-year tax liability. 'All or nothing' claim – cannot make a partial claim. If income is too low, it could waste tax credits and/or only benefit at the lower tax rate.
Section 382 TCA 1997	Losses may be carried forward and set against future profits of same trade. Unrelieved trading charges are added to the loss to carry forward (section 390).	Automatic relief – no claim is necessary. Applies to losses remaining after a section 381 claim, or if no section 381 claim is made.	Only shelters future trading income, loss relief is delayed.
Section 385 TCA 1997	Terminal loss relief – carry back to the three preceding years prior to the last 12 months of trading; claim against latest period first and against trading income.	No time limit for the claim.	Only shelters past trading income and there may be a tax refund.

1.7.1 Current-year Loss Relief under Section 381 TCA 1997

Under section 381 TCA 1997, a Case I trading loss can be offset against a sole trader's other gross taxable income, or against income of his or her jointly assessed spouse in the tax year in which the loss arises.

Example 1.5

Kevin has Schedule E employment income (i.e. a salary) of €100,000, but he also conducts a trade as a sole trader. Kevin's sole trade business generated a loss of €20,000 for the tax year 2022. If Kevin makes a loss relief claim under section 381, the tax loss will have the effect of reducing his gross income liable to income tax as follows:

	€
Schedule E income	100,000
Section 381 loss relief claim	(20,000)
Taxable income after loss relief	80,000

On submission of the section 381 loss relief claim in Kevin's 2022 income tax return, a refund of tax that was deducted through PAYE may be generated (€20,000 × 40% = €8,000).

If a taxpayer chooses to claim relief under section 381 they cannot choose to use only part of the loss against part of their income. Instead, if a claim for relief is made, the full loss must, in so far as possible, be set off against all of the taxpayer's income. Equally, if that individual is jointly assessed they cannot choose to claim relief against only their own income and not against their spouse's/civil partner's income, i.e. the claim must be made against their joint income. Losses in excess of the individual's other income must first be offset against **trading income** of their spouse/civil partner, with any remaining excess offset against other income of their spouse/civil partner.

The taxpayer must make a claim for loss relief under section 381 not later than two years after the end of the year of assessment to which the claim relates. The claim for relief must be made on Form 11 or Form 12, as appropriate, by entering the amount of the loss to be set off against other income of the taxpayer or their assessable spouse.

Pre-trading expenses that are deductible under section 82(3) TCA 1997 (see **Section 1.5**) are not permitted to create or augment a claim for a loss under section 381.

Interaction with Capital Allowances

Section 392 TCA 1997 provides that an individual may treat the current-year trading capital allowances as an amount to be deducted in computing the profits or loss of that trade when making a claim for relief under section 381. If the section 381 loss (as augmented or created by the section 392 election) exceeds the individual's other income, the section 381 relief is treated as having been given first in respect of the tax loss of the trade in priority to the capital allowances, thereby leaving the capital allowances not set off under the claim to be carried forward to the following tax year.

Capital allowances carried forward from previous years cannot be used to directly create or enhance a section 381 loss relief claim. However, the losses brought forward may be used to shelter any current-year balancing charges and to reduce current-year profits.

Example 1.6

John has been in business for many years and prepares his annual accounts to 30 September. His tax-adjusted profit for the year ended 30 September 2022 is €28,000.

Unutilised capital allowances brought forward from 2021 are €30,000. The capital allowance position for 2022 is as follows:

	€
Wear and tear allowances	(21,000)
Balancing allowances on sale of assets	(1,500)
Balancing charges	2,400

The 2022 tax-adjusted profits will be computed as follows:

	€
Case I tax-adjusted profit	28,000
Less: 2021 capital allowances b/f	(28,000)
2022 taxable profit	Nil
Add 2022 balancing charge	2,400
Less: balance of 2021 capital allowances b/f	(2,000)
Less: 2022 capital allowances	(22,500)
Current-year Case I loss*	(22,100)

*Available for utilisation against other income as a section 381 loss relief claim.

As demonstrated by **Example 1.6**, prior-year capital allowances can be used to eliminate the current-year balancing charges and profits, with the result that the current-year capital allowances generate a Case I loss that can be used under section 381 for offset in the current year against other income (either John's or that of his jointly assessable spouse).

Restriction for Passive Trades

Section 381B TCA 1997 limits the use of loss relief where the business owner is not actively involved in the business, i.e. the trade is passive or a 'hobby' trade. An individual is deemed to be carrying on a trade in a non-active capacity if they do not work for the greater part of their time on the day-to-day management of the trade. The individual must spend an average of at least 10 hours per week personally engaged in the activities of the trade. In addition, those activities must be carried out on a commercial basis. Where the individual is deemed to be carrying on a trade in a non-active capacity, the loss relief available is limited to €31,750 or, if lower, the actual amount of the loss sustained.

1.7.2   Carry Forward of Unused Trading Losses under Section 382 TCA 1997

Section 382 TCA 1997 provides that a loss in respect of which relief is not given under section 381 TCA 1997 is carried forward and set against the next available profits of the same trade that gave rise to the loss in the first place. For this purpose, the profits of the trade of the next year available to cover the loss carried forward are the taxable profits for that year after deducting the capital allowances. If those profits (after capital allowances) are insufficient to fully absorb the tax loss carried forward, the balance is again carried forward to the following year of assessment and so on until the loss is fully used up. If the trader does not generate a future profit for the same trade, then the benefit of loss relief carried forward is lost.

Example 1.7

Jim's only source of income is his travel agency business, which he has carried on for many years. He prepares his annual accounts up to 30 June each year. Recent tax-adjusted results are as follows:

2020 tax-adjusted loss	(€50,000)
2021 tax-adjusted profits	€60,000
2022 tax-adjusted profits	€130,000

Jim is single and his personal tax credit entitlement is assumed to be €3,400 per annum. Jim's tax assessment (ignoring PRSI/USC) will be as follows:

	2020	2021	2022
	€	€	€
Case I	0	60,000	130,000
Less: Case I loss b/f	0	(50,000)	0
Assessable Case I	0	10,000	130,000
Less: relief	0	0	0
	0	10,000	130,000
Taxed as follows:			
€10,000/€36,800 @ 20%	0	2,000	7,360
Balance @ 40%			37,280
	0	2,000	44,640
Less: credits	(3,400)	(3,400)	(3,400)
Tax due	0	0	41,240

Jim is obliged to use the loss relief brought forward to the first year in which Case I profits are generated. This occurs in 2021 and means a loss of personal tax credits of €1,400. It would be more beneficial for Jim if he could defer claiming loss relief until 2022, but the deferral of losses is not allowed in such circumstances.

Key Issue

Losses carried forward must be used against the first available profits generated in a sole trader's business.

1.7.3 Planning Points for Loss Relief and the Sole Trader

It is important for a sole trader to consider the utilisation of loss relief in the early years of their business. If the sole trader has other income and the trade is likely to be loss-making for a number of years, there may be merit in continuing to operate as a sole trader (rather than as a company), and so obtain the benefit of loss relief against their other income and that of their jointly assessed spouse. The tax relief could in turn help fund the trading activity.

The decision on whether or not to incorporate a company will arise at some point in a sole trader's business (see **Chapter 2**). The question of loss relief may be a key issue in this decision and when is the best time to incorporate. One of the main benefits of operating through a company is the low rate of corporation tax that will attach to trading profits. If profits do not exist, then income tax loss relief could be beneficial to a sole trader.

There is no obligation on the taxpayer to claim loss relief against other personal income in the current year under a section 381 claim. If trade profits are expected to arise in the next year (and are due to be liable at the higher rate of tax), there may be merit in carrying the loss forward to the next year to maximise the tax advantage.

Example 1.8

2021 Tax Year	€
Trading loss Case I	(10,000)
Other income	25,000
2022 Tax Year	
Anticipated Case I trade profits	100,000
Other income	25,000

The taxpayer will be liable to the 20% rate of income tax on their 2021 taxable income.

If the taxpayer does not claim loss relief in 2021 against other income of €25,000, the loss of €10,000 can carry forward for offset against the anticipated 2022 trading income of €100,000. The value of the loss relief claim in 2022 is €10,000 × 40% = €4,000, compared to the value of the loss relief claim of only €2,000 (€10,000 × 20%) in 2021.

1.8 Cessation of a Sole Trade

The date of cessation of a sole trade will be established by virtue of the facts surrounding the trade/activity. For example, the cessation point could be when all of the trade's stock has been sold. A subsequent sale of the business's capital assets at a later date would not extend the cessation date. The existence of sales would also indicate that a trade has not yet ceased.

If the ownership of a business changes, for tax purposes the date of cessation is the date of sale/transfer of the business. From that date the sole trader selling the business will no longer be deemed liable for income tax/CGT on the profits/gains of the business. A sole trade is also deemed to have ceased where a business is transferred to a company; or on the death of the sole trader (unless the surviving spouse/civil partner continues the same trade after the death).

Following a cessation to trade, receipts collected by the sole trader will be liable to income tax as Case IV income (i.e. not as Case I trading income).

1.8.1 Basis of Assessment Rules on a Permanent Cessation

On the cessation of a trade, the profits liable to tax will be those profits from 1 January to the date of cessation. An adjustment to taxable income in the year prior to cessation may also be required. The prior year's profits will be revised to an actual basis (i.e. January to December in the year prior to cessation). If those profits on an actual basis are higher than the profits originally assessed, the sole trader's assessment will be revised in line with the higher actual Case I profits.

Example 1.9
John Jones ceased to trade on 31 July 2022. His sole trade profits over the last three years were as follows:

	€
31 July 2022	20,000
31 January 2022	90,000
31 January 2021	50,000
31 January 2020	60,000

Final Year – 2022
John's profits liable to income tax in the year of cessation will be those profits arising between 1 January 2022 and 31 July 2022:

	€
€90,000 × 1/12	7,500
€20,000	20,000
Total 2022 taxable profits	27,500

Prior Year – 2021
The 2021 tax year profits, under an ongoing trading basis, liable to tax were €50,000 (i.e. Case I year ended 31 January 2021). However, as the trade has ceased, an adjustment of 2021 to an actual basis is required if it gives a higher taxable profit:

	€
€50,000 × 1/12	4,167
€90,000 × 11/12	82,500
Revised 2021 taxable profits	86,667

Under self-assessment, John must advise Revenue of the "prior year adjustment", i.e. the uplift in profits assessable.

Example 1.10
A sole trader's business ceases on 31 December 2021. Prior to this, accounts are prepared to 30 April each year. Profits as per the accounts are:

	€
Year to 30 April 2020	40,000
Year to 30 April 2021	60,000
8 months to 31 December 2021	55,000

The prior-year adjustments are:

	€
Year 2019 profits to 31 December 2020	53,334
Year 2020 profits to 31 December 2021	75,000
	128,334

As the business ceased in December 2021, the amount of taxable profits for tax year 2020 increases by €13,334.

If the sole trader has control of when the trade ceases, i.e. on incorporation (see **Chapter 2**), they should consider delaying the cessation of the business until 31 January 2022. For the month 1 January to 31 January 2022, the business has taxable profits of €7,000. Taxable profits would be as follows:

	€
Year 2022 profits to 31 January 2022	7,000
Year 2021 profits to 31 December 2021	75,000
	82,000

By delaying cessation of the trade until 2022, an overall tax saving has been achieved because the taxable profits for 2020 did not require adjusting, thus avoiding the increase in taxable profits of €13,334.

Short-lived Businesses
The profits liable to income tax for a business that commences and ceases within the first three years will be the actual profits (i.e. on a January to December basis).

1.8.2   Terminal Loss Relief

A loss incurred by a sole trader in the last 12 months of a discontinued trade that cannot be otherwise relieved may be carried back and set against the profits of the same trade for the three preceding years. This relief, known as terminal loss relief, is dealt with under the provisions of section 385 TCA 1997. The key features of terminal loss relief are:

- it applies only to either a sole trader or a partner in a partnership;
- to be entitled to the relief, the trade or profession must have been permanently discontinued;
- the loss sustained in the last 12 months of trade of a business is available for terminal loss relief;
- relief is given against the trading profits from the same trade giving rise to the loss of the last three fiscal years of the business, taking the most recent years first;
- the loss is not to displace relief already given or capable of being given for losses carried forward from earlier periods.

The amount of the terminal loss is the sum of the following:

- the adjusted loss generated in the final 12 months of trading (which may include a portion of the prior year of assessment figures); and
- capital allowances available in that final 12-month period (which may include a pro rata proportion of capital allowances for the period in the prior year of assessment).

Timing of Cessation
A trade is deemed to be permanently discontinued or to have ceased when there has been a change of ownership. The **transfer of a trade to a company** constitutes a cessation of trade and hence terminal loss relief could be available and a review of losses and profits within the prior three-year period should be undertaken.

A planning point would be to ensure that there are profits within the prior three years to avail of terminal loss relief. The timing of the transfer should be considered to ensure maximum benefit of terminal loss relief (i.e. attract profits that were taxed at the 40% rate of income tax).

The timing of the incorporation and transfer of a business to a limited company is discussed in detail in **Section 2.4**. The issue of terminal loss relief, and its timing, should be considered in conjunction with the CGT transfer of a business relief.

Example 1.11: Timing of transfer of a business
Stephen Byrne carries on a sole trade. To date, his accounting year-ends have been 31 December. He plans to transfer his business to a limited company on 30 September 2022.

The profits, losses and capital allowances of his trade are as follows:

	Capital Allowance	Profit/Loss
	€	€
2018	(3,000)	5,000
2019	(2,500)	6,500
2020	(3,500)	2,000
2021	(2,500)	6,000
9 months to 30/09/2022	(2,500)	(7,000)

continued overleaf

Prior Tax Assessments

	2018	2019	2020	2021
	€	€	€	€
Profit/loss	5,000	6,500	2,000	6,000
Less: capital allowances	(3,000)	(2,500)	(3,500)	(2,500)
Taxable profit/loss	2,000	4,000	(1,500)	3,500
Loss relief b/f claim				(1,500)
Taxable profits	2,000	4,000	0 *	2,000

* Assume section 381 loss relief was not claimed in 2020.

Since Stephen plans to transfer his business to a limited company on 30 September 2022, the trade will therefore cease and terminal loss relief can be claimed. The terminal loss in the final 12 months is computed as follows:

	€
Loss up to 30 September 2022	(7,000)
Add: capital allowances	(2,500)
Total loss for nine months	(9,500)

Three months of prior year (i.e. 2021 period)

As there was no loss in this three-month period, the terminal loss for the 12-month period is €9,500. Terminal loss relief will be taken as follows to the preceding three years of assessment:

	Profits Assessed	Terminal Loss	Revised Assessment
	€	€	€
2021	2,000	(2,000)	Nil
2020	Nil	Nil	Nil
2019	4,000	(4,000)	Nil

Key Issue
In **Example 1.11**, if Stephen decided to defer the transfer of the business to a limited company until 2023, he would only be able to claim terminal loss relief for the three preceding taxable periods prior to 2023 (being 2022, 2021 and 2020). This would result in losing the benefit of terminal loss relief in 2019 (being the last tax year with substantial profits). As such, it is more beneficial from a tax perspective for Stephen to cease trading in 2022.

1.9 Compliance Obligations of a Sole Trader

A sole trader will be considered a chargeable person for income tax purposes. By contrast, individuals who do not have income other than Schedule E employment income (i.e. salary on which payroll is operated) would not be considered chargeable persons. Proprietary directors are an exception to this as they are regarded as chargeable persons and hence must file tax returns under the self-assessment system. A proprietary director is one who can control directly or indirectly 15% of the ordinary share capital of the company.

Key Issue
It is important that students are familiar with the key differences between chargeable and non-chargeable persons (and the filing requirements).

All chargeable persons are required to:

- Make a return of income to Revenue for each year that they are chargeable persons. The prescribed return form is Form 11, which must be filed electronically. In exceptional cases a paper Form 11 will be accepted.
- The return, if permitted to be filed in paper format, should include a declaration by the taxpayer regarding the income and gains earned in the period, along with any deductions claimed by the taxpayer during that period.
- File a 'self-assessment' (i.e. calculation of the tax liability for the year).

Failure to file a return will lead to the imposition of penalties and interest by Revenue, which also reserves the right to impose more serious penalties, including imprisonment.

Chapter 1 Summary

Does a trade exist?	• Badges of trade • Deductibility of expenditure • Capital versus revenue
Operating as a sole trader	• Special rules for allocating profits/losses to tax years on commencement • Loss reliefs available to a sole trader – how to maximise tax relief and cash flow • Implication if trade ceases

Questions

Review Question
(See Suggested Solutions to Review Questions at the end of this textbook.)

Question 1.1

Joe Smyth, a sole trader trading as Lemon Fresh, a manufacturer of toilet cleaning products, ceased to trade on 30 June 2023 due to a decline in demand for its product. Joe Smyth prepared his accounts to 31 December. He had the following results for the periods below:

Period to 30 June 2023 trading loss	(€55,000)
Y/E 31 December 2022 trading loss	(€5,000)
Y/E 31 December 2021 trading profit	€25,000
Y/E 31 December 2020 trading profit	€22,000
Y/E 31 December 2019 trading profit	€15,000

Requirement

Calculate the terminal loss claim, ensuring that loss relief claimed is maximised and assuming that Joe Smyth had no income other than his trade income.

Challenging Question

(Suggested Solutions to Challenging Questions are available through your lecturer.)

Question 1.1

You had a recent meeting with a potential new client, Ted Hickey. Ted is married, and his wife works on a part-time basis. Her annual salary is €25,000. While Ted has been working as an employee, his annual salary is normally in the region of €70,000. He also has an active interest in horticulture and garden design.

He has been dabbling in this area a lot more recently and, in the last year, he won a competition to design a garden for the Bloom Garden Festival in 2022. In 2022, his employer asked him to work a three-day week until things pick up again. With this extra time on his hands, Ted wants to try to start a garden design business to capitalise on his appearance at the Bloom Garden Festival. He has incurred a loss of some €70,000 to date on this activity as he has acquired lots of tools and equipment. He has also attended courses costing €5,000 and wants to claim these as business expenses. Ted thinks his initial commissions in 2022 may end up costing him about €10,000 as he wants to build his reputation and create some good examples of his work, but he cannot afford to charge the clients enough to pay for his time. Ted is unsure of the future prospects but, if things go well, he may perhaps break even in 2023.

Ted's wife inherited a substantial sum from her aunt and this was invested in different types of investment properties. She has Case V income of €260,000 for 2022 and Case V losses of €60,000 carried forward from 2021.

Requirement

Ted asks for a letter to set out their expected income tax position for 2022 and advice on the best use of all initial trading losses in his business. As he is not great with tax things, he would like any "technical parts" explained with simple calculations.

The Incorporation Decision and Tax Relief for Funding a New Company

Learning Objectives

By the end of this chapter you will be able to:

■ Analyse the potential tax implications for a business trading through a company, with particular reference to:

- consideration of reasons to incorporate a business;
- comparison of sole trade profits to incorporated profits;
- cessation issues for a sole trader;
- optimum use of incorporation (section 600 TCA 1997) relief.

■ Understand the following tax reliefs available to help fund the company:

- Employment and Investment Incentive (EII); and
- Start-up Relief for Entrepreneurs (SURE).

In almost every business the question will arise as to how to structure the business. Often a business commences as a sole trade, and it can remain that way for its lifetime; sometimes the sole trader may decide to incorporate – to become a limited company. In some cases, though it is not common, a limited company can be transferred to a sole trade. And of course, a limited company can be set up from the outset to commence the trading activities.

2.1 Advantages and Disadvantages of Operating as a Sole Trader

There are advantages and disadvantages to operating as a sole trader. Often it will come down to an individual's business and their particular circumstances, preferences and priorities. Some of the general advantages and disadvantages of operating as a sole trader are summarised in the table below.

Advantages of Operating as a Sole Trader	Disadvantages of Operating as a Sole Trader
▦ Offers a degree of flexibility to the trader.	▦ No limited liability protection.
▦ Low professional costs in respect of annual filings.	▦ Could be difficult to introduce outside investors into a non-corporate structure.
▦ Loss relief can be utilised against other income, which can help finance ongoing trading activities and expansion.	▦ Limited scope for pension planning. Tax benefits are limited by reference to earnings and the person's age.
▦ Cash is received directly from trading activities, therefore no cash extraction issues compared to a company.	▦ Profits liable to the higher rate of income tax (compared to a 12.5% rate for companies).
▦ Direct ownership of trading assets. Proceeds of a future sale will be received directly.	▦ May be difficult to raise finance to fund trade expansion.

2.2   Incorporation of a Company: Critical Issues

2.2.1   Incorporation Decision Matrix

Some of the key issues or conditions that might prompt the incorporation of a limited liability company are:

1. Anticipation of significant profits and the benefit of the 12.5% rate of corporation tax (as opposed to income tax rates).
2. Tax exemption for start-up companies (see **Chapter 3, Section 3.2**).
3. If incorporating an existing business and there are losses carried forward, these will effectively be lost. Consideration must also be given to Case I cessation rules and their implications. Note that these 'historical' issues have no relevance for the individual who has never operated as a sole trader and commences trading through a company from the beginning.
4. Availability of R&D credit (see **Chapter 3, Section 3.7**).
5. Need for limited liability protection.
6. As a vehicle for raising capital/borrowings.
7. Borrowings could be repaid out of post-12.5% income, which should facilitate a quicker repayment of borrowings.
8. Multiple owners of the business and a means to facilitate shared ownership of a business.
9. Creation of clear ownership structure of the business.
10. Means to formalise a business structure.
11. Introduction of new investors into a business and the requirement to be a limited company.
12. Banking requirements (trade expansion, audit and security issues).
13. Plans for future disposal of a business (share sale requirement).
14. Pension planning opportunities are limited for sole traders/individuals.
15. Funding the business – Employment and Investment Incentive (EII) scheme (EIIS) and Start-up Relief for Entrepreneurs (SURE) (see **Section 2.4**).
16. Staff schemes such as share options, etc.
17. After-tax profits of 87.5% are available for an incorporated company to invest in business expansion and growth, compared to after-tax profits of 45% for a sole trade.

Some issues that may influence the decision **not** to incorporate a company are:

- Complexity and administration.
- Case I losses not available for offset against an individual's other income if the business is incorporated.
- Significant close company legislation (see **Chapter 3, Section 3.4**).
- Cash extraction issues on an ongoing basis. How can funds be extracted from a company tax efficiently?
- A company is a separate legal entity and valuable assets would not be directly held by shareholders. This is often a key issue and generally arises where a valuable property asset is held by individuals.
- Additional costs, such as legal costs.
- Lifestyle funding requirements of the individual – cash extraction issues.
- Potential for double CGT charge if the business/assets are sold by the company (and cash is extracted by way of a liquidation/capital distribution to shareholders).

The decision to incorporate a company can also link in with other more long-term strategies. For example, an individual wishing to build up a business for a future sale may wish to incorporate a company if it is likely that the purchaser of the business will want to purchase shares in a company rather than in a sole trade operation.

Key Issue
Consider all of the other tax charges and reliefs (including CGT and stamp duty) when considering the structure of a new or existing business. It is likely that there will be many issues to consider, and it is important that consideration is always given to future events rather than short-term plans.

2.3   The Decision to Incorporate a Business

The following questions should be addressed before deciding whether or not to incorporate.

Is the business likely to be profitable?
- If not, it may be more tax-efficient to operate as a sole trader and obtain section 381 TCA 1997 loss relief until such point as profits are anticipated. The sole trade business can be transferred to a company at a future stage, at which time transfer of a business relief may be available.
- If the trade is to be operated as a sole trade, the first three years' profits/losses will be computed by reference to the commencement basis of assessment rules.
- If significant profits are anticipated, it may be beneficial to incorporate a company from the outset (rather than setting up as a sole trader) to avail of the tax exemption for new start-up companies (see **Section 3.2**). If the business has been carried on as a sole trader, then there is the benefit of the lower corporate rate of tax of 12.5% on trading profits.

How will the business be funded?
- If the business is to be funded by a bank loan, it is likely to be easier for for an incorporated company, rather than a sole trader, to make the loan repayments from after-tax funds (as its profits are either exempt for the first three years or liable to the 12.5% rate of tax).
- The Employment and Investment Incentive (EII) could provide a means of introducing funding to a qualifying company; the Start-up Relief for Entrepreneurs (SURE) could be used to assist the funding of a qualifying new trading company. (See **Section 2.5**.)

- Other tax reliefs, such as the research and development (R&D) tax credit, could help fund the business of a company. The R&D tax credit allows for a either a tax credit or a tax refund even where a corporation tax liability does not exist. (See **Section 3.7**.)
- If the shareholders fund a company by way of subscription for share capital, the amount paid for the shares will be their CGT base cost on a future disposal of those shares.

Often there is a mixture of share capital subscription and an element of loans from the shareholders to the company. These loans can be repaid tax-free to the shareholders; however, any interest charged on these loans could be treated as a distribution for tax purposes as per the close company rules (see **Section 3.4**).

Is the business likely to be subject to significant commercial risks?
- If yes, it is perhaps best to establish a company as soon as possible to protect the individual's personal assets if the business were to fail (i.e. limited liability protection).

What is the spouse's level of involvement in the business?
- Does the spouse have their own source of income? If no, can they legitimately draw a salary from the business that can utilise personal income tax bands and tax credits?
- Drawing a salary could create a pensionable employment and allow for the funding of a private pension scheme for the spouse. Also, PRSI contributions would be payable on the salary, which may entitle the spouse to a State contributory pension (assuming sufficient PRSI contributions are paid).
- If the spouse is to be a shareholder and the shares are to be subsequently disposed of, consider appointing the spouse as a director (for the required time on either a part-time or full-time basis) to allow access to CGT retirement relief in the future.

Does the taxpayer intend to sell the business?
- If yes, it may be beneficial to conduct the business through a company to maximise business growth/development (i.e. with the 12.5% tax rate applying to profits generated). Also, a purchaser may prefer to purchase a business by way of share purchase since stamp duty on shares is only 1% (as opposed to 7.5% on a trade/asset purchase).
- Retirement relief may be available on the future disposal of shares in a trading company. Consider transferring shares to a spouse before the transferor is aged 55 years, and then, if all other conditions are met, claims for retirement relief can be maximised.
- A holding company structure could be put in place. This could facilitate the exempt sale of the shares in a trading subsidiary by the holding company. The tax-free funds could then be used for either further investment, or be extracted out of the holding company by way of liquidation.
- If the business has a property element, consideration should be given at the outset to its ownership, i.e. whether it will be owned by the individual or the company. See below under 'Property issues'.

Does the taxpayer intend to gift the business to their family/children?
- If yes, tax reliefs such as retirement relief (for CGT) and business asset relief (for CAT) should be considered. These reliefs can facilitate a tax-efficient transfer of assets to the next generation.

Property issues
- Factors such as a purchase of the property by a company could lead to issues if the company ceases trading and the property is subsequently sold. If a third-party purchaser wishes to purchase the property only (as opposed to buying the shares in the company from the shareholders), a double charge to tax could arise on extracting cash from the company. This would arise as follows:
  - CGT at 33% on a disposal by the company of the property.
  - CGT at 33% (ignoring revised entrepreneur relief) on a liquidation of the company and distribution of cash to the shareholders.

▦ It may be a planning point to consider purchasing the property personally and renting it to the company. This will generate rental income for the shareholders personally and also keep the property out of the corporate regime. The rental income could be used to finance bank borrowings taken out to purchase the property. A Case V tax deduction should be available in respect of interest repayments on bank loans. However, the shareholder may not have sufficient income after tax to pay back the loan and therefore will need another source of funds to repay some of the loan.

▦ One incentive to purchase property through a company is that it may be easier to fund bank borrowings for the property (as company profits will be liable to 12.5% tax as opposed to higher income tax rates).

2.4 Transfer of a Sole Trade Business to a Company

A number of taxes across a range of tax heads are triggered on the incorporation of a sole trade business. Each of the tax heads and the potential reliefs are considered in this section.

2.4.1 CGT Relief for the Transfer of a Business to a Company

On making the decision to incorporate a company, a sole trader will transfer the existing business to their new company, which will involve a disposal of the trade by the trader to the company. The question will arise as to how this can be done and what the tax implications are. A limited company is a distinct legal entity, legally separated from its shareholders.

The trade will, most likely, contain at least one capital asset, namely the goodwill of the trade. The goodwill is the value of the trade over and above the value of the underlying assets.

Where there is a disposal/transfer of chargeable assets between connected persons, a charge to CGT may arise based on the market value of those assets, despite the fact that money is not changing hands in the transaction.

CGT on the disposal of business assets to a company may be deferred under section 600 TCA 1997, provided that the business and all its assets (other than cash) are transferred in consideration for the issue of shares in the company. To avail of this relief, the business must be transferred as a going concern to the company, and the transfer must be for bona fide commercial reasons and not part of a tax avoidance scheme. The deferral continues until the shares are disposed of by the individual who transferred the assets to the company. The net gain on the transfer of the chargeable assets to the company is calculated and the gain proportionate to any cash or deemed cash consideration is assessed immediately. The deferred gain is apportioned over the shares received, thereby reducing the base cost of these shares for the purposes of any subsequent disposal.

If any liabilities of the business are taken over by the company this is treated as a cash payment to the former proprietor and the deferred gain is reduced, triggering an upfront CGT liability. A similar treatment applies if part of the consideration is satisfied by the creation in the company of a loan account in favour of the individual, or the payment by the company of pre-incorporation taxation or other personal liabilities of the individual.

When the normal gain arising on the transfer of the chargeable assets to the company has been calculated, the amount to be deferred is calculated by applying the formula:

$$\frac{\text{Consideration in form of shares}}{\text{Total value of gross assets taken over}} \times \text{Chargeable gain (after indexation relief)}$$

If more than one class of shares is issued, the deferred gain is deducted from the cost of the shares on the basis of the relative market values of each class of shares at the time of acquisition.

Limitations of the Relief

The fact that the liabilities of the trade taken over by the company are treated as cash consideration for the purposes of calculating the deferral relief reduces the benefit to be gained from claiming the relief. In practice, however, where an individual transfers a business to a company in exchange for shares only, and assets exceed liabilities, bona fide trade creditors taken over will not be treated as consideration.

In order to claim section 600 relief, all the assets of the business must be transferred from the sole trade to the company. However, it is generally not tax-efficient to hold assets that can appreciate in value (such as property) in a company because a double charge to CGT will arise on the ultimate extraction of value from the appreciating asset. The first charge to tax is CGT arising on the disposal of the assets by the company and the second charge to tax is triggered on the extraction by the shareholder of the after-tax profits out of the company, which can give rise to an income tax liability or CGT liability depending on the method of extraction (see **Chapter 4**). Therefore, section 600 relief may not be appropriate to claim if it means the transfer of property or buildings to a company. The owners of trading companies commonly hold the trading premises personally and rent the property to the company. A subsequent sale of the property does not then give rise to a double tax charge.

There is no equivalent relief to section 600 for stamp duty purposes. Therefore the company taking a transfer of assets, such as the property and goodwill from the sole trade business, will incur a stamp duty liability. As all assets of the business must be transferred, claiming section 600 for CGT purposes can reduce planning opportunities for the minimisation of stamp duty.

The reduced rate of CGT of 10% under revised entrepreneur relief cannot be claimed on gains arising on non-share consideration taken in conjunction with a section 600 relief claim if the transfer is not for bona fide commercial reasons. This issue is addressed in **Chapter 9**.

Example 2.1

On 30 March 2022, Jane Morgan transferred the sole trade business she had established 30 years earlier to a company, JM Ltd. All the sole trade's assets and liabilities, other than cash but including a personal tax liability of €10,000, were transferred.

In consideration for the transfer to the company, JM Ltd issued 10,000 €1 ordinary shares at par fully paid. It also created a loan account in favour of Jane of €100,000 and paid Jane €30,000 in cash. The incorporation of the sole trade was undertaken for bona fide commercial reasons.

At the date of transfer, the balance sheet of the sole trade business was as follows:

	€
Assets:	
Goodwill at cost (owned for 30 years)	5,000
Trading stock	100,000
Debtors	60,000
Building at cost (owned for 30 years)	35,000
Cash	25,000
	225,000

continued overleaf

Liabilities:

Trade creditors	50,000
Personal tax liability	10,000
Proprietor's capital account	<u>165,000</u>
	225,000

At the date of transfer the market value of the assets was as follows:

	€
Goodwill	100,000
Trading stock	100,000
Debtors	60,000
Buildings	<u>690,000</u>
Gross value of assets transferred	950,000
Less:	
Trade creditors	(50,000)
Personal tax liability taken over by JM Ltd	(10,000)
Cash payment	(30,000)
Loan in Jane's favour	<u>(100,000)</u>
Net value of assets transferred	**760,000**

The value of the shares is therefore €760,000, which is equal to the net value of assets transferred. The chargeable gains are computed as follows:

	€
Adjusted base cost:	
Goodwill: €5,000 indexed at 1.406	7,030
Buildings: €35,000 indexed at 1.406	42,210
Chargeable gains (current market value – adjusted base cost):	
Trading stock (non-chargeable asset)	Nil
Goodwill (€100,000 – €7,030)	92,970
Buildings (€690,000 – €49,210)	<u>640,790</u>
Total gain	733,760
Less: deferred gain (Note 1)	<u>(587,008)</u>
Chargeable gain	146,752
Less: annual exemption	<u>(1,270)</u>
	145,482
CGT @ 10% (Note 2)	14,548
Allowable cost of shares for any future disposal:	
Value of shares	760,000
Less: deferred gain	<u>(587,008)</u>
Cost for subsequent disposals of the shares issued to Jane	172,992

If Jane decided not to claim section 600 relief but instead transferred all the sole trade assets and liabilities, other than the building, to the company, the position would be:

Chargeable gains	€
Gain on goodwill transferred to company (as above)	92,970
No gain on building	Nil
	92,970
Less: annual exemption	(1,270)
	91,700
CGT @ 10% (Note 2)	9,170

Value of shares transferred

Assets:	
Goodwill	100,000
Trading stock	100,000
Debtors	60,000
	260,000

Liabilities:	
Trade creditors	(50,000)
Cash due to Jane	(30,000)
Director's loan account	(100,000)
Jane's personal tax bill	(10,000)
	(190,000)
Net assets/value of shares issued to Jane	**70,000**

Notes:

1. As Jane is taking shares and cash from the company and the company is taking over her personal tax liability and will create a loan account in her favour, the trade creditors of €50,000 will be treated as cash consideration when calculating the deferred and current CGT liability arising on the incorporation of the business. The deferred gain is calculated as:

$$\frac{\text{Consideration in form of shares}}{\text{Total value of gross assets taken over}} \times \text{Chargeable gain (after indexation relief)}$$

$$= \frac{€760,000}{€950,000} \times €733,760 = €587,008$$

2. It is assumed that Jane satisfies all conditions necessary to avail of the reduced 10% CGT entrepreneur relief (see **Chapter 9** for a full discussion of entrepreneur relief) and that the decision to incorporate the sole trade was for bona fide commercial reasons and did not form part of a tax avoidance arrangement.

Jane will save €5,378 by not claiming section 600 relief, being the difference between the CGT liability arising on the transfer of the business under section 600 (€14,548) and the CGT arising on the disposal of goodwill to the company (€9,170).

All future uplifts in the value of the building will accrue directly to Jane and she will incur a single charge to CGT on the future disposal of the building.

In addition, the company will save stamp duty of €51,750 (€690,000 × 7.5%) if the building is not transferred to the company. The company will incur a stamp duty liability of €19,500 (€260,000 × 7.5%) on the transfer of the assets of the business to the company. See **Section 2.4.3** for a full discussion of stamp duty implications on the incorporation of a sole trade.

> **Key Issue**
> A sole trader should consider whether it would be of benefit to retain some assets (e.g. property) and transfer the balance of the trade to a new company. This could involve an immediate tax charge in favour of the avoidance of a future greater gain and the avoidance of stamp duty (see **Section 2.4.3**).

2.4.2   VAT Treatment on the Transfer of a Trade

Usually when a VAT-registered business, such as a sole trade, disposes of assets on which a VAT input credit has been claimed, then VAT must be charged on a sale or transfer of those assets to the purchaser. The VAT charge is based on the price plus VAT (at the same class of rate as the VAT-registered business incurred on the acquisition of the asset). For example, if a VAT-registered business disposes of a building on which VAT was incurred on acquisition, then (depending on the VAT history of the building) VAT at 13.5% may have to be charged on the sales price. If equipment, furniture, and intangible assets, such as goodwill, intellectual property, etc., are transferred, VAT at 23% applies.

However, VAT does not apply if all of the following conditions are satisfied:

1. the purchaser is a VAT-registered person; and
2. is entitled to claim a **full** (i.e. 100% recovery) input credit for any VAT charged to it; **and**
3. the transfer **must** constitute an undertaking, or part of an undertaking, capable of being operated on an independent basis.

This is commonly referred to as "transfer of business relief". The relief is set out in section 20(2)(c) VATCA 2010 and section 26 VATCA 2010. These sections effectively deem such a transaction not to be a supply of goods or services and to be outside the scope of VAT. In order for the relief to apply, the seller must transfer a mixture of assets that would be capable of assisting in the operation of a business. In a typical sale of a business, a vendor is likely to be disposing of assets such as stock, premises, staff, cash/bank, contracts, goodwill, debtors, plant and equipment, etc. It is not necessary for **all** of these items to be disposed of for the relief to apply, but it is likely that at least several of them should be present.

VAT should therefore not arise on the incorporation of a sole trade business provided that the company is registered for VAT in advance of taking a transfer of the assets and that the business is transferred as an undertaking, or part of an undertaking, capable of being operated on an independent basis. It is important to note that where the conditions for transfer of business relief are satisfied, the treatment is mandatory and no VAT should be charged or claimed. If VAT is charged in error, Revenue could deny an input credit to the purchaser.

2.4.3   Stamp Duty Issues on the Transfer of a Trade

There are no stamp duty reliefs available on the transfer of assets on incorporation of a sole trade business. Assets transferred are subject to *ad valorem* duty. Certain assets, such as plant and machinery, may 'pass by delivery' and hence are not subject to stamp duty. The concept of pass by delivery is covered in the CA Proficiency 2 course. Briefly, it means that ownership of certain assets can be legally transferred without the requirement of a legal document and therefore stamp duty can be avoided. However, where consideration for the transfer of assets takes the form of a share issue, company law stipulates that a contract or written document must be in place and that all assets must be listed in this contract. It is therefore not possible to minimise stamp duty where the transfer of trade is by a share issue.

Where a company issues shares in exchange for the assets of a sole trade business under section 600 TCA 1997 (transfer of business relief) as set out in **Section 2.4.1**, stamp duty at a rate of 7.5% is payable on the assets exchanged for shares.

2.4.4 Income Tax Issues for the Sole Trader

The sole trader must carefully consider the income tax implications of incorporating the sole trade business as it can give rise to additional income tax liability under cessation of a trade rules and balancing charges. Careful consideration must also be given to the use of losses accruing to the sole trade before the business is incorporated. These issues are discussed in **Chapter 1**, but the key considerations on incorporation are briefly set out again below.

Cessation of the Sole Trade
When a sole trader transfers their trade to a company, the sole trade will cease and the income tax cessation provisions (section 67 TCA 1997) will apply as set out in **Section 1.8**. These cessation provisions require a penultimate year review to take place. Where the actual profits for the penultimate year are higher than the profits originally assessed, additional income tax will be due.

Balancing Adjustment
As a result of the cessation of the sole trade, possible balancing charges may arise in respect of tangible movable assets, such as plant and machinery and fixtures and fittings, under section 298 TCA 1997. A balancing charge would increase the income tax payable by the sole trader in the tax year the business ceases. However, section 312 TCA 1997 provides that assets can be transferred at their tax written down value (TWDV) rather than at the deemed market value to a company controlled by the transferor. A formal election by both parties is required for this section to apply. Therefore, no balancing allowance or charge will arise on the sole trader.

In certain circumstances it may be advantageous not to make the election to transfer the assets at TWDV. For example, if a sole trade business has losses that will absorb the balancing charge, there will be no additional income tax cost, and at the same time the base cost of the assets to the company for capital allowance purposes will be increased.

Loss Relief for a Sole Trade
Where a loss is incurred by the sole trade business in the 12 months to cessation, a terminal loss relief claim may be made as set out in **Section 1.8.2**. Unutilised trading losses of a sole trade business cannot be carried into the company on incorporation.

Loss relief for sole traders is not as extensive as that for companies. For example, if a sole trader makes a profit in one period and makes a loss in the following period, there is no mechanism for setting the loss back against the profits of prior years. However, a company in the same circumstances could generate tax refunds by setting the losses back against profits in earlier years. Loss relief for corporates is discussed in detail in the CA Proficiency 2 course.

2.4.5 Corporation Tax Issues on the Transfer of a Trade

The impact of close company provisions (see **Chapter 3, Section 3.4**) should be considered as the company that has taken over the trade will be closely held if it is owned by the sole trader or a family member.

The start-up company exemption (see **Section 3.2**) from corporation tax is not available on the incorporation of a sole trade. The exemption specifically excludes any trade that was previously "carried on by another person or formed part of another person's trade".

2.5   Funding the New Company

Raising capital is a key objective for companies seeking growth and the ability to raise it tax-efficiently is worthy of consideration. The Employment and Investment Incentive (EII), Start-up Relief for Entrepreneurs (SURE) and the Start-up Capital Incentive (SCI) are schemes that provide tax relief on investment in certain corporate trades.

The EII aims to raise funding for companies to promote job creation and encourage R&D activities; SURE offers tax incentives to individuals to start their own business, while SCI seeks to attract equity investment for early-stage micro-enterprises.

While these reliefs are attractive in principle, the qualifying criteria can be complex, which may act as a disincentive to potential investors. These schemes are only available when the qualifying trade is operated as a company, i.e. sole traders are not eligible.

The main rules applying to these schemes are found in Part 16 of the TCA 1997. The main issues for consideration on use of this relief are:

- A company can raise EII funding up to a total of €15 million, subject to a maximum of €5 million in any one 12-month period. There is a lifetime limit of €500,000 that can be raised under SCI, and a limit of €4.2 million that can be raised under SURE.
- The shares issued in respect of an individual's SURE investment must not carry any preferential rights to dividends, assets or redemption. However, an EII investor can acquire preference shares and qualify for tax relief.
- The investor must not dispose of the shares for at least four years, and there must be no attempt to pass the investment back to the investor during that period. Furthermore, the investor must not enter into any agreement, arrangement or understanding that would eliminate the risk from the investment.
- The company must be an unquoted company resident in Ireland or the EEA.
- The company must be a micro-enterprise (less than 10 employees and an annual turnover and/or annual balance sheet total not exceeding €2 million); a small enterprise (less than 50 employees and an annual turnover and/or annual balance sheet not exceeding €10 million); or a medium-sized enterprise (less than 250 employees and an annual turnover not exceeding €50 million or an annual balance sheet total not exceeding €43 million). If the company is a medium-sized enterprise it must be in an "assisted" area of Ireland. If the company is in a "non-assisted" area (i.e. Dublin, Meath, Kildare, Wicklow or Cork, other than the Cork Docklands), it can only qualify if it is in its "seed" or start-up stage of development, as defined.
- The schemes are available for the management and operation of nursing homes and internationally traded financial services (as defined), subject to conditions (see **Section 2.5.2**).
- The company must use the amounts invested for the purposes of job creation or increase in R&D.
- A system of "self-certification" is in place whereby the company raising the EII and SURE finance issue statements of qualification to the investor and the investor then self-assesses his/her own qualification before claiming tax relief. The "self-certification" system is subject to interest and penalties in the event that the company or the investor incorrectly operates the tax relief.
- EII is currently available until 31 December 2024.

2.5.1   Start-up Relief for Entrepreneurs

SURE is designed to provide an incentive for individuals who intend to start up their own business. The relief is available to a specified individual who makes a relevant investment in a company. The individual must also be employed by that company.

The relief is granted in respect of that person's investment in the share capital of a new Irish resident (or EEA resident) company. This new company must be a trading company or the holding company of a trading company,.

The method for granting SURE allows that person to elect to have the amount invested in the new company claimed as a deduction and thereby receive a refund of tax paid in any of the six years immediately prior to that investment. The relief is effectively designed as a refund of PAYE paid by the individual in prior years.

The individual can effectively claim relief on €700,000, i.e. €100,000 in the year of investment and €600,000 for the previous six years (maximum investment per year is €100,000).

The rules applicable are as follows:

- The person must become a full-time employee of the company in the tax year in which the investment is made in the share capital. The person must also remain employed for a minimum of one year.
- The qualifying investment may be made in two investments, the second investment being made within two years of the end of the tax year in which the first investment was made.
- The individual must own at least 15% of the ordinary share capital of the company for a period of one year from the date of issue or date from which trade commences, whichever is later.
- The individual must not have had a beneficial interest of more than 15% in any other company within 12 months prior to commencing employment in the new company.
- SURE is designed for those who have mainly PAYE income in the previous four years. Excluding the year prior to the investment year, if the individual's non-employment income is in excess of the lower of their PAYE income or €50,000, the relief will not be available. The relief is essentially designed for former employees who wish to start their own business.
- The company must be carrying on a trade that would qualify for EII relief (see **Section 2.5.2**).
- If any of the relief conditions are breached, there will be a clawback of the relief.
- The individual must hold the shares for a period of four years from the date of issue.

The relief is designed to generate income tax refunds for the investor. To qualify for the relief, the company must be carrying on a new business. For example, the business could not have been operated by the individual as a sole trader and subsequently transferred to a limited company.

The relief is achieved by deeming the investment to have been made in each of the six years prior to the issue of the new share capital. For each of the six years, the refund is limited to the total tax paid with an upper limit relief claim of €100,000 per tax year. SURE is a very attractive source of funds to an individual embarking on a new venture. The actual tax paid by the investor will be a critical issue to establish. To maximise the relief it should be targeted for those years in which the investor paid the most income tax.

The claim for tax relief must be made within two years of the end of the year of assessment in which the investment is made and shares issued, e.g. a claim for an investment made in 2022 must be claimed by 31 December 2024.

Where any part of the investment cannot be relieved in a tax year due to insufficiency of income in that year, the balance unused may be used against another year (i.e. the individual may pick the year(s) with the highest income).

Example 2.2

John, a qualifying individual for SURE, invested €180,000 in a qualifying investment on 1 March 2023. His taxable salary income for the previous six tax years was as follows:

	2017	2018	2019	2020	2021	2022
	€	€	€	€	€	€
Taxable income	45,000	40,000	45,000	92,000	80,000	125,000

John will be entitled to make a claim for tax relief subject to the maximum claim in any one year of €100,000. The refund due to John will depend on the rate of tax applicable to his income in each of the relevant tax years.

To maximise the relief, John should select the tax year within the last six years (in which the investment is deemed to occur) in order to maximise tax relief. As John's earnings have been higher in recent years, the tax paid will also be higher in those years. John should target those years to maximise the tax refund due.

The nominated tax years for the claim will be 2020 and 2022 as these years, taken together have the highest amount of tax paid.

	2017	2018	2019	2020	2021	2022
	€	€	€	€	€	€
Taxable income	45,000	40,000	45,000	92,000	80,000	125,000
Less: SURE	0	0	0	(80,000)	0	(100,000)
Revised taxable income	45,000	40,000	45,000	12,000	80,000	25,000

If John had selected 2017 as his nominated year, tax relief would not be maximised, as a significant portion of his income in 2017, 2018 and 2019 was only taxed at the standard rate of tax (i.e. 20%). The tax relief should target years in which the top rate of tax applied.

2.5.2 EII and SCI

The EII and the SCI provide income tax relief to an individual by reference to their investment in the share capital of certain qualifying companies. The scheme is designed to attract investors to Irish businesses and is designed to encourage investment in relevant companies and to stimulate and encourage further employment of staff. The investee company benefits from funding and the investor benefits from the income tax relief by reference to the amount invested in the company.

Qualifying Company

A qualifying EII/SCI company must be:

- unquoted;
- incorporated in Ireland or another EEA state;
- be resident in Ireland (or else be a resident of an EEA state and carry on a business in Ireland through a branch or agency); and
- be a trading company, which for these purposes excludes activities such as land development, professional services (e.g. accountants, pharmacists, solicitors, doctors), and the forestry, coal, steel and shipbuilding industries, share dealing and film production.

Other Conditions

Other more particular conditions include:

- The company must use the funds raised for the purposes of carrying on relevant trading activities or, if the company has not yet commenced to trade, in incurring expenditure on R&D.

- Relief is available in a full tax year, subject to a maximum amount of €250,000. If the investor commits to a seven year or more period of investment, relief is available on a maximum investment of €500,000.
- If more than €250,000 is invested by an investor, the excess over that amount is deemed to have been invested in the following tax year and tax relief may be claimed in that next year.
- If full relief is not possible in the year of investment (due to the investor not having sufficient income), the unutilised amount can be carried forward to the next tax year.
- EII/SCI relief is deducted from total income before the investor's tax liability is calculated. If the investor does not have sufficient taxable income this can have the effect of wasting annual tax credits and the 20% standard rate band. The relief is, therefore, more tax efficient for a marginal rate taxpayer.
- EII relief may not be claimed where an individual is connected to the investee company. This occurs where the individual or their relative/associate own any share capital, loan capital, voting rights or rights to the assets on a winding up within the company. This rule is relaxed in the case of investment under the SCI for a micro-enterprise (defined as one with less than 10 employees, and an annual turnover and/or annual balance sheet total not exceeding €2 million) to facilitate tax relief for investments by friends and family in start-up companies.
- Both a husband and wife and civil partners can obtain relief for up to €250,000 each in a tax year. The investment by the husband and wife or civil partners must be separate, however, and each party should have sufficient personal income (i.e. the EII relief is non-transferable between spouses/civil partners).
- An individual cannot claim any other tax relief in respect of borrowings drawn down to make an EII investment.
- A claim for tax relief must be made within two years of the end of the tax year in which the shares were issued.
- Tax relief is clawed back if the shares are sold within four years of the investment.
- If the shares are disposed of and a gain is realised, the full cost of acquisition is allowable as a base cost for CGT purposes. If the disposal results in a loss, the full cost of acquisition is reduced by the amount of the EII relief, which restricts the amount of loss relief available.

Designated Funds

An individual may obtain EII relief by investing in an EII-designated fund, an investment limited partnership or a limited partnership. Such EII funds are subject to the same conditions as those of a single investment as outlined above. While a single investment is subject to a €250 minimum investment, no such minimum applies for a designated fund.

Since 1 January 2020, for all designated fund investments, the tax relief is only available in the year the amount was subscribed to the fund. An SCI investment must be made directly to a company and cannot be made by way of a designated fund investment.

> **Key Issue**
> Always consider EII if the company is a qualifying company and funding is required.

SCI Investments

The only difference between the investors qualifying for EII and SCI is in relation to the restriction placed on associates of investors. EII is not available for investors whose associates have an interest in the company; SCI is available to such associates.

2.5.3   *Withdrawal of SURE and EII/SCI Relief*

SURE and EII/SCI relief will be withdrawn if the investor disposes of the shares within four years of issue of the shares.

If a company in which an individual has made an investment under the EII/SCI:

- repays any debt to the individual (other than an ordinary trade debt);
- makes a loan to the individual or generally attempts to circumvent the requirements of the EII/SCI by providing a benefit for the individual;
- transfers an asset to the individual without any consideration; or
- attempts to pass back to investors the money which they have invested,

then the individual is deemed to have "received value" from the company and their benefits under the EII/SCI will be reduced accordingly.

If the relief does have to be withdrawn from the investor, the investor's liability to income tax in the year in which the relief was originally given is reassessed and interest and/or penalties may arise.

Chapter 2 Summary

Incorporation decision	<ul><li>Consider how well the sole trade is performing before incorporating</li><li>Compare tax savings to be made on incorporating</li><li>Consider the tax implications of incorporation – cessation of trade, balancing adjustments, VAT</li><li>Consider the non-tax implications of incorporating</li><li>Consider future plans for exiting the business – sale, retirement, etc.</li></ul>
Before incorporating	<ul><li>Consider assets to be transferred</li><li>Consider if any assets should be retained personally</li><li>Consider tax implications (CGT, stamp duty, VAT) on the disposal and if reliefs are available</li><li>Consider income tax implications, i.e. cessation of trade rules and balancing charges</li><li>Consider losses of the sole trade – unutilised losses cannot be carried forward on incorporation</li></ul>

Changes on incorporation	• Separate legal entity • Corporation tax regime applies to profits • No longer self-employed • More favourable loss relief rules
Funding the company	• EII/SCI and SURE provide tax relief for investent in certain corporate trades • Start-up company exemption not available on incorporation of sole trades

Questions

Challenging Question
(Solutions to Challenging Questions are available through your lecturer.)

Question 2.1

Mr Bear is a long-established client of your firm. Mr Bear is 53 years old and the sole proprietor of his trading business, Bear Toys, which manufactures cuddly toys, and which was set up over 10 years ago.

Bear Toys trades from a property owned by Mr Bear. The current market value of the property is €450,000 and was purchased for €150,000 when Mr Bear commenced trading.

The business was slow to take off, with losses incurred in the opening years. However, over recent years business has been good and Mr Bear has recently undertaken a programme of restructuring to allow the trade to progress further. This, together with capital allowances claimed on the capital investment, has resulted in current year losses.

Mr Bear currently takes drawings of €40,000 from the business and has no other sources of income.

Mr Bear has provided you with projections in respect of the next two trading years. He has estimated that profits will be in the region of €230,000 per annum and will continue at this level for the foreseeable future.

Mr Bear wishes to talk to you about how best to progress his business in the future, and is keen on the idea of incorporating the trade. You have reviewed the projections, together with the current market position of the business, and have estimated that the goodwill on incorporation would be €200,000; Mr Bear is of the view it would be €1 million (both figures to be considered).

Requirement

Prepare a report on the potential incorporation to cover the following areas:

(a) A broad outline of the potential tax savings on incorporating the trade against trading as a sole trader.
(b) The potential CGT liability arising on the incorporation.
(c) Any reliefs that may be available to reduce the CGT liability.
(d) Advice on whether the property should be transferred to the new limited company or held outside in personal ownership and the implications of the goodwill.
(e) Any tax relief available on the pre-incorporation tax losses.

Tax Considerations for Trading and Investment Companies

Learning Objectives

By the end of this chapter you will be able to:

■ Analyse the potential tax implications for a business trading through a company, with particular reference to:
- differing rates of corporation tax;
- tax exemption for start-up companies;
- brief reminder on use of corporate losses;
- anti-tax avoidance rules for close companies and service companies;
- special tax rules for investment and rental companies;
- Research & Development tax credit;
- the Knowledge Development Box; and
- relief for specified intangible assets.

3.1 Rates of Corporation Tax

A sole trader's profits are liable to tax according to the income tax rules, whereas profits earned by a limited company will be taxed according to corporation tax rules. Corporation tax rates are lower than income tax rates, which as we have seen, can influence the incorporation decision.

A company's Case I income (trading income) is liable to corporation tax at a rate of 12.5%; whereas a company's non-trading income (commonly known as 'passive income') is subject to a 25% rate of corporation tax. Passive income is typically income earned from investments and includes:

■ **Case III income:**
- Irish bank interest income;
- foreign interest income;
- foreign dividend income (some taxable at 12.5%);
- foreign rental income;
- income of a foreign trade; and
- any other foreign income.

- **Case IV miscellaneous income:**
  - royalty income; and
  - all other miscellaneous income (not taxed under Cases I, II, III, or V).

- **Case V rental income:**
  - Irish rental income.

In some instances non-trading income can be liable to an **additional 20% tax**, the "close company surcharge". In this regard, students should bear in mind that if a close company has passive income, due consideration should be given to its exposure to a close company surcharge (see **Section 3.5**).

Other types of income and applicable rates of corporation tax are:

- Franked investment income   Exempt
- Income from minerals (an 'excepted trade')   @ 25%
- Petroleum activities (an 'excepted trade')   @ 25%
- Land-dealing income (an 'excepted trade')   @ 25%

3.2 Tax Relief for Start-up Companies

A limited five-year corporation tax relief for new companies is available in accordance with section 486C TCA 1997. To be eligible for the relief, the company must:

- be incorporated on or after 14 October 2008;
- commence a new qualifying trade between 1 January 2009 and 31 December 2026; and
- be taxable at 12.5%.

This relief reduces the corporation tax on the profits of a new trade and gains on disposal of any assets used for the purposes of the new trade by the amount of PRSI paid for each employee, subject to a maximum of €5,000 per employee and an overall limit of €40,000.

The relief will apply to a new company in any of its first five years of operation where the corporation tax payable by the company is less than €40,000, i.e. a maximum relief of €200,000 over three years.

3.2.1 Conditions of the Relief

A **qualifying trade** is one that does **not** include any trade:

- carried on previously by another person and to which the company has succeeded (which would rule out the incorporation of a business by a sole trader/partnership), including trades transferred between connected companies;
- the activities of which were previously carried on as part of another person's trade or profession;
- that is an 'excepted' trade (e.g. land developers, mining and petroleum activities – see **Section 3.1**), which are trades taxed at the 25% rate; or
- the activities of which, if carried on by a close company with no other income, would result in that company being considered a service company for the purposes of the close company surcharge (which rules out newly incorporated professional services practices).

The relief is limited by the amount of employer PRSI contribution paid by the company. This is calculated by adding the PRSI paid for each employee, subject to a maximum of €5,000 per employee.

Example 3.1

Innu Ltd is a newly formed company qualifying for relief under section 486C. Its first year of trading is 2022. The corporation tax payable for 2022 is €38,500 before start-up relief is claimed. Employer's PRSI paid on behalf of employees for 2022 is as follows:

Employee	Employer PRSI 2022	Specified Contribution
Ms P	€2,500	€2,500
Mr J	€3,200	€3,200
Ms L	€8,700	€5,000
Ms B	€6,400	€5,000

As the corporation tax liability is less than €40,000, start-up relief is restricted to the amount of PRSI paid, subject to a maximum of €5,000 per employee. Total PRSI specified contribution is €15,700. The revised corporation tax payable is as follows:

	€
Actual corporation tax liability	38,500
PRSI restriction	(15,700)
Revised corporation tax liability	22,800

3.2.2 Relevant Corporation Tax Liability

Start-up relief applies to income from a qualifying trade and is computed by reference to "relevant corporation tax". Relevant corporation tax is the total corporation tax exclusive of:

- close company surcharges under sections 440 and 441 TCA 1997;
- profits attributable to dealing in residential development land under section 644B TCA 1997;
- the corporation tax chargeable on the profits of the company attributable to chargeable gains for the period; and
- the corporation tax chargeable on profits charged at the 25% rate.

Example 3.2

James Mead decides to set up a new manufacturing company, James Mead Ltd, in 2022. He owns 100% of the shares. The tax-adjusted trading profits for the year ending 31 December 2022 are €200,000 and the company also has investment income of €20,000. The company paid €40,000 in employer's PRSI in 2022.

James's understanding is that the company has no corporation tax to pay. Is he correct?

No. Assuming James Mead Ltd meets all the conditions set out above, the €25,000 corporation tax on trading profits (€200,000 × 12.5%) would be reduced to nil. However, the company has non-trading income which is liable to €5,000 corporation tax (€20,000 × 25%) and this is due to be paid.

If James Mead Ltd carried on engineering services trade rather than a manufacturing trade, the outcome would be different. Engineering is a professional service activity which is excluded as a qualifying trade under section 486C relief. The company would therefore be liable to the €25,000 corporation tax on the "trading profits" in addition to the €5,000 corporation tax on the investment income (plus potentially a close company surcharge if the after-tax income is not distributed).

3.2.3 Marginal Relief

Marginal relief applies where the total corporation tax is between €40,000 and €60,000. In this instance, the sum of corporation tax on income from the qualifying trade and the corporation tax on chargeable gains from the disposal of qualifying assets is reduced by reference to the formula:

$$3 \times (T - M) \times \frac{(A + B)}{T}$$

where:

    T is the total corporation tax payable by the company for the accounting period;

    M is the lower limit, i.e. €40,000;

    A is the corporation tax payable by the company on income from the qualifying trade for the accounting period; and

    B is the corporation tax payable by the company for that accounting period on chargeable gains on the disposal of qualifying assets.

Example 3.3

A company has trading profits of €400,000 and non-trading profits of €20,000. All of the qualifying conditions for section 486C relief are met. The corporation tax due for the year ended 31 December 2022 is calculated as follows:

Corporation tax on trading profits: €400,000 @ 12.5%	€50,000
Corporation tax on non-trading profits: €20,000 @ 25%	€5,000
	€55,000

Marginal start-up relief therefore applies. Applying the formula:

$$3 \times (€55,000 - €40,000) \times \frac{(€50,000 + €0)}{€55,000} = €40,909$$

Therefore, the total corporation tax bill for the company will be €40,909 + €5,000 = €45,909.

3.2.4 Unused Relief Carried Forward

Unused relief from the first five years of trading may be carried forward for offset against qualifying profits. Unused reliefs occur when:

▤ the company's corporation tax liability in the first five years of trading does not exceed €40,000 **in each accounting period**; and

▤ the company's employer's qualifying PRSI liability exceeds its total corporation tax liability, i.e. before the application of the section 486C relief, for those years (this amount is referred to as the "specified aggregate").

Example 3.4

	Year 1	Year 2	Year 3	Total
	€	€	€	€
Case I trading profits	20,000	150,000	80,000	
Corporation tax @ 12.5%	2,500	18,750	10,000	
Total employer PRSI	15,000	15,000	15,000	
Corporation tax after section 486C relief	0	3,750	0	
Specified aggregate	12,500	0	5,000	17,500

continued overleaf

	Year 4
	€
Case I trading profits	150,000
Corporation tax @ 12.5%	18,750
Total PRSI	18,000
Specified aggregate b/f*	17,500
Corporation tax after section 486C relief	1,250

* If the employer's PRSI in Year 4 was less than the corporation tax liability, say, €16,000, then the specified aggregate brought forward would be limited to €16,000 in Year 4 with the unused balance of €1,500 carried forward to Year 5.

Some points to bear in mind:

- Not all types of profit qualify (e.g. non-trading gains or income) and not all types of trading companies qualify (e.g. professional services).
- A combination of start-up corporation tax relief plus investment incentives for the company could give a very good tax result to a start-up company. For example, EII could be used to attract investment into the company and start-up relief could reduce the company's tax liability, which should free up capital to help build the business.

> **Key Issue**
> This exemption has the potential to assist a lot of start-up companies by reducing their overall effective tax liabilities. A start-up company previously carried on as a sole trade **cannot** access start-up company relief.

3.3 Overview of Trading Loss Relief for a Company

Loss relief rules within a single company are covered in detail in CA Proficiency 2. A brief recap of the key points is set out in the table below.

Legislative reference	Use of the loss	Claim required
Section 396(2) TCA 1997 – Case I (25% rate)	Set-off against other profits in the same or preceding accounting period of same length.	Within two years of the end of the accounting period.
Section 396(1) TCA 1997 – Case I	Carry forward against future profits of the same trade.	Automatic.
Section 396A TCA 1997 – Case I (12.5%)	Set-off against other relevant trading income in the same or preceding accounting period of same length.	Within two years of the end of the accounting period.
Section 396B TCA 1997 – Case I (12.5%)	Set-off on value basis against corporation tax on profits of the same or preceding accounting period of same length.	Within two years of the end of the accounting period.
Section 396(1) TCA 1997 – Case III trade	Carry forward against future Case III profits.	Automatic.
Section 397 TCA 1997 – terminal loss	A loss in the last 12 months of trading can be set back against trading income of the preceding three years.	Must be made after all other possible claims are made.

3.4   Close Company Provisions

Close company provisions are anti-tax avoidance measures designed to prevent situations where the profits of close companies are accumulated rather than distributed to shareholders, in whose hands the distributions would attract income tax at the higher rate. The anti-avoidance close company provisions are also designed to prevent "participators" extracting funds or value from a close company in a manner that avoids or reduces potential tax liabilities. These rules are covered in detail in CA Proficiency 2. A summary of the provisions are provided here by way of a recap.

A close company is an **Irish tax resident** company that is:

- controlled by five or fewer participators; or
- controlled by any number of directors who are also participators; or
- where, on a full distribution of its income, more than half the income would be paid to five or fewer participators or to participators who are directors.

3.4.1   Definition of Terms

It is necessary to consider a number of the terms used in the definition of a close company.

Participator

A participator is a person having a share or interest in the capital or income of a company and includes anyone holding:

- present or future rights to share capital, voting rights;
- any loan creditor of the company (except in respect of an ordinary bank loan);
- rights to share in any distribution by the company;
- rights to share in any premium on redemption of loan capital; and
- any other rights under which the person could secure that present or future income or assets of the company could be applied directly or indirectly for the person's benefit.

Control

Control is also an essential aspect of deciding if a company falls within the definition of "close". A person is regarded as having control of a company if the person possesses, or is entitled to acquire, more than 50% of the company's share capital, income if it were distributed, or assets in a winding up.

Associates

Crucially, the rights and powers of a person's "associates" are also attributed to the individual for the purposes of determining control. An associate includes:

- the person's close relatives, which includes a husband, wife, civil partner, ancestor, lineal descendant, brother or sister, but excludes, for example, the brother or sister of a spouse or civil partner;
- the person's business partners;
- the trustees of any settlement made by the person or by any close relative; and
- if the person is interested in any shares or obligations of the company as a beneficiary of a trust or of a deceased person's estate, any other person interested in those shares or obligations.

Director

The term "director" includes any person occupying the position of director by whatever name called, any person in accordance with whose directions or instructions the directors of a company are accustomed to act, and any manager who alone or with associates owns or controls 20% or more of the ordinary share capital of the company. The definition of a close company specifies that once a company is controlled by directors, it is a close company, regardless of the number of directors included in the "control", and there is no need to consider how many participators control the company.

Non-resident Companies

Close company rules apply to Irish tax resident companies, so an Irish branch of a foreign company will not be subject to close company provisions. However, an Irish tax resident company **owned** by foreign shareholders will be subject to close company rules if the control tests set out above are satisfied.

Quoted Companies

Close company provisions do not apply to quoted companies where:

■ shares carrying 35% or more of the voting rights are held by the public; and
■ the shares have been traded on a stock exchange during the previous 12 months; and
■ not more than 85% of the voting power is in the hands of the principal members.

3.4.2   Implications of Close Company Status

A close company is subject to anti-avoidance measures aimed at ensuring that closely held companies are not used to:

■ shelter income that would be taxable at higher rates if distributed to participators; or
■ to withdraw profits or value from the company without paying tax.

As a general rule, close company anti-avoidance provisions are designed to make any monies or value passing from a company to its shareholders liable to income tax (as opposed to being either exempt or liable to lower CGT rates of tax).

Students should be familiar with the close company anti-avoidance measures from previous studies. Briefly, the main disadvantages associated with close companies are:

■ benefits and expense payments to participators or their associates are treated as distributions;
■ interest in excess of a specified rate paid to directors or their associates are treated as a distribution;
■ loans to participators or their associates are penalised and, if the loan is forgiven, it will be treated as income in the hands of the recipient;
■ transfer of assets at undervalue will also be penalised;
■ undistributed investment, rental and service company income is liable to a 20% surcharge; and
■ certain settlements of money, or money's worth, made by a close company are treated as a distribution and certain receipts by individuals or their relatives from settlements are treated as Case IV income.

Example 3.5

Mike and Mary are the shareholders and directors of Double M Ltd. Their 20-year-old son Marty is in college and wants to work in Boston for the summer. The return flight is €600, which is paid for by Double M Ltd. Marty doesn't work for Double M Ltd.

The tax impact of the payment for the airline ticket is:

■ it is deemed a distribution and is a non-deductible expense for Double M Ltd;
■ Double M Ltd is obliged to apply dividend withholding tax (DWT) on the deemed distribution to Marty;
■ Marty is liable to income tax on the gross deemed distribution under Schedule F with a credit for the 25% DWT applied at source by Double M Ltd.

3.4.3 *Close Company Surcharge*

The close company surcharge is an extra layer of tax designed to discourage the retention of investment, estate and professional earnings (see **Section 3.5**) within the close company. A close company that does not distribute its after-tax estate and investment income is liable to a surcharge of 20% on such income.

The surcharge does not apply to the after-tax estate and investment income where such income is €2,000 or less.

Trading and professional service companies are entitled to a 7.5% trading deduction when calculating "distributable estate and investment income" (or relevant income) for the purposes of calculating the close company surcharge.

If a distribution of the relevant income is made by way of dividend within 18 months of the end of the accounting period, no surcharge arises. Where individual shareholders are receiving the distribution, consideration should be given to whether it costs less in tax terms for the company to incur the surcharge rather than make the dividend payment. The effective tax rate on the surchargeable income in the company is approximately 40%, whereas the individual could be liable to income tax, PRSI and USC of up to 55% on taking a dividend taxable under Schedule F.

No surcharge applies if there are insufficient distributable reserves in the company because the surcharge does not apply to any income that a company is by law precluded from distributing,

---

Example 3.6

Gamma Ltd is a close company and had the following income in the year ended 31 December 2022:

Case I	€100,000
Case III	€2,000
Case V	€6,000

Gamma does not pay dividends to its shareholders. The close company surcharge is payable on its distributable estate and investment income, to the extent that it is not distributed. Therefore:

	€
Estate and investment income	8,000
Corporation tax @ 25%	(2,000)
	6,000
Trading deduction 7.5%	(450)
Distributable estate and investment income	5,550
Less: dividends paid/payable within 18 months	Nil
Liable to surcharge	5,550
Surcharge @ 20%	1,110

3.4.4 *Election for Two Close Companies to Ignore a Distribution*

In the case of a corporate shareholder, a dividend or a distribution received from a subsidiary may have close company surcharge implications if the group is close. This is the case even though corporation tax does not apply on dividends or franked investment income. However, a paying company and a receiving company **may jointly elect** not to have the dividend or distributions treated as such for the purpose of the close company surcharge. Thus a company can avoid the surcharge on dividends received where a valid election is in place.

Where the election is made, the paying company cannot use the amount of the dividend to reduce its own distributable estate and investment income. Although the paying company may have a surcharge liability, the facility to elect prevents multiple surcharges arising as a dividend is paid up through a number of tiers of corporate ownership.

The election operates best when a trading company is making a distribution to its parent, because the trading company will not have a close company surcharge to contend with. However, if the paying company does have a close company surcharge, the election may not generate a tax-efficient outcome as highlighted by the following example.

Example 3.7

HoldCo is a close company. It is the 100% owner of AlphaCo, a trading company that does not have any non-Case I source income. AlphaCo pays a dividend (FII) of €25,000 to HoldCo, on which HoldCo is facing a potential close company surcharge of €5,000. Both companies can make a joint election that HoldCo is not surchargable on the dividend.

However, say AlphaCo had rental income of €30,000. The election to treat the dividend payment to HoldCo as non-surchargable would not then be tax efficient. AlphaCo is entitled to a deduction for the dividend paid to HoldCo in the calculation of its own close company surcharge as follows:

	€
Estate and investment income	30,000
Corporation tax @ 25%	(7,500)
	22,500
Trading deduction 7.5%	(1,687)
Distributable estate and investment income	20,813
Less: dividends paid/payable within 18 months	(25,000)
Liable to surcharge	Nil

If AlphaCo cannot use the dividend of €25,000 paid to HoldCo in its close company surcharge calculation, then it would incur a surcharge of €4,163 (€20,813 @ 20%).

This provision works best where the paying subsidiary is a trading company without surchargeable income of its own. By making the election, the receiving company does not suffer a surcharge, nor does it need to make a distribution to avoid one; and the paying trading company does not have a surcharge to avoid in the first place.

Key Issue

When passive income is included in a company's income, always consider if there is a close company surcharge issue.

3.5 Professional Service Companies

A 'professional services surcharge' also applies to income generated by professional service companies. This surcharge is designed to discourage professionals who would otherwise run their business as a sole trade (and so be liable to the higher rate of income tax) from incorporating and sheltering income at the lower corporation tax rates.

A service company is one carrying on a profession, or providing professional services or exercising an office or employment. "Professionals" include accountants, actors, actuaries, archaeologists, architects, auctioneers/estate agents, barristers, computer programmers, dentists, doctors, engineers, journalists, management consultants, opticians, private schools, quantity surveyors, solicitors, veterinary surgeons.

The surcharge is applied to 50% of the distributable trading income at a rate of 15%. Passive income is still levied at 20%. A *de minimis* limit applies where no surcharge arises if the income liable to the professional service company surcharge and the close company surcharge is less than €2,000.

Example 3.8

Accounting Ltd is a professional service company with the following results for the year ended 31 December 2022:

	€
Professional income (after costs)	1,200,000
Deposit interest	300,000
	1,500,000

The company also paid a dividend of €100,000 in this accounting period.

Distributable estate and investment income is calculated as:

	€
Investment income	300,000
Less: tax @ 25%	(75,000)
	225,000
Less: 7.5%	(16,875)
	208,125

Trading income = €1,500,000 minus €300,000 = €1,200,000.

The distributable trading income is the trading income minus the amount of corporation tax payable on that income, i.e. €1,200,000 – (€1,200,000 @ 12.5%) = €1,050,000.

Surcharge calculation	€	€
Distributable estate and investment income	208,125	
Dividend paid	(100,000)	
	108,125	
Surcharge €108,125 @ 20%		21,625
Distributable trading income: €1,050,000 × 50%	525,000	
Surcharge €525,00 @ 15%		78,750
Total surcharge		100,375

3.6 Investment Companies

Special tax rules exist for Irish investment companies to provide, under certain conditions, a tax deduction for their management expenses when calculating the company's tax liability. An investment company is defined in section 83 TCA 1997 as being:

> "any company whose business consists wholly or mainly of the making of investments and the principal part of whose income is derived from the making of investments"

The concept of "wholly and mainly" has been considered by the courts over the years. A degree of investment **activity** is required for a company to be in the business of making investments.

When considering the income of the company, it is reasonable to take a long-term view of income projections, rather than merely one accounting period. The question can then arise as to whether a company is a genuine investment company, or merely a holding company (holding shares, etc.). A holding company will not qualify for the special tax rules pertaining to investment companies. The mere holding of investments by a company does not automatically qualify it for investment company status.

An Irish resident investment company may, in computing its taxable profits, deduct management expenses incurred during a taxable period. The entitlement to this deduction is a key benefit attaching to investment company tax status. Without this specific tax treatment, an investment company could not obtain a tax deduction for its costs of operation.

3.6.1 Deduction for Management Expenses

Management expenses are not defined in tax legislation. Once again, the concept of what a management expense is has been the source of extensive case law. The following expenditure has been determined as being deductible for tax purposes:

- Costs such as the keeping of the investment company share register, annual accounts and the holding of annual shareholder meetings.
- Costs incurred in respect of stock exchange quotations.
- Maintenance and repair costs in respect of premises used by the investment company.
- Director's remuneration (subject to not being in excess of 10% of the company's gross investment income excluding chargeable gains).
- Payments in respect of Revenue-approved retirement schemes.
- Redundancy costs.
- Charges on income (e.g. interest, etc.).

The following are specifically **not** considered an expense of management:

- Professional fees in respect of land held as investments.
- Cost of appraising investments.
- Brokerage, commissions and stamp duty in respect of investments.
- Costs of raising capital.

The management expenses of an investment company are deductible against investment income (e.g. dividends, bank interest, etc.) in the applicable taxable period. An excess of unused/unutilised management expenses may be carried forward to the next accounting period. It is also possible to surrender excess management expenses to a fellow group member and claim group relief.

Example 3.9

Quasi Investments Ltd reported the following results for the year ended 31 December 2022 in its management accounts.

	€	€
Investment Income – 2022		
Irish dividend income	20,000	
Bank interest (received gross)	2,000	
Chargeable gain on disposal of shares (adjusted for corporation tax purposes)	50,000	
Foreign dividend income from non-treaty country	8,000	
Gross income	80,000	80,000
Management Expenses – 2022		
Director's remuneration	10,000	
Appraisal costs	2,000	
Shareholder meeting costs	3,000	
Rent of office	2,000	
Repairs to office door	1,000	
Total expenses	(18,000)	(18,000)
Net profit per management accounts		62,000

The tax computation of Quasi Investments will be as follows:

	€	€
Irish dividend income	Exempt	
Bank interest	2,000	
Foreign dividend income	8,000	
Total taxable gross income	10,000	
Chargeable gain	50,000	
Total profit	60,000	60,000
Less: management expenses:		
Shareholder meeting costs	3,000	
Director's remuneration (limit of 10%)	3,000	
Office rent	2,000	
Repairs	1,000	
Total management expenses	(9,000)	(9,000)
Taxable profit		51,000

Corporation tax:

€50,000 @ 12.5%	6,250
€1,000 @ 25%	250
Corporation tax due	6,500

An investment company, like any other company, returns details of its income in an annual corporation tax return (Form CT1). This return must be submitted approximately nine months after the company's year end.

3.6.2 Property Rental Companies

Revenue accepts that a property rental company can come within the definition of an investment company for corporation tax purposes. However, it has also been indicated by Revenue that a property rental company should contain some of the following characteristics in order to obtain the same tax treatment as an investment company:

- The company must hold more than one property.
- A company that holds only one property must also hold other classes of investment assets.
- The company must derive its income from the property (i.e. there must be an active rental operation carried on by the company).

The expenses deductible by a property rental company are:

- Those normally deductible for Case V purposes, i.e. bank interest, repairs, property management fees, insurance, letting fees, etc.
- Management costs deductible under the investment company rules (as detailed in **Section 3.6.1**).

A tax deduction for a director's remuneration is limited to 10% of the company's gross income (excluding chargeable gains). There is, however, an increased deduction of 15% of gross rental income where the director devotes a substantial part of their time to the management of the company's investment properties.

Example 3.10

Quasi Property Ltd, whose director devotes a substantial part of her time to the management of the company's investment properties, reported the following results for the year ended 31 December 2022 in its management accounts.

	€	€
Investment Income – 2022		
Irish dividend income	20,000	
Bank interest (received gross)	2,000	
Rental income	50,000	
Foreign dividend income from non-treaty country	8,000	
Gross income	80,000	80,000
Expenses – 2022		
Director's remuneration	(12,000)	
Appraisal costs	(500)	
Shareholder meeting costs	(2,500)	
Property management fees	(2,000)	
Repairs to premises	(1,000)	
Total expenses	(18,000)	(18,000)
Net profit per management accounts		62,000

The tax computation of Quasi Property Ltd is as follows:

	€	€
Franked investment income	Exempt	
Schedule D, Case III (interest)	2,000	
Schedule D, Case V (Note 1)	47,000	
Schedule D, Case III (foreign dividend)	8,000	
Total gross income	57,000	57,000
Less: management expenses:		
Shareholder meeting costs	(2,500)	
Director's remuneration (limits of 10% and 15%)	(10,500)	
Total management expenses	(13,000)	(13,000)
Taxable income		44,000
Corporation tax:		
Cases III and V €44,000 × 25%		11,000

Note 1: Case V income is calculated as €50,000 less property management fees (€2,000) and repairs (€1,000).

3.6.3 Close Company Surcharge Issues

An investment company and a property rental company could come within the scope of a close company surcharge (as set out in **Section 3.4.2**) and an additional 20% tax may also arise on any undistributed investment and estate income net of tax. This close company surcharge issue should be considered when reviewing the tax liability of an investment company.

Example 3.11

Taking the details from **Example 3.10**, Quasi Property Ltd's close company surcharge position is as follows:

- the company's rental and investment income is calculated;
- the company's FII is then added to this figure and a deduction taken for non-trade charges and expenses of management; and
- the tax payable is deducted from this result to arrive at the distributable rental and investment income.

The relevant figures for Quasi Property Ltd for year ended 31 December 2022 are:

	€
Rental and investment income	57,000
Allowable management expenses	(13,000)
	44,000
Less: corporation tax @ 25%	(11,000)
Net after-tax income	33,000
Add FII	20,000
Distributable total	53,000
Surcharge @ 20%	10,600

The surcharge of €10,600 is payable **unless** distributions are made in respect of this accounting period. Distributions made up to 30 June 2024 will reduce or eliminate the surcharge.

3.7   Research and Development (R&D) Tax Credit

Tax relief for expenditure on R&D is a very important tax incentive for Irish companies as well as for international businesses looking for investment opportunities or to undertake R&D activity in Ireland. The availability of the relief is significant for companies as it represents a potential 25% tax credit against the corporation tax liability or a tax refund.

The relief is by way of a 25% credit (in addition to a 12.5% corporation tax deduction for R&D expenditure).

3.7.1   Calculation of the R&D Tax Credit

For accounting periods commencing on or after 1 January 2015, section 766 TCA 1997 provides that all qualifying R&D expenditure incurred by a company, or group of companies, is eligible for the 25% tax credit. Prior to that date, the R&D tax credit was granted at a rate of 25% of incremental expenditure incurred by a company.

The credit available is in addition to the normal tax deduction as a trading expense, which means a potential tax saving of 37.5% for the company.

Only expenditure incurred in carrying on R&D activities qualifies for the tax credit. Expenditure on plant and machinery can be treated as qualifying R&D expenditure but must be eligible for wear and tear capital allowances as well as being used for R&D activities. R&D is a "qualifying activity" if it satisfies all of the following conditions, which provide that the expenditure must be:

1. for systematic, investigative or experimental activities;
2. in a field of science or technology; and

3. involve one or more of the following categories of R&D:
   (a) basic research;
   (b) applied research; or
   (c) experimental development.

In addition it must "seek to achieve scientific or technological advancement, and involve the resolution of scientific or technological uncertainty".

Qualifying expenditure **excludes**:

- expenditure that is deductible for tax purposes in another jurisdiction;
- expenditure qualifying for a capital allowance as scientific research under section 765 TCA 1997;
- expenditure claimed as a capital allowance under the intangible assets regime (see **Section 3.9**);
- royalty payments paid to a connected party that are exempt from tax in the hands of the recipient or if the amount paid exceeds an arm's length amount that would be paid between unconnected parties;
- interest;
- expenditure funded by grants from the EU, EEA or the Irish State.

The company must file a claim for the R&D credit within 12 months of the end of the accounting period in which the expenditure was incurred.

Expenditure on R&D activities **outsourced** by a company to subcontractors also qualifies for the R&D tax credit, but are subject to the following limits/conditions:

- For expenditure paid to third-level institutions and unconnected third parties, the amount which can be claimed by the paying company is 15% of its R&D expenditure or €100,000, whichever is greater.
- Third parties must be notified in writing in advance of payment that the paying company intends to claim the R&D credit for the expenditure so that the third-party subcontractor does not also make a claim for the R&D credit.

Example 3.12

In the 12-month accounting period ended 31 December 2022, Beta Ltd had sales of €100,000 and incurred €40,000 of qualifying R&D expenditure. Its corporation tax computation is as follows:

	€
Sales	100,000
Qualifying R&D expenditure	(40,000)
Taxable profits	60,000
Corporation tax @ 12.5%	7,500
Credit for R&D expenditure (€40,000 × 25%)	(10,000)
Corporation tax liability	Nil
Excess R&D credit available to carry forward (€10,000 – €7,500)	2,500

3.7.2 Use of the R&D Tax Credit

Use of the R&D credit is as follows:

1. The credit is first set against the company's current-period corporation tax liability (under section 766(2) TCA 1997).
2. Any unused excess can be carried back to offset corporation tax of the preceding accounting period of equal length (under section 766(4A) TCA 1997).

3. Where a company has offset the credit against the corporation tax of the preceding accounting period, or where no corporation tax arises for that period and an excess still remains, the company may make a claim to have the amount of that excess paid to them by Revenue in three instalments.
4. The three instalments will be paid over a period of 33 months from the end of the accounting period in which the expenditure was incurred. The first instalment to be paid will amount to 33% of the excess and may be payable by the filing date for the accounting period in which the expenditure was incurred.
5. The remaining balance will then be used to first reduce the corporation tax of the next accounting period and, if any excess still remains, a second instalment amounting to 50% of that remaining excess will be paid to the company 12 months after the due date of the filing of the corporation tax return that gave rise to the original claim. For example, if a company made a claim in respect of expenditure incurred in the accounting period ending 31 December 2022, the 50% in question (i.e. the second instalment) would be refunded 12 months after the filing of the 31 December 2022 return, i.e. on or after 23 September 2024.
6. Any further excess may then be used to reduce the corporation tax of the following accounting period and, if an excess still remains, under section 766(4B) TCA 1997, that amount will be paid to the company as the third instalment, 24 months after the filing of the corporation tax return that gave rise to the original R&D credit. Following the example above, the final refund would issue 24 months after the filing of the return for the period ended 31 December 2022, i.e. on or after 23 September 2025.

The maximum cash refund payable to a company is limited to the greater of:

1. the corporation tax payable by the company for accounting periods ending in the 10 years prior to the relevant period, or
2. the payroll taxes remitted by the company to Revenue in the relevant period and the previous period.

Payroll liabilities include the Universal Social Charge, along with income tax and PRSI payable by the company.

Example 3.13
Innovation Ltd commenced to trade in the year ended 31 December 2021. In the 12-month period ended 31 December 2022, it incurred R&D on qualifying activities of €1,400,000. Its payroll liabilities for the tax year 2022 are €85,000 and for the 2021 tax year amounted to €65,000. Its corporation tax liability is €50,000 for 2021; for 2022 it is nil; and for 2023 it is €40,000. The R&D tax credit in 2022 is €1,400,000 at 25% or €350,000.

Effect	Excess Credit
	€
Step 1 It has no corporation tax liability in 2022 and seeks to make a claim for payment of the credit.	350,000
Step 2 In the 2021 financial year, its corporation tax liability was €50,000 and the credit can be used to offset this.	(50,000)
	300,000
Step 3 The excess credit of €300,000 can be claimed as a refund up to a maximum of €150,000 (i.e. payroll liabilities for 2022 plus 2021) and the balance not refunded can be used as a credit.	
Step 4 33% of €150,000 or €50,000 will be repaid to the company no earlier than 21 September 2023.	(50,000)
	250,000
Step 5 The remaining excess of €250,000 is treated as a credit for the financial year ended 31 December 2023. The company has no R&D in that year, but has a corporation tax liability of €40,000, which is offset with the 2022 credit.	(40,000)
	210,000

continued overleaf

Step 6 50% of the remaining refundable excess of €100,000 (i.e. €150,000 – €50,000) or €50,000 will be repaid no earlier than 12 months after the filing date, i.e. 21 September 2024.	(50,000)
	160,000
Step 7 The remaining €160,000 will be a tax credit for 2024 and will offset any corporation tax liability of that year. We will assume that the company had no corporation tax liability in that year.	
Step 8 The remaining refundable excess of €50,000 will be repaid no earlier than 24 months after the filing date, i.e. 21 September 2025.	(50,000)
Step 9 The remaining amount after claiming a credit for tax liabilities for the accounting years 2021, 2022 and 2023, and on claiming a refund up to the maximum of €150,000, can be used as a credit against future years' corporation tax liabilities of Innovation Ltd.	110,000

3.7.3 Remuneration of Key Employees

Relief is available for the remuneration of key employees engaged in the R&D process. Qualifying R&D companies may surrender all or part of the R&D tax credit to key employees who have been or are central to the R&D activity. A "key employee" is defined in section 472D TCA 1997 as an individual who:

- is not, or has not been, a director of the company and is not connected to a director of the company;
- does not have, or has never had, a material interest in the company or is not connected with a person who has a material interest in the company;
- performs at least 50% of their activities "in the conception or creation of new knowledge, products, processes, methods and systems"; and
- has 50% or more of their emoluments which qualify for the R&D tax credit.

The quantum of credit that can be surrendered to the employee is limited to the amount of corporation tax due by the company prior to taking the R&D credit into consideration (i.e. the company must be paying tax in the first instance). The effective rate of tax payable by the individual employee cannot be reduced below 23%. Employees allocated the R&D tax credit by their employer must file a tax return under the self-assessment system to Revenue to receive an income tax refund.

3.7.4 R&D Buildings

In addition to the relief available under section 766 TCA 1997, a tax credit of 25% is available under section 766A TCA 1997 for expenditure on buildings/structures used for R&D. The company must be entitled to claim industrial buildings capital allowances on the building/structure to qualify for the credit. The section 766A R&D credit excludes expenditure qualifying for a capital allowance as scientific research (under section 765).

The corporation tax of the company may be reduced by 25% of the expenditure (net of grant and cost of the site) in the year in which the expenditure is incurred. If only part of the building/structure is used for R&D activities, the expenditure qualifying for relief must be apportioned accordingly. The 25% credit is given in addition to any capital allowances.

Example 3.14

Beta Ltd incurred expenditure of €2 million in the accounting period ended 31 December 2022 in respect of a building used for R&D activities. The R&D activities to be carried on by the company in that building over the specified relevant period will represent 40% of all activities carried on in the building or structure.

The tax credit is calculated as follows:

Specified relevant expenditure:	€2,000,000 @ 40%	€800,000
Tax credit:	€800,000 × 25%	€200,000

Clawback

If the building/structure is sold or ceases to be used for the purposes of carrying on R&D activities within 10 years, any relief already given is withdrawn. The company will be assessed under Case IV Schedule D to an amount equal to four times the credit granted and this amount is then taxed at 25%, i.e. the credit given is clawed back.

3.7.5 R&D Tax Credit – Incorrect Claims

Where a company deliberately overstates an R&D tax credit claim or makes a false claim, it is chargeable under Case IV on an amount equal to eight-times the amount over-claimed, e.g. if a company is found to have deliberately overstated its qualifying R&D expenditure by €100,000 and claimed an additional R&D credit of €25,000, it will be liable to corporation tax under Case IV on an amount of €200,000 (8 × €25,000). If the additional claim had been due to an error rather than deliberate behaviour, the amount assessable under Case IV would be €100,000. The Case IV deemed income cannot be reduced by losses or R&D tax credits available to the company.

Where a company has made an incorrect claim for an R&D tax credit and surrenders an amount of that credit to a key employee, the tax foregone is recovered from the company instead of from the key employee. The tax foregone is recovered by assessing the company on Case IV profits of four-times the amount of the credit to which it was not entitled.

3.8 Knowledge Development Box

The Knowledge Development Box (KDB) is provided for under sections 769G–769R TCA 1997. It is designed to supplement the R&D credit by providing a special tax rate on profits generated from related R&D or intellectual property activities. The KDB rate is effectively a tax rate of 6.25%, which applies to accounting periods that begin before 1 January 2023. While the legislation does not provide for a 6.25% corporation rate; an additional tax deduction is granted that, when factored into the calculation of taxable profits and the 12.5% rate is applied, results in an effective rate of 6.25%.

Ireland's KDB is seen as the first such scheme to comply with the OECD's guidelines to prevent tax avoidance. It is hoped that Ireland's compliance with these high international standards will offer businesses, both foreign and indigenous, certainty and confidence in investing in intellectual property activities in Ireland.

The KDB applies the 'Modified Nexus Approach' designed by the OECD, which calculates tax relief using the proportion of qualifying R&D expenditure expended by the Irish company in comparison with the entity's overall R&D spend worldwide. Therefore, the higher the proportion of R&D that takes place in the Irish entity, the greater the proportion of qualifying income/profits from a "qualifying asset" that may qualify for the 6.25% rate. The company must be carrying on a "specified trade".

A **specified trade** is one that satisfies one or more of the following criteria:

1. The managing, developing, maintaining, protecting, enhancing or exploiting of intellectual property.
2. The researching, planning, processing, experimenting, testing, devising, developing or other similar activity leading to an invention or creation of intellectual property.
3. The sale of goods or the supply of services that derive part of their value from activities described in 1. and 2. above, where those activities were carried on by the relevant company.

Where the above activities form part of the trade of a company, the specified trade will be deemed to be a separate trade and the results for this specified trade must be separated from the overall activities of the company.

"**Qualifying assets**" are specific qualifying intellectual property as follows:

- computer programs, within the meaning of the Copyright and Related Rights Act 2000 (this includes computer programs that represent a derivative work or an adaptation of an original work);
- inventions protected by a qualifying patent or certain supplementary protection certificates; and
- medical or plant breeders' rights within the meaning of section 4 of the Plant Varieties (Proprietary Rights) Act 1980.

"**Qualifying expenditure**" under the KDB is expenditure that must be incurred "wholly and exclusively" in the carrying on of R&D activities in an EU Member State, the consequences of which lead to the development, improvement or creation of the qualifying asset. When R&D activities are outsourced to a third-party entity that is not a member of the corporate group, this also constitutes qualifying expenditure. Costs of acquiring the qualifying asset also comprise qualifying expenditure.

The cost of R&D outsourced to related parties, i.e. members of the same corporate group, along with the cost of acquiring intellectual property is not treated as qualifying expenditure. To take account of such excluded expenditure, an additional 'up lift' allows qualifying expenditure to be increased by the lower of:

- 30% of qualifying expenditure; or
- the aggregate of amounts paid to related parties and the cost of acquiring intellectual property.

"**Qualifying profit**" is the profit of the specified trade relevant to the qualifying asset. In the case of the KDB this includes royalties, licence fees, insurance, damages or compensation, and the portion of income from sale of a product or service that relates to the intellectual property (calculated on a "just and reasonable" basis). Companies must also deduct costs expended in earning the income; therefore, the amount that qualifies for the effective rate of 6.25% is the net profit attached to the qualifying asset and is achieved as follows:

$$\frac{QE + UE}{OE} \times QA$$

where:
QE is the qualifying expenditure on the qualifying asset;
UE is the uplift expenditure;
OE is the overall expenditure on the qualifying asset; and
QA is the profit of the specified trade relevant to the qualifying asset.

Example 3.15

Bloks Ltd is a specialist IT company. The following data is relevant for its financial year ended 31 December 2022:

	€
Outsourcing costs incurred (related group company)	295,000
Direct acquisition cost of patent	195,000
Qualifying expenditure on R&D activities	375,000
	865,000
Total qualifying profits from R&D activities	1,980,000
Other profits (non-R&D activities)	400,000

Formula to calculate qualifying profits:

$$\frac{(QE+UE)}{OE} \times QA = \frac{(€375,000 + €112,500*)}{€865,000} \times €1,980,000 = €1,115,896$$

KDB relief is therefore €1,115,896 × 50% = €557,948

* UE is lesser of:

- Qualifying expenditure €375,000 × 30% = €112,500 **or**
- Outsourcing costs plus cost of patent = €490,000

Corporation tax computation	€
Qualifying profits from R&D activities	1,115,896
Non-qualifying profits from R&D activities	864,104
Total profits from R&D activities	1,980,000
Other profits (non-R&D activities)	400,000
	2,380,000
Less: KDB relief	(557,948)
	1,822,052
Corporation tax @ 12.5%	227,757

3.8.1 Operation of the Relief

The qualifying profits of the specified trade calculated using the above formula equal the profits qualifying for the KDB relief. As demonstrated in **Example 3.15** above, the KDB relief is calculated in such a way that it gives the company an 'allowance' of 50% of qualifying profits (treated as a trading expense) in that period. This 50% allowance is how the effective corporation tax rate of 6.25% is achieved.

Where the specified trade results in a loss, the above formula is used to calculate the "qualifying loss". Therefore relief for losses incurred in a specified trade is given after reducing the loss by 50%.

Losses from a specified trade can be relieved against the other profits of a company or a group on a value basis, as is the case when using trading losses against income taxable at, say, the 25% corporation tax rate (see **Section 3.3**). For example, an R&D company has losses of €100,000 (calculated using the formula above), of which a €10,000 loss is offset against non-R&D trade leaving a loss balance of €90,000. The loss utilised is treated as 200%, i.e. €20,000 (€10,000 × 200%), leaving the balance of the loss at €80,000. In effect, this gives relief for the losses on a value basis.

A claim for KDB relief must be made within 24 months of the end of the accounting period to which the claim relates.

3.9 Relief for Specified Intangible Assets

Ireland's attractiveness as a knowledge-based economy and as a holding company location for foreign groups with worldwide patent brands is supported by the relief available for expenditure incurred by companies on "specified intangible assets". The relief is provided for in section 291A TCA 1997.

For an asset to qualify for the relief it must be regarded as an intangible asset under generally accepted accounting practice, and it must be included in the list of specified intangible assets (SIAs) as defined in section 291A. The definition of SIAs is quite broad and includes patents, patent rights, design rights, trademarks, brand names, licences, copyright, computer software, know-how, goodwill associated with the foregoing intangible asset categories and customer lists, provided they are not acquired as part of a business as a going concern.

3.9.1 Operation of the Relief

The relief is in the form of a capital allowance and is available for expenditure incurred, including expenditure incurred prior to the commencement of the trade, on the provision of an SIA for the purposes of the trade. The amount of the allowance available for tax purposes will generally follow the accounting treatment applicable to the acquisition of intangible assets, i.e. the company's amortisation policy. The company also has an option to spread the expenditure over a 15-year period (7% in years 1–14, and 2% in year 15).

If a company wishes to avail of relief under section 291A, it must make a claim within 12 months from the end of the accounting period in which the expenditure giving rise to the claim is incurred.

3.9.2 Restrictions on the Relief

The amount of allowances available under section 291A is subject to a restriction. Interest relief available to the company in respect of a loan taken out to acquire the SIA is subject to the same restriction.

The aggregate of the allowances and any related interest incurred on acquisition of the SIA cannot exceed 80% of the company's income from "relevant activities", which includes the managing, developing and exploiting of intangible assets. Income from "relevant activities" is treated as income from a separate trade, known as the "relevant trade". Therefore, if a company has other trading income it is necessary to separately identify the income from "relevant activities" and the income from the other trade to calculate the relief available.

Example 3.16

In 2022, NTM Ltd acquired patents for €15,000,000 and trademarks for €5,000,000, financed by a loan subject to 1% interest per annum. It uses these to manufacture and sell industrial panels. The company makes up its accounts to 31 December each year.

In 2022, NTM Ltd showed a loss before tax of €500,000; in 2023 it posted a profit before tax of €2,000,000. Amortisation on the patents is over 10 years, i.e. €1,500,000 per annum; and on the trademarks, over 16 years, i.e. €312,500 per annum.

What tax deductions can NTM Ltd claim for the capital cost of acquiring the intellectual property? Both the patents and trademarks qualify as SIAs under section 291A.

Option 1: Amortisation per accounts

- Patents = €1,500,000 p.a.
- Trademarks = €312,500 p.a.

Option 2: Over 15 years

- Patents = €15,000,000 × 7% = €1,050,000 p.a.
- Trademarks = €5,000,000 × 7% = €350,000 p.a.

NTM Ltd chooses the accounting amortisation option for the patents, and spreads the trademark allowances over 15 years. The annual capital allowance is therefore €1,500,000 + €350,000 = €1,850,000.

The maximum claim that NTM Ltd can make is subject to the annual restriction of 80% of its relevant profits. Taking the years given:

	2022	2023
	€	€
Profit/(loss) before tax	(500,000)	2,000,000
Add back amortisation:		
Patents	1,500,000	1,500,000
Trademarks	312,500	312,500
Taxable profits	1,312,500	3,812,500
Maximum of 80%	1,050,000	3,050,000
Deduct interest	(200,000)	(200,000)
Capital allowance claim made in year	(850,000)	(2,850,000) (carried forward + current)
Assessable Case I profits	262,500	762,500
Carried forward amount	1,000,000	Nil

3.9.3 Balancing Charge on Disposal of SIAs

Prior to Finance Act 2020, no balancing charge (i.e. a clawback of capital allowances previously claimed) arose if the SIA had been held for more than five years. Finance Act 2020 makes an amendment to provide that all capital expenditure incurred on the provision of SIAs on or after 14 October 2020 is subject to a balancing charge on a subsequent disposal, regardless of when the balancing event may occur.

Chapter 3 Summary

Rates of corporation tax

- In general, trades are taxed at 12.5%
- Certain trades and passive income taxed at 25%

Anti-avoidance provision for companies

- Close company anti-avoidance provisions impact the majority of Irish companies
- Service companies are also subject to close company provisions
- Investment and rental companies are subject to special rules for expenses deductions and to close company surcharge

Reliefs available for companies

- Start-up exemption (section 486C TCA 1997 relief)
- Relief for trading losses
- R&D tax credits
- The Knowledge Development Box
- Intangible assets scheme

Questions

Challenging Question

(Solutions to Challenging Questions are available through your lecturer.)

Question 3.1

Teckno Ire is an Irish incorporated, fully owned subsidiary of Teckno Global Inc. (Teckno Inc.). The Irish operation manufactures and distributes specialist audio products from its plant in Shannon. A recent detailed analysis of Teckno Ire's R&D activities carried out by technical experts uncovered additional qualifying but unclaimed expenditure of €300,000 in respect of the year ended 30 November 2021.

The original R&D expenditure in 2021 was calculated as €250,000 and was the amount reflected in the company's tax return for 2021. Qualifying expenditure on R&D activities incurred by Teckno Ire in 2022 is €100,000, plus qualifying expenditure of €400,000 on R&D carried out in a Northern Ireland branch of Teckno Ire.

In 2024, Teckno Ire is considering investing €5 million in a state-of-the-art new research facility in Shannon to be used exclusively for R&D activities. Enterprise Ireland will provide a grant of €1 million towards the total cost of €5 million. Teckno Ire intends spending €100,000 on the acquisition of registered designs and €75,000 on authorisations to sell certain medicines to complement the products to be developed in the new R&D centre. Teckno Ire's amortisation policy for intangible assets is on a straight-line basis over 10 years.

The trading results and tax liabilities of Teckno Ire are as follows:

- Year ended 30 November 2021 – trading profits of €1,500,000; corporation tax paid of €125,000. PAYE, PRSI/USC costs amounted to €525,000.
- Year ended 30 November 2022 – projected trading losses of €50,000. PAYE, PRSI, and USC projected to cost €550,000.
- Year ending 30 November 2023 – projected trading profit of €800,000; corporation tax projected at €75,000.

Requirement

(a) What are the tax implications for Teckno Ire in making an additional claim for R&D expenditure for 2021?
(b) Calculate Teckno Ire's 2022 R&D tax credit and state how this credit can be used tax-efficiently.
(c) What tax relief entitlement will Teckno Ire have in respect of the proposed expenditure on the new R&D centre in Shannon?

Cash and Wealth Extraction from a Company

Learning Objectives

By the end of this chapter you will be able to:

■ Analyse the tax consequences of extracting profits from a company in the form of :

- salaries and termination payments;
- pension contributions;
- distributions;
- liquidation of companies; and
- share buy-back provisions to avail of CGT treatment.

A company is a separate legal entity to its shareholders. Therefore the money earned by a company does not constitute immediate earnings by the shareholders, and the funds earned by a company must be extracted in an appropriate manner. There are strict tax laws (in particular, close company rules) and company law rules that impact how a shareholder can extract cash/wealth from companies.

The extent to which cash/wealth is extracted from a company will depend on a number of factors. One shareholder may be happy to leave the cash to accumulate in a company for many years; another may require immediate access to the cash. If cash is extracted on a frequent basis, it is most likely paid out by way of salary or annual dividend. In the hands of the shareholder, this income will be liable to income tax.

4.1   Emoluments

The most common form of cash extraction takes the form of a salary, bonus, a director's fee, benefit in kind, etc. These forms of payments, known as "emoluments", are in respect of an employment or office held by an individual under a contract of services. Emoluments are liable to income tax under Schedule E and the employer is obliged to operate PAYE at source and pay the after-tax emolument to the employee.

A shareholder can therefore extract cash from the company by means of an emolument if that shareholder holds an employment, e.g. an executive directorship, or if that shareholder holds an office, e.g. as a non-executive director, company secretary, etc. The employer can take a tax deduction for the gross emolument in the calculation of its taxable profits, provided the payment was "wholly and exclusively" incurred for the purpose of its trade.

Example 4.1

Jane O'Malley set up her own company called JOM Ltd. She is the main shareholder, with 99% of the share capital, and her husband, Kevin, holds 1%. Jane works full-time for the company as an executive director and holds a contract of employment. Jane is also a non-executive director of the company and participates at board meetings and the AGM.

Kevin is the company secretary and looks after JOM Ltd's company law obligations while also working full-time as a PAYE worker elsewhere.

The company has available cash of €100,000 for payments to its members in the year ending 31 December 2022. Jane, as an employee of the company, takes a salary of €90,000 and the following PAYE is operated by JOM Ltd as her employer:

	€	€
Gross salary		90,000
Income tax:		
€36,800 @ 20%	7,360	
€53,200 @ 40%	21,280	
	28,640	
Less: Personal Tax Credit	(1,700)	
Earned Income Credit	(1,700)	
	25,240	
PRSI @ 4%	3,600	
USC:		
€12,012 @ 0.5%	60	
€9,283 @ 2%	186	
€48,749 @ 4.5%	2,194	
€19,956 @ 8%	1,596	
	4,036	
Total USC and PRSI	7,636	
Total deductions	32,876	
Net salary		57,124

Jane also takes a fee of €5,000 in respect of her office as a non-executive director. Kevin also takes a fee of €5,000 in respect of his office as company secretary. JOM Ltd must operate PAYE on the payment of these fees.

Jane	€	Kevin	€
Fee	5,000	Fee	5,000
Income tax 40%	2,000	Income tax 40%	2,000
PRSI 4%	200	PRSI 4%	200
USC 8%	400	USC 8%	400
Total tax	2,600	Total tax	2,600
Net fee	2,400	Net fee	2,400

Employer's PRSI will apply in respect of salary paid on salaries to non-controlling shareholders. From 1 January 2022, the rate of employer's PRSI is 11.05% on a salary above €410 per week. Employer's PRSI is not levied on a salary paid to a controlling shareholder or on fees paid to non-executive directors. This is a tax advantage for a company paying salary as a means of facilitating shareholder cash extraction.

While taking cash out of the company through an emolument is the most common form of regular cash extraction, it also involves a significant tax cost in the hands of the recipient due to the high rates of income tax arising on such payments.

4.1.1 Termination Payments

The payment of a tax-free termination payment or an ex-gratia payment can provide a tax-efficient method of extracting funds from a company. Termination payments apply where the working shareholder is ceasing active involvement in the company, either by way of resignation or retirement.

The tax-exempt portion of a termination payment is computed using the **highest** of:

1. the "basic exemption" of €10,160 plus €765 for each complete year of service; or
2. the "increased exemption" being the basic exemption (1. above) plus €10,000, less any tax-free payment received or receivable from a pension scheme (assuming that within the last 10 years the individual has not claimed either the increased exemption or 3. below); or
3. the standard capital superannuation benefit (SCSB).

The maximum amount that an employee can take tax-free under the above calculations is subject to a lifetime cap of €200,000.

An employee who is entitled to a tax-free lump sum under their pension must deduct the present value of the lump sum from the additional €10,000 under option 1 and option 3 when calculating the tax-exemption available under these options.

The exemption under the SCSB is based on the length of service and level of remuneration of the employee. Therefore, individuals who have both a significant number of years of service with a company and a high salary would typically benefit from the SCSB. However, the value of a tax-free lump sum from a pension scheme is deducted in arriving at the SCSB amount. The SCSB is computed by reference to the formula:

$$\frac{E \times Y}{15} - L$$

where,

E = Average remuneration* for the three years prior to termination of employment;
Y = Number of complete years of service of the person with the company; and
L = Tax-free lump sum** that the person is entitled to receive from the company pension scheme on retirement (or the actuarial value of any future right to receive a tax-free lump sum).

* Remuneration means pay, before pension deductions, plus any benefits in kind.
** An individual may make an irrevocable claim to waive entitlement to the tax-free lump sum, which would increase the value of the SCSB.

The SCSB can be used as a planning tool, where the level of Schedule E salary being received in the employee's final years may be adjusted to maximise the level of the SCSB relief.

Where the amount of the termination payment exceeds the limits as calculated, the excess is treated as salary and is subject to PAYE and USC. Employee and employer's PRSI are not due on this excess.

Example 4.2

John Swan is a director and non-controlling shareholder of Swanlake Ltd. He is due to retire on 30 November 2022 and will immediately begin to draw down his pension. He commenced employment with the company on 1 January 2002. His average salary for the last three years has been €90,000. He is due to receive a tax-free lump sum from the company pension scheme of €100,000, which you can assume is the present value of this sum. Swanlake Ltd wishes to make an ex-gratia payment to John of €200,000 and the aim is to make this payment as tax-efficiently as possible. The €200,000 ex-gratia payment does not include taxable remuneration, such as holiday pay, bonus, etc. to which he may also be entitled.

Compute the net amount of John's termination package.

The tax-exempt portion of John's termination payment is the highest of:

Option 1: Basic exemption: €10,160 + (€765 × 20) = €25,460

Option 2: Increased exemption: This is a negative figure, i.e. €25,460 + Nil [€10,000 – €100,000]

Option 3: The SCSB:

$$\frac{€90,000 \times 20}{15} - €100,000^* = €20,000$$

The tax-exempt portion is therefore the basic exemption (€25,460). The net amount of John's termination package is:

	€
Gross termination package	200,000
Tax-free portion	(25,460)
Taxable termination payment	174,540
Income tax @ 40%	69,816
USC @ 8%	13,963
Net termination package	116,221

*As John has 20 complete years' service and he is coming up to retirement, it is not advisable for him to waive the right to receive a tax-free lump sum from his pension scheme. If he does, then the lump sum remains in the fund and will be taxable when he draws down his pension.

The taxable portion of the termination payment is taxable in the year in which the employment ceases. In this regard, the date on which the payment is made to the employee will establish the period in which the tax is due. The company will not receive a tax deduction in respect of termination payments where:

- the termination payment relates to the proceeds from the sale of shares in the company; and
- the termination payment is made after the company ceases to trade.

4.2 Pensions

Tax relief is available for both employer's contributions and employee's/director's contributions to a Revenue-approved corporate pension scheme, subject to certain conditions. Corporate pension funding is a tax-efficient cash extraction tool for retiring directors or employees of a company where the correct tax rules are properly applied.

4.2.1 Corporate Pension Schemes for Directors/Employees

There are significant benefits in setting up a Revenue-approved corporate pension scheme. The main tax advantages are:

1. Contributions paid by the company (as employer) to the pension scheme are fully tax deductible (subject to a restriction where the contributions are excessive).
2. The company receives a tax deduction by reference to the pension payments made.
3. Contributions paid by the company are not subject to the same restrictions as those for personal contributions by the employee/director.

The corporation tax deduction for pension contributions is only available on a paid basis. This means that pension contribution accruals reflected in the company accounts at year end must be added back when doing the tax computation.

Example 4.3: Pension accruals

	€
Opening pension accrual at 1 January 2022	50,000
Closing pension accrual at 31 December 2022	200,000

The increase in the accrual of €150,000 must be added back in the tax computation to arrive at the tax-adjusted profit/loss. The accrual movement would be reflected in the profit and loss account as an expense.

The key issues in relation to company pension schemes are:

- A corporate pension scheme provides a means of extracting cash in a tax-efficient manner in the future. The amounts invested in the pension scheme can be invested solely for the benefit of the relevant director/employee.
- A commercial advantage is that the company pension scheme is protected from the creditors of the company should the company experience trading difficulties or even go into liquidation.
- All contributions made by the company to a Revenue-approved pension scheme do not give rise to a benefit in kind for the employee/director.
- Revenue-approved pension schemes are permitted to not only fund pensions but also life cover, disability cover and permanent health insurance. Therefore, such benefits can be provided to the employee/director on a tax-efficient basis.

Top-up Pension Fund (Lump Sum Pension Payments)

The annual pension payment generated by an occupational pension fund cannot exceed a set percentage, depending on the employee's/director's length of service and final remuneration. The maximum pension available for individuals with 40 years of service is two-thirds of the individual's final remuneration as per section 772(3)(a) TCA 1997. In circumstances where the occupational pension scheme is not sufficiently funded to provide for such a pension (i.e. two-thirds of the individual's final salary), the company may make lump sum top-up payments on a periodic basis to maximise the fund and meet future pension requirements.

These top-up pension payments may not be fully tax deductible for corporation tax purposes in the accounting period in which they are paid, and may be subject to a 'spreading adjustment'. If the spreading adjustment applies, the tax deduction for the lump sum pension payment will be spread over a period of up to five years. The actual period of the spread is determined by taking the lesser of five years or a sum under the following formula:

$$\frac{\text{Once-off lump sum payment}}{\text{Annual recurring pension contributions}}$$

Example 4.4

PC Futures Ltd pays a pension contribution of €200,000 per annum on behalf of its three key directors and equal shareholders. The pension fund will be required to pay two-thirds of the directors' final pensionable salary on their retirement.

In 2022, in order to meet future pension requirements, the company pays a lump sum of €1 million to the pension fund. This lump sum is inclusive of the annual ordinary pension contribution of €200,000. The 2022 tax deduction for total pension contributions will be:

	€
Ordinary pension contribution	200,000
Special lump sum contribution*	200,000
Total tax-deductible payment in 2022	400,000

* The lump sum contribution of €800,000 is to be spread for corporation tax deductibility purposes as follows:

€800,000/€200,000 = four years spread (i.e. €800,000 × ¼ = €200,000)

Note: if the above computation produced a result above five years, the lump sum would be spread over five years for tax deductibility purposes.

4.2.2 Personal Pension Contributions

The tax relief for personal pension contributions is subject to certain restrictions, which take the form of an age limit and an earnings limit. These two limits apply for both sole traders paying into a PRSA/personal pension plan and for personal contributions paid by an employee/director to a corporate pension scheme. As stated above, corporate contributions are not subject to the same restrictions where paid to a Revenue-approved corporate pension scheme. Therefore, the use of a corporate pension scheme can facilitate much higher contributions to a pension scheme for the company's director/employee. This has a big advantage over the sole trader contributor.

The personal tax relief limits are based on the taxpayer's age as follows:

Age	% of net relevant earnings
Under 30	15%
30 to 39	20%
40 to 49	25%
50 to 54	30%
55 to 59	35%
60 or older	40%

The director's/employee's personal pension contributions are also subject to an earnings cap of €115,000.

Example 4.5

John Sheridan is 32 years old and has net relevant earnings of €200,000. He is a member of his employer's Revenue-approved corporate pension scheme. The maximum personal pension contribution John can make and still qualify for tax relief is €23,000 (€115,000 × 20%)).

If John makes a contribution of €40,000 in a tax year, he can only get tax relief in that year of €23,000. The excess contribution of €17,000 can be carried forward for tax relief to the following tax year.

> **Key Issue**
> Pension contributions to a Revenue-approved corporate pension scheme are not subject to the same level of tax restrictions as those of individual contributions by its directors/employees. This is a significant issue for the sole trader who cannot avail of such a scheme unless they incorporate.

4.2.3 Pension Planning on Retirement

On the director's/employee's retirement, a portion of the pension fund may be paid as a tax-free lump sum. Broadly, there are two options:

1. If a director/employee has 20 years of pensionable service with the company, this entitles the director/employee to a maximum tax-free lump sum payment from their pension fund of 1.5 times their "final pensionable remuneration". In some cases this can be the entire accumulated fund. Where there is a fund remaining, this is used to purchase an annuity (which will effectively be the investment that will fund the pension).
2. The alternative is to take up to 25% of the accumulated fund as a cash lump sum and with the balance either:
   (a) invest in an approved retirement fund (ARF);
   (b) purchase an annuity;
   (c) take as taxable cash; or
   (d) a combination of (a), (b) and (c).

   Again, the ARF or the annuity will effectively be the investment that will fund the pension.

The tax-free lump sum amount is, however, subject to a lifetime limit of €200,000 and any excess up to €500,000, i.e. a maximum of €300,000, is taxed at 20%. This tax-free lump sum is also exempt from USC. Where the individual's lump sum exceeds €500,000, the excess is taxed at the individual's marginal rate of income tax plus USC. The pension provider must operate PAYE for the year of assessment in which the lump sum is paid.

Final Pensionable Remuneration
For an employee/director who does not hold more than 20% of the ordinary share capital, there are three different methods of determining final pensionable remuneration. It can be based on:

1. basic remuneration of any 12-month period of the five years preceding the retirement date, to include the average of any fluctuating emoluments of three or more consecutive years ending on the retirement date; or
2. the average of the total emoluments for any three or more consecutive years ending not earlier than 10 years before the retirement date; or
3. the rate of basic pay at the retirement date or at any date within the year ending on that date plus the average of any fluctuating emoluments calculated in 1. above.

However, for a director who holds more than 20% of the ordinary share capital, final pensionable remuneration must be the average of the total emoluments for any three or more consecutive years ending not earlier than 10 years before the retirement date.

The above computed final pensionable remuneration forms the basis of computing the relevant tax-free lump sum. In practice, final pensionable remuneration is not a tax issue – the pension company or agent will provide the final pensionable remuneration amount to the tax advisor who will calculate the relevant tax-free lump sum.

If steps are put in place in respect of the director's/employee's final level of remuneration, either in the final year or in the final 10-year period, the tax-free lump sum can be maximised. This could be a key planning step for executives within the corporate scheme who are due for retirement. However, care must be exercised to ensure that the pension scheme rules are not contravened.

4.2.4 Pension Planning and Sale of a Business

If a sale of a business is planned, pension planning can be used in conjunction with any other tax relief associated with the future sale of a business (e.g. retirement relief; see **Chapter 7**). If, for example, a sale of an existing business is planned in the foreseeable future, the current shareholders/directors may take proactive steps to maximise cash extraction from the business prior to its sale. In addition to retirement relief, pension planning could (indirectly) achieve significant tax-efficient cash extraction from the business.

Example 4.6

Tim Mullane is 57 years of age with no children. He runs a transport and haulage business, Trans-Speed Ltd, which he has operated for 25 years. Tim is a 100% shareholder in the company.

Tim has never invested in a pension scheme. Instead, he retained all surplus funds in the company to build it up. The company is now valued at approximately €1 million. Tim has taken an annual salary from the company of €50,000 for the last 10 years. The company currently has €400,000 in cash.

Tim plans to sell the company by his 60th birthday. He is confident that a buyer can be easily found as he has received many offers from local investors over the years to purchase the business from him. Tim will sell the company by way of 100% share sale.

Tim is conscious that the company has significant cash reserves and would like to utilise this cash in a tax-efficient manner prior to the sale of the company. He does not want to draw all the cash down as a salary immediately, as he knows that this will lead to a large income tax liability.

Taking into account Tim's lack of pension provision and his intention to sell the business within the next three years, the following steps could be put in place to maximise the tax-efficient extraction of the €400,000 cash holding from the business:

- The company sets up a Revenue-approved pension scheme.
- By increasing Tim's salary to €120,000 per annum for the next three years, the company could invest €180,000 in a corporate pension scheme, i.e. the amount that he could receive tax-free up to a maximum of €200,000 (average annual remuneration of €120,000 × 1.5).

On Tim's retirement, assume he could take a tax-free pension lump sum of €180,000 (being 1.5 times final salary). Assuming a corporation tax rate of 12.5%, the net cost (after tax) to the company over the three years would be:

	€
Additional salary	210,000
Allowable pension lump sum	180,000
	390,000
Less: corporation tax relief	(48,750)
Company's after-tax cost	341,250

Tim would personally receive the following cash from the company over the three-year period:

	€
Additional salary	210,000
Less: PAYE* on salary	(84,000)
Net income	126,000
Tax-free lump sum**	180,000
Tim's total after-tax funds	306,000

continued overleaf

---

* Assuming marginal tax rate at 40% and ignoring PRSI and USC.

** Ignoring costs and income/gains/losses earned.

If Tim had withdrawn the company's significant cash holding by way of salary or dividend, the tax rate alone applicable to that income would be 40%. Following the above pension/tax planning steps, the effective tax rate applying to the funds paid to Tim would be as follows:

€84,000/€390,000 = 21.5% effective tax rate

Tim may, on his 60th birthday, dispose of his shares in his trading company. Tim should qualify for retirement relief for CGT purposes. This will provide an additional tax saving for Tim.

Let us further consider what would happen if the company wishes to pay him a termination payment and he is to receive a tax-free lump sum of €180,000 and his pay has been increased to €120,000 for three years. Tim has 25 complete years' service.

Basic exemption:	€10,160 + (€765 × 25) = €29,285
Increased exemption:	This is a negative figure, i.e. €29,235 + €10,000 − €180,000

SCSB:

$$\frac{€120,000 \times 25}{15} - €180,000 = €20,000$$

As can be seen, the amount of the termination payment is significantly reduced due to the tax-free sum from the pension. Therefore, while the pension tax-free lump sum is attractive, it does significantly reduce the tax-free sum under a termination payment.

A substantial extraction of cash from the company (such as the termination payment and salary payments to Tim) may reduce the market value of the company, which in turn would reduce the taxable gain for CGT purposes and potentially bring the proceeds on the sale of the company within the thresholds for CGT retirement relief (see **Chapter 7**).

Key Issue

There may be opportunities for pension planning where:

- Director/shareholder has sufficient funds for their personal lifestyle and the company has excess cash holdings. There may be scope to implement a corporate pension scheme and invest the excess cash.
- Director/shareholder has been building up the business for a number of years and has neglected their pension planning. A corporate pension scheme could be put in place to fund their retirement.
- Consider the level of remuneration being paid to key directors/employees in the final years of employment. This is relevant to the level of tax-free lump sum payments that can be made to them on their retirement. This is particularly relevant if the individual has more than 20 years' service with the company.
- A sole trader is operating a profitable business and is making the maximum allowable pension contributions but is still subject to significant income tax on the remaining taxable profits. There may be benefit in transferring that trade to a company and setting up a corporate pension scheme to maximise tax relief.

4.3   Loans to Directors/Shareholders

A director/shareholder may decide to take a loan from their company, with repayment terms generally at the shareholder's discretion. There is, however, significant legislation in respect of loans to shareholders. Company law prohibits loans in excess of 10% of the company's net assets and violation is considered a very serious offence. If loans exceed this level, the shareholder's loan will be illegal and the company's auditors must report the violation to the Office of the Director of Corporate Enforcement.

From a tax perspective, close company tax rules (see **Chapter 3**) also impact a company's ability to make loans to directors/participators (and their associates). In addition a benefit in kind (BIK) charge will apply if the loan is provided at an interest rate below the allowable rates set by Revenue (4% for a loan related to a principal private residence and 13.5% in all other cases). Income tax, PRSI and USC on the BIK must be operated through the company's payroll.

Under close company rules, a company must operate a withholding tax on loan to a shareholder/participator (or an associate of the participator). The loan will be treated as being a net annual payment, and subject to a re-grossing adjustment. The payment due to Revenue is 20/80ths of the loan and is payable as part of the company's corporation tax payment obligations. Revenue will refund this withholding tax when the loan is repaid by the shareholder.

The above withholding tax treatment will not apply where:

- the amount of the loan (taking into account any other loans to that person and their associates) does not exceed €19,050; and
- the borrower works full time for the company; and
- the borrower does not have a material interest in the company (a material interest being defined as more than 5% of the ordinary share capital of the company).
- the loan is repaid to the company by borrower within nine months of the accounting year end.

Example 4.7

Joe Malone took an interest-free loan of €12,000 from his company in December 2022. When preparing Form CT1 for his company, the tax treatment will be as follows:

	€
Deemed net loan	12,000
Re-grossing adjustment	15,000
Income tax to be withheld	3,000

The withholding tax of €3,000 must be paid to Revenue unless the loan is repaid to the company by Joe Malone within nine months of the accounting year end. When the loan is repaid in full, or in part, the appropriate portion of the withholding tax will be repaid to the company.

As Joe's loan is interest-free, a BIK charge will also apply and the company must account for PAYE on the relevant BIK on the interest free loan.

If, at a later date, a company writes off a loan advanced to a director/shareholder, the individual will be assessable to income tax under Case IV on the loan advanced. The amount assessable is the gross loan, i.e. the cash advanced plus the income tax withheld by the company. A credit is available for the income tax paid by the company in computing the individual's tax liability.

Example 4.8

M Ltd is a close company and made interest-free loans to the following shareholders during the accounting period ending 31 December 2022.

	€
Mr X, who owns 30% of the share capital	50,000
Mr Y, full-time director with 3% share capital	10,000
Mr Z, who owns 2% of the share capital and is not a director/employee	15,000

The loan to Mr Y is not subject to the withholding tax provisions as he is a full-time working director of the company, his shareholding does not exceed 5% and the loan does not exceed €19,050.

Mr Y will be liable to BIK on the interest deemed to apply to the loan. If the loan is not a principal private residence- related loan, a BIK will arise at an interest rate of 13.5%. The BIK will be accounted for through the company's payroll operation and will be liable to income tax, PRSI and the USC.

continued overleaf

Mr X and Mr Z – income tax is payable by the company in respect of loans to Mr X and Mr Z. The income tax due will be computed as follows:

	€
Mr X	50,000
Mr Z	15,000
Total	65,000
Tax due (20/80)	16,250

We assume that all of this income tax will have been paid to Revenue by 23 September 2023 (the date by which all corporation tax must be paid). If, for example, Mr X repays €25,000 on 30 December 2023, the company would be entitled to the following refund of income tax paid:

	€
Loan repaid	25,000
Withholding tax repaid	6,250

The refund is claimed in the company's next CT1 return.

4.4 Distributions

A shareholder who does not have an office or employment will generally take regular payments of cash from the company in the form of dividend distributions. As set out in the CA Proficiency 2 course, distributions are not tax deductible when calculating the paying company's liability to corporation tax. In addition, the company is obliged to deduct dividend withholding tax (DWT) at a rate of 25% at source from distributions to shareholders and to pay the tax withheld directly to Revenue within 14 days from the end of the month in which the dividend was paid.

The dividend is taxable in the hands of the recipient as Schedule F income. If the dividend is paid to an individual, they will be liable to income tax on the dividend at their marginal rate of income tax and must also pay PRSI and USC on the dividend appropriate to their rates and threshold.

Example 4.9

	€		€
Gross dividend	35,000 (A)	Gross dividend	35,000
Income tax @ 40%	14,000*	Tax exempt	35,000
PRSI @ 4%	1,400		
USC @ 8%	2,800		
Total tax	18,200 (B)		
Dividend after tax	**16,800** (A) – (B)	**Dividend after tax**	**35,000**

If the dividend is payable to a shareholder who is an Irish resident company, then the payment is treated as franked investment income and is not liable to corporation tax. While the dividend will not be liable to corporation tax, consideration would need to be given to close company surcharge implications.

Other forms of wealth extraction, such as use of company assets by shareholders, are also treated as distributions under close company rules and are subject to the same income tax treatment outlined above based on the market value of the asset in question. Likewise, the company must withhold income tax at 25% on the deemed distribution and pay the tax owing to Revenue within 14 days of the end of the month in which the distribution was made. In addition, the company is not entitled to a tax deduction for the deemed distribution paid to the shareholder.

Example 4.10

Monique Ware Ltd paid for a holiday worth €6,000 for its shareholder Mr Dempsey in September 2022. Mr Dempsey is not an employee of the company.

The provision of the holiday is deemed to be a distribution of €8,000 (i.e. the deemed net dividend of €6,000 re-grossed at 25% to cover the DWT liability of Monique Ware Ltd).

The company is obliged to pay €2,000 to Revenue by 14 October 2022 and will incur interest on any late payments. Mr Dempsey is liable to income tax on the €8,000 at his marginal rate, taking a credit for the 25% withholding tax applied by the company as well as appropriate PRSI and USC on this deemed distribution.

The company must take into account whether it has sufficient distributable reserves to make a distribution. This is a key requirement for company law purposes as distributable reserves must exist.

The practical differences between salary and dividends are summarised in the table below.

Salary	Dividend
Salary is subject to PAYE/PRSI/USC at source and the shareholder receives a net income. Salary income is therefore not likely to be liable to any further taxes in the hands of the shareholder.	The shareholder receives 75% of the dividend after 25% DWT is applied. The dividend is liable to income tax plus USC and possibly PRSI in the hands of the shareholder, with a credit available for the 25% DWT.
The company must remit the PAYE/PRSI/USC under the PAYE system.	The company must remit the DWT to Revenue in the month following the distribution.
The salary (and employer's PRSI where applicable) is deductible for tax purposes against the company's profit. This represents a 12.5% tax benefit to the company (i.e. an allowable deduction).	A dividend is not deductible for tax purposes against the company's profit.
Employer's PRSI is payable by the company if the salary is paid to a non-controlling shareholder.	Employer's PRSI will not arise on dividends paid to shareholders.
Ongoing/set salary payments represent a significant cash outflow for a company as cash may be required for working capital purposes.	A dividend may be declared at year end, when the company is in a position to establish the extent to which a dividend can be paid (by reference to the previous trading period and future trading projections).
Salary can increase the capacity to boost pension contributions and can also increase the SCSB figure if a termination payment is being made in the future.	The dividend will reduce the distributable after-tax investment income of the company and hence lower/eliminate the close company surcharge liability.
The shareholder's income tax burden in respect of this income will be accounted for through the company's payroll. The shareholder will, however, have to make a declaration of this salary in an annual tax return.	The shareholder will have to declare this dividend in their annual tax return and pay any additional tax/PRSI/USC where due.

4.5   Company Buy-back of Shares

For tax purposes, any amount receivable by a shareholder in respect of their shares is treated as a distribution under section 130 TCA 1997 and is subject to income tax under Schedule F, with the exception of capital distributions (see **Section 4.6.3**). Therefore, sums received by a shareholder for the purchase, repayment or redemption of their shareholding from a limited company in which the shares are held is subject to income tax, PRSI and USC in the hands of the shareholder.

There is an exception to this rule under section 176 TCA 1997, which provides that the distribution received under a buy-back scheme will be subject to CGT at 33% provided certain conditions are met. See **Chapter 9, Section 9.2** for how the tax treatment of a buy-back scheme interacts with the revised entrepreneur relief for CGT.

It should be noted that section 175 TCA 1997 provides that, unless there is an anti-avoidance purpose, amounts received by a shareholder of a quoted company for the redemption, repayment or purchase of the shares in that company are subject to CGT regardless, and are to be distinguished from the tax treatment of shares in a limited company.

The qualifying conditions for section 176 to apply are outlined in sections 177 and 183 TCA 1997, and can be summarised as follows:

- The company must be an unquoted trading company or an unquoted holding company of a trading company.
- The buy-back must be made principally to benefit a trade carried on by the company (or its subsidiaries).
- The shares must have been owned by the shareholders for the previous five years prior to disposal (except for inherited shares where the ownership period is three years). If a scheme of reconstruction is undertaken, then the new shareholding takes on the same base cost and acquisition date as the old holding prior to the reorganisation.
- The shareholder must be resident and ordinarily resident in the State.
- The shareholder's remaining interest in the company does not exceed 75% of the interest held by them before the buy-back.
- The disposing shareholder's holding and that of their associates must be less than a 30% interest in the company after the buy-back.

4.5.1   Disposing of Shareholder's Interest

Where a company does not buy back all of a shareholder's shares, the shareholder's interest in the company must be substantially reduced (by a minimum of 25%). In assessing the interest of a disposing shareholder in a company, the interests of the disposing shareholder's associates also have to be taken into account. An associate's interest in the company acquiring its own shares is only brought into the reckoning if, immediately after the acquisition by the company of its own shares, the associate owns shares in the company. For the purpose of determining whether a disposing shareholder's interest has been substantially reduced, the interests of any associates are treated as those of the disposing shareholder.

Example 4.11

Multichem Ltd has an issued share capital of 5,000 €1 shares, of which 1,000 are owned by Conor Maguire and 250 by his wife, Mrs Maguire. If Multichem Ltd purchases 250 shares from each of them, Mrs Maguire will own no shares after the purchase and the comparison to determine the reduction in Conor's interest will ignore Mrs Maguire's former holding. Before the purchase, Conor's interest is 20% (1,000/5,000) and, after the purchase, is 16.67% (750/4,500), which is a reduction of at least 25%.

The comparison to determine the reduction in Mrs Maguire's interest will need to include Conor's holding, because he still owns shares after the transaction. Mrs Maguire's interest (including that of her associate) is reduced from 25% (1,250/5,000) to 16.67% (750/4,500), which is reduced by at least 25%.

If, instead, Multichem Ltd purchased 500 shares from Conor and none from Mrs Maguire, the comparison to determine the reduction in Conor's interest will include Mrs Maguire's holding because she still owns shares after the transaction. His interest is reduced from 25% (1,250/5,000) to 16.67% (750/4,500), which is a reduction of at least 25%.

> **Key Issue**
> To qualify for CGT treatment, the shareholding after the share buy-back must represent a minimum 25%
> reduction in the original holding. When calculating the former as a percentage of the total issued share
> capital, remember that the issued share capital is reduced by the amount of shares bought back.

4.5.2   Trade Benefit Test

Under the 'trade benefit test' it must be demonstrated that the sole or main purpose of the buy-back is to benefit the trade carried on by the company. The test is not fulfilled where the sole or main purpose of the buy-back is to benefit the shareholder or to benefit a business purpose of the company other than a trade.

Circumstances in which the Trade Benefit Test Applies
The company buy-back of shares route has proved to be a very effective exit mechanism in the following circumstances:

1.   **Dissident shareholders:** Revenue will normally regard a buy-back as benefiting the trade where there is a disagreement between the shareholders over the management of the company, and that disagreement is having, or is expected to have, an adverse effect on the company's trade, and where the effect of the buy-back is to remove the dissenting shareholder.
2.   **Retiring shareholder:** the company buy-back of shares treatment can satisfy the trade benefit test when a controlling shareholder is retiring as a director and wishes to make way for new management. This relief is very useful when used in conjunction with retirement relief under sections 598 and 599 TCA 1997. In many cases, the retiring shareholder will have no base cost other than the nominal value of the shares. This can provide a tax-free gain on proceeds up to €750,000 or €500,000 (depending on the age of the retiring shareholder).
3.   **Inheritance of shares:** the trade benefit test under the company buy-back treatment could also be satisfied where the personal representatives of a deceased shareholder wish to realise the value of the shares or a legatee of a deceased shareholder does not wish to hold shares in the company.

The above examples envisage the shareholder selling their entire shareholding and making a complete break from the company. If the company is not buying all the shares owned by the vendor, or if the vendor is selling all the shares but retaining some connection with the company (e.g. continuing as director), it would seem unlikely that the transaction would benefit the company's trade. However, the trade benefit test may still apply where, for sentimental reasons, a retiring director of a company retains a small shareholding in the company provided the conditions outlined above are fulfilled. However, this is at Revenue's discretion. Revenue's *Tax and Duty Manual*, Part 06-09-1 sets out its interpretation of the trade benefit test in more detail. In exceptional cases Revenue may, if requested, provide an advance opinion in relation to the trade benefit test.

Example 4.12
Darren Philips is a 60% shareholder and director in Philips Trading Ltd. Darren is 60 years of age. He has two sons (aged 30 and 25) working in the company who each hold a 20% shareholding. The company has distributable reserves of €1 million. Darren's 60% shareholding is currently valued at approximately €700,000. Darren originally subscribed €7 for his 60% shareholding on setting up the company in 2004.

In the interest of ensuring the continued success of the company, Darren decides to retire as a director and shareholder of the company and let his sons take over as they are effectively coming up with the best management and strategy ideas for the business. The company undertakes a scheme of share buy-back whereby all but 1% of Darren's shares are redeemed for a payment of €688,333. All the conditions are in place to meet the trade benefit test and Darren has substantially reduced his shareholding and is allowed to retain the 1% shareholding for sentimental reasons.

continued overleaf

The payment to Darren is treated as a distribution under section 130 TCA 1997 to the extent that it exceeds the €7 he originally paid for the shares. However, share buy-back relief means that the distribution will be subject to CGT rather than income tax.

Darren's sons' shareholdings do not need to be taken into consideration to determine if Darren's shareholding has been substantially reduced. This is on the basis that the sons are not minor children.

Darren may also qualify for retirement relief (see **Chapter 7**), which means that the distribution he received from the company in respect of the buy-back is tax-exempt, provided certain conditions are fulfilled. Note that Darren is 60 years of age, meaning that the €750,000 limit applies and not the €500,000 limit.

Example 4.13

Mark has been a director of ABC Ltd since the company was incorporated in June 1990. Mark is 50 and intends to retire. His original investment was €10,000 in €1 ordinary shares. His brothers Sam and Billy own 10,000 €1 shares between them and they will continue to run the business after Mark retires. Mark had his shares valued and they are worth €500,000. How can these shares be sold tax-efficiently and control kept within the family? You can assume that Sam and Billy cannot raise the funds to buy the shares from Mark.

If the conditions are met for share buy-back, Mark is liable to CGT:

	€
Proceeds	500,000
Cost €10,000 × 1.442	(14,420)
Gain	485,580
Less: annual exemption	(1,270)
Taxable	484,310

CGT would be payable on €484,310 at either 10% or 33%, depending on eligibility for revised entrepreneurs' relief.

If conditions are not met for share buy-back, Mark is liable to income tax, USC and possibly PRSI as follows:

	€	
Schedule F	490,000	(€500,000 – €10,000 cost)
@55%	269,500	

Tax saving when liable to CGT @ 33% = €109,678. The company will also be obliged to deduct DWT.

Example 4.14

The facts are the same as in **Example 4.13**, except Mark is 60 years old and intends to retire. Would your advice be any different?

As we have already seen, if the conditions are met for share buy-back, Mark is liable to CGT. If, however, in addition to that relief he also meets the conditions for retirement relief, since the proceeds are less than €750,000 they are exempt from CGT. In that case, the CGT calculation would be as follows:

	€
Proceeds	500,000
Retirement relief	(500,000)
Gain	NIL
CGT @ 10%/33%	NIL
CGT saving @ 33%	159,822

The use of CGT treatment under share buy-back and retirement relief (covered in detail in **Chapter 9**) is restricted if the transferor is over 66 years of age. On a transfer of shares in a family company to a child and to a company **controlled** by that child, the value of the shares transferring under both transactions is aggregated when calculating the €500,000 lifetime limit on transfers to third parties. For example, €3 million worth of shares are transferred to a child and the transferor is over 66 years old. If there were a further disposal of shares worth up to €500,000 to a company **controlled** by that child, retirement relief could not be claimed on this second transaction.

4.6 Liquidation/Winding Up of a Company

There are two types of liquidation, or winding up, of companies:

1. compulsory winding up by a court; and
2. voluntary winding up initiated by the shareholders or creditors.

When a company commences to be wound up, it ceases to be the beneficial owner of its assets and the **custody and control of those assets pass to the liquidator**.

4.6.1 Status of Liquidator

A liquidator is not an agent of the company or of the creditor, nor is the liquidator an officer of the company.

Prior to liquidation, a company is both the legal and beneficial owner of its assets. When the company is put into liquidation, it ceases to be the beneficial owner and it no longer retains control of the assets. The liquidator holds the assets for the purposes of distributing them, or what remains of them, to the ultimate beneficial owners.

4.6.2 Tax Implications of Liquidation

Liquidator's Responsibilities

A company is chargeable to corporation tax on profits arising in the winding up of a company. **During the course of the winding up the liquidator has the responsibility of accounting for corporation tax on income received and on capital gains arising on the disposal of chargeable assets**. Therefore, the liquidator must pay the corporation tax by the due date and submit any corporation tax returns. If there is a disposal of development land, which is liable to CGT, the liquidator is responsible for paying the CGT and submitting the return.

End of an Accounting Period for Corporation Tax

When a company commences to be wound up, an **accounting period ends** and a new one begins; thereafter, an accounting period may not end otherwise than on the expiration of 12 months from its beginning or by the completion of the winding up. The ending of an accounting period can affect the following:

■ the due date for payment of corporation tax;
■ the date the company's corporation tax return must be submitted; and
■ the extent to which trading losses may be offset against the total profits of the immediately preceding period, or against fellow group members' total profits on a claim to group relief.

As regards the due date for the corporation tax return and the balance of tax, where an accounting period ends on or before the date of commencement of the winding up of a company and the specified return date in respect of that period would fall on a date after the commencement of the winding up but not within a period of three months after that date, then the specified **return date becomes the date which falls three months after the date of commencement of the winding up**, but in any event not later than day 23 of the month in which that period of three months ends.

Example 4.15

Axel Ltd was trading for a number of years and had a 31 December year-end. On 30 June 2022 a liquidator was appointed and the company commenced to be wound up.

Accounting period 1 January 2022 to 30 June 2022:

Assuming Axel Ltd is a 'small' company for preliminary tax purposes, 90% of the corporation tax liability for the period (or 100% of the corporation tax for the corresponding accounting period) must be paid by 23 May 2022.

The corporation tax return and the balance of tax must be submitted on or before 23 September 2022.

Accounting year 1 January 2021 to 31 December 2021:

The company's tax return must be filed by 23 September 2022. As this is within three months of the commencement of winding up on 30 June 2022, the return date is not changed. If the commencement of winding up were on, say, 30 April 2022, then the return for the year ended 31 December 2021 would be due on 23 July 2022 (three months after commencement of winding up), instead of 23 September 2022.

Ranking of Creditors and Revenue Priority

On the occasion of a company being put into liquidation, creditors are ranked in the following order in respect of payments due to them:

1. creditors with a fixed charge (proceeds from that particular asset);,
2. liquidation costs;
3. preferential creditors;
4. creditors with a floating charge;
5. unsecured creditors; and, finally,
6. shareholders.

The main preferential creditors are Revenue, employees and local authorities in respect of rates due. There is legislation outlining the exact periods for which taxes are preferential.

4.6.3   Capital Distributions to a Shareholder

Generally, distributions are treated as Schedule F income when received by an individual, or as exempt franked investment income when received by a body corporate. However, capital distributions made in the course of the winding up of a company are treated as a disposal for CGT purposes, and will give rise to a chargeable event for both corporate and individual shareholders.

Under section 583 TCA 1997, a shareholder will be treated as making a disposal of an interest in shares where they receive a capital distribution from the company in respect of those shares.

A capital distribution can be thought of as the market value payment to the shareholder on the extinction of their shares because the company is put into liquidation. In general, the capital distribution payable to the shareholder is essentially funds remaining after the liquidator has sold the assets of the company and paid all debts, loans and professional liquidation fees.

An individual shareholder will be liable to CGT at 33% on the capital distribution received in respect of their shareholding. Subject to the individual shareholder's personal circumstances, and if the shares are considered to be chargeable business assets, the 33% rate may be reduced to 10% if the CGT entrepreneur relief can be availed of.

A corporate investor will also be liable to corporation tax at a rate of 12.5% on the adjusted gain arising on a capital distribution. However, Revenue practice tends to allow a corporate investor to be exempt from tax under section 626B TCA 1997 (see **Chapter 5**) if the capital distribution is in respect of a disposal by way of liquidation of its shareholding in a qualifying subsidiary. This treatment applies where the subsidiary trades almost up to the point of being placed into liquidation.

On liquidation, a capital distribution is paid in respect of the shareholding, so the original cost of the shares must be considered when calculating any CGT arising on the disposal. An investor will commit funds to a company by way of an equity investment or by way of a loan. The form of the investment will impact on the CGT liability arising on an individual shareholder on the ultimate sale of shares or liquidation of the company.

Example 4.16

Billy formed a property investment company on 1 July 1976. He paid €200,000 for 10,000 €1 ordinary shares. The company operated successfully as a property rental company but was subsequently liquidated on 1 November 2022. The liquidator realised €600,000 on disposal of the company's assets after all creditors, including taxation and the liquidator's fees, had been paid. This was distributed to Billy. The date of disposal is the date of the liquidator's distribution.

The gain is calculated as follows:

	€
Capital distribution to Billy	600,000
Deduct: €200,000 indexed at 5.238	(1,047,600)
No gain/no loss	Nil
Net cash extracted	**600,000**

Indexation relief was abolished for capital assets acquired on/after 1 January 2003. Funding a company by a loan also provides the shareholders with greater accessibility to their funds because the company can repay the loan, if cash flow permits, without any tax implications. This is in contrast to funding by way of an equity investment as full repayment of the funds invested in shares is only accessible by either share sale or liquidation, both of which are likely to result in CGT liabilities.

Anti-avoidance and Section 817 TCA 1997

It is generally more tax-efficient for an individual to have funds taxed under CGT rates of 33% (or potentially 10% if entrepreneur relief is available), rather than income tax rates of up to 55%. Section 817 TCA 1997 is an anti-avoidance provision aimed at preventing a shareholder in a close company from avoiding or reducing a charge to income tax under Schedule F by converting a dividend from a close company into a capital receipt, i.e. a capital distribution from a close company.

When the section applies, it treats the proceeds of the disposal of the shares in the close company as a distribution liable to Schedule F, which is subject to income tax rates. Section 817 does not apply to a disposal of shares where:

- the shareholder has directly or indirectly significantly reduced their interest in the company in question; and
- the disposal is made for bona fide commercial reasons and is not part of a tax-avoidance arrangement.

4.6.4 Tax Impact of a Company Selling Assets and Subsequent Liquidation

A liquidation generally follows the disposal of the business carried on by a company. Therefore, there are two exposures to taxation on the liquidation of a company. First, the disposal by the company of its business and assets may give rise to a CGT liability; secondly, there is a CGT exposure to the shareholders on receipt of the capital distribution in respect of their shares.

Example 4.17

A company pays €2.75 million corporation tax on the realised capital gains on the sale of the asset for €11 million. The shareholders pay CGT on liquidation of the company (assuming that the reduced entrepreneur relief rate is not applicable) as follows:

	€ million
Net cash distribution to shareholders (€11m – €2.75m)	8.25
(Base cost of €100 as indexed is irrelevant) CGT@ 33%	2.72
Corporation tax paid	2.75
Total taxes	**5.47**

A liquidator could also transfer capital assets *in specie* to the shareholders in exchange for their shares. This is an alternative to the sale of the assets followed by a transfer of the cash proceeds by the liquidator to the shareholders in exchange for their shares. Two exposures to tax arise on a distribution *in specie*:

1. CGT on any gains accruing to the company because it is deemed to dispose of the assets at the market value to the shareholders in accordance with the connected person rules under section 547 TCA 1997; and
2. CGT on the individual shareholders, calculated on the basis of the net value of the assets/cash received from the liquidator for the effective disposal of their shareholdings.

A distribution *in specie* is generally only possible when the company has sufficient cash to clear all its debts and loans. If the company does not have sufficient cash to clear its debts, then the liquidator will have to sell some or all of the company's assets to generate funds to settle all outstanding debts and loans, and only then can the remaining assets be distributed to the shareholders in respect of their shares in the company.

Example 4.18

Oscar Ltd owns commercial premises worth €1.2 million, which it originally purchased for €500,000 in 2005. The company has ceased to trade and the shareholders would like to take a distribution *in specie* of the property. However, the company has debts of €500,000 and professional liquidator fees of €50,000. It does not have cash to clear these debts.

The liquidator must therefore sell the premises to generate funds to clear the company's liabilities and will distribute the balance to the shareholders as a capital distribution. The following taxes arise:

	€
Corporation tax payable by the company:	
Sales of premises	1,200,000
Base cost	(500,000)
Gain	700,000
CGT @ 33%	231,000
Net funds available to clear debts	969,000
Less: company debts	(500,000)
Less: liquidator fees	(50,000)
Net funds available for distribution	419,000

A distribution of assets *in specie* by a liquidator to shareholders of an Irish company in the course of a winding up is not chargeable to stamp duty. The legitimate avoidance of stamp duty, which is chargeable at the rate of 7.5% on the market value of the asset, is a substantial saving for the recipient of an asset distributed *in specie*. However, a charge to stamp duty can be incurred in the course of the distribution of assets *in specie* if:

- the asset distributed is the subject of a mortgage or charge and is transferred subject to that charge; or
- the company has a debt to a third party and the shareholders agree to assume liability for that debt in consideration of the distribution; or
- the company owes a debt to the shareholders and the shareholders agree to forgive the debt in consideration of the distribution.

The result is that the transaction will be treated as a sale for the amount of the liabilities taken over or mortgage transferred, and stamp duty will apply based on the liability or mortgage assumed as per section 41 SDCA 1999. Therefore, all mortgages and debts on the asset itself must be cleared before it can be distributed *in specie* in order to avoid a charge to stamp duty.

Example 4.19

Lucinda set up a company in 2007 and subscribed at par for share capital of 200,000 €1 ordinary shares. The company purchased a commercial property for €550,000 in 2009, which was part-funded by a mortgage. Lucinda decided to liquidate the company and take a distribution *in specie* of the property, which is valued at €750,000.

The company has sufficient cash balances to pay its debts and CGT arising on the distribution *in specie*. However, Lucinda will take over the outstanding mortgage of €100,000 on taking a distribution of the property.

	€
Disposal by the company	
Market value	750,000
Less: base cost	(550,000)
Gain	200,000
CGT @ 33%	66,000
Distribution *in specie* to Lucinda	
Net proceeds	750,000
Less: consideration paid	(100,000)
Less: base cost	(200,000)
Gain	450,000
CGT @ 33%	148,500

4.6.5 Insolvent Liquidations

Where a company is liquidated and the company is not solvent, the shareholders will not receive a payment from the liquidator. As a result, the shareholder will have a loss. While there is no actual disposal until the liquidation is complete, a loss may be claimed under the rule that a claim may be made when an asset has negligible value. However, this is subject to the negligible loss claim being accepted by Revenue. When the liquidation is complete and the company is dissolved, at that stage the shareholder will be treated as having made a disposal of shares for CGT purposes (when an asset ceases to exist this is a disposal for CGT purposes) and can claim relief for the loss on shares without having to make a negligible value claim.

Chapter 4 Summary

Cash extraction from company

- There are many ways to extract cash from a business, each with its own tax implications
- Consider need and tax position of shareholders and company combined
- Salary versus dividend decision – the advantages and disadvantages of both
- Pension contributions are generally a tax-efficient way of extracting cash
- Termination payments have advantages in limited circumstances

Buy-back of shares from shareholder

- The funds from a share-buy back are under first principles a distribution in the hands of a shareholder
- If certain conditions are fulfilled, then the shareholder will qualify for CGT on the funds under the buy-back scheme

Liquidation of company

- Tax implications of a liquidation
- Cash extraction by way of liquidation
- Distribution of assets *in specie*

Questions

Review Question
(See Suggested Solutions to Review Questions at the end of this textbook.)

Question 4.1

(a) During the period of liquidation of a company, who is liable for the payment of tax on any gains on the disposal of assets that the company owned at the time the liquidator was appointed?
(b) A company has prepared its financial statements for the year ended 30 June 2022. A liquidator is appointed on 15 September 2022. What corporation tax returns must be filed and by what date(s)?
(c) John Murphy, an Irish tax resident individual, acquired shares in Burst Ltd, an Irish tax resident company, on 1 May 2002 for €50,000. The company traded successfully for several years but has been loss-making in recent years. When its main lender received the financial statements for the year ended 31 August 2022, it was very concerned and a liquidator was appointed to wind up Burst Ltd. On 1 December 2022, the liquidator advised that the liabilities of the company significantly exceeded its assets and that shareholders will receive no payment. What are the tax consequences for John?

Challenging Question
(Suggested Solutions to Challenging Questions are available through your lecturer.)

Question 4.1

Mr and Mrs Jones are equal shareholders in their trading company, Jones Ltd. The company was set up over 10 years ago when Mr Jones incorporated his shoe shop trade. Mr Jones takes a salary of €80,000 and Mrs Jones does not take anything. The dividend policy of the company has been to pay an annual dividend of €5,000 per shareholder.

Mr Jones is the major influence on the business, but Mrs Jones helps out with the company's administrative duties, such as taking phone calls, following up orders and sorting payments as required. She has no other income. The company currently employs 20 staff and Mr Jones is keen to incentivise his key members of staff in a tax-efficient manner, but is unsure if this is possible.

Mr Jones advises you that he has not started to plan for the future yet, but anticipates that he will require an annual income of €30,000 on retirement to maintain his current lifestyle.

The couple has been made an offer of €1 million for the business.

Requirement
Prepare a report for Mr and Mrs Jones addressing the following issues:

(a) The tax efficiency of the present remuneration arrangements from the company.
(b) Other forms of cash extraction from the company.
(c) The tax consequences of selling the business for €1 million.

Corporate Groups

Learning Objectives

By the end of this chapter you will be able to:
- Analyse and evaluate the taxation implications at all stages of a group of company's business life cycle, including:
  - use of trading losses and excess charges in a group scenario;
  - CGT provisions relating to group transfers;
  - stamp duty relief on transfers between associated companies; and
  - exemption from CGT in case of gains on a disposal of a subsidiary.
- Consider the implications of business taxation decisions at the individual entity level.

Note: group relief is covered extensively in CA Proficiency 2, and students should review this material before reading this chapter.

5.1   Reasons for a Group Structure

A business could form a group structure to run its various business activitities for many commercial, practical and/or tax reasons. For example, if a company has a number of trading interests, or indeed very distinct activities, it may wish to separate those trading interests into separate companies to:

- Operate separate trades capable of individual measurement.
- Separate strong and weak trades.
- Manage the performance of each entity.
- Isolate certain activities from other group activities.
- Manage any exposure to bad debts/trade failure, creditor pressures, etc.
- Separate companies/trades/assets for sale to third parties.
- Separate poorly performing trades for liquidation/cessation.
- Form one company to hold all employees.
- Form a company to hold all assets/shares in other subsidiaries.
- Form a company to facilitate once-off commercial transactions (often known in practice as "special purpose companies").
- Create a holding company structure to avail of reliefs, such as the participation exemption (section 626B TCA 1997 – CGT exemption in respect of a disposal of shares in a trading subsidiary; see **Section 5.8**).
- Claim interest as a charge for investment in subsidiaries by a holding company.

While the above list is not exhaustive, it nevertheless demonstrates the numerous reasons why a corporate group may exist. In practice, as a business expands, additional companies are often created to facilitate growth/expansion or new business ventures.

5.2 Corporation Tax Group: Key Tax Issues

A company is a distinct legal entity. Tax reliefs are available where a qualifying group exists. An example of a corporation tax group is illustrated below.

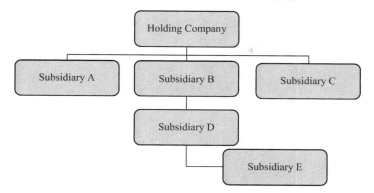

In general, the specific tax reliefs available in qualifying group situations are:

- Relief from withholding tax obligations on annual payments between group members.
- Group loss relief for tax losses.
- Relief from tax on the transfer of capital assets between group companies.

Each of these tax group provisions require a specific shareholding relationship and are also subject to specific conditions set out in the discussion for each tax group provision as follows.

5.3 Group Payment Relief: Obligation to Withhold Income Tax

Certain payments made by one company to another company may create a withholding tax obligation on the paying company. The withholding tax rate is the standard income tax rate (currently 20%). The payments on which there is a requirement to withhold income tax include:

- yearly interest;
- annuities;
- patents; and
- other annual payments.

The withholding tax liability is returned and paid by the payer company as part of its annual corporation tax payment obligation.

A company is not required to withhold the 20% tax when there is a 51% shareholding relationship between the paying company and the recipient company. (Remember, a company is a 51% subsidiary of another company if more than 50% of its ordinary share capital is owned directly or indirectly by that other company.) Non-Irish companies qualify for the relief if they are resident in any country with which Ireland has a DTT, or if the non-Irish parent company's shares are traded on a recognised stock exchange. In cases where the recipient company is not resident in Ireland, then the payment must also be taxable in the recipient's country to avoid the obligation to operate withholding tax.

> **Key Issue**
> Students should pay particular attention to situations where annual payments are being made by a company.
> There may be a requirement to withhold 20% tax by the payer company if it is not a 51% group member.

5.4 Corporation Tax Group: Loss Relief

When a corporate group exists, a key tax objective for the group is to efficiently manage its overall tax liability. If one company in the group makes a loss, that loss should, if possible, be available for use in another profit-making group entity.

Corporation tax group relief allows for an off-set of losses in one group company against the profits of another group company.

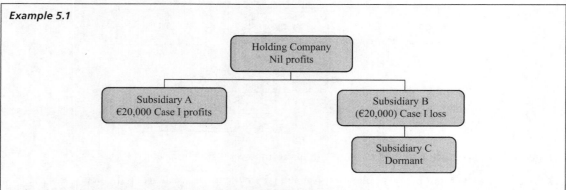

Example 5.1

In the absence of group relief, Subsidiary A will be liable to corporation tax at 12.5% on its €20,000 profits. Subsidiary B will not have a corporation tax liability as it is in an overall loss position.

However, if the conditions for group relief are in place, then the Case I loss in Subsidiary B should be surrendered to Subsidiary A for offset against its taxable Case I profits and the group should achieve an overall nil tax liability on optimisation of group relief.

Section 420 TCA 1997, and the related sections 420A and 420B, provide for corporation tax group relief. The following are available for surrender to other group members:

- Trading losses.
- Certain excess capital allowances.
- Management expenses (i.e. of an investment management company).
- Charges on income (e.g. yearly interest, patents, etc.).

To claim group loss relief, a 75% relationship must exist between the relevant group members. This 75% relationship is satisfied if one company holds, directly or indirectly, at least 75% of the ordinary share capital of the other company. It will also apply where two or more companies are 75% subsidiaries of a company (usually known as a 'parent' or holding company). The parent must be entitled to 75% of the profits on a winding up and 75% of the assets on distribution.

A qualifying group structure may include indirect shareholdings, provided they are owned by a company that is either:

- resident in Ireland;
- resident in an EU Member State;
- resident in an EEA state that has a double tax treaty (DTT) with Ireland;
- resident in any country with which Ireland has a DTT; or
- resident in any country, provided the company's principal class of shares are substantially and regularly traded on a recognised stock exchange.

Example 5.2: Group relief

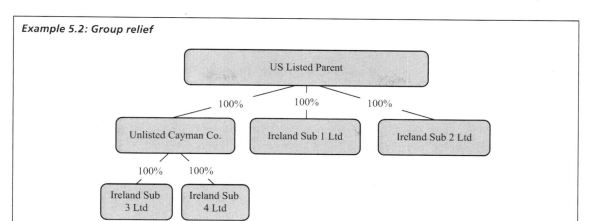

Only two of the Irish subsidiaries (Sub 1 and Sub 2) form part of a group since their immediate parent is listed on a recognised stock exchange. Sub 3 and Sub 4 do not form part of a group since their immediate parent is not resident in a country with which Ireland has a DTT.

In addition to the 75% shareholding test, for group relief to apply, the company must also:

- be entitled to not less than 75% of the profits of another company; and
- be entitled to not less than 75% of the assets of another company if that company were wound up.

Losses can be surrendered up through the group, down through the group or sideways through a group. The key requirement at all times is that the 75% tests must be met.

Example 5.3

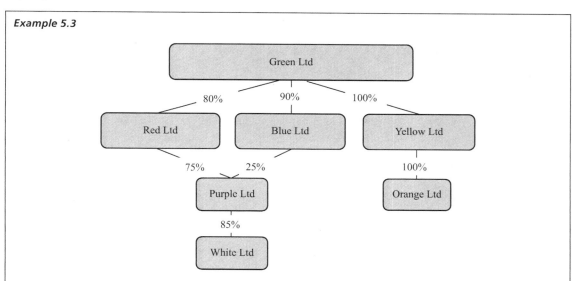

The Green Group consists of Green Ltd, Red Ltd, Blue Ltd, Yellow Ltd, Purple Ltd and Orange Ltd.

Purple Ltd is a member of the group as Green Ltd owns more than 75%, i.e. 82.5%, of the shares once the combined shareholding is taken into consideration.

White Ltd has only a 70.125% shareholding and so does not satisfy the 75% overall shareholding condition. However, as there is a group relationship between Purple Ltd and White Ltd, group relief applies between those two companies.

5.4.1 Tax Residency Issues

The question of tax residency must be carefully considered when assessing the application of group relief. The company seeking to claim group relief must be either resident in Ireland or be an Irish branch of a DTT company. In other words, the claimant company must be liable to Irish corporation tax to avail of the relief.

Group relief in respect of Case I losses incurred outside of Ireland is only available for relief upwards, i.e. from the foreign subsidiary to its Irish parent. The loss must be surrendered to an Irish parent of a 75% subsidiary that is tax resident in a EU/EEA Member State. Irish tax relief is only available when it is established that there is no other means of using the loss in the foreign subsidiary. This form of loss relief has very narrow application and was introduced following the outcome of *Marks & Spencer v. Inspector of Taxes* (2006) (Case C–446/03).

5.4.2 Key Questions when Considering Group Relief

The first question to ask is:
- Does the company have current-year trade losses?

   If the answer is yes, then ask:
   - Is the company a member of a tax group, i.e. is the required 75% common relationship in place?

      If yes, then ask:
      - Is there another group member with taxable profits?

         If yes, then ask:
         - Does the company meet the required residency rules?

            If yes, then ask:
            - Are there any issues which might impact on the use of group relief (e.g. late filing of returns, failing to meet time limits, etc.)?

If the answer to the last question is no, then group relief applies and the trading losses may be offset against trading profits or used on a 'value basis' against corporation tax of the group.

5.4.3 Claiming Group Loss Relief

Both the surrendering and claimant company must agree to the utilisation of group relief. A claim for group relief can be made on the company's CT1 Form (for both the surrendering company and the claimant company).

Group relief may be **restricted** on late submission of corporation tax return (section 1085 TCA 1997). This restriction applies where either the surrendering company or the claimant company files a late return. It is very important, therefore, that all companies within a group that wish to claim group relief file their tax returns on time. The restriction is as follows:

- Where the return is less than two months late, the group relief claim is restricted to 75% of the relief, subject to a maximum restriction of €31,740.
- Where the return is more than two months late, a 50% restriction applies, subject to a maximum restriction of €158,715.

Group relief claims require the consent of the surrendering company and must be made within two years of the end of the surrendering company's accounting period in which the loss arises.

> **Key Issue – Time Limits**
> Goup relief must be claimed within two years of the end of the surrendering company's relevant accounting period (a claim is not available beyond that period). This includes amendments of previous claims for group relief.

Losses brought forward from a prior period must also be utilised by a claimant company before it can avail of group relief.

Group relief in respect of Case I trading losses is claimed in the following order:

1. Relevant trading losses against other group trading income (section 420A TCA 1997).
2. Group relief as a credit against corporation tax on a "value basis" (section 420B TCA 1997).

Example 5.4

	€
Subsidiary A Case I loss	(80,000)
Subsidiary B Case I profit	100,000
Subsidiary B Case I loss b/f	(50,000)

Subsidiary B must first utilise the Case I loss brought forward, and then use the available loss relief, best illustrated as follows:

Subsidiary B	€
Case I profit	100,000
Less: loss b/f	(50,000)
	50,000
Less: loss relief surrender from A	(50,000)
Taxable profits	Nil

Subsidiary A has a Case I loss for carry forward of €30,000.

Value Basis Relief

As set out in CA Proficiency 2, the 'value basis' for loss relief involves an offset of a 12.5% trading loss against other income and gains such that only the 12.5% value of the loss is used against income taxable at 25%. Due to the different corporate tax rates, a euro-for-euro offset of a 12.5% loss against profits taxable at 25% would create a tax advantage which is countered by the value basis principle.

Example 5.5

	€
Subsidiary A Case I loss	(100,000)
Subsidiary B Case III profit	40,000

Subsidiary B's Case III profits are taxed as €40,000 × 25% = €10,000.

The value basis for loss relief means that Subsidiary A must use €80,000 of its losses to shelter the €10,000 tax liability arising in Subsidiary A, i.e. the value of €80,000 × 12.5% = €10,000.

Subsidiary A now has a trading loss balance for carry forward of €20,000 (€100,000 less losses surrendered under group relief of €80,000).

Payments for Group Relief

In practice, a claimant company may pay a surrendering company for group loss relief. There is no requirement or obligation to do so, but it may arise for commercial reasons within groups, i.e. different cost centres must be reimbursed or where a third party owns a 10% minority interest in a company that is a group member, they may wish to see some benefit accruing to the surrendering company if it is surrendering tax losses to that company.

The amount paid is typically the same value as the tax benefit received by the claimant company. If the payment for the group relief does not exceed the amount of loss relief actually claimed, then:

■ the payment is not considered to be taxable income or a deductible expense in the hands of either company; and
■ the payment is not considered a dividend to the recipient of the payment.

Impact of Accounting Periods

Group relief can only be availed of where the accounting period of the surrendering company (i.e. the 'loss-maker') and the claimant company (i.e. the 'profit-maker') correspond wholly or partly. If both companies have, for example, a year end of 31 December, no further consideration is required as the accounting periods correspond equally. If, however, the accounting periods correspond partially, group loss relief is computed on a time-apportionment basis. This is done by computing the losses and profits for those corresponding periods and the group relief claim then equals **the lower** of the time-apportioned profit or loss.

To maximise group loss relief, the accounting periods immediately before and after the corresponding periods should also be considered for losses or profits of group members that might be available to offset. Note that, although the claimant and surrendering companies must be in a group throughout any overlapping accounting period, they need not be in a group relationship at the time the relief is claimed.

Example 5.6
Take **Example 5.4** above, but assume that Subsidiary A's accounting period is the 12 months to 30 September 2022 and Subsidiary B's is the 12 months to 31 December 2022.

	€
Subsidiary A Case I loss	(80,000)
Subsidiary B Case I profit	100,000
Subsidiary B Case I loss b/f	(50,000)

Subsidiary B must first utilise the Case I loss brought forward, and then use the available loss relief as follows:

Subsidiary B	€
Case I profit	100,000
Less: loss b/f	(50,000)
	50,000
Less: loss relief surrender from Sub. A (Note)	(37,500)
Taxable profits	12,500

Note: establish the profit and loss of the corresponding accounting period and take the lower figure:

9/12 × €80,000 = €60,000
9/12 × €50,000 = €37,500

Subsidiary A has a trading loss carry forward of €42,500.

We should also consider the extent to which the accounting periods immediately before and after these periods correspond. For example, A's loss for the three months to 31 December 2021 might be available for offset against any profits of B for the corresponding accounting period. Similarly, if A has losses for the year ended 30 September 2023, the portion that corresponds with B's period to 31 December 2022 could be used.

5.4.4   Computational Example: Group Loss Relief

Example 5.7

Take the corporation tax group below, where X Ltd is the parent company and the year end for all group members is 31 December 2022. All profits/losses shown are Case I trade related.

Loss relief can be surrendered as follows:

	€
X Ltd	
Case I profits	1,000,000
Less: surrender of loss – Z Ltd	(1,000,000)
Profits liable to corporation tax	0
Y Ltd	
Case I profits	500,000
Less: surrender of loss – Z Ltd	(500,000)
Profits liable to corporation tax	0
H Ltd	
Case I profits	500,000
Less: surrender of loss – Z Ltd	(500,000)
Profits liable to corporation tax	0
Z Ltd – Tax Loss Memo	
Current-year loss	(2,000,000)
Surrender to X Ltd	1,000,000
Surrender to Y Ltd	500,000
Surrender to H Ltd	500,000
Balance c/f at 31/12/2022	0

The key points to note in the above example are:

1. Z Ltd did not have profits in the prior year that could have benefited from a carry back of the loss.
2. Z Ltd did not have other income that would have been reduced by loss relief before group relief.
3. There is no particular order to claim the group relief; the above example could have started with A Ltd benefiting from the group relief.

4. If Z Ltd was paid by the group members for the relief, a charge to tax would not arise for Z Ltd on the payment (subject to the required conditions discussed previously).
5. If any of the corporation tax returns of the relevant companies were late, group relief would be restricted. This is a key point to be aware of when claiming relief.

5.5 Consortium Relief

A consortium exists where at least 75% of the share capital of a company is owned by:

■ five or fewer companies;
■ all of which are EU resident or resident in a country within the EEA and with which Ireland has a double taxation treaty; and
■ no single investor company on its own owns 75% or more of the company.

The company owned by a consortium must be either a trading company, or a company that owns a minimum 90% holding in trading entities. The consortium structure of a trading company might look like this:

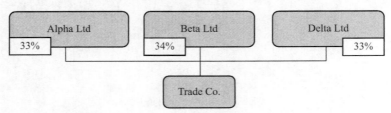

The consortium structure where there is a holding company could look like this:

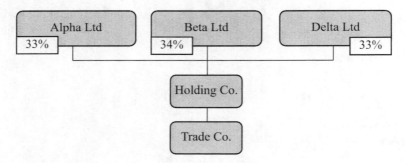

Consortium loss relief is a type of corporation tax group relief. However there are distinct differences between consortium loss relief and corporation tax group loss relief outlined in **Section 5.4.** The first difference is that the 75% group relationship between one parent and the trading company does not exist for consortium relief purposes. In fact, for consortium relief to apply, one company alone must not own 75% or more of the trading subsidiary. The consortium members (of which there will be five or less in number) must hold at least 75% of the trading company. A member's share in a consortium is the lower of:

■ its percentage holding in the trading company/holding company of a trading group;
■ its percentage entitlement to profits available to equity holders; or
■ its percentage entitlement to assets on a winding up.

The second issue to note is that losses may only be surrendered upwards (which is different to normal loss relief). In effect, this means that Trade Co. will surrender losses to its consortium owners in proportion to its percentage holdings.

Example 5.8

Trade Co., which incurred a trading loss of €2 million, is owned by four companies with different shareholdings. Trade Co.'s €2 million loss can be surrendered upward as follows:

	Shareholding	Loss relief available
A Ltd	20%	€400,000
B Ltd	40%	€800,000
D Ltd	30%	€600,000
G Ltd	10%	€200,000

5.6   Capital Gains Tax Group

Group relief also exists in respect of the transfer of chargeable assets between group members. Remember, where ownership of a chargeable asset changes, there will be a disposal of that asset for tax purposes. Also, where that disposal occurs between connected parties, the transaction will be deemed to happen at the market value of the asset passing. As a reminder, examples of chargeable assets can include property, goodwill, shares and other such capital assets.

The transfer of revenue items (e.g. stock or debtors) does not give rise to CGT issues. The group-relieving provisions provide that the transfer of the chargeable asset is to occur as if a no gain/no loss situation were to arise. The purchaser or recipient of a property will take on the original base cost and date of acquisition of the vendor/transferor. If an asset is transferred intragroup numerous times, the base cost and date of acquisition attaching to that property will not change until the company leaves the group or the property is sold to a third party.

5.6.1   Intragroup Sales/Transfers of Capital Assets

A principal company and its effective 75% subsidiaries form a CGT group. Where a principal company itself is a member of a group (as being itself an effective 75% subsidiary), that group comprises all of its effective 75% subsidiaries.

A "principal company" is a company of which another company is an effective 75% subsidiary (directly or indirectly). A company is an effective 75% subsidiary of another company, the parent, if the parent:

1. owns, directly or indirectly, not less than 75% of its ordinary share capital;
2. is beneficially entitled to not less than 75% of any profits available for distribution; and
3. would be beneficially entitled to not less than 75% of the assets of the company available for distribution on a winding up.

The distinction between a group for loss relief purposes and for CGT purposes is that where a principal company is itself an effective 75% subsidiary, it and all its effective 75% subsidiaries will be part of the same CGT group as its parent, even though a sub-subsidiary of the ultimate parent may be less than 75% owned by that parent. For example: P Ltd owns 75% of S Ltd. A Ltd acquires 75% of P Ltd. Even though A Ltd does not control 75% of S Ltd, it is in the A Ltd CGT group.

The member companies must be resident in Ireland, the EU/EEA or in a country with which Ireland has a double tax treaty, or be a company quoted on a recognised stock exchange. However, the asset transferred must continue to be within the charge to Irish tax post-transfer.

The thrust of CGT group relief is that where an asset is transferred between members, the transfer is deemed to occur at a price that would give rise to a no gain/no loss position. This is a compulsory condition and has the effect that there cannot be a capital loss on intragroup transfers of capital assets.

For accounting purposes, the transfer may occur at the book value of those assets. For tax purposes, the consideration (if any) that actually passes is ignored. The tax relief is structured in such a manner that it is deemed to be at no loss/no gain.

Subsequently, if there is a disposal of an asset by a member of a group to a person outside the group and that asset had been acquired by the company making the disposal from another group member, the acquisition cost for the disposal is the original base cost and date of acquisition of the first member to acquire the asset.

CGT group relief does not remove the requirement on the transferor company to obtain CG50 clearance from Revenue in advance of the disposal. Notwithstanding that the transfer results in a no gain/no loss situation for the transferor, Revenue could seek to apply penalties to the transferee if CG50 clearance is not in place (see **Section 12.5**).

The pre-entry losses of a company joining a group are subject to an anti-tax avoidance measure with a similar objective to the restriction on buying a company's trading losses (see **Chapter 6, Section 6.2.2**). The pre-entry losses of a joining company cannot be offset against subsequent gains within the group. The restriction applies to:

■ losses arising in the company before it became a group member (i.e. on a past disposal); and
■ subsequent losses arising on assets held by the company when it became a group member.

Capital losses restricted under this anti-avoidance provision can be offset against the joining company's own gains under normal CGT rules.

5.6.2 Clawback of Relief

As with most tax reliefs, there is a provision for clawback of that relief (section 623 TCA 1997 in this case). In general, the clawback will occur where the company that acquired the asset leaves the group still holding that asset. The clawback period exists for 10 years following the transfer of that asset.

Example 5.9

Company A transfers a building to Company B on 1 July 2014. If Company B were to leave the group before 1 July 2024, there will be a clawback of group relief from Company B.

Where a company ceases to be a member of a CGT group, the assets it has acquired and on which group relief was claimed will be deemed to have been sold and immediately reacquired at market value at the date of the original transfer by the company holding the asset. Note therefore that CGT group relief is effectively, for that 10-year period, a deferral of the CGT that should have arisen on that intragroup transfer. It is not a full exemption without further implication to the CGT group.

If the 10-year period expires, there will not be a clawback of group relief if the 75% relationship is broken. Group relief clawback should be considered if any of the following occurs:

■ New investors into a group (i.e. the 75% relationship is broken).
■ Disposal of a subsidiary to a third party.
■ Liquidation of a subsidiary and the passing of assets to members (see below for exception).

The above scenarios could give rise to clawbacks of group relief.

Occasions where Group Relief Clawback Does Not Occur

A clawback of group relief will not typically occur where:

▨ the asset has been held by the company leaving the group for more than 10 years; or

▨ a company leaves the group by virtue of being wound up or dissolved. This dissolution of the company must occur for bona fide commercial reasons and not for the purposes of tax avoidance.

Example 5.10

Take the following group structure:

```
            ┌─────────────────────────┐
            │ Steel Frame Holdings Ltd │
            └─────────────────────────┘
         ┌───────────────┴───────────────┐
 ┌──────────────┐              ┌─────────────────────┐
 │ Iron Ore Ltd │              │ Steel Fabricators Ltd │
 └──────────────┘              └─────────────────────┘
```

The two subsidiaries are owned by Steel Frame Holdings Ltd. It purchased a property in 2014 for €20 million, which in 2022 is valued at €30 million. This property is where the group's steel products are manufactured. In recent years, Iron Ore Ltd has reduced its activity as Steel Fabricators Ltd now directly sources all its own materials. Steel Fabricators Ltd is the main trading entity, with turnover of €200 million per annum, and is profitable.

To streamline the business, in 2022 Steel Frame Holdings Ltd is going to transfer the property to Steel Fabricators Ltd. Without group relief, the following would occur:

▨ Steel Frame Holdings Ltd would be deemed to dispose of the property at market value. A chargeable gain of €10 million would arise, taxable at an effective rate of 33%.

▨ Steel Fabricators Ltd would acquire the asset and its base cost would be €30 million.

Group relief provides that the following applies:

▨ Steel Frame Holdings Ltd will dispose of the property for a deemed consideration that will give rise to a no gain/no loss situation. It will not have a tax liability on the transfer.

▨ Steel Fabricators Ltd will acquire the asset and will take on the base cost and date of acquisition of Steel Frame Holdings Ltd (i.e. €20 million and acquired in 2014).

If Steel Fabricators Ltd were to leave the group within 10 years, the following would occur:

▨ Steel Fabricators Ltd would be deemed to have disposed of and immediately reacquired the property (by reference to the date it took ownership – 2022). A chargeable gain of €10 million would arise and, as such, Steel Fabricators Ltd would trigger a €3.3 million tax liability for itself in the absence of loss relief.

If Steel Fabricators Ltd does not leave the group but sells the property to a third party in the future, then:

▨ Steel Fabricators Ltd would be liable to CGT on the disposal of the property. For computational purposes, it will have a base cost of €20 million and an original date of acquisition of 2014.

5.7 Stamp Duty: Associated Companies Relief

Stamp duty relief is also available for the transfer of assets between group members. If two companies involved in a property/asset transfer are 90% related by virtue of:

▨ direct or indirect ownership of 90% of ordinary share capital;

▨ entitlement to not less than 90% of any profits available for distribution; and

▨ entitlement to not less than 90% of assets available on a winding up, then an exemption from stamp duty can be claimed. The profit and assets tests here are similar to the tests applied in establishing if a group exists for the purposes of transfers of corporation tax losses between group companies as set out in above sections of the chapter.

Section 79 of the Stamp Duty Consolidation Act 1999 (SDCA 1999) legislates for this exemption. The exemption will apply to an instrument that executes for the transfer of any of the following:

- Conveyance or transfer on the sale of any stocks or marketable securities.
- Conveyance or transfer on sale of a policy of insurance or a policy of life insurance where the risk to which the policy relates is located in the State.
- Conveyance or transfer on the sale of any property other than stocks or marketable securities, a policy of insurance or a policy of life insurance

In practice, one is most likely to encounter a transfer of shares, stocks and property.

This stamp duty exemption is a valuable relief, particularly if property is the asset being transferred as it subject to the higher (7.5%) rate of stamp duty.

Key Issue
Where there is a transfer of assets intragroup, there may be an entitlement to an exemption from stamp duty if the provisions of section 79 SDCA 1999 are met. This is a valuable relief.

This stamp duty relief is subject to clawback if the two companies cease to be associated within two years of the transfer. However, a clawback will not occur if there is a liquidation or merger within the two-year period. These exceptions are on the basis that the beneficial interest in the property continues to be held by the transferee and that the beneficial ownership of the transferee remains unchanged for two years after the transfer. The transfer of the property or the liquidation of the company must be for bona fide commercial reasons.

Example 5.11
All entities within the A Ltd group are 100% subsidiaries.

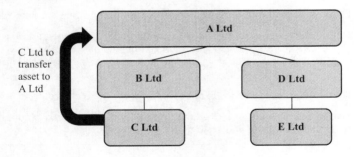

If C Ltd were to transfer a property asset to A Ltd, a claim for stamp duty associated companies relief is available.

If the 90% association between C Ltd and A Ltd is broken within two years of the transfer, there will be a clawback of the associated companies relief, unless the breaking of the relationship due to a liquidation or merger.

Note that CGT group relief can also be claimed and the transfer can effectively take place tax-free.

5.8 Disposal of a Subsidiary (Section 626B TCA 1997)

Section 626B TCA 1997 provides an exemption from Irish CGT where a capital gain is made by a company on the disposal of a shareholding in a subsidiary. The exemption applies if the relevant conditions are met, and it is therefore not necessary that a formal claim for the exemption be made by the company making the gain.

Certain conditions must be met before a gain can be exempt:

- First, the investor company must have a minimum shareholding in the investee company. The investor is required to have a minimum holding of at least 5% in the investee company for a continuous period of at least 12 months at any time in the two years prior to the disposal.

- Secondly, the investee company must carry on a trade, or the business of the investor company and its investee company, taken as a whole, must consist wholly or mainly of the carrying on of a trade or trades. As per Revenue's *Tax and Duty Manual,* Part 20-01-14, "wholly or mainly" means greater than 50%. The primary tests are the proportion of net trading profits and the proportion of net trading assets, though other factors may be taken into account. These lesser considerations might include trading turnover as a proportion of gross receipts or the proportion of employees' time devoted to trading and non-trading activities.

- Finally, at the time of the disposal the investee company must be resident in an EU Member State or a country with which Ireland has a tax treaty.

The exemption does not apply on the disposal of a company with shares that derive the greater part of their value from land in the State, or from minerals or rights or interests in relation to mining or minerals or the searching for minerals. Anti-avoidance provisions are in place to prevent the value of shares attributable, directly or indirectly, to Irish land/buildings being reduced by an arrangement that involves the transfer of money or other assets to the company by a connected person before the disposal of the company where the main purpose is the avoidance of tax. Therefore, it is essential to review the balance sheet of a subsidiary to consider if more than 50% of the company's value is derived from land and buildings, minerals, or mining rights and interests when assessing if section 626B can be applied.

In addition, the exemption under section 626B does not apply to disposals regarded as no gain/no loss transactions, such as CGT group transfers under section 617 TCA 1997. The exemption excludes disposals deemed to take place under section 627 TCA 1997, which provides that the cessation of residence of a company triggers a charge to either corporation tax or, where appropriate, CGT.

Example 5.12

Jones Holding Ltd owns 100% of the ordinary share capital of Software Dynamics Ltd, a trading company carrying on a business of software development. Jones Holding Ltd has owned the shares in Software Dynamics Ltd for three years. Both Jones Holding Ltd and Software Dynamics Ltd are tax-resident in Ireland. Jones Holding Ltd has received an offer from Macro-soft Ltd for the entire issued share capital of Software Dynamics Ltd, which will generate a capital profit for Jones Holding Ltd of €5,000,000.

Due to the exemptions available under section 626B, Jones Holding Ltd will not pay tax on the €5,000,000 gain.

If Software Dynamics were tax-resident in Germany, Jones Holding Ltd would still be entitled to the exemption as its subsidiary was resident in the EU.

5.8.1 Section 626B Interaction with Capital Gains Groups

In order to determine whether the company disposing of shares has held them for the required holding period under section 626B, the period of ownership of shares by a company can be extended where the shares were acquired in a transaction that is treated as giving rise to neither a gain nor a loss, such as the transfer of shares within a group of companies as per Schedule 25A TCA 1997. No gain or loss is treated as arising on the intragroup transfer of shares, but the new owner takes over the assets for CGT purposes at their original base cost.

In these circumstances, the new owner is allowed to extend the period of ownership by the same length of time the shares were held by the previous owner on any further disposals qualifying for section 626B relief.

5.8.2 Loss Relief and Section 626B

A loss cannot be an allowable loss if a gain on the same transaction would not be a chargeable gain. Therefore a loss arising on the disposal of shares in a company is disregarded because the gain would have been exempt under section 626B. In addition, a company may not claim relief for a loss in value of shares that have negligible value if a gain on a disposal of the shares would be exempt under section 626B.

This means that companies may lose out on the benefit of capital losses on the disposal or write-off of loss-making subsidiaries. As section 626B is an automatic exemption, an Irish company with latent losses on subsidiaries may want to take steps to ensure that the participation exemption will not apply before realising the loss on making a disposal or making a negligible loss claim.

5.9 Benefits of a Holding Company Structure

There are limited benefits in keeping various business interests in separately owned companies, i.e. not within a group structure. Problems can arise using this type of structure, for example in respect of the financing of each individual entity. Therefore, a holding company structure is often put in place to maximise commercial and tax efficiencies.

A holding company is a company whose business consists wholly or mainly of holding shares in subsidiary companies. The benefits of a holding company can be summarised as follows:

- Facilitates group loss relief in respect of tax losses between subsidiaries.
- Facilitates CGT group relief in respect of the transfer of assets between members.
- Interest as a charge may be claimable by the holding company.
- Section 626B TCA 1997 (participation exemption) may apply on a future disposal of shares by the holding company.
- Creates a vehicle to allow third-party investors entry at the top company level.

Putting a holding company in place in a tax-efficient manner will be considered in **Chapter 7**.

Chapter 5 Summary

Corporation tax losses for groups

- Facilitates the transfer of losses to ensure the overall profit/loss position of a group is recognised for tax purposes
- Need a 75% relationship overall
- Losses available include trading losses, excess management expenses and excess capital allowances and charges on income
- Impact on loss relief where tax returns are filed late

Consortium relief

- Surrender/claim losses in proportion to ownership
- Needs consent of all members
- Group relief takes priority over consortium relief

Capital gains groups

- Need 75% ownership, with overall control of the group
- Assets are transferred at no gain/no loss
- Clawback may apply on member leaving the group

Other group issues

- Stamp duty – relief where 90% relationship exists
- Clawback of relief if member leaves group
- Participation exemption – relief from CGT on sale of subsidiary

Questions

Review Questions
(See Suggested Solutions to Review Questions at the end of this textbook.)

Question 5.1

In the year ended 31 March 2022, GAS Ltd is a 75% subsidiary of OIL Ltd. The accounts and computations of the companies for the 12-month accounting period to 31 March 2022 show the following:

	€
OIL Ltd	
Current-year management expenses	15,000
Management expenses brought forward	2,500
Case III income	3,200
GAS Ltd	
Trading profits	10,000
Charges paid	600

GAS Ltd claims group relief from OIL Ltd, with the consent of OIL Ltd.

Requirement
(a) Calculate the amount of group relief available to GAS Ltd.
(b) Calculate the revised profits chargeable to corporation tax for the group for the year ended 31 March 2022.

Question 5.2

Company A is a 75% subsidiary of Company B. Both companies make up their accounts to 31 December. The accounts and computations of the companies for the 12-month accounting period to 31 December 2022 show the following:

	€	€
Company B		
Management expenses		2,000
Capital gain	3,200	
Less: capital losses brought forward	(1,800)	1,400
Case III income		1,000
Non-trade charges paid		5,500
Company A		
Case I profit		1,000
Case III income		500
Non-trade charges paid		200

Requirement
Calculate the maximum amount of group relief claim between Company A and Company B.

Question 5.3

Tree Ltd is owned as follows:

The following information in respect of the members of the consortium is available:

- Garden Ltd had trading profits of €290,000 in respect of the year ended 31 December 2021.
- Park Ltd had trading profits of €200,000 in respect of the year ended 31 March 2022. In addition, Park Ltd had a non-trade charge of €75,000.
- Pitch Ltd had trading profits of €160,000 and Case III income of €40,000 for the year ended 31 March 2022.
- Tree Ltd has trading losses of €400,000 and Case III income of €45,000 in respect of the year ended 31 March 2022.

Requirement
(a) Calculate the maximum amount of losses available for consortium relief.
(b) Calculate the corporation tax liabilities for the above companies, assuming all relevant claims and elections are made.

Challenging Question
(Suggested Solutions to Challenging Questions are available through your lecturer.)

Question 5.1

During the year ended 31 December 2022, QuikPhones Group had the following trading results:

- QuikPhones Ltd is a trading company involved in the manufacture of mobile phones. During the year ended 31 December 2022, it had trading profits of €256,065 with capital losses brought forward of €60,000.
- Phunkyfones Ltd has Schedule D Case I profits of €67,994 before deducting capital allowances of €34,000. The company also has trading losses of €446,086 brought forward, together with capital losses of €44,000.

- CallTime Ltd incurred trading losses of €369,402 during the year.
- SpeakUp Ltd had trading profits of €72,100 and a capital gain of €135,000.
- The shareholding in AnsMe Ltd was acquired by QuikPhones Ltd on 1 August 2022. Its results for the year ended 31 December 2022 showed a Schedule D, Case I profit of €155,866.

The financial controller advises you of the following transactions due to take place in the coming months:

- An offer of €1,750,000 for a property owned by SpeakUp Ltd has been received by an unconnected third party. The property was originally transferred from NoMob Ltd in January 2014 when an offer of €1.25 million was turned down, as it was needed in the trade of SpeakUp Ltd. Due to recent changes in the company, it is no longer required and the offer is too good to refuse. QuikPhones is to transfer a smaller property that is not currently being used to SpeakUp Ltd. The property was acquired in February 1983 and indexation from then to 2003 is 2.253.
- NoMob Ltd is to be sold to an unconnected third party. The purchaser is interested in a property that is held by the company and which was originally bought by QuikPhones in January 1986 for €45,000. The property was transferred to NoMob Ltd in November 2011, when it was worth €178,000. Indexation from January 1986 to 2003 is 1.713.

Requirement
(a) State the members of the group relief CGT for corporation tax purposes.
(b) State the members of the CGT group.
(c) Calculate the corporation tax liability of the group, on the basis that all claims and elections are made to minimise the tax position.
(d) Advise on the actual and proposed capital transfers during the year.

Acquisition and Disposal of a Business

Learning Objectives

By the end of this chapter you will be able to:

- Analyse and evaluate the taxation implications of an acquisition or disposal of a business, including:
  - share sales;
  - trading losses and loss-buying restrictions;
  - taxation warranties and indemnities requirements; and
  - asset/trade sales.

6.1　Types of Acquisition and Disposal

The sale or acquisition of a business can take various forms. Each of the various approaches gives rise to a different commercial, tax and legal consequence that influences the way in which the transaction is structured. In summary, the different forms of a business sale or acquisition can include:

- Share sale/purchase.
- Sale/purchase of a trade as a going concern.
- Sale/purchase of assets.

The purchaser and the vendor will have different objectives with regard to the buying and selling of the business assets or shares of a company; each will look to achieve a more favourable tax outcome for themselves. This chapter looks at several ways of acquiring/disposing of a business from both the vendor's and the purchaser's point of views, having regard to the tax, legal and commercial consequences of the transactions.

How a business is eventually sold will be a matter for negotiation between the two parties. A restructuring or reorganisation of a business prior to a sale may be required to enable a particular type of sale, one that is satisfactory for the purchaser and/or the vendor.

Example 6.1
A purchaser may only want to buy the share capital of a company and not the specific business assets/trade of the company. In this case, specific steps are necessary to facilitate the share sale. For example, assets held by the company not intended for sale will need to be moved out of the company, requiring a restructuring of the company prior to the share sale.

Example 6.2

A purchaser may not wish to purchase the shares of a company, for example to avoid taking on responsibility of any historical tax issues or latent gains associated with the company. The seller must therefore take appropriate steps to ensure that an asset sale can be facilitated. The vendor must take into account how to extract the cash proceeds from the company following the sale of the asset/s. The challenge of tax-efficient extraction of cash is often a key issue associated with an asset sale for the vendor.

Example 6.3

A company wants to sell a 100% shareholding in a subsidiary. However, the company and its subsidiary are members of a CGT and a stamp duty group and tax relief on an assets transfer has been claimed by the group in recent years. The sale of the subsidiary will trigger a clawback of tax relief claimed. Therefore the company will need to carefully consider the implications of selling the subsidiary and the timing of the sale.

Key Issue

Prior to the sale of a business, **the vendor** must consider the tax implications associated with the various sale options. In the case of an asset/trade sale by a company, the shareholder of the vendor company should carefully evaluate how cash can be extracted from the company. It may be the case that the shareholder wishes to retain cash in the company for further investment. Issues such as the base cost of assets will be relevant as the vendor is likely to have to consider a CGT liability at both company level and at shareholder level. Retirement relief (see **Chapter 9, Section 9.3**) is a key planning relief and if available can prove very beneficial to the vendor.

From a tax perspective, **the purchaser** will want to buy the business tax-efficiently. This includes not just reducing the tax liability on the transaction itself, but also consideration of future tax implications such as latent gains or the possibility of availing of capital allowances on the purchase of assets. Consideration should also be given to the purchaser's future or intended exit from the business. Stamp duty will be a key consideration for the purchaser, with a share purchase offering the most favourable stamp duty result. However, tax issues should be assessed alongside commercial and legal considerations rather than in isolation.

Whatever the disposal method chosen, the proceeds received will be subject to either CGT on the chargeable gain (if sold by an individual) or corporation tax on the chargeable gain (if sold by a company).

Retirement relief may apply to reduce or fully relieve the CGT liability in the case of an individual liable to gains on a disposal of business assets or shares and this topic will be fully discussed in **Chapter 9**. The gains arising on the disposal of shares in a company may qualify for tax exemption under section 626B TCA 1997 as set out in **Chapter 5**.

6.2 Share Sale/Purchase

As already highlighted, the purchaser and the vendor will have different motives for preferring a share sale rather than an asset sale. A purchaser may wish to acquire shares for a number of reasons, such as:

■ The business can continue uninterrupted.
■ The lower rate of stamp duty on the purchase of shares (1%) compared to stamp duty on transactions involving commercial land and buildings and business assets such as goodwill (7.5%).
■ Unused tax reliefs, such as losses available for carry forward, continue to be available, subject to anti-avoidance provisions on the change of ownership.
■ The vendor may not be willing to sell anything other than the shares.

A vendor may prefer to sell the shares in the business because:

■ If the vendor is an individual, they will receive the cash personally from the share sale. CGT, at a current rate of 33% (or 10% if entrepreneur relief is available), will apply to the chargeable gain arising. The vendor may also qualify for retirement relief (see **Chapter 9**).

■ It avoids a double tax charge: (a) the tax on gains arising on the disposal of assets at company level; and (b) CGT on the subsequent cash distribution to the shareholders following the liquidation or winding up of the company and payable by the individual shareholders. **This is a key tax planning issue to remember: as the asset sale by a company does not give the individual the direct benefit of the sale proceeds, further steps are required to extract cash from the company.**

■ If a holding company is disposing of one of its trading subsidiaries, the participation exemption under section 626B TCA 1997 (see **Section 5.8**) may be available, thus exempting the share disposal from tax.

6.2.1 Tax Consequences of a Share Sale

A sale of shares is a disposal for CGT purposes. If the entire sale consideration is in cash, as opposed to a swap for shares in another company (see **Chapter 7**), the vendor is taxed on the full amount received after deducting the base cost and other allowable costs associated with the original acquisition of the shares. There is a continuation of the company's trade and no balancing charge/allowance is triggered on a transfer of asset on which capital allowances are claimed.

Existing tax losses may be carried forward within the company, subject to the anti-avoidance provisions, i.e. if there is a change in the nature or conduct of a trade following the change in ownership. These provisions are discussed in more detail in **Section 7.3**.

VAT does not arise in the case of a share sale because a sale of shares is not a VATable supply. However, as will be discussed further in **Chapter 7**, VAT input credits on professional fees and other costs cannot be claimed by the purchaser of shares.

Note that a share purchase may not be the best choice for the purchaser since a share purchase carries with it a number of risks, i.e. taking on the 'history' of the company, including any bad debts and outstanding liabilities.

A restructuring of the business may be required to separate items held by the company that are not intended to form part of the sale. Corporate restructuring is considered in detail in **Chapter 7**.

Stamp Duty Considerations: Share Purchase
Stamp duty is a cost for the purchaser, so it is sensible from their perspective to seek to structure the transaction to minimise stamp duty. As the rate of stamp duty on the purchase of shares is 1% as opposed to 7.5% on the purchase of assets, the purchaser is likely to prefer a share purchase. The question of stamp duty will not arise in isolation, however, as other commercial and tax issues will impact on the transaction structure.

Latent Gains Attaching to Property
A frequent tax consideration when dealing with a share sale/purchase, is the question of 'latent gains' attaching to a company's assets. Remember that on a share purchase all assets remain in the ownership of the company and their base cost is unaffected. A latent gain can arise where the company (now under the ownership of the purchaser) incurs a capital gain on the disposal of an asset (e.g. property). This arises where the property has a low base cost but has appreciated in value while in the ownership of the company. Where such latent gains are identified before the share sale/purchase, the purchaser will no doubt want to be compensated for this potential liability by negotiating a lower price for the shares.

Key Issue
In valuing the shares for the share sale, the value comes from the market value of the underlying assets of the company at the date of sale. On a purchase of shares in a company, the base cost for a future disposal will be the price paid for the shares. However, if the company is disposing of its assets (e.g. property) subsequent to the share sale, the assets retain their original base cost.

Example 6.4
Steven Ryan purchased the shares of a trading company, Blue Ink Ltd, for €15 million. The assets of the company comprised a trade worth €5 million and a property worth €10 million. The property was purchased by Blue Ink Ltd many years ago for €100,000. Steven has now received an offer to acquire the Blue Ink Ltd's trade and assets for €16 million. The purchaser doesn't want to acquire the shares in the company.

Steven thinks he will only be liable to CGT on the gain of €1 million. Is that correct?

It is not. One of the key issues driving the high value of the company is that the property is worth at least €10 million. If that property is sold at its current market value, the company will be liable to corporation tax on a significant chargeable gain of nearly €10 million. This is because the base cost is very low compared with the market value. In other words, the €15 million paid by Steven is not considered when the company is making the asset sale. The €15 million paid by Steven is the base cost of the shares only; the key asset, i.e. the property, is still held within the company and retains its very low base cost (€100,000).

Steven should try to negotiate a share sale rather than an asset sale. If properly advised, the purchaser may be reluctant to accept this without being adequately compensated as, at a future date, it is likely they will face the same latent gain issue.

Where a latent gain is identified in advance of a share acquisition, a purchaser may decide instead to only buy the trade/assets of the company. There would, however, be the higher rate of stamp duty (7.5%) payable on the purchase of assets.

Example 6.5
Philip Loughran is considering the purchase of Travel Ltd from an unconnected third party. Travel Ltd's accounts show a premises with an original base cost of €200,000. The current market value of the premises is €1 million.

Philip knows that the premises will be surplus to requirements once the company is bought as he has his own premises from which the new business will trade.

The latent gain in the company is as follows (ignoring any indexation):

	€
Current market value	1,000,000
Base cost	(200,000)
Potential gain	800,000
Corporation tax liability @ 33%	264,000

Philip will want to ensure that this latent liability is reflected in the purchase price negotiations for Travel Ltd, as ultimately it will be his liability.

6.2.2 Loss-buying Provisions

An investor's motive in buying shares in a company may be to acquire a company to access existing tax losses. If the investor is confident that they can make the company profitable, then the existing tax losses constitute a future benefit or asset of the company (i.e. the tax losses can be used to shelter future profits and avoid tax). Case I trading losses can be carried forward and set against future profits from the same trade. However, where there is a change in ownership of a company, existing trading losses can sometimes be disallowed. This is commonly known as the loss-buying anti-avoidance rule. The losses will be disallowed where, within a three-year period:

- there is a change in the ownership of the company; **and**
- there is also a major change in the activities carried on by that company; **or**
- where, at the time of the change in ownership, the company was almost dormant in terms of activity.

A major change in the nature of the trade of the company can include a change in the stock, property or services sold by the company, or a major change in the company's customer or market base.

Key Issue

The purchaser of shares may be confident that they can turn a loss-making business into a profitable one. If the company has significant tax losses accumulated (which could be common in companies that require significant growth/development investment), these tax losses represent an asset to the purchaser of shares. The key issue is to ensure that losses carried forward by the company are not jeopardised by any change in the nature of the trade or level of activity in the three years following the change of ownership.

6.2.3 Due Diligence Process

If a share purchase is to take place, the purchaser will carry out a due diligence review of the company to ascertain the level of any hidden/potential liabilities within the company. The due diligence process is similar to an audit of the company's affairs. The due diligence review of a company will normally involve a detailed review of the accounts of the target company for at least the previous three years and is a vital part of a share sale. The intention is to discover any potentially hidden liabilities in the company, but it is also an important tool for assessing whether or not to proceed with the deal. The purchaser will typically use any discoveries to negotiate a more realistic sale price. If the investor's confidence in the company is reduced following the findings of a due diligence review, the investment may not take place.

Due diligence tax checks can:

- Elicit the history of outstanding tax returns across all tax heads.
- Establish if tax returns have historically been submitted on time (to establish exposure in respect of potential interest and penalties).
- Conduct a review of the company's VAT history from records available.
- Ensure that the company has applied the correct VAT rate to its supplies.
- Establish the extent to which the company is entitled to VAT recovery (and comparison with what has actually been recovered).
- Establish the key VAT history of property within a company/group.
- Establish if the PAYE/PRSI affairs are in order, including the extent to which payments have been made to individuals without operation of PAYE.
- Obtain confirmation of the last period in which there was a Revenue audit and the outcome.
- Cross-check VAT and PAYE records to key financial data (e.g. the financial statements).
- Establish indicators of any aggressive tax planning in the company.
- Analyse intragroup/inter-company transactions to establish if the share sale will trigger a clawback of reliefs such as group relief and stamp duty relief.

6.2.4   *Tax Warranties and Indemnities*

Tax warranties are an important part of a share purchase agreement. The rationale of tax warranties is to impose a legal liability on the vendor if there are any discrepancies between the tax position as reported and the actual tax position.

If, as part of the due diligence process, any outstanding or potential future liabilities are discovered, the purchaser will want a commitment from the vendor that the vendor will be responsible (indemnified) for these should they arise. These tax warranties and indemnities can be included as part of the share purchase agreement or covered in a separate legal document.

Key Issue

If shares in a company are being purchased, it is very important that the history of the company is checked. For example, if a company is purchased on 1 July 2022, and one week later that company receives notification of a PAYE and VAT audit for the 2019 tax year. Any tax liabilities that arise from that audit would be the responsibility of the new shareholders.

The due diligence process will help to identify any such risks pre-purchase. Appropriate warranties and indemnities should be documented in the share purchase agreement or a similar legal document.

Examples of tax warranties include:

- that VAT compliance is up to date and no historical filing penalties will accrue to the new investors;
- that PAYE obligations have been met and no historical filing penalties will accrue to the new investors;
- that historical corporation tax affairs are in order and no historical filing penalties will accrue to the new investors;
- that the computation of tax losses carried forward is accurate and correct;
- those in respect of prior-year CGT/stamp duty group relief claims; and
- to establish who will benefit from future tax refunds by reference to the periods prior to the share purchase (e.g. a back-dated claim for tax relief, etc.).

6.2.5   *Group Relief Clawback Provisions*

As set out in **Chapter 5**, transfers of chargeable assets (e.g. property, goodwill, shares, etc.) between group companies related by virtue of 75% common ownership can happen without triggering a charge to tax on any gain. This is commonly known as 'CGT group relief'. The assets are deemed to transfer between the group members in such a way that would give rise to a no gain/no loss position.

There is a clawback of CGT group relief if the 75% group relationship is broken prior to the expiry of a 10-year period following the asset transfer. If the group relationship is broken, the company holding the asset is deemed to sell and immediately reacquire the asset at the market value on the date it took ownership. The company leaving the group will be liable to tax on the chargeable gain arising, and this tax must be remitted to Revenue.

This is an issue, therefore, for an investor purchasing a company that holds an asset on which group relief was previously claimed (e.g. where group relief was claimed on an asset transfer within the previous 10 years).

It might not be obvious to the investor that group relief had been claimed previously. Sufficient investigation as a part of the due diligence process should be undertaken and, in addition, warranties should be put in place in the share purchase agreement.

A similar issue can arise for stamp duty associated companies relief (see **Section 5.7**). In this situation, if the 90% relationship is broken between the transferor and the transferee of property within two years, a clawback of stamp duty relief will arise.

6.2.6   Summary: Share Sale

Some of the key advantages and disadvantages associated with a share sale are outlined in the table below.

Vendor's Perspective	Purchaser's Perspective
Reduced consideration receivable due to company's latent gains (i.e. cost paid for shares is not the base cost of underlying assets).	Due diligence process is likely to be costly, but a key requirement in advance of completing the sale.
Shareholders benefit by receiving cash directly from the sale.	Sufficient warranties will be required.
Liable to once-off CGT rate of 33% (assuming retirement relief or entrepreneur relief does not apply).	Provision for latent gains should be reflected in the purchase price.
No balancing charges in respect of assets held by the company.	Lower stamp duty (1% on share purchase).
No liquidation costs (when compared to a sale of trade/assets by a company and subsequent liquidation to distribute the net proceeds to the shareholders).	If purchasing a company from a group, is there potential for clawback of CGT/stamp duty reliefs previously claimed on intragroup transfers?
No VAT considerations as a share sale is not a VATable supply.	VAT will not arise on share purchase.
If the vendor is a company, section 626B TCA 1997 (participation exemption) relief may be available.	May purchase tax losses within a company – but bear in mind that anti-avoidance loss-buying provisions and restrictions apply.

6.3   Sale/Purchase of a Trade and/or Assets

6.3.1   Trade Sale/Purchase

A disposal of a trade and/or assets by a company or a sole trader may trigger a chargeable gain on the disposal. The chargeable assets for tax purposes are likely to be land and buildings and the goodwill of the business.

The **purchaser** may wish to only acquire the trade and/or assets of a company. It is often easier and more straightforward to acquire assets rather than shares and it may be less costly. For example, a due diligence is not likely to be required if an asset purchase is planned. The main reasons for the purchaser to acquire the trade/assets are:

- Can choose which assets to acquire.
- The assets are acquired at their market value, rather than at their base cost in the case of a share purchase, therefore the issue of latent gains is not relevant.
- Capital allowances may be claimed on the purchase of plant/machinery/equipment, etc. on their purchase price.
- The requirement for tax warranties and indemnities may not arise.
- Issues such as a clawback of CGT group relief or associated company stamp duty relief are not relevant.

Purchaser's Disadvantage

The major disadvantage to the purchaser of acquiring assets is that the higher stamp duty rate of 7.5% will apply on the acquisition of the shares compared to a stamp duty rate of 1% on a share purchase.

Vendor's Disadvantage

On a sale of the asset/trade by a company, the company will receive the consideration. The company will be liable to corporation tax at a rate of 33% on the chargeable gain arising, and may also be liable to a balancing charge triggered on the sale of assets if capital allowances have been claimed (e.g. industrial building, plant, etc.).

The next matter to consider is how the shareholder can extract the after-tax gain arising from the sale of the asset from the company. If funds relating to the gain are extracted by way of dividend or salary, the funds will be subject to additional 40% income tax and PRSI/USC (see **Chapter 4**). If the company is liquidated, a 33% CGT charge will arise for the shareholders on the disposal of their shares (see **Chapter 4, Section 4.6**). Therefore, a double tax charge arises at company level on the sale of the assets and at shareholder level on the extraction of the gain on the assets disposal from the company.

Example 6.6: Trade/asset sale

Jones Ltd is disposing of its trade and assets for €500,000 and John Jones intends to extract the remaining cash from the company post-sale by way of dividend.

	€	
Proceeds of sale of assets	500,000	
Cost of assets per balance sheet	(225,000)	
Gain arising in company	275,000	
Less: corporation tax on gain @ 33%	(90,750)	
Proceeds available for distribution	409,250	
Less: DWT @ 25%	(102,312)	
Additional income tax due on distribution*	(61,388)	(@ 40% – 25%)
Net proceeds received by shareholder	245,550	(taking account of taxes due)

* Assuming John Jones is a 40% rate taxpayer and ignoring PRSI/USC for illustrative purposes.

The sale of assets and subsequent cash extraction by way of dividend has been very tax inefficient for John Jones. A tax charge has arisen twice on the proceeds received from the sale – first as corporation tax on the gain and then as DWT on the distribution of the proceeds.

John Jones's intention is for immediate cash extraction from the company to individual shareholders, in which case a share sale has obvious advantages over a trade/asset sale. If the intention was to keep the cash in the company for further investment, then an asset sale may well give the best tax result.

Key Issue
Always establish the intention of the vendor if an asset sale is planned. Timely tax advice may highlight the benefits of a share sale and lead to a change in the structure of a transaction.

6.3.2 Tax Consequences of Sale of Trade and/or Assets

The sale of a trade by a **company** will result in a cessation of the trade for corporation tax purposes and trigger the end of an accounting period. In the case of a cessation of a trade, unused tax reliefs and trading losses carried forward cannot be utilised. Terminal loss relief may be available on the cessation of the trade, which could utilise loss some of all available loss relief.

The sale of a trade by an individual will result in a cessation of the trade for income tax purposes. The tax implications of a cessation to trade for a sole trader are considered in **Chapter 1**.

CGT will arise on the disposal of chargeable assets, such as property or goodwill, for both a company and an individual trader. In the case of a company, if there are current-year trading losses available these may be used to reduce the corporation tax on the gains arising. An individual trader may have current-year CGT losses or CGT losses forward for offset against the gains arising on the disposal of the asset/s of the trade.

A balancing adjustment is triggered on the sale of assets on which capital allowances were claimed and balancing charges arising will give rise to additional taxes for the vendor. The sale of stock may give rise to a profit, which will be taxed as a trading receipt.

VAT is chargeable on the sale of assets on which VAT was incurred, unless the transfer of a business as a going concern treatment applies (see **Chapter 2, Section 2.4.2**). For this relief to apply, the purchaser must also be a VAT-registered entity.

Stamp duty will influence how the purchaser will want to structure the acquisition of a business. Stamp duty considerations for the purchaser will focus on the rate of stamp duty – 1% on the purchase of shares, 7.5% on the purchase of assets.

In general, the legal title to plant, equipment, fixtures, fittings and stock can be transferred by physical delivery and are therefore not stampable as there is no document transferring title (stamp duty only arises on instruments passing legal title). To avoid the charge to stamp duty, a sale agreement should, at the most, only note that the title to such assets will pass by delivery. However assets such as property and goodwill require a written agreement or instrument to pass the legal title and so will be liable to stamp duty at 7.5%.

6.3.3 Commercial Considerations

It is important to identify precisely the assets/liabilities transferred from a legal point of view. Leases may need to be reviewed. The assignment of a lease may require a VAT review. Employee legislative and pension rights must be considered to avoid any potential liabilities arising after the sale if a business is being purchased as a going concern.

6.3.4 Summary: Trade/Asset Sale

The key advantages and disadvantages associated with a trade/asset sale are outlined in the table below.

Vendor's Perspective	Purchaser's Perspective
Advantages	
Vendor likely to benefit from higher price as the question of latent gains and significant warranties may not arise if the assets are sold directly to purchaser.	Due diligence is not likely to be required, providing a cost saving to the purchaser.
Further tax planning may be required to extract cash proceeds from the company – this may be a key disadvantage.	Warranties may not be critical.
The company making the sale will be liable to an effective corporation tax rate of 33% on any chargeable gain arising.	The question of latent gains will not arise as the purchase price will be the base cost of the assets on a future disposal.

Vendor's Perspective	Purchaser's Perspective
Disadvantages	
Possible balancing allowances/charges in respect of assets being disposed of.	Higher stamp duty charge is likely to be an issue.
Liquidation of the company may be required post-sale, which could be a lengthy and costly process.	Capital allowances will be based on the acquisition price paid for assets.
VAT will need to be considered as part of the sale of the trade/assets.	VAT recovery should be considered if it is going to arise on the purchase of assets/trade.
	Tax losses will not be purchased if assets are purchased.

Chapter 6 Summary

Share sale/purchase

- Depending on the circumstances this may be the vendor's preferred method of sale
- Disposal for CGT purposes
- Will require a due diligence/warranties/indemnities
- Purchaser takes on history of the company, indemnity e.g. latent gains
- Various reliefs available
- Lower rate of stamp duty
- Losses of target company might be unavailable

Sale of trade and assets

- Depending on the circumstances, this may be the purchaser's preferred method of sale
- Disposal for CGT purposes
- Potential double tax charge on the ultimate shareholder
- Higher rate of stamp duty

Questions

Review Questions
(See Suggested Solutions to Review Questions at the end of this textbook.)

Question 6.1

Rose Ltd produces golf balls. The company has divisions in Ireland, the UK, France and Spain. However, recent trading results have been poor and accumulated trading losses amount to €400,000. In particular, the Spanish division has had extremely poor results.

McIlroy Ltd wishes to buy Rose Ltd and make the following changes:

- Change the machinery being used – McIlroy Ltd feels it is out of date and needs modernising.
- Close the Spanish division.
- Include a teaching app with each set of golf balls, with lessons on how to get the best value from the golf balls.
- McIlroy Ltd sees Germany as a new market that could benefit from the product and will open a division there in the near future to help regenerate sales.

Requirement
Advise McIlroy Ltd on whether it can utilise the trading losses.

Question 6.2

Rover Ltd owns 8% of Ford Ltd and 70% of Porsche Ltd. Porsche Ltd also owns 4% of Ford Ltd.

Requirement
(a) Rover Ltd sells its entire shareholding in Ford Ltd on 1 July 2022. Can the participation exemption apply?
(b) The directors of Porsche Ltd are considering selling its shareholding in Ford Ltd. Advise on the latest date the transaction should take place.

Challenging Questions
(Suggested Solutions to Challenging Questions are available through your lecturer.)

Question 6.1

Rattles Ltd is involved in the manufacture and distribution of baby rattles. It is wholly owned by Sharon Williamson, who started the business almost 22 years ago. Following a period of poor sales and results, Sharon now wishes to retire and has been approached by another company, Shakes Ltd, with an offer for the trade and assets of Rattles Ltd.

Sharon is reluctant to sell the trade and assets, and would prefer a share sale, as she will have only one tax charge on the sale of the shares. Shakes Ltd has indicated that a share sale might be possible, but at a reduced sales price to take account of various issues that could arise from the tax due diligence review.

Shakes Ltd is involved in the production of baby milkshakes, but wishes to expand its operations into the baby market further and is confident that it can turn the trade of Rattles Ltd around and make it profitable once again.

The balance sheet of Rattles Ltd for the year ended 31 December 2022 is as follows:

	€		€		€
Fixed assets (Note 1)		150,000	Share capital		1,000
Cash at bank		30,000	Accumulated profits		80,300
Debtors		3,500			
Creditors:					
Trade creditors	60,000				
PAYE (Note 2)	23,750				
VAT	4,450				
Other (Note 3)	14,000	(102,200)			
Net assets		81,300			81,300

Notes:
1. The fixed assets of €150,000 include:
   - Plant and machinery with a net book value of €5,000 and a TWDV of €2,250.
   - Goodwill of €25,000 relating to the goodwill of Sharon's trade on incorporation of the business in March 1999. It has a current market value of €45,000.
   - Business premises which are included at a cost of €120,000 and have a market value of €500,000.
2. The PAYE liability includes €2,000 in relation to an additional liability as the result of a recent PAYE inquiry.
3. Other creditors of €14,000 relate to a contingent liability for a trade dispute between Rattles Ltd and various customers over a faulty batch of rattles. This is the best estimate of the amount to be paid out.

In addition, Rattles Ltd has trading losses carried forward of €87,000 and current-year losses of €18,000.

Requirement

(a) Calculate the minimum price that Sharon Williamson should accept, and calculate the maximum amount that Shakes Ltd should be willing to pay for the business. You can assume that the sale takes place on 31 March 2023.
(b) Advise how the sale proceeds should be allocated, and indicate how this will affect Rattles Ltd.
(c) What tax indemnities should Shakes Ltd include within the share purchase agreement?
(d) Advise Shakes Ltd on whether the accumulated trading losses of Rattles Ltd can be used.
(e) Assuming the two parties meet in the middle in respect of the sale consideration, calculate the CGT liability of Sharon Williamson, indicating any reliefs that may be available to reduce her gain.

Company Reorganisations

There are many reasons why the business of a company might be reorganised. The shareholders may wish to prepare for the sale of a particular trade and therefore reorganise the trade by hiving it into a new company. The shareholders may wish to partition two trades held in the same company into two separate companies to facilitate succession planning or efficiencies in running the business. There may be a reorganisation of share capital within the company for the purposes of raising new finance. The reorganisation of a business in a company generally triggers tax charges for both the shareholders and the company, in particular CGT and stamp duty. However, provided that the reorganisation is for bona fide commercial reasons and is not part of a scheme to avoid tax, various tax reliefs can be applied to ensure that the reorganisation of a company is tax-efficient for the shareholders and the company itself.

As set out in **Chapter 5**, transactions involving the transfer of assets with a group of connected companies qualify for CGT and stamp duty relief which are predicated on the group relationship of the companies involved. The reliefs set out in **Section 7.2**, are designed to facilitate a change of ownership and the application of relief to both individuals and companies involved in the transactions.

7.1   Reorganisation of Share Capital within the Company

Ordinarily, if a shareholder sells shares or receives a capital distribution for shares then a disposal has taken place and CGT is likely to arise. However, where shares in a company are simply exchanged for a different holding of shares in the same company, and the shareholder ends up with a similar shareholding to that held before the exchange, this transaction is treated as a reorganisation of the company's share capital. Section 584 TCA 1997 will treat the share-for-share exchange as if no disposal had taken place and the new shares will be deemed to have been acquired at the same date and cost as the original shares.

Example 7.1

Mary bought 5,000 €1 unquoted ordinary shares for €8,000 in Hanover Ltd, a trading company, in January 1979. Due to trading difficulties, the company was forced by its creditors to reorganise its share capital and Mary received 2,000 non-voting unquoted ordinary shares in February 1981 in exchange for her old shareholding. In December 2022, Mary sold her 2,000 non-voting shares for €60,000. The following CGT treatment is applied:

The exchange of shares in February 1981 is not treated as a CGT disposal under section 584 TCA 1997 as Mary got nothing tangible out of the company (i.e. all Mary received was shares in the second company, she did not receive any other form of consideration).

The sale of the shares in December 2022 gives rise to the following CGT treatment:

		€
Sale proceeds		60,000
Cost	January 1979 €8,000	
	Indexed @ 4.148 (factor for a 1978/79 acquisition)	(33,184)
Gain		26,816
Less:	Annual exemption	(1,270)
		25,546
CGT @ 10%		2,555

It is assumed that Mary satisfies all conditions for the 10% CGT rate to apply.

7.1.1 New Shares Acquired for Old Shares and New Consideration Payment

Where the original shares plus the new consideration are exchanged for new shares in the same company, the new shares take on the original cost of the old shares and the acquisition date of the old shares, and the new consideration is treated as enhancement expenditure incurred at the date of payment.

Example 7.2

Frances purchased 1,000 unquoted ordinary shares in Frank Ltd on 1 May 1976 for €6,000. On a reorganisation of Frank Ltd in June 1982, Frances received 2,000 non-voting unquoted ordinary shares in exchange for her original holding plus an additional cash payment by her of €1,000. On 30 November 2022, she sold her holding for €93,000.

The exchange of shares in June 1982 is not treated as a CGT disposal under section 584 TCA 1997 as Frances effectively received no value from the company. The consideration of €1,000 is treated as enhancement expenditure.

The sale of the shares in November 2022 gives rise to the following CGT treatment:

	€
Sale proceeds	93,000
Deduct: Cost of original shares:	
May 1976 = €6,000, indexed @ 5.238	(31,428)
Enhancement expenditure:	
June 1982 = €1,000, indexed @ 2.253	(2,253)
Gain	59,319
Less: annual exemption	(1,270)
	58,049
CGT @ 10%	5,805

It is assumed that Frances satisfies all conditions for the 10% CGT rate to apply.

7.1.2 Exchange of Old Shares for New Shares Plus Cash (or other Property)

Where the original shares are exchanged for new shares in the same company plus other consideration, there is a deemed part disposal for a consideration equal to the cash or value of the other assets received. The new shares are treated as having the same acquisition date as the original shares and the same cost as the original shares less the amount allocated to the part disposal.

Example 7.3

Alan acquired 4,000 €1 ordinary shares in Zig Ltd on 1 July 1976 for €5,000. As a result of a reorganisation in July 1989, he received €4,000 in cash and 3,000 new "A" ordinary shares in Zig Ltd. The market value of the 3,000 "A" ordinary shares in July 1989 was €10,000. Alan subsequently sold the "A" ordinary shares for €42,000 in August 2022. The exchange of shares in July 1989 is treated as a part disposal for CGT purposes as Alan has received cash of €4,000 out of the company.

CGT 1989/90 Part disposal		€
Sale proceeds		4,000
Deduct:		

$$€5,000 \times \frac{€4,000}{€4,000 + €10,000} = €1,429$$

Indexed @ 3.485 (1976/77 to 1989/90 factor)		(4,980) No gain/no loss

The sale of the shares in August 2022 gives rise to the following CGT treatment:

		€
Sale proceeds		42,000
Deduct: Original cost	€5,000	
Used cost 1981/82	(€1,429)	
	€3,571	
Indexed @ 5.238 (factored for 1976/77 acquisition)		(18,705)
Gain subject to exemption		23,295
Less: annual exemption		(1,270)
Taxable gain		22,025

It is assumed that Alan does not satisfy all conditions for the 10% CGT rate to apply.

7.2 Reorganisations Involving a Change of Ownership

Relieving provisions apply where one company exchanges its "paper" for the shares or undertaking of another company in an amalgamation or take-over situation provided certain conditions are fulfilled. Amalgamations can take the following form.

A "**share-for-share exchange**" arises where a shareholder exchanges shares in one company for shares in another company.

A "**share for undertaking three-party swap**" arises where a company (target company) transfers all or part of its business to another company (acquiring company) in exchange for shares in that company being issued to the shareholders of the target company, i.e. the target company does not receive any consideration. The three parties to the swap are the target and acquiring companies and the shareholders of the target company.

A "**share for undertaking two-party swap**" arises where a company (target company) transfers all or part of its business to another company (acquiring company) in exchange for shares in that company. The two parties to the swap are the target company and the acquiring company.

We will now review the tax reliefs available under the various tax heads for each of the above-mentioned types of amalgamation/reorganisation.

7.2.1 Share-for-Share Exchange

A share-for-share exchange takes place when the shareholders in one company (target company) exchange their shareholding for shares in another company (acquiring company). The result of such an exchange is that the target company becomes directly owned by the acquiring company, as outlined in **Example 7.4 below.** This transaction will trigger a possible CGT liability in the hands of the shareholders of the target company and a possible stamp duty liability for the acquiring company. Therefore, we need to consider available reliefs under both tax heads to minimise the tax cost of a share-for-share exchange.

CGT Relief for Shareholders: Section 586 TCA 1997
Relief under section 584 TCA 1997, as outlined in **Section 7.1**, is extended to company amalga-mations by exchange of shares under section 586 TCA 1997.

The main conditions which must be satisfied under section 586 are:

1. the acquiring company must gain control of the target company; or
2. if the acquiring company makes a general offer to the second company, it must be made on such conditions which, if satisfied, would give the acquiring company control of the second company.

The reconstruction/amalgamation must be effected for bona fide commercial reasons and should not form part of any arrangement/scheme the main purpose of which is the avoidance of tax.

Example 7.4

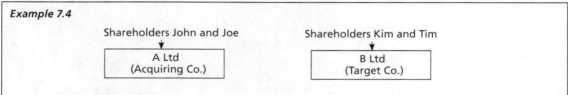

A Ltd wants to acquire B Ltd's shares.

A Ltd acquires B Ltd by issuing additional A Ltd shares to Kim and Tim as the shareholders of B Ltd in exchange for their shares in B Ltd.

New structure after the takeover is as follows:

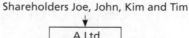

As per section 586, Kim and Tim are not treated as having made a disposal of their shares in B Ltd for CGT purposes, as the paper-for-paper exchange of B Ltd shares for A Ltd shares has resulted in the acquiring company, A Ltd, taking control of the target company, B Ltd.

Stamp Duty Relief for Acquiring Company: Section 80 SDCA 1999
Stamp duty relief under section 80 SDCA 1999 will apply on the transfer of shares in the target company to the acquiring company provided certain conditions are satisfied. The level of stamp duty saving on application of a section 80 share for share exchange is 1% of the value of the shares. The following conditions must be fulfilled to avail of this relief:

■ The scheme of reconstruction/amalgamation must be undertaken for bona fide commercial reasons and must not involve tax avoidance as one of its principal objects.

■ The acquiring company must have the objective of obtaining, and actually obtain, at least 90% of the issued share capital of the target company.

■ In general, the 90% holding must be achieved in a single transaction.

■ The consideration for the acquisition, excluding liabilities of the target company taken over, must be paid by way of at least 90% in the issue of new shares in the acquiring company to the shareholders of the target company. The balance of the consideration may be paid in cash or other benefits paid in another form.

■ The acquiring company must issue shares to the shareholders of the target company in proportion to their shareholdings in the target company.

■ The acquiring company must be a limited company and must be Irish or EU registered.

■ The target company (limited or unlimited) can be registered anywhere in the world.

■ The acquiring company must be incorporated or its nominal share capital must be increased with a view to the acquisition of the shares in the target company.

A clawback of relief under section 80 will arise if the acquiring company does not retain beneficial ownership of all the shares acquired in the target company for at least two years. Relief is not lost if the acquiring company does not retain beneficial ownership of shares as a result of liquidation. However, if relief were obtained on the basis of false information, interest is payable from date of original transaction. Interest of 0.0219% per day is due from the date that beneficial ownership is lost.

The shareholders are not required to retain the consideration shares in the acquiring company for any particular length of time. As noted above, a key requirement for section 80 relief is that the shares must be issued to the shareholders in proportion to their holding in the target company, but once the exchange is complete, they can dispose of their shareholding in the acquiring company. However, a clawback of the relief will be triggered if the acquiring company disposes of the shares in the target company within two years of claiming relief. The relief operates on a self-assessment basis.

7.2.2 Share for Undertaking Three-party Swap

A share for undertaking three-party swap arises when a company (target company) transfers all or part of its business to another company (acquiring company) in exchange for shares in the acquiring company being issued to the shareholder of the target company. On completion of a successful three-party share for undertaking swap, the undertaking is owned by one company, which is in turn owned by the original target company's shareholders and the acquiring company's shareholders, as outlined in the example below.

Tax relief under a share for undertaking three-party swap allows for a change of ownership of the company involved in the transaction, with the relief extending to the individual shareholders as well as the companies involved in the transaction. The relief here is therefore more flexible than CGT and stamp duty group reliefs as set out in **Chapter 5**, which only apply to companies in a static group relationship and where relief is clawed back if the group relationship between the companies involved in the transaction is broken.

The disposal of the target company's business/undertaking is a disposal for the target company itself and for the shareholders of the target company as value will have passed out of their shareholding in exchange for shares in the acquiring company. In addition, as the acquiring company will take a transfer of an undertaking, a stamp duty event will be triggered. Therefore consideration needs to be given to available reliefs for CGT at the shareholder level and at the company level as a result of the transfer or the undertaking; and to stamp duty reliefs for the acquiring company on acquiring the undertaking.

CGT Relief for Shareholders: Section 587 TCA 1997

Share for undertaking exchanges may qualify for relief under section 587 TCA 1997. The "share for undertaking" transaction is treated as an exchange of shares and comes within the rules applicable to a reorganisation of share capital under section 584, as discussed in **Section 7.1**, so that the new holding is treated in the hands of the shareholders as if it were the original holding with no resulting charge to CGT at the time of the exchange.

Relief under section 587 is not dependent on the acquiring company gaining control of the target company on completion of the transaction. Relief will not apply, however, unless the transaction is for bona fide commercial reasons and not part of a tax avoidance scheme.

There is also a possible exposure to income tax for the shareholders on a deemed distribution under section 130 in respect of the transfer of business assets to a company controlled by shareholders. However, Revenue practice is not to invoke a charge under section 130 where the provisions of section 587 and section 615 apply.

Tax Relief on Capital Gains for Target Company: Section 615 TCA 1997

A tax-efficient share for undertaking transaction also relies on relief under section 615 TCA 1997 to provide for a no gain/no loss position on the transfer of chargeable assets, such as goodwill and property, to the acquiring company. In order to claim the relief a number of conditions must be satisfied:

1. The amalgamation or reconstruction must be effected for bona fide commercial reasons and does not form part of a scheme the main purpose of which is the avoidance of a liability to tax.
2. Any scheme of reconstruction or amalgamation must involve the transfer of the whole or part of a company's business to another company.
3. At the time of transfer both companies must be resident in the State or an EU Member State or EEA Member State with which Ireland has a tax treaty, or the assets before and after the transfer must be chargeable assets for CGT purposes.
4. The target company must receive no consideration for the transfer other than the taking over of its liabilities of the business by the acquiring company. The relief does not apply to the transfer of trading stock.

There is no provision for a clawback of relief granted under section 615.

> **Key Issue**
> Structure the transfer of company assets under a section 615 arrangement rather than through an intercompany transfer of assets under section 617. Remember, a clawback will arise under section 617 if the group relationship is broken within 10 years of the intragroup transfer of chargeable assets; no clawback arises under a section 615 claim.

Stamp Duty Relief for the Acquiring Company: Section 80 SDCA 1999

Relief from stamp duty is also available on the transfer of assets from the target company to the acquiring company where consideration for the transfer consists of shares in the acquiring company. Under section 80 SDCA 1999, there is a potential 7.5% stamp duty saving.

The assets transferred must constitute an "undertaking" or "part of an undertaking". Case law has determined that the term "undertaking" means a level of activity as opposed to the mere ownership of assets. A key condition for section 80 relief in a share for undertaking three-party swap is that at least 90% of the consideration (apart from any liabilities of the target company which are taken over) provided by the acquiring company must consist of its own shares. The shareholders are not required to hold the shares for any minimum period of time on completion of the swap. However, relief is not available if a subsequent sale of shares by the shareholders is contingent on the reconstruction.

A clawback and corresponding interest will arise if the relief was originally granted on the basis of false information.

Example 7.5

Two companies, A Ltd and B Ltd, are structured as follows:

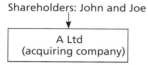

Shareholders: John and Joe

A Ltd
(acquiring company)

Shareholders: Kim and Tim

B Ltd
(target company)

A Ltd wants to acquire B Ltd's trade, i.e. an undertaking.

A Ltd acquires B Ltd's trade by issuing additional A Ltd shares to Kim and Tim as the shareholders of B Ltd.

The new structure after the takeover is as follows:

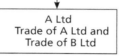

Shareholders Joe, John, Kim and Tim

A Ltd
Trade of A Ltd and
Trade of B Ltd

As per section 587 TCA 1997, Kim and Tim are not treated as having made a disposal of their shares in B Ltd for CGT purposes. If they dispose of their shares in A Ltd, they will use the original base cost and acquisition date of their shareholding in B Ltd.

As per section 615 TCA 1997, B Ltd will be treated as having transferred the undertaking to A Ltd for a no gain/no loss. A Ltd will use the original base cost and date of acquisition for any future disposals of the undertaking.

A claim for section 80 SDCA 1999 relief will ensure that stamp duty does not arise on the value of the undertaking passing.

7.2.3 Share for Undertaking Two-party Swap

A share for undertaking two-party swap occurs when a company transfers all or part of its business to another company in exchange for shares in that company.

CGT Relief for Target Company – Section 631 TCA 1997

As the target company transfers its undertaking to the acquiring company, a disposal has taken place and a potential CGT liability on chargeable assets may arise. Section 631 TCA 1997 provides relief where a company transfers a trading operation carried on in the State to another company in return for securities in the second company. Such a transaction does not give rise to a corporation tax charge or a CGT charge, or to a balancing allowance or balancing charge in relation to capital allowances on any of the assets transferred. A claim for relief under section 615 TCA 1997 would not be possible in a share for undertaking two-party swap as the target company is receiving consideration, i.e. shares in the acquiring company. As set out in the discussion above on conditions for section 615, a key condition to that relief is that the target company must receive no consideration other than taking over the liabilities of the business by the acquiring company. Relief under section 631 also goes further than the relief provided by section 615 because section 615 does not remove the possibility of a balancing adjustment on transfers of assets on which capital allowances have been claimed.

The acquiring company, on taking over the trading operation, is regarded as having acquired the assets at their original cost and as having received any allowances that the transferring company received.

Section 631 provides that, where the shares acquired in consideration for the trading operation are sold within six years, the base cost of those shares for CGT purposes is reduced by the gain deferred on the assets transferred.

As the share for undertaking two-party swap does not involve the shareholders of the target company, there is no disposal at shareholder level and it follows that there is no need to invoke the provisions of sections 584 to 587 TCA 1997.

Stamp Duty Relief: Section 80 SDCA 1999

The rules for relief are the same as the rules for the three-party swap. The main difference in a two-party swap is that the consideration shares are issued to the target company itself. If the target company is going to remain in existence, then it is more common to issue the shares to the company rather than to each shareholder.

However, a share for undertaking two-party swap is subject to a clawback of relief if the target company (the company which received shares in exchange for the undertaking) does not retain beneficial ownership of the shares in the acquiring company (the company which acquired the undertaking) for at least two years.

Stamp duty becomes payable, together with interest, from the date when beneficial ownership of the shares is lost. If relief was obtained on the basis of false information, interest applies from date of original transaction.

Relief is **not** clawed back if beneficial ownership is lost as the result of liquidation or further reconstruction or amalgamation.

Example 7.6

Taking **Example 7.5**, if instead A Ltd were to acquire B Ltd's trade by issuing additional A Ltd shares to B Ltd, the new structure after the takeover would be as follows:

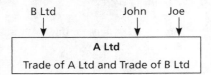

The transaction occurs between B Ltd and A Ltd, resulting in B Ltd becoming a shareholder of A Ltd.

The transfer of the trade to A Ltd does not qualify as an amalgamation/restructuring under section 615. However, section 631 provides that a no gain/no loss arises on the point of transfer of the trade to A Ltd.

Stamp duty will also be avoided on claiming section 80 SDCA 1999 relief. However, B Ltd must hold its shareholding in A Ltd for two years to avoid a clawback of relief.

7.3 Company Reorganisations without a Change of Ownership

Up to now, this chapter has focused on share reorganisations within a company and reorganisation involving a change of ownership and the capital taxes implications. As a reorganisation can also take the form of a "hive out" of a business or part of a business to a new company in such circumstances that the overall ownership of the business remains the same, we also need to consider the implications for capital allowances and any losses in the business.

Section 400 TCA 1997 provides certain relief where a trade carried on by one company (or a part of a trade carried on by one company) is transferred to another company as a going concern. The section provides for the transfer of capital allowances and losses from one company to another where a trading company ceases to carry on a trade or part of a trade and, following the cessation, another company carries on the same trade. Such a transfer is allowed only where there is substantial common identity of not less than 75% in the ownership of the trade both before and after the change. Where the conditions of the section are fulfilled, the successor company, in effect, steps into the shoes of the predecessor for the purposes of capital allowances and losses. The relief permits the transferor company to:

- transfer assets at tax written down values without triggering balancing allowances or balancing charges; and
- transfer the benefit of unutilised tax deductible trading losses to the successor company.

In the absence of this provision, it would be impossible for one company to transfer the benefit of unutilised trading losses carried on by it to a successor company to which the trade is transferred or sold.

This relief only applies to transfers of unutilised trading losses between body corporates and does not apply to transfers between a company and a sole trader or *vice versa*.

The conditions for this relief are that:

- the same persons must own at least a 75% share in the trade at some time within one year before the change and at any time within two years after the change; and
- the trade must, between those times, have been carried on by a company or companies within the charge to corporation tax (this condition would not be satisfied if, for example, at any time between those times the trade was carried on by an individual or a partnership of individuals).

The following losses are not included under section 400 relief for transfer to the successor company:

1. Case V losses;
2. unused Case V capital allowances; and
3. capital losses.

7.3.1 Restriction on the Transfer of Losses

The right of the successor company to utilise the losses transferred from the predecessor company is, however, subject to the general anti-avoidance provisions contained in section 401 TCA 1997 regarding the loss-buying provisions (see **Section 6.2.2**). The effect of the section is to deny carry-forward relief for the unrelieved trading losses (and certain capital allowances) of a company where, in association with a change in ownership of the company, there is a major change in the activities of its trade or, at the time of the change of ownership, the company's trade is near dormant.

Example 7.7

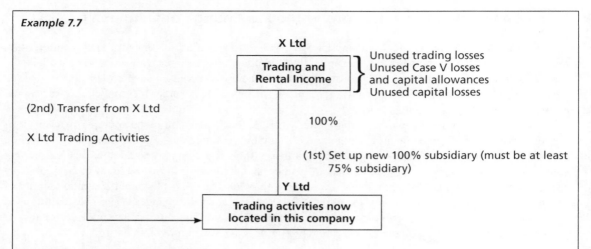

Section 400 relief provides the following:

▨ Transfer of assets at tax written down value (TWDV), i.e. equipment/buildings – no balancing charges.

▨ Transfer of unused trading losses to Y Ltd permitted.

▨ The unused Case V losses/capital allowances and the unused capital losses cannot be transferred to Y Ltd.

▨ Transfer of assets in a 75% capital gains group under section 616 TCA 1997 without triggering taxable chargeable gains under section 617 TCA 1997, e.g. goodwill, land and buildings.

▨ Transfer of assets in a 90% stamp duty group under section 79 SDCA 1999 avoids stamp duty for acquiring companies.

Other Issues
What reliefs would be lost if Y Ltd was immediately bought by a group of investors (individuals or company)?

If Y Ltd leaves the XY group (capital gains group under section 616 TCA 1997), any gains on capital assets transferred to Y Ltd by X Ltd would be triggered but the liability is payable by Y Ltd (section 623 TCA 1997).

Any stamp duty avoided by Y Ltd on transfer of assets is lost as a clawback liability for Y Ltd if the 90% shareholding relationship is lost within two years of claiming section 79 SDCA 1999 relief (see **Chapter 5, Section 5.7**).

The new owners of Y Ltd would still be entitled to use the unused trading losses transferred from X Ltd, provided section 401 TCA 1997 does not prevent this (i.e. no change in nature or conduct of trade, etc.).

7.3.2 Terminal Loss Position

The company transferring the trade to the successor company is not entitled to any terminal loss relief (section 397 TCA 1997) on the occasion of the transfer to the successor.

If, however, the successor terminates the trade more than four years after the succession, having incurred a loss in the 12 months immediately before the trade ceased, it would be able to get full terminal loss relief itself.

If the successor company's cessation takes place within the total period of four years, and the successor's income from the trade is not sufficient for the allowance of the full terminal loss relief available, the balance of the relief may be given to the predecessor company against its income arising from the same trade subject of course to the normal 36 months maximum throwback period, i.e. in no case can the period over which the relief be given extend further back than four years from the date the trade actually ceased.

7.4   Capital Losses and Debt Write Off

Section 552 TCA 1997 defines what items of expenditure can be taken into account for the purposes of the base cost. Typically, this includes expenditure incurred on the purchase, improvement and repair of qualifying capital assets. Where the base cost exceeds the net sales proceeds, a loss will arise for capital gains tax purposes.

Where a taxpayer acquired assets, e.g. land and buildings, which were financed by borrowed money, section 552 would have provided that the amount of the loss for CGT purposes was to be calculated without taking into consideration the fact that the loan had been wholly or partially written off by the financial institution. This resulted in a mismatch between the monetary loss and the tax loss.

Section 552(1B) takes into consideration the amount of debt written off by the financial institution. The effect of this is to restrict the amount of the capital loss arising on the disposal of the capital asset to the actual monetary loss arising. Consequently, the monetary and capital loss positions are realigned. It should be noted that the legislation only applies to restrict losses; it does not affect the computation of gains where they arise.

This provision applies to disposals made on or after 1 January 2014, whether or not the debt was released before, on or after that date.

7.4.1   Debt Released on or before Date of Disposal

Where an asset is acquired and financed by debt, and the borrower has been released in whole or in part from repaying the debt (e.g. the borrower has gone into receivership), that part of the cost of acquisition or enhancement expenditure not actually borne, will not be treated as an allowable cost.

Example 7.8

Tom borrows €750,000 from a bank and buys a property for €1 million in May 2005. However, due to financial difficulties Tom can no longer meet the repayments on the loan. The July 2022 value of the property is €500,000.

Tom enters into an agreement with the bank in November 2021, under which he agrees to sell the property as soon as possible and pay the proceeds to the bank. The bank in turn agrees to forgo the remainder of the debt of €300,000. The property is sold in August 2022 for €500,000.

Position pre-section 552(1B)

	€
Sale price	500,000
Cost price	1,000,000
Loss for CGT	(500,000)

Position with section 552(1B)

	€	€
Sale price		500,000
Cost price	1,000,000	
Less: debt released	(300,000)	700,000
Net loss for CGT		(200,000)

Section 552(1B)(b) reduces the cost price by the amount of the loan waived by the bank.

7.4.2 Debt Released in Year of Assessment Subsequent to Date of Disposal

It is feasible that a debt may be written off in a year of assessment subsequent to that in which the asset was sold. Where this occurs, and on the basis that it was not known that the debt would be written off, at the date of disposal of the asset the base cost could not have been adjusted. Section 552(1B) provides that a balancing adjustment is required in the year of assessment in which the write off occurs.

The legislation provides that where the write off is in a subsequent year of assessment, then a chargeable gain equal to the amount of the debt released is deemed to accrue in the year of assessment in which the debt is released.

Example 7.9
The facts are the same as **Example 7.8**, except that the bank does not release Tom from the remainder debt of €300,000 until March 2023, i.e. the year after the year of disposal.

2022
The loss for CGT purposes on the disposal of the property is:

	€
Sale price	500,000
Cost price	1,000,000
Loss for CGT	(500,000)

No restriction applies in 2022 – on the basis that the debt has not been released.

2023
The debt is subsequently released by the bank in 2023. Consequently, there is a deemed chargeable gain of €300,000 arising in 2023. This is equal to the amount of the debt released.

The net position over the two years is:

	€
2022: CGT loss	(500,000)
2023: CGT deemed gain	300,000
Net loss over the two years	(200,000)

The overall net loss position at the end of the two-year period is the same as the final position in **Example 7.8**.

7.5   Deemed Conveyance on Sale

The stamp duty rate and treatment of a transaction must also be carefully considered when advising on the tax consequences of cash extraction plans, reorganisations and liquidations. The following sets out the key rules for establishing the stamp duty implications of such transactions.

7.5.1   Consideration Consists in All or in Part of Shares

Person Transfers Property for Cash Plus Shares
The instrument conveying the property (e.g. land and buildings) is liable to stamp duty as a deemed conveyance on sale. The consideration for stamp duty purposes is the **cash plus the value of the shares**.

The transfer of the shares is also liable as a conveyance on sale of stock or marketable securities at 1% (unless new shares are issued). The vendor is responsible for this payment.

Person Transfers Property for Shares Only

The conveyance is a deemed conveyance on sale with the consideration being the **market value of the shares**. In such circumstances, the transfer of the shares is not separately stampable and only the purchaser is liable to pay the stamp duty.

Example 7.10

Large plc, an Irish registered company, has offered to purchase an office building from Tiny Tim, who will receive shares in Large plc as consideration.

Tiny Tim is Irish resident and the agreements and conveyances to sell the property are executed here. The share transfer certificates are drawn up. The stamp duty consequences are:

1. The conveyance of the office building is stampable at 7.5%. The consideration is the value of the shares transferred.
2. The share transfer certificates are not liable to stamp duty.

Example 7.11

The facts are the same as outlined in **Example 7.10** above only Tiny Tim is to receive a mixture of shares plus cash.

Both the conveyance of the buildings and the share registration forms are stampable at 7.5% and 1% respectively.

7.5.2   Conveyance in Consideration of Debts

Consideration involving the satisfaction or assumption of a debt is chargeable consideration for stamp duty. Where property is conveyed in satisfaction of a debt, stamp duty is charged on the amount of the debt plus any cash consideration.

Example 7.12

Eamonn owes Kathleen €80,000. He transfers property with a market value of €100,000 to her for €20,000 in forgiveness of the debt.

Stamp duty is chargeable on the cash consideration of €20,000 plus the value of the debt forgiven – €80,000, i.e. €100,000 in total.

7.5.3   Contracts Treated as Conveyance on Sale

A contract is not necessarily the instrument which conveys a property. Accordingly, in the past it was possible to avoid stamp duty by letting a transaction rest at contract stage.

Anti-avoidance provisions were introduced whereby certain contracts which are not conveyances are deemed to be conveyances for stamp duty purposes. These include:

1. contracts for the sale of equitable estates or interests in property (e.g. sale of long lease, sale of life interest, etc.); and
2. contracts for sale of any estate or interest in property, except:
   (a) immovable property in the State (already subject to stamp duty);
   (b) property located outside the State;
   (c) goods and merchandise;
   (d) stocks and marketable securities (already subject to stamp duty); and
   (e) ships, vessels or aircraft.

In practice this provision means that contracts for the sale of intangible assets are deemed conveyances on sale. Contracts for sale of assets such as goodwill, trademarks, copyrights, patents, designs, licenses, book debts, cash on deposit at bank and the benefit of contract are deemed conveyances on sale. However, sales or other dispositions of intellectual property are exempt.

Example 7.13

John sells the Irish goodwill of his business to Bob for €100,000. A contract is drawn up to evidence the agreement. The contract will be a deemed conveyance on sale and will be liable to 7.5% stamp duty.

Bob is a tax client of the firm where you are employed. He rings your manager, who is at a meeting, and asks to be put through to a person working for your manager. Bob explains to you that his friend has suggested that he redraft the contract and change the consideration to €50,000 and give John cash of €50,000. In this way Bob could pay stamp duty on only €50,000. What should you do?

What Bob is suggesting is not legal and is not ethical. As Bob is a client of your manager, it is more appropriate that your manager would explain this to him. Therefore, you should advise Bob that you will get your manager to ring him when his meeting ends. You should tell your manager about the call.

Example 7.14

Bill sells an Irish patent to Ann for €100,000. A contract is drawn up to evidence the agreement. The sale is exempt from stamp duty as it is intellectual property.

Resting in Contract

In the past, in order to avoid stamp duty, in some cases even though the full consideration was paid under a contract for the sale of land (including buildings), no conveyance would be executed. This was known as "resting in contract". However anti-avoidance legislation is now in in place to treat contracts for the sale of land (including buildings) as a conveyance on sale where at least 25% of the consideration payable under the contract has been paid.

If a stamp duty return is filed in relation to a conveyance made in conformity with the contract and payment is made within 30 days of the payment under the contract being made, then this anti-avoidance rule does not apply. Also, if stamp duty has been paid under this legislation, it does not arise again when the land is actually conveyed to the new owner.

There is similar anti-avoidance legislation in respect of agreements for leases in excess of 35 years and agreements or licences to develop land.

Example 7.15

Peter buys land from his sister-in-law, Kate. They sign a contract under which Peter acquires the land on 25 July 2022 and the price is €105,000. Although the contract is signed, the legal title to the land is not conveyed to Peter.

What are the stamp duty consequences if Peter:

1. Makes no payment to Kate?

2. Pays €10,000 to Kate?

3. Pays €50,000 to Kate?

Even if the conveyance has not taken place, he has to pay the full stamp duty if 25% or more of the consideration has been paid. Therefore, he would not have to pay stamp duty where he has made no payment, or where he has paid €10,000 (situations 1. and 2.) as this is not 25% or more of the consideration being paid.

Under situation 3., he would have to pay the full stamp duty due as 25% or more of the consideration has been paid, i.e. he will have to pay €105,000 × 7.5% = €7,875.

Chapter 7   Summary

Reorganisation of share capital in a company	• Triggers CGT on the shareholder. • Reliefs apply and CGT depends on if the shareholder receives value from the company at the time of the reorganisation
Reorganisation involving change of ownership	• Share-for-share exchange – shares one company exchanged for shares in another • Share for undertaking three-party swap – transfer of a business from target company to acquiring company in exchange for shares in acquiring company issued to shareholders of target company • Share for undertaking two-party swap – transfer of a business from target company to acquiring company in exchange for shares in acquiring company
Tax consequences of reorganisation involving change of ownership	• CGT (corporation tax on chargeable gains) for companies on the transfer of assets, businesses or shares • CGT for shareholders where shares are sold or swapped • Stamp duty where assets, businesses or shares are acquired • Corporation tax for companies, where assets on which capital allowances were claimed are transferred • VAT on the transfer of assets • Tax reliefs available to mitigate these tax liabilities (subject to general anti-avoidance provision, i.e. reorganisation is for bona fide commercial reasons

Questions

Review Questions
(See Suggested Solutions to Review Questions at the end of this textbook.)

Question 7.1

The directors of Derry plc are considering purchasing Casey Ltd, which has a modern factory facility where production could be expanded to provide much needed capacity to Derry plc. The approximate total value of the shares in Casey Ltd is €3.5 million. The underlying market value of the business is as follows:

Factory	€2,500,000
Goodwill	€1,000,000

The chairman of Derry plc has been in discussions with the owner of Casey Ltd, Pat Casey, to discuss how to structure the purchase. In particular, they have discussed the options of Derry plc issuing shares to Pat Casey in exchange for the undertaking of Casey Ltd.

Requirement
What are the tax implications of this option for Derry plc and Pat Casey?

Challenging Questions
(Suggested Solutions to Challenging Questions are available through your lecturer.)

Question 7.1

Janice Dickinson is the managing director of High Fashions Ltd, a clothing distribution company. Since 1990, she has owned 75% of the company and her husband, Andy, has owned the remaining 25%. The company owns and operates from premises off Grafton Street in Dublin. The premises is currently valued at €1.5 million. A modest mortgage of €50,000 is outstanding on it. The company has surplus cash reserves of €200,000 after taking account of all its debts and liabilities.

Although previously extremely profitable, the company has suffered losses in recent years, with an accumulated trading loss for corporation tax purposes of €150,000. However, Janice is sure that the business will pick up as she has recently secured new customer contracts, negotiated substantial discounts from her suppliers and rationalised the business by letting a number of staff go. Janice also plans to relocate the business to a more accessible location for orders and delivery of goods and will sell the Grafton Street premises at the first available opportunity.

As their marriage has broken down and they do not have any children, Janice and Andy have decided to formally separate and split their assets. Both are Irish tax resident and Irish domiciled. Currently they are legally married but living apart, with no prospect of a reunion. The separation will be subject to a court order to ensure that no CGT will arise on the transfer of their assets.

While Janice and Andy are satisfied that they can tax-efficiently divide their personal assets, the main area of dispute arises in the division of their interests in High Fashions Ltd. Andy's 25% shareholding has been professionally valued at €400,000. After months of legal negotiations, it is now agreed that High Fashions Ltd will undertake a 'hive out' of the trade into a new company (NewCo). The property in the old company will be sold and then liquidated and a distribution of the surplus will be made to Janice and Andy.

Andy's share in NewCo will then be transferred by way of court order to Janice free of CGT. No CAT or stamp duty will arise as they will be still legally married. This will leave Janice with the trade intact in a new company.

Requirement

Set out the tax implications of the proposal to divide the wealth in High Fashions Ltd between Janice and Andy.

Capital Tax Valuations

8.1 Introduction

The valuation of an asset is a key factor in the calculation of stamp duty, CAT and CGT, and is a key driver in how much tax is ultimately payable. Given the central role of asset valuations, it is not surprising that there are specific tax laws that govern how assets should be valued for tax purposes. In fact, each of the capital taxes has its own particular rules for the valuation of assets on direct and indirect acquisitions and disposals, along with anti-avoidance provisions, which we will examine in the following sections.

8.2 Valuation of an Asset for CGT Purposes

The general rule for CGT purposes is that tax is calculated on the gain generated by the seller on the disposal of an asset. The consideration paid for an asset also forms part of the base cost in the calculation of gains arising on the subsequent disposal of the asset.

Example 8.1

Mary purchases a commercial premises for €300,000 from Ken. Ken has made a disposal of the commercial premises for a consideration of €300,000 and his CGT liability will be based on the difference between what he originally paid for the asset and the consideration received of €300,000. Mary sells the premises a year later for €315,000. Her CGT liability is calculated on the difference between the consideration she originally paid for the asset of €300,000 and the consideration she receives on the sale of the asset of €315,000.

Consideration is not defined in the legislation and, thus, has been discussed and interpreted in a number of court cases. However, broadly it takes the general meaning of "money or money's worth".

There are a number of situations where the CGT legislation will also apply a notional consideration for a disposal to replace the actual consideration paid in the calculation of a taxable gain or loss. These situations can be summarised as follows:

- assets owned at 6 April 1974;
- disposals between connected parties;
- disposal not for a bargain at arm's length;
- transfers between group companies; and
- shareholder exchange of shares.

8.2.1 Assets Owned at 6 April 1974

All assets held at 6 April 1974 are deemed to be sold and reacquired at market value on that date. This is the case because CGT did not exist before 6 April 1974 and, in the interests of fairness, it is appropriate to allocate a value equivalent to a valuation on the date CGT law came into effect. Therefore, when calculating CGT arising on a subsequent disposal of an asset, such as property, which was acquired before 6 April 1974, that asset will be treated as having a base cost equal to the 6 April 1974 valuation. An asset such as goodwill developed by a sole trader or company will generally have no base cost if the asset was not purchased. However, goodwill developed before 1974 will be deemed to be sold and reacquired at market value at 6 April 1974 and will, therefore, acquire a 1974 valuation, even though no consideration was paid by the sole trader or company for the goodwill.

8.2.2 Disposals between Connected Parties/Not for a Bargain at Arm's Length

In certain circumstances, the CGT legislation requires that the actual price at which an asset passes from one person to another be ignored and instead, under section 547 TCA 1997, it substitutes a deemed price, usually the market value of the asset at the date of the transaction. Market value is substituted in place of consideration (if any) given or received on transfers not made for a "bargain at arm's length", including gifts. This is because either there is no actual purchase/sale price or the price does not represent the true value of the asset.

Under section 547(1), the cost of the acquisition of an asset is deemed to be equal to the market value of the asset in the following situations:

- Where the asset is not acquired by way of a bargain at arm's length, including a gift situation.

> **Example 8.2**
>
> Jim gifts his art collection to his friend, Gene. Jim has made a disposal for CGT purposes and he is deemed to have received consideration based on the market value of the art collection on the date of disposal.

- Where the acquisition of the asset is by way of a distribution from a company to a shareholder.

> **Example 8.3**
>
> Liquid Ltd makes a distribution *in specie* of property to its shareholders. The property must have market value rules applied. CGT is payable by the company based on the market value of the property on the date of distribution and also by the shareholders as this is the value they are deemed to receive for their shares.

- Where the acquisition of the asset is wholly or partly for a consideration that cannot be valued, such as an acquisition in consideration of natural love and affection; in consideration of marriage; on discharge of a personal undertaking; a right to unliquidated damages; or the acquisition on the occasion of the loss of employment, the reduction of emoluments or in consideration of past services.

The rule that the market value is substituted for the consideration given on the transfer of an asset, in the absence of a preventive measure, may be open to abuse in cases where an asset is acquired for less than the market value, but the person from whom the asset is acquired is not regarded as having made a disposal of the asset for CGT purposes.

A person will not be regarded as having acquired an asset at market value where:

- there is no corresponding disposal of the asset; and
- there is no consideration paid, in money or money's worth, for the asset, or the value of the consideration is less than the market value of the asset.

Examples of assets being acquired without a corresponding disposal include:

- non-purchased goodwill of a business;
- shares acquired on the issue of those shares by a company;
- the right to sue, arising from negligence;
- statutory rights to compensation; and
- a non-purchased patent.

Section 547(4) provides that the consideration for the disposal of an asset is deemed to be equal to the market value of the asset in the following circumstances:

- where the disposal is otherwise than by means of a bargain at arm's length, including in particular a gift; and
- where the consideration cannot be valued.

Example 8.4

Kevin sold his shares in the family company to his daughter, Jane, for €300,000. The open market value of the shares on the date of disposal was €400,000. Therefore, under section 547(4), Kevin will be treated as having received consideration of €400,000 and will pay CGT based on consideration of €400,000.

Acquisitions and disposals between connected persons are treated as if they were not bargains at arm's length under section 549 TCA 1997, bringing the transaction within the scope of section 547 TCA 1997.

8.2.3 Who/What is a Connected Person?

Connected persons for CGT purposes are defined under section 10 TCA 1997, subsections (3) to (8). Connected parties are as follows:

1. A husband, wife or relative. A "relative" includes a brother, sister, uncle, aunt, niece, nephew, ancestor, or lineal descendant. Relatives-in-law are also connected persons.
2. A trustee of a trust is connected with the settlor if the settlor is an individual, but a trustee will not be connected with the settlor if the settlor is a company. The trustee is also connected with any person connected with that settlor.

3. A person is connected with his/her partner and with the husband or wife or relatives of his/her partner. A bona fide commercial arrangement for the acquisition or disposal of partnership assets does not invoke the connected party rules.
4. A company is connected with another company:

   (a) if the same person has control of both, or a person has control of one and persons connected with him, or he and persons connected with him, have control of the other; or

   (b) if a group of two or more persons has control of each company and the groups consist of the same persons or could be regarded as consisting of the same persons if a member of either group was replaced by a person connected with that member.

5. A company is connected with another person if that other person has control of it, or if he and persons connected with him together have control of it.

For the purposes of section 432 TCA 1997, a person is regarded as having control of a company if the person has or is entitled to:

- the majority of the issued share capital or voting power;
- such part of that capital as would entitle the person on a total distribution of income to more than 50% of such distribution; or
- such rights as would entitle the person on a winding up or otherwise to more than 50% of the distributable assets.

Under section 549(3), relief for a loss on a disposal to a connected person is restricted so that the loss may be allowed only against a chargeable gain on some other disposal by the disponer to the same connected person.

Example 8.5

Alison sells her farm to her son for €1,500,000. The farm had a market value of €2,000,000 at the time of sale. Alison originally inherited the farm when it had a market value of €2,750,000. Her CGT calculation on the disposal is as follows:

	€
Market value of assets (section 547 rules)	2,000,000
Less: value of asset on acquisition	2,750,000
Loss	(750,000)

Under section 549(3), this loss can only be used against a CGT liability arising on the disposal of further assets by Alison to her son.

8.2.4 Valuation of Assets

Section 548 TCA 1997 contains rules for determining the market value where this is required under transfers by means of bargains not at arm's length. The basic rule is that market value is the price that an asset might reasonably be expected to fetch on a sale in the open market.

In addition, the market valuation must not take into account any reduction in value as a result of a large number of the same assets "flooding" the market on the same date. In general, the value of shares is to be taken as the value for one share which emerges from bargains of normal size and condition in those shares, multiplied by the number of shares.

Valuation of Shares

The valuation of unquoted shares is based on the concept of a willing buyer and a willing seller. The general commercial rules which are normally applied in valuing shares in private companies are applied in arriving at the market value for CGT purposes. The distinction between a controlling interest and a minority holding for commercial valuation purposes on the open market is well recognised, with the value of a minority holding usually significantly smaller than that of a majority stake. The commercial valuation methods referred to include:

1. asset value;
2. capitalisation of profits;
3. dividend yield method;
4. earnings yield (or profits available for dividend) method;
5. earnings per share method or its reciprocal – the price–earnings method; or
6. other methods.

These valuation methods are outside the scope of this textbook but are mentioned here for the purpose of identifying the commercial valuation methods with the accepted market valuation method used for CGT purposes.

Quoted Shares

The valuation of shares or securities listed in the Irish Stock Exchange Official List is the lower of:

- the price at which bargains in the particular shares were last recorded; and
- where bargains (other than special bargains) in the particular shares were recorded in that list for the relevant date, the price at which the bargains were so recorded or, in a case where more than one price was so recorded, a price halfway between the highest and the lowest prices recorded.

For shares or securities listed on the London Stock Exchange Daily Official List, the valuation is the lower of:

- the lesser of the two prices shown for the particular date plus 25% of the difference between the two prices; or
- where bargains (other than special bargains) are recorded for the relevant date, the price recorded or, where more than one price is recorded, a price halfway between the highest and lowest prices recorded.

Where shares or securities are listed on both lists on the same date, the lower relevant valuation is taken.

8.2.5 Married Couples and Civil Partners

As outlined in **Section 8.2.3**, married couples and civil partners are connected persons for the purposes of section 549 TCA 1997. In the absence of any special rules, transfers between spouses/civil partners would be subject to market value rules under section 547 TCA 1997. The CGT legislation provides a "no gain/no loss" rule in respect of transfers between married couples/civil partners who actually live together as married couples/civil partners at the time of disposal. Under section 1028 TCA 1997, the spouse making a disposal will be treated as making the disposal for a consideration equal to a no gain/no loss, and the acquiring spouse/civil partner will take over the tax history of the asset, including base cost and year of acquisition of the disposing spouse/civil partner, so long as they are married and living together at the time of disposal.

Example 8.6

Mr Smyth purchased a rental property in 2008 for €500,000. Mr Smyth transferred 50% of the property to his wife in 2012 when the property had a market value of €750,000. Under section 1028, Mr Smyth is treated as having made a disposal of 50% of his property for a consideration which gives rise to no gain/no loss. Mrs Smyth sells her 50% share of the property in 2022 for €300,000 to an unconnected party. She has the following CGT liability:

	€
Consideration on sale	300,000
Base cost on purchase of property in 2008*	(250,000)
Less: annual exemption	(1,270)
Taxable gain	48,730

* Mrs Smyth is treated as having acquired 50% of the property on the same date and for the same cost as her husband acquired it.

Taking **Example 8.6**, if Mr and Mrs Smyth were not actually living together at the time of the 2012 transfer, then section 1028 would not apply. Instead the market value rules under section 547 would be invoked in the calculation of CGT arising on the disposal in 2012 by Mr Smyth and on the base cost available to Mrs Smyth on the disposal in 2022. Therefore, it is essential to note that, not alone must the couple be legally married to avail of this special CGT treatment, but that they must also be living together as a married couple on the date of the transfer in order to benefit from section 1028. If a couple are living apart on a permanent basis, then any assets transferred on foot of a court order or formal separation agreement will be treated as transferred on a no gain/no loss basis.

The no gain/no loss rule under section 1028 does not apply to trading stock of the disposing spouse/ civil partner or where the asset will be used as trading stock by the acquiring spouse/civil partner.

The no gain/no loss rule only applies to transfers which take place in the lifetime of the spouse making the disposal. Therefore, a disposal on the death of a spouse to a surviving spouse/civil partner will not give rise to a CGT liability, and the surviving spouse will be treated as acquiring the assets for the market value on the date of death of the deceased spouse/civil partner.

8.2.6 Transfers between Group Companies and Shareholders' Exchange of Shares

The transfer of capital assets from one company to another will generally give rise to corporation tax on chargeable gains unless the companies are closely related and group relief provisions apply. The effect of group relief under sections 616 and 617 TCA 1997 is to treat intragroup transactions and transfers as if they take place for a consideration that produces no gain/no loss. In such a case, there are two consideration figures, one of which is the actual consideration (if any) and the other being the deemed consideration for the purposes of the no gain/no loss rule. The no gain/no loss treatment also applies to shareholders who exchange their shareholding in a company for different shares in the same company under section 584 TCA 1997, or shares in another company under sections 586 and 587 TCA 1997. The no gain/no loss treatment available under group transfers and shareholder exchange of shares is discussed in detail in **Chapter 7**.

8.3 CAT Valuation Rules

8.3.1 General Valuation Rule

CAT is charged on the taxable value of a taxable gift and taxable inheritance. Similar to CGT, the first step in arriving at the taxable value of property is to ascertain its market value.

Section 26(2) of the Capital Acquisitions Tax Consolidation Act 2003 (CATCA 2003) sets out the main rule for estimating market value by stating that:

> "Subject to this Act, the market value of any property for the purposes of this Act is estimated to be the price which, in the opinion of the Commissioners, such property would fetch if sold in the open market on the date on which the property is to be valued in such manner and subject to such conditions as might reasonably be calculated to obtain for the vendor the best price for the property."

Therefore, section 26 CATCA 2003 is similar to section 548 TCA 1997 for CGT purposes in that the market value of an asset is the best price available on the open market if the asset were sold in such a manner to obtain the best price for the vendor. Again, as with the section 548 provision, in estimating the market value of any property, Revenue will not allow a reduction in value if a large quantity of the same asset is placed on the market at the same time.

8.3.2   Valuing Shares in a Private Company

Section 27 CATCA 2003 deals with the market value of shares in a private company. The valuation of minority shareholdings in a private company for CGT and stamp duty purposes follows commercial minority valuation methods. However, for CAT purposes, section 27 imposes a specific rule for valuing minority shareholdings which says that, where a beneficiary, together with his relatives, nominees and trustees, controls the company, the value of the shares received by the beneficiary is to be valued as a proportionate part of the value of the company as a whole. Therefore, if a beneficiary acquires 10% of the shares and his relatives own another 70%, the 10% value is taken as 1/8th of the value of the 80% owned by the individual and his relatives. Under normal commercial valuation rules, the shareholding would be a 10% minority holding. However, for CAT purposes, the shareholding is valued on a proportionate basis as 1/8th of an 80% holding.

A "private company" for the purposes of section 27 is an unquoted company under the control of not more than five persons. The term "under the control of not more than five persons" means that the company is under the control of not more than five persons, if any five or fewer persons together can control the company, directly or indirectly, with the following groups treated as a single person:

- relatives (married couples, parents, grandparents/grandchildren, siblings, uncles/aunts, nieces/ nephews, first cousins, and in-laws);
- partners; or
- trustees of any settlement whose objects include the beneficiary or relatives of the beneficiary.

The term "control" includes having:

- over 50% of voting power;
- control of the board of directors;
- title to more than 50% of dividends and interest on debentures; or
- title to 50% or more of the nominal value of the shares of the company.

8.3.3   Surcharge for Undervaluation

Section 53 CATCA 2003 provides that, where an accountable person (generally the beneficiary) submits a return and the estimate of the market value of an asset included in the return is less than 67% of Revenue's market valuation of that asset, a surcharge will be applied. The net effect is that Revenue will review what the valuation should be and, if the taxpayer's return shows a figure which is less than 67% of that, then a surcharge must be paid.

The extent of the surcharge varies with the extent of the undervaluation as follows.

Revenue's opinion of the market value of the asset in the return as % of the market value returned	Surcharge
Equal to or greater than 0% but less than 40%	30%
Equal to or greater than 40% but less than 50%	20%
Equal to or greater than 50% but less than 67%	10%

8.3.4 *Treatment of Gifts to or by Private Controlled Companies*

Section 43 CATCA 2003 provides that, where a private company makes or receives a gift or inheritance, the liability to CAT on that gift/inheritance is determined by "looking through" the company to the individual shareholders of that company. Each shareholder is deemed to have provided/received the benefit in the proportion of his/her entitlement to the assets of the company on liquidation.

Example 8.7

Grian Ltd is a private company, the shares of which are owned equally by Kevin Dolan, Sean Ryan and Báisteach Ltd (which is 100% owned by Alice Kenny).

For the purposes of section 43 The 'owners' of Grian Ltd, are:

- Kevin Dolan = 33%
- Sean Ryan = 33%
- Alice Kenny = 33% (Báisteach Ltd is 'looked through' and any gifts to the company are attributed to Alice).

Kevin Dolan is owed €100,000 by Grian Ltd and he writes off the debt without receiving any consideration. The release of the debt is a taxable gift allocated as follows:

- Kevin is deemed to have taken a gift of €100,000 @ 33% = €33,333, but no tax is payable as a taxpayer is not liable to CAT on a gift from him/her self.
- Sean Ryan is deemed to have taken a gift of €100,000 @ 33% = €33,333.
- Alice Kenny, as the 100% owner of Báisteach Ltd, is deemed to have taken a gift of €100,000 @ 33% = €33,333.

For CAT purposes these gifts will be treated as coming from Kevin and the Group C tax-free threshold and the small gift exemption will be available to Sean and Alice (if not already utilised on other gifts) in their respective CAT liability calculations.

If the company involved is itself owned by another company, or a chain of companies, then the trail behind the second and subsequent companies must be followed until the ultimate beneficial individual shareholders are established for the purposes of calculating the tax arising on the gift passing (as is the case for Báisteach Ltd in **Example 8.7** above where Alice Kenny is treated as the beneficiary).

It should be noted that these special rules only apply to a private company for the purposes of section 27 CATCA 2003 (as previously defined in **Section 8.3.2**), which is an unquoted company under the control of not more than five persons.

In addition, special rules apply in the case of a debt write off by a financial institution and Revenue generally does seek CAT on the debt write-off. These rules are outside the scope of this textbook and should not be confused with the treatment under section 43 CATCA 2003 for private companies and shareholders as described above.

A gift by or to a company, which is not a private company, or a discretionary trust is treated as a gift to or by the company itself or the discretionary trust, and the Group C threshold of €16,250 applies in the calculation of tax arising on a gift or inheritance.

When tracing the beneficial ownership of a chain of private companies with a view to determining the ultimate beneficial shareholders, any shares held by a public company are treated as shares held by a non-corporate shareholder for this purpose. Thus, there is no "look through" to see the ultimate beneficial owners, and that company is seen as the beneficial owner.

8.4 Stamp Duty

8.4.1 Valuation Rule for Stamp Duty Purposes

The value of an asset, which is the subject matter of a stampable instrument or document, must also be established for stamp duty purposes. Valuations are commonly required for gifts or transfers for less than market value, where the transfer involved shares and stocks or where the consideration is unascertainable.

Under section 19 SDCA 1999, the principles set out in section 26 CATCA 2003 are also applied for valuations for stamp duty purposes, as outlined in **Section 8.3.1**. To reiterate, section 26 states that the market value of any property is:

> "…the price which, in the opinion of the Commissioners, such property would fetch if sold in the open market on the date on which the property is to be valued in such manner and subject to such conditions as might reasonably be calculated to obtain for the vendor the best price for the property."

It should be noted that special CAT rules for valuing shares in an unquoted privately controlled company as set out under section 27 CATCA 2003 are not applicable for stamp duty purposes. Therefore, normal commercial valuation methods for minority shareholdings may be applied in arriving at the valuation of shares in an unquoted private company.

8.4.2 Undervaluation for Stamp Duty Purposes

A fixed penalty of €3,000 applies for failure to file a correct return under section 8A SDCA 1999. Interest will also be charged on the underpayment of stamp duty at a rate of 0.0219% per day.

Under section 134A SDCA 1999, tax-geared penalties can also apply where the taxpayer is considered to have acted deliberately or carelessly in relation to their stamp duty obligations.

8.5 Close Company Transferring Assets at Undervalue

As highlighted in the preceding sections of this chapter, there are extensive anti-avoidance measures to discourage interference with market values, such as surcharge on undervaluation, as well as detailed rules in tax legislation, e.g. section 27 CATCA 2003, on how particular minority shareholdings should be valued. Anti-avoidance is also provided for in the close company anti-avoidance provisions, which ensure that a transfer of company assets or values to shareholders is discouraged by reducing the base cost of the shares on a subsequent disposal. (The definition of a close company is set out in **Chapter 3, Section 3.4**.)

Section 589 TCA 1997 covers the situation where a close company, or a company that would be a close company if resident in the State, transfers an asset to any person other than by means of an arm's length bargain and for a price less than the market value. Where section 589 applies, then the difference between the consideration received for the asset and its market value is apportioned among the issued shares of the company, so that on the disposal of any of those shares the cost of acquisition is reduced by the proportionate part of that difference.

Under section 589, the reduction in the cost price of the shares for the purposes of any subsequent disposal of those shares by a shareholder is made from:

1. the original cost price of the shares where they have been acquired on or after 6 April 1974; or
2. the market value at 6 April 1974 in the case of shares held at that date.

The deduction is made before the application of indexation relief.

The transfer of assets at an undervalue may also give rise to a Schedule F distribution treatment under section 130(3) TCA 1997, which provides that, where a company transfers assets to its members, the amount by which the market value of the assets transferred exceeds the amount or value of any new consideration given is treated as a distribution. The company is obliged to operate withholding tax on the value of the distribution and the shareholder is obliged to pay income tax at his/her marginal rates on the distribution.

The market value rules of section 547 TCA 1997 will also be invoked in calculating the CGT payable by the company on the disposal of the asset based on the market value rather than the consideration paid (if any) by the shareholder.

The transfer of assets to a director of a company may trigger a BIK charge, resulting in an income tax liability payable under PAYE. Section 118 TCA 1997 is the general BIK charging provision and is widely drafted to impose an income tax liability on living accommodation, entertainment, domestic or other services, or other benefits or facilities of whatever nature, provided to a director or employee by a company.

Chapter 8   Summary

Valuation rules for CGT purposes	• Basic rule is based on market value, i.e. the price that an asset might reasonably be expected to fetch on the open market • Market value used for assets passing on death, transfers by gift and other transfers by means of bargains not at arm's length, transactions between connected parties and assets owned at 6 April 1974 • Additional tax, interest and penalties will arise if the correct market value is not used
CAT valuation rules	• Similar to CGT, i.e. market value – the best price available on the open market if the asset were sold in such a manner to obtain the best price for the vendor • Special rules for valuing shares in a private company • Additional tax, interest and a surcharge apply if correct market value not used

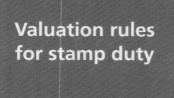

Valuation rules for stamp duty

- Market value of any property is regarded as the price which, in the opinion of Revenue, it would fetch if sold in the open market on the date on which the property is to be valued to obtain for the vendor the best price
- Additional tax, interest, a fixed or a tax-geared penalty will apply if the asset is undervalued

Questions

Review Questions
(See Suggested Solutions to Review Questions at the end of this textbook.)

Question 8.1

Henry Cullen makes a gift of a business he established in 1972 to his son, Ronan, and to Ronan's girlfriend, Gina, in equal measures in November 2022. The value of the business assets are as follows:

	Value in 1972 €	Value on 6 April 1974 €	Value on date of gift €
Goodwill	Nil	10,000	150,000
Premises	11,000	15,000	250,000

Requirement

(a) Advise Henry of the CGT consequences of the gift of the business to Ronan and Gina in November 2022, along with a calculation of CGT arising on the transfer.

Ronan and Gina split up one year later. Under the terms of the settlement reached, Gina agrees to transfer her share of the business to Ronan in exchange for Ronan's share of the house they shared as their principal private residence. The 50% share in the house is significantly greater in value than the 50% share in the business.

(b) Advise Ronan and Gina of the CGT consequences of the proposed split of assets.

Question 8.2

Strange Trading Ltd is an unquoted family company owned equally by Mr and Mrs Kenny. A professional valuer has valued the company at €2 million in total. The professional valuer has also provided a value of €125,000 on the minority shareholding of 10%.

In May 2022 Mrs Kenny decides to gift 10% of her shares to her daughter, Aisling, for a consideration of natural love and affection. They are appalled with the tax liabilities generated from the valuations provided, and are willing to chance their luck and submit a value of €75,000 to Revenue in respect of the gift of 10% of the company.

Requirement

(a) Advise the Kennys of the CAT and stamp duty implications of the gift of the 10% shareholding to Aisling.

(b) Advise the Kennys of the implications of submitting a lower valuation than that provided by the professional valuer to Revenue. Assume that Aisling has already utilised her group a tax-free threshold.

Challenging Question

(Suggested Solutions to Challenging Questions are available through your lecturer.)

Question 8.1

O'Neill Ltd is a family-owned company with the following shareholders:

Aidan O'Neill	20% shareholding
Anna O'Neill	20% shareholding
Sean O'Neill	20% shareholding
Tommy O'Neill	20% shareholding
Tina O'Neill	20% shareholding

Aidan, Sean, Tommy and Tina are siblings; Anna is Aidan's daughter and inherited the shares from her grandmother.

The total issued share capital in the company is 50,000 shares issued at par. These shares were originally issued at par on the formation of the company in September 1973. The market value of a 10% shareholding in the company on 6 April 1974 was €11,500.

On 1 October 2022, O'Neill Ltd sold a commercial property to Anna for €60,000 cash. The market value of the property at the date of sale was €80,000. In December 2022, Aidan decides to sell his 20% shareholding in the company to a third party. He receives €100,000 in proceeds for his 20% shareholding.

Requirement

Provide full analysis of the tax consequences of the transfer of the property to Anna under each relevant tax head.

Capital Tax Reliefs and Planning Tools

Learning Objectives

By the end of this chapter, you should be able to identify the opportunities to apply the main reliefs available under both capital acquisitions tax (CAT) and capital gains tax (CGT) legislation, and show the differences in qualification for similar reliefs, including:

- revised entrepreneur relief (CGT)
- retirement relief (CGT);
- relief for the transfer of a site to a child (CGT);
- agricultural property and business reliefs (CAT);
- relief for surrender of Government securities (CAT);
- relief for surviving spouse of a deceased person (CAT);
- favourite nephew/niece relief (CAT);
- negligible value relief; and
- credit for CGT against CAT on the same transaction.

You should also be able to demonstrate a detailed working knowledge of the events that trigger the charges to CAT, CGT and stamp duty, with particular focus on the following themes:

- transfer or gift of a business to a family, a third party or on a death; and
- retirement planning.

9.1 Introduction

A gift or an inheritance of a business can trigger tax charges under three tax heads: CGT, CAT and stamp duty.

The tax charge under CGT will arise to the disponer on the difference between the market value of the assets of the business on the date of transfer and the base cost of the assets on the date of original purchase by the disponer. **Section 9.3** outlines how retirement relief under section 598 or section 599 TCA 1997 may be claimed to reduce or eliminate the CGT arising on such gifts, provided certain conditions are fulfilled. We will also discuss how retirement relief can be claimed on the sale of a business or business asset at arm's length prices to an unconnected third party. Individuals may also be entitled to apply a lower rate of CGT of 10%, the revised entrepreneur relief, on gains arising on disposals of certain business assets (see **Section 9.2**).

The beneficiary will also be liable to CAT on the market value of business assets transferred less any consideration paid by them for the assets. The beneficiary may also be entitled to relief on taking a gift of a business under sections 90 to 101 CATCA 2003 and on taking a gift of a farm under section 89 CATCA 2003, provided certain conditions are fulfilled as outlined in **Section 9.4**.

A gift of a business will also trigger a charge to stamp duty payable by the beneficiary. Business assets such as property and goodwill, which must pass under an executed written document, will attract stamp duty at 7.5% of the market value of the assets on the date of transfer. Consanguinity relief may be available to reduce the stamp duty liability in the case of transfers of farmland, provided certain conditions are satisfied.

The availability of reliefs, and other capital tax reliefs outlined in this chapter, should ensure that the family business can be passed to the next generation with less of a burden to tax.

9.2 Entrepreneur Relief

Entrepreneur relief (ER) was originally introduced by Finance (No. 2) Act 2013 and implemented by section 597A TCA 1997. ER applied to individuals who, in the period 1 January 2014 to 31 December 2018, reinvested the proceeds of disposals of chargeable business assets made on or after 1 January 2010 in new business ventures. In its original form, ER was not extended beyond 31 December 2018. Although in theory it can still be claimed, it is to all intents and purposes superseded by 'revised entrepreneur relief' (section 597AA), which applies to disposals of chargeable business assets made on or after 1 January 2016.

9.2.1 Revised Entrepreneur Relief

Section 597AA TCA 1997 outlines the revised ER and provides that a lower rate of CGT (10%) applies to an individual who disposes of chargeable business assets if that individual is a **"relevant individual"** or **"qualifying person"**. The lower rate of CGT is 10% for disposals on or after 1 January 2017.

Under section 597AA, chargeable business assets include:

- assets, including goodwill, plant and machinery, fixtures and fitting, and land and buildings, used for the purposes of a **qualifying business** carried on by the individual; or
- ordinary shares in a qualifying company carrying on a qualifying business (or ordinary shares in a holding company of a qualifying group), provided that the individual selling the shares owned 5% or more of the ordinary share capital in the company being sold.

Anti-avoidance measures were introduced in Finance Act 2017 which provide that goodwill and/or shares disposed of by an individual to a company will not be considered as qualifying assets for the purpose of this relief if the individual is connected with the company immediately after the transfer. However, this restriction does not apply if it would be reasonable to consider that the disposal was made for bona fide commercial reasons and did not for part of a scheme or arrangement the main purpose, or one of the main purposes, of which was tax avoidance. If arrangements are made to circumvent the connected parties test, the reduced rate of CGT will not apply.

A **"qualifying business"** is a business that does not include:

- the holding of shares/securities held as investments;
- the holding development land; or
- the development or letting of land.

Disposals by Sole Traders/Partners

The qualifying business assets must have been owned by that individual for a continuous period of three years in the five years immediately prior to the disposal of those assets. Periods of ownership by spouses cannot be aggregated for the purpose of the three-year continuous ownership condition.

In the case of a partnership, relief can apply to the interest of an individual in the assets of a partnership in which he or she is a partner, where those assets were used for the purposes of a qualifying business carried on by the partnership and the individual was actively involved in the business.

Disposals by Shareholders

Where a business is carried on by a company, individuals seeking to qualify for the relief must satisfy the following conditions:

■ The individual owns not less than 5% of the ordinary shares in the qualifying company or 5% of the ordinary shares in a holding company of a qualifying group. A holding company means a company whose business consists wholly or mainly of the holding of shares of **all** companies that are its 51% subsidiaries. A qualifying group means a group where the business of **each** 51% subsidiary (other than a holding company) consists wholly or mainly of carrying on a qualifying business. This means that relief will not apply where there is a dormant company in a group, or where one of the subsidiaries is not a trading company.

■ The individual must have been a director or employee of the qualifying company (or companies in a qualifying group) who is, or was, required to spend not less than 50% of his or her time in the service of the company or companies in a managerial or technical capacity and has served in that capacity for a continuous period of three years in the five years immediately prior to the disposal of the chargeable business assets.

■ The individual must have owned the shares for at least a continuous three-year period. Any period during which an individual owned shares in or was a director or employee of a company that qualified for relief under sections 586 or 587 TCA 1997 (share-for-share exchange, see **Section 7.2.1**) will be taken into account for the purpose of the three-year continuous ownership requirement. However, periods of ownership of assets before incorporation of a business (e.g. periods of ownership of assets of a business carried on by a sole trader or partners in a partnership) is not counted for the purposes of this relief.

The relief operates by applying the 10% CGT rate to disposals of chargeable business assets by a qualifying individual. There is a lifetime limit of €1 million of chargeable gains that qualify for the 10% rate. Chargeable gains that exceed €1 million are taxable at the rate of 33% on the amount in excess of €1 million.

Example 9.1

Tom Griffin disposed of a chargeable asset in 2022 for €300,000, on which he made a gain of €125,000. Assuming he has not already used up his €1 million threshold, this gain of €125,000 is chargeable at 10%. The CGT is therefore €12,500.

9.2.2 Interaction of Revised Entrepreneur Relief with Other Tax Reliefs

Buy-back of Shares

Relief can apply where the share buy-back is within the charge to CGT (see **Section 4.6**).

Company Liquidations

Relief can apply on the liquidation of a company (see **Chapter 4, Section 4.6**), provided the company was carrying on a qualifying business up to the time the liquidator was appointed and the liquidation was completed within a reasonable period of time. For this purpose, Revenue regard a period of two years as being reasonable.

Double Holding Company Structures

Relief can apply in a double holding company structure where a holding company holds another holding company which, in turn, holds a trading company. In this connection, section 9(1)(a) refers to more than 50% of the ordinary share capital of a company being owned directly or indirectly by another company.

Relief for the Transfer of a Business to a Company

Relief for the transfer of a business to a company under section 600 TCA 1997 is covered in **Chapter 2, Section 2.3** Revised entrepreneur relief may be restricted where an individual transfers a business to a company pursuant to section 600. Relief will not be available on the portion of the gain which relates to non-share consideration (i.e. cash) received out of the assets of the company in respect of the disposal. However the restriction does not apply in relation to bona fide commercial disposals which do not form part of a tax avoidance arrangement.

9.3 CGT Retirement Relief

Retirement relief under sections 598 and 599 TCA 1997 is a CGT relief on certain disposals of business assets by an individual aged 55 years or over. Companies and trusts do not qualify for the relief. If the conditions are satisfied, gains realised on the disposal of relevant business assets are relieved from CGT. Full relief from CGT will only apply under section 599 where the **disposal is to a child** and takes place on or after 1 January 2014 by an individual who is aged 55 to 65. Where the individual making the transfer is aged 66 or over, an upper limit of €3 million on retirement relief will be imposed.

If the disposal is to a person/entity other than a child, by an individual who is aged 55 to 65, a threshold of €750,000 applies under section 598. Where the disposal is made by an individual aged 66 or over, then the €750,000 threshold is reduced to €500,000 when the disposal is on or after 1 January 2014. The value of any disposals to children under section 599 is disregarded for the purpose of calculating the total consideration received for section 598.

Typically, the relief is claimed where an entire business is being sold. However, the relief also applies to disposals of individual assets, even when the person making the disposal continues to trade. For example, a farmer aged over 55 years could sell sites while continuing to carry on his farming business and retirement relief would apply to any gains on the disposals of the sites. While the relief is referred to as retirement relief, there is no requirement that the person actually retires.

There are, however, wide-ranging anti-avoidance provisions associated with this relief to protect against abuse.

9.3.1 Conditions for Relief

The relief applies where the disposal is made:

- by an individual, who is
- aged 55 years or more at the time of the disposal,

and the disposal is:

- of a qualifying asset (as outlined in **Section 9.3.2**), which is
- owned by that individual for the qualifying period (as outlined in **Section 9.3.3**).

The requirement that the individual should be aged 55 years or over is relaxed by Revenue where the individual is in severe or chronic ill health. Revenue has indicated that they will consider claims for retirement relief where an individual disposes of qualifying assets before their 55th birthday if all of the following conditions are met:

- due to severe or chronic ill health the claimant is unable to continue in employment, including farming, a trade, profession, office or employment or as a working director in a relevant company;
- at the time of disposal of the qualifying assets, the conditions for relief (other than the age requirement) are satisfied;
- at the time of disposal the claimant is within 12 months of their 55th birthday; and
- the claimant can provide medical evidence of the illness and outline the circumstances in which the relief is being claimed.

9.3.2 Qualifying Assets for Retirement Relief

The relief applies to the disposal of qualifying assets. Qualifying assets may comprise actual assets used in a trade or profession or shares in trading companies. Investment assets such as quoted shares and rental properties do not qualify for the relief. If these assets are held within a trading company, an apportionment would be required to see what amount of the consideration would qualify for the relief.

Qualifying assets comprise:

1. **Land, buildings and goodwill** owned for at least 10 years and used for the purposes of the trade or profession continuously throughout the 10-year period. Goodwill disposed of by an individual to a company where the individual is connected with the company immediately after the transfer is excluded as a qualifying asset for retirement relief purposes. However, the connected company exclusion does not apply where it is considered that the disposal is for bona fide commercial reasons and is not for tax avoidance purposes.

2. **Plant, machinery or motor vehicles** used for the purposes of the trade or profession. Plant, machinery and motor vehicles do not have to be owned for a 10-year period prior to disposal. This is in recognition of the fact that such assets rarely have a useful life of up to 10 years. In practice, it would be very rare for a capital gain to arise on a disposal of plant, machinery or motor vehicles as they are wasting assets. However, it is very important to bear in mind that they are qualifying assets and the value of such assets must be included in the calculation of the €750,000 threshold.

3. **Shares in a family trading company or farming company or holding company of a trading group** where the shares have been held by the individual making the disposal for a period of not less than 10 years ending on the disposal and the individual has been a working director of the company for 10 years, five of which years he/she has been a full-time working director of the company. A company is a family company in relation to an individual who is disposing of the shares, if:

   (a) he or she owns at least 25% of the shares; or
   (b) he or she owns at least 10% of the shares and his or her family, including the individual's own holding, owns at least 75% of the shares. Family means a spouse, a relative and relative of a spouse. A relative means a brother, sister, ancestor and lineal descendant.

Tests (a) or (b) above must be satisfied throughout the 10-year period immediately prior to the disposal of the shares in order for the shares to be qualifying assets.

Shares disposed of by an individual to a company where the individual is connected with the company immediately after the transfer is excluded as a qualifying asset for retirement relief purposes unless the disposal is for bona fide commercial reasons and is not for tax avoidance purposes.

4. **Assets owned by the individual but used by the family company**. Therefore, assets such as buildings and plant and equipment owned personally by the shareholder for a period of 10 years ending on the disposal, but used by the company for the purposes of carrying on its trade or profession, qualify for relief if the assets are transferred at the same time as the shares in the company in which the assets are used. This provision mirrors the business property relief for CAT as outlined in **Section 9.4**, although different tests apply to each, e.g. for retirement relief to apply the recipient need not control the company, whereas that is a condition of CAT business relief. Many Irish family businesses operate on the basis that a limited company carries on the trade or profession while the individual who owns the company personally purchases the land or building used by the company to carry on its trade or profession and rents the property to the company (see **Chapter 2, Section 2.3**).

5. **Qualifying assets relevant to the agricultural land and property** are as follows:

   ◼ chargeable business asset of the individual which he/she has owned for at least 10 years up to the disposal date and which have been chargeable business assets throughout that 10-year period;
   ◼ Single Farm Payment entitlements where these are disposed of at the same time and to the same person as land, to the extent that the land would support a claim to payment in respect of those payment entitlements;
   ◼ land leased under the Scheme of Early Retirement from Farming where, for a period of not less than 10 years prior to the land being leased, it was owned by the individual claiming relief and used by him/her for the purposes of farming throughout that period;
   ◼ land that was let during a five-year period prior to its disposal under a compulsory purchase order for the purpose of road construction and, prior to its first letting, the land was farmed for 10 years by the person making the disposal;
   ◼ land that was let at any time during the 25 years before disposal but, prior to its first letting, was farmed for 10 years by the individual making the disposal and the disposal is to a child;
   ◼ land that was leased on a long-term basis (for a minimum of five years and a maximum of 25 years) but, prior to its first letting, was farmed for 10 years by the owner and the disposal is to a person other than a child. Where the land was let under one or more conacre agreements (short-term eleven-month land rentals) before 31 December 2016, this will not impact the land owner's entitlement to relief, provided the conacre agreement is replaced with a formal long-term lease before 31 December 2016.

For disposals made on or after 1 January 2018, entitlement to retirement relief will not be affected by the fact that solar panels are installed on land suitable for farming, where the area of the land on which the solar panels are installed does not exceed half the total area of the land concerned.

Example 9.2
Mark is aged 56. He sold his stationery business to Mary (unrelated third party) for €770,000 on 10 March 2022. The sales consideration comprised the following:

	€
Shop owned for 15 years	440,000
Delivery van owned for two years	10,000 (cost €16,000)
Stock valued	40,000
Debtors valued	20,000
Shelving valued	10,000 (cost €15,000)
Computer system valued	20,000 (cost €30,000)
Goodwill valued	230,000

continued overleaf

First, we must establish if the total proceeds in respect of qualifying assets (i.e. assets used for the purpose of the business and which could result in a capital gain on disposal) exceed €750,000. If they do not, it is not even necessary to calculate any potential gains. The qualifying assets are the shop, goodwill, the van, the shelving and the computer system. The shelving, van and the computer system are chargeable assets for CGT purposes even though it is obvious that no chargeable gain arises on the disposal of these assets. Note that the stock and the debtors are not qualifying assets as these are not chargeable assets for CGT purposes.

Proceeds on Qualifying Assets	€
Shop	440,000
Goodwill	230,000
Van	10,000
Shelving	10,000
Computer system	20,000
Total	**710,000**

As the proceeds, in respect of qualifying assets, are less than €750,000, retirement relief applies regardless of the level of any gains arising on the disposal of individual assets. A clawback of relief can arise for the seller of the business assets if the cumulative lifetime sale proceeds to third parties after the seller has reached 55 years of age exceeds €750,000 (€500,000 in the case of disposals made on or after 1 January 2014 and where the seller is 66 years or older).

9.3.3   Qualifying Periods of Ownership

The following points should be noted in relation to the "10-year period of ownership" rule:

1. The asset must be owned and actually used in the trade for the 10-year period immediately before the disposal. For example, an individual may have owned a warehouse for the last 20 years. For the first 18 years, it was let but had been used for the purposes of the trade for the last two years. Such an asset would not be a qualifying asset as, while it was owned for more than 10 years, it was not used for the purposes of the trade throughout the 10-year period immediately before the disposal.
2. A period of ownership of a spouse/civil partner or a deceased spouse/civil partner is taken into account in assessing the 10-year period of ownership. For example, a woman may have owned a building for seven years for the purposes of carrying on her trade before gifting the building and the trade to her husband. If he then disposes of the building after a further three years having used the building for the trade, the asset would be a qualifying asset.
3. Where the qualifying assets are shares in a family company, which was previously run as a sole trade or partnership, and section 600 TCA 1997 relief on the transfer of a business to a company in exchange for shares was claimed, then the period the business was run as a sole trade will also qualify for the purposes of the 10-year test. The period the individual ran the business as a sole trade will also count for the purposes of assessing if the working director test of 10 years ending on the date of disposal is satisfied.

9.3.4   Disposal of Shares in a Company

The value of the shares in a company is determined by different factors, including the assets on the balance sheet. All assets held by the company might not be business assets. Therefore, a portion of the value of the company may not qualify for business relief. The formula to calculate the proportion of the sales proceeds that relates to the chargeable business assets is:

$$\text{Sales proceeds} \times \frac{\text{(Chargeable business assets)}}{\text{(Total chargeable assets)}}$$

In this way, non-chargeable assets, such as stock and debtors, are excluded from the calculation.

Example 9.3

Susan, aged 58, sold her 80% shareholding in NER Publishing Ltd for €750,000. She originally purchased her shares in 2005 for €150,000. Since then she has worked full-time in the company and been a full-time working director. The company's assets at the date of sale were as follows:

	€
Factory premises	600,000
Plant and machinery	50,000
Debtors	10,000
Stock	15,000
Investments	20,000
	695,000
Less: creditors	(25,000)
	670,000

Susan qualifies for retirement relief on the disposal of her shares.

Step 1 – calculate the gain arising

Proceeds of sale	€750,000
Less: base cost	(€150,000)
Gain	€650,000

Step 2 – compute the portion of relief due

Chargeable assets are:

Factory premises	€600,000
Plant and machinery	€50,000
	€650,000

The debtors and the stock are not chargeable assets. The investment of €20,000 is not a chargeable business asset but is a chargeable asset. The portion, therefore, of the value of the shares being transferred attributable to chargeable business assets is €750,000 × €650,000/€670,000 = €727,611.

Step 3 – compute the gain relieved from tax

€650,000 × €727,611/€750,000 = €630,597

Step 4 – tax the remaining gain

Taxable gain	€650,000
Less: retirement relief	(€630,597)
Remaining gain	€19,403
Taxed at 10%	€1,940 (assuming revised entrepreneur relief applies)

9.3.5   *Marginal Relief*

If the sales proceeds on disposals to third parties under section 598 relating to qualifying trading assets exceed €750,000, retirement relief is not available. However, a measure of marginal relief under section 598(2) TCA 1997 may be available providing that the total CGT payable on the various assets disposed does not exceed 50% of the excess of the proceeds over €750,000.

It is first necessary to compute the total CGT arising on the disposal. The maximum CGT payable will be the lower of:

- the actual capital gains tax computed; or
- 50% of the excess of the sales proceeds relating to qualifying assets over €750,000. Marginal relief will also be available in respect of disposals to third parties where the disponer is aged 66 and over and the proceeds exceed €500,000

Example 9.4

Martin, aged 64, disposed of his business to a third party on 10 December 2022. He had commenced to trade in 1976. The total sales proceeds were €840,000, allocated as follows:

	€
Goodwill	280,000
Premises	395,000
Plant	110,000
Stock	25,000
Debtors	30,000
	840,000

He purchased the premises in June 1980 for €40,000. No capital gain arises on plant. The proceeds in respect of qualifying assets are as follows:

	€
Goodwill	280,000
Premises	395,000
Plant	110,000
Total	785,000

As the proceeds in respect of qualifying assets exceed €750,000, full retirement relief is not available. However, marginal relief may be available.

First, calculate the CGT payable.

Goodwill

Martin has no base cost for goodwill as it was not purchased. The full €280,000 represents a capital gain.

Premises	€
Proceeds	395,000
€40,000 @ 3.240	(129,600)
Gain	265,400

Summary of gains	
	€
Goodwill (no base cost)	280,000
Premises	265,400
Total	545,400
Less: annual exemption	(1,270)
	544,130
CGT @ 10%	54,413

Secondly, calculate the excess of the proceeds of qualifying assets over €750,000.

As the proceeds in respect of qualifying assets are €785,000, the excess is €35,000. 50% of the excess is €17,500. As 50% of the excess is less than the CGT on individual assets of €54,413, then the final CGT payable is €17,500.

If the marginal relief in the above example did not provide a saving, then CGT under normal rules would be payable.

It is assumed for the purposes of the above calculations that Martin satisfies all of the conditions to avail of the reduced 10% CGT entrepreneur relief rate.

9.3.6 Clawback of Retirement Relief (section 598 TCA 1997)

Provisions are made for a clawback of relief where an individual, who has claimed retirement relief on disposals to persons other than a child, makes a further disposal of qualifying assets after the individual has reached the age of 55, which would qualify for retirement relief, and the aggregate proceeds exceed the threshold (€750,000). Therefore, if an individual claims retirement relief under section 598 TCA 1997 and subsequently makes a further disposal of qualifying assets, then CGT relief on the original claim will be clawed back. The clawback calculation would be based on the lower of the actual CGT liability on the aggregate disposals or CGT based on marginal relief.

Where the individual is 66 or older and makes a subsequent disposal of qualifying assets, the aggregate consideration will be limited to €500,000. A clawback of relief will arise if the total aggregate consideration is in excess of this amount. The amount of tax payable should not exceed 50% of the difference between the consideration and the €500,000 limit, i.e. marginal relief.

9.3.7 Disposals to a Child

For the purposes of retirement relief, under section 599 TCA 1997 a child includes a niece or a nephew who has worked substantially on a full-time basis in the business for the five years ending with the date of disposal. The definition of a child includes a qualifying foster child, a child of a deceased child and a child of a civil partner. A qualifying foster child is a child who was under the care of the individual making the disposal, and was maintained at the expense of the individual throughout a period of five years prior to the child reaching 18 years of age.

For individuals aged 55 to 65, there is no monetary limit on the amount of consideration that can qualify for relief in relation to disposals to a child. Where an individual who is 66 years or older disposes of the whole or part of their qualifying assets to his or her child and the market value of the qualifying assets is €3 million or less, full relief will be given on any gain accruing. Where the market value is in excess of €3 million, relief will be limited to the gain attributable on the capped €3 million proceeds. Amounts received in excess of the €3 million cap will be taxable in the normal manner.

An anti-avoidance measure applies in the case of disposals involving shares in a family company to a child. Where an individual aged 66 years or over disposes of shares or securities of a family company to a child, the consideration in respect of such a disposal must be aggregated with any disposal of shares or securities by the individual to a company controlled by that same child, for the purpose of calculating the €500,000 threshold limit for relief under section 598 TCA 1997. The objective of this anti-avoidance measure is to prevent tax planning involving the use of the €3,000,000 threshold on transfers to a child and the €500,000 threshold on transfers to a third party that ultimately benefits the same child. This provision is not subject to a bona fide test and therefore applies even if there is a commercial reason for the transaction.

Clawback of Retirement Relief (section 599 TCA 1997)

Under section 599(4)(a) TCA 1997, if a child receives assets under a disposal that attracts retirement relief, he must not dispose of those assets for at least six years after the date of disposal. If there is a disposal within the six-year period, the CGT avoided on the disposal by the parent becomes payable by the child. There is no requirement that the child should continue trading with the asset on which retirement relief was claimed by his/her parent. For example, a child could lease the assets of the trade without triggering a clawback of the relief. If the assets received by the child are shares in a family company, the six-year holding period applies to the shares. There is no restriction on the company disposing of some of its trading assets within the six-year period.

In calculating the amount of clawback, it is necessary to first ascertain if the parent would have qualified for retirement relief under section 598 TCA 1997 on that disposal. In computing a clawback on a child, any relief that would have been available to the parent had the original disposal been to a third party must be allowed. Marginal relief is also available when computing the clawback.

Example 9.5

Robert, aged 57 years, transferred all his business assets to his daughter, Eleanor. The market value of the qualifying assets at the date of the transfer was €1.5 million. CGT of €100,000 was avoided by availing of retirement relief. Eleanor carried on the business for three years, but then disposed of it.

Because Eleanor did not retain ownership of the assets for six years, she must pay the €100,000 CGT avoided by her father on his transfer of the business to her. It is clear that no form of retirement relief would have been available to the father had the original disposal been to a third party as the €1,500,000 proceeds means that marginal relief would not be claimed, i.e. (€1.5 million − €750,000) @ 50% = €375,000 > €100,000 actual CGT. It should be noted that Eleanor may also have a CGT exposure in relation to her own period of ownership of the assets.

There is no clawback of the relief if the child dies within the clawback period, i.e. six years. As you will recall, death is not a CGT event.

9.3.8 Disposals to Spouses

Normally, disposals between spouses are treated as a no gain/no loss with the transferee spouse deemed to have acquired the asset at the same date and cost as the transferor spouse. Where the asset disposed is a qualifying asset and the transferor spouse is aged 55 years or more, the asset is deemed to be transferred at market value for the purposes of the €750,000 or €500,000 threshold. This is an anti-avoidance provision and is designed to prevent asset transfers between spouses, to effectively increase the €750,000 or €500,000 threshold. All disposals between spouses before reaching age 55 continue to be treated as transferred at no gain/no loss and do not utilise any part of the transferor's €750,000 threshold.

One exception to the rule outlined arises where all of the qualifying assets of one spouse are transferred to the other spouse. In this case the transfer is made at cost regardless of age. This is a logical exception as the transferor spouse cannot avail of retirement relief as they have now divested themselves of all their qualifying assets.

9.3.9 Liquidation and Retirement Relief

A capital distribution of cash and assets to a shareholder following the appointment of a liquidator is broadly a CGT disposal by the shareholder of his shares, as outlined in **Chapter 4**. Retirement relief may be available on capital distributions if the necessary conditions are satisfied.

Technically, retirement relief does not apply as, at the time of liquidation, the assets of the company consist of the proceeds of disposal of the business and not the business itself. Section 598(7) TCA 1997 allows the relief in the case of capital distributions received by an individual in the course of the dissolution or winding-up of a family company in the same manner as if the individual had disposed of the shares or securities in the company. By concession, the relief will apply if the company assets are sold not more than six months prior to liquidation and were sold with the intention of liquidating the family company.

Retirement relief is not available if a shareholder receives a capital distribution *in specie*, i.e. physical transfer of ownership of assets without a sale of company assets by the liquidator.

9.3.10 Interaction of Retirement Relief with Other Tax Reliefs

Transfer of a Business to a Company Relief

As outlined in **Chapter 2**, if a sole trade is transferred to a company under section 600 TCA 1997, the period of ownership of the sole trade is recognised for the purposes of the 10-year tests applicable to qualifying shares and qualifying periods of directorship of a family company.

As stated in **Section 9.3.2**, goodwill disposed of by an individual to a company where the individual is connected with the company immediately after the transfer is excluded as a qualifying asset for retirement relief purposes unless it can be demonstrated that the disposal is for bona fide commercial reasons and is not for tax avoidance purposes. Restrictions apply under section 598(7C) and (7D) TCA 1997, which directly impact on the availability of retirement relief with section 600 (transfer of a business to a company) relief. Retirement relief is available on the portion of the gain that relates to non-share consideration received out of the assets of the company for disposals under a section 600 transfer. However, the restriction will not apply where it is reasonable to consider that the disposal is made for bona fide commercial reasons and does not form part of a tax avoidance arrangement.

The interaction of the two reliefs can also yield other negative results. For example, if a child takes a transfer of qualifying trading assets under section 599 TCA 1997 relief and incorporates the business within six years from the date of the retirement relief claim, then the transfer of the business to the company is a disposal for CGT purposes. This will trigger a clawback of retirement relief originally claimed by the parent, notwithstanding the fact that the actual CGT arising on the transfer of the business to the company qualifies for CGT relief under section 600.

Unquoted Company Buy-back of Shares

Section 176 TCA 1997 provides that a distribution received under a scheme of buy-back will be subject to CGT, provided certain conditions are met (see **Chapter 4, Section 4.6**). One of the tests of the relief is to show that the buy-back of shares was carried out for the benefit of the trade. This test may be satisfied when a controlling shareholder is retiring as a director and wishes to make way for new management.

The distribution treated as a CGT event may then qualify for retirement relief under section 598, provided all the other conditions for the relief are fulfilled. Any payments received which qualify for the CGT treatment on the buy-back of company shares must be taken into account for the €750,000/€500,000 lifetime threshold under section 598.

The use of CGT treatment under a share buy-back (see **Chapter 4**) and retirement relief is restricted in the case of a transferor aged over 66 years. On a transfer of shares in a family company to a child and to a company controlled by that child, the value of the shares transferring under both transactions is aggregated for the purposes of calculating the €500,000 lifetime limit on transfers to third parties. For example, if an individual aged over 66 years transfers €3 million worth of shares to a child, and then in a further disposal transfers shares worth up to €500,000 to a company **controlled** by that child, retirement relief cannot be claimed on the second transaction. This provision is not subject to a bona fide commercial test and can apply to genuine commercial transactions.

CAT Business Relief and Agricultural Relief

Retirement relief provides relief for gifts of businesses and farms which might otherwise give rise to a CGT liability on the disponer. However, the business and farm may be a taxable gift in the hands of the recipient for CAT purposes. Therefore, the provision of advice to a client on retirement relief may also involve a review of the recipient's circumstances in order to ensure that business relief or agricultural relief for CAT purposes can also be claimed.

Revised Entrepreneur Relief

Revised entrepreneur relief reduces the rate of CGT from 33% to 10%, while retirement relief operates by exempting proceeds (subject to the applicable threshold) based on the disponer's age and the relationship with the donee (i.e. a child or a third party). Therefore both reliefs can arise on a disposal of the same asset(s) if the conditions are all met. Retirement relief and revised entrepreneur relief are mandatory reliefs, i.e. where the conditions apply the reliefs apply automatically, which means there is no scope to defer one relief to maximise the other if the conditions for both are met. It is possible that a disposal of assets qualifying for retirement relief on proceeds of €750,000 will also use up €750,000 of the lifetime threshold of gains of €1,000,000 under revised entrepreneur relief where the conditions for both reliefs apply.

9.3.11 Retirement Relief Planning Points

There are many planning points associated with maximising the benefit of retirement relief. The relevant planning points will depend on the facts of the particular case but, in general, the following points should be noted for implementation before **the individual's 55th birthday** (these actions are designed to minimise CGT that may arise on the disposals of qualifying assets after the age of 55):

1. Gift assets or shares to spouse/civil partner. In some cases, this will mean that two €750,000/€500,000 thresholds become available. Where it is not possible to make such a gift, it may be possible to ensure that maximum benefit is derived from one €750,000 threshold by ensuring that the transferor spouse has exactly €750,000 worth of assets which qualify for relief. Ideally, the assets which count for the €750,000 threshold should attract the largest gain and CGT liability, and thereby yield the greatest saving.
2. Sell qualifying trading assets that are surplus to requirements. It may be possible that certain assets are no longer vital to the running of the business. For example, certain items of plant and motor vehicles could be disposed of in preparation for a retirement relief claim before age 55. Assets such as plant and motor vehicles are unlikely to generate capital gains, but these assets could eat into the €750,000 threshold.

3. Sell and lease-back certain trading capital assets on which there are either no latent gains or relatively small latent gains. If possible, certain trading assets with minimal gains should be disposed of before the owner's 55th birthday. For example, a premises used in a business may be worth €400,000 but, due to indexation relief/substantial base cost, no capital gain would arise on disposal. The premises could be sold to an investor and leased back for continued use in the business. A future claim for retirement relief would not include the leased asset.

4. Where a disposal of a business to a third party would be for an amount significantly in excess of €750,000/€500,000, it may be possible to sell or gift some assets to a child on the basis that the child will not sell the assets until after the requisite six-year holding period. The proceeds of the asset taken by the child under a section 599 claim are disregarded for the purposes of the €750,000/€500,000 test under the section 598 claim and are not aggregated with the proceeds of sale to third parties.

5. In the case of a business carried on through a company, long-term planning could be implemented by appointing a spouse/civil partner as a working director for a minimum of 10 years and ensuring that the spouse is a full-time working director for at least five years. A surviving spouse may aggregate the period of the deceased spouse's directorship, but no aggregation is allowed for the period of director-ship of a living spouse.

6. Where the value of shares exceeds the €750,000/€500,000 threshold, reduce the value of the shares by extracting value from the company in a tax-efficient manner, which essentially means reducing the overall tax burden. For example, it may be possible to use available cash to increase the company's contribution to the pension fund or it may be possible to pay a tax-free termination payment or, in some cases, it may be tax-efficient to pay additional salary or directors' fees, thereby extracting cash and reducing the value of the shares that qualify for retirement relief to below the €750,000/€500,000 threshold.

7. Where it is intended to transfer or sell a business to a niece or nephew, employ that person in the business with a view to transferring or selling the business to them after five years.

9.4   CAT Business Relief and Agricultural Relief

9.4.1   CAT Business Relief

As noted above, the gift of a business will in general also give rise to a CAT liability on the recipient. A gift, or indeed an inheritance, of a family business or shares in a family company may qualify for a generous relief known as business relief under sections 90 to 101 CATCA 2003 provided certain conditions are fulfilled. The relief takes the form of reducing the market value of qualifying business property by 90%. There is currently no upper ceiling of the value to which the 90% reduction applies.

Example 9.6

Caroline inherited shares with a market value of €120,000 in an unquoted trading company from her cousin on 10 April 2022. On 20 June 2022, her mother gifted 100% of the shares in another unquoted company to Caroline with a market value of €400,000. The shareholdings in both companies qualify for business property relief. Caroline had not received any other taxable benefits on/after 5 December 1991. The business relief is calculated as follows:

continued overleaf

	€
Inheritance from cousin April 2022, market value	120,000
Less: business relief @ 90%	(108,000)
Taxable value of inheritance	12,000
Less: annual gift exemption (not available as not a gift)	(Nil)
Taxable value (covered by Group C threshold of €16,250)	12,000
Tax payable	Nil
Gift from mother June 2022, market value	400,000
Less: business relief at 90%	(360,000)
Taxable value of gift	40,000
Less: annual gift exemption	(3,000)
Taxable value (covered by Group A threshold of €335,000)	37,000
CAT payable	Nil

9.4.2 Conditions for Business Relief

In order for assets, which are the subject of a gift or inheritance, to qualify for business relief, the assets must qualify as "relevant business assets", defined as:

1. **Property or any asset (such as goodwill, trading premises, debtors, trading stocks, etc.) of an unincorporated business,** e.g. sole trader or partnership carrying on a trade or profession, or an interest in a business, whether or not the business is carried on in Ireland or abroad.

    Individual assets that are used in the business, e.g. the business premises, do not qualify for the relief if they are transferred to the recipient without the transfer of the business.
2. **Land, buildings, machinery or plant, which immediately before the gift or inheritance were used wholly or mainly for the purpose of a business** carried on by a company controlled by the recipient, the spouse or civil partner of the recipient or by a partnership in which the recipient was a partner. To qualify for relief under this heading, the disponer must also simultaneously transfer shares in the company which qualify as relevant business property or an interest in the partnership which qualifies as relevant business property. The land, buildings, plant and machinery must continue to be used for at least six years by the company to avoid a clawback of the relief.
3. **Unquoted shares of a trading or professional company**, provided the recipient satisfies one of the following conditions on the valuation date, after taking into account the gift/inheritance received:
    - he/she must control more than 25% of the voting rights of the company in their own name; or
    - the company is, after taking the gift or inheritance, under the control, i.e. more than 50%, of the recipient and his/her relatives; or
    - he or she controls 10% or more of the issued share capital of the company and has been a full-time working director or employee of the company or of any company in the same group of companies throughout the period of five years ending on the date of the gift or inheritance.

The shareholding tests above apply to the recipient and not to the disponer. For example, the disponer might hold 9% of the voting rights of a company and gift this holding to a recipient who already holds 20%. After receiving the gift, the recipient would then hold more than the necessary 25% of the voting power and, accordingly, the shares would qualify for business relief.

Shares in foreign incorporated companies may qualify for the relief. Shares in farming companies qualify provided the above conditions are satisfied.

The trading or professional activity of the company must continue to be carried on for at least six years to avoid a clawback of the relief.

4. **Quoted shares or securities of a company** carrying on a business provided they would have qualified for the relief if it is assumed they were unquoted, were in the beneficial ownership of the disponer immediately prior to the transfer and were unquoted on 23 May 1994 or, if later, the date of commencement of that beneficial ownership.

Examples of non-qualifying property for the purposes of business relief include shares in investment or property rental companies, quoted shares in most resident and non-resident companies and investment properties owned by landlords and private investments in antiques, paintings, jewellery, etc.

9.4.3 Other Points Affecting the Definition of Qualifying Business

A business or an interest in a business will qualify as relevant business property if, on the date of the gift or inheritance, the business was carried on wholly or mainly either inside or outside the State.

Any type of business may be carried on by a company whose shares qualify as relevant business property, subject to the following exclusions: currency dealing, share dealing, dealing in land or buildings, or a business of making or the holding of investments.

Agricultural property, as defined for agricultural relief purposes, may be treated as a qualifying business property, but only if it does not first qualify for agricultural relief. Business property relief can only be claimed if a farming business is actually carried on by the recipient. For example, if the recipient simply rented the farm to a third party, then business property relief could not be claimed. There is no similar condition for agricultural relief and a beneficiary qualifying for agricultural relief can rent the farm to a third party.

9.4.4 Minimum Period of Ownership Condition for Disponer

A minimum period of ownership test must be satisfied by the disponer before a beneficiary can qualify for the benefit of business relief in respect of a gift or inheritance. To qualify for business relief, the asset must have been continuously in the beneficial ownership of the disponer, or of the spouse/civil partner of the disponer, for the following minimum periods:

1. two years prior to the date of the inheritance (in the case of an inheritance taken on the death of a disponer), or, in any other case, five years immediately prior to the date of the gift;
2. a period of ownership by a disponer's spouse/civil partner or by a trustee may be included for the purpose of the two- and five-year tests;
3. the five-year test also applies to gifts/inheritances taken from trusts. However, the period of ownership of the trust and that of the disponer (i.e. the settlor) may be aggregated to satisfy this test.

9.4.5 Replacement Property

When a qualifying business property has been replaced with other property within the minimum ownership period, that relevant business property will qualify for the relief if the property it replaced would have qualified as relevant business property. In dealing with the replacement property, as some time may elapse between the sale of one business and its replacement with another, the minimum ownership periods are extended from two years and five years, to three years and six years respectively. However, the assets must have been owned for a minimum of two of the three years or five of the six years respectively.

Similarly, in the case of gifts or inheritances arising other than on the death of the disponer, the minimum ownership period requirements would be satisfied if the disponer owned the original and replacement properties for five years out of the six years immediately preceding the date of the benefit.

There is no requirement that the replacement property be of a similar nature to the property it replaces.

9.4.6   Quick Succession Relief

The two-year minimum ownership rule is waived in the case of an inheritance taken on the death of an individual where all of the following conditions are satisfied:

1. the disponer had acquired the property less than two years before the date of the inheritance as a result of an earlier gift or inheritance;
2. the property that the disponer acquired less than two years earlier would have qualified as relevant business property; and
3. the property in question would satisfy all other conditions, apart from the two-year rule, to qualify as relevant business property.

9.4.7   Valuation Rules

The value of the business to which business relief will apply is defined as being its "net value". This net value is arrived at by taking the market value of all the assets used in the business, including goodwill, as reduced by the aggregate value of any liabilities incurred for the purposes of the business. The normal CAT rules for valuing shares in private companies are used for the purposes of business relief.

Special rules apply, however, to the valuation of shares in a holding company of a group if the group contains a company which carries on a non-qualifying activity. In such circumstances, the shares in the holding company of that group must be valued as if the company carrying on the non-qualifying activity was not a member of the group.

A similar rule applies where the holding company owns quoted shares of another member or members of the group. Again, the value of those quoted shares is excluded from the valuation of the holding company's shares. This latter rule is subject to the exception whereby certain quoted shares can qualify for business relief.

9.4.8   Property Not Qualifying as Relevant Business Property

Certain assets are specifically excluded from the benefit of relevant business property relief. These are:

1. **Excepted Assets** An asset that has not been used wholly or mainly for the purposes of the business throughout the two years to the date of the gift or inheritance (or for the entire period of ownership if it has been owned for less than two years) is an excepted asset and the value of the asset will not qualify for relief. Any asset used at any time during the period of ownership for the personal benefit of a company director will also be an excepted asset.
2. **Excluded Property** Where the relevant business property consists of shares in a company, the value of such shares qualifying for business relief will be reduced in respect of the value of any business or interest in a business which has been owned for less than five years before the date of the gift or inheritance. This rule is relaxed to two years in the case of an inheritance arising on the death of the disponer.

9.4.9 Withdrawal of Relief: Clawback Event within Six Years

Where relief has been claimed but the qualifying property ceases to be qualifying business property or is sold within six years of the valuation date, then the relief originally granted is withdrawn.

Example 9.7
An unincorporated hotel business is inherited. The beneficiary decides he does not wish to operate it and rents the hotel to a third-party operator. This will result in a loss of business relief.

Example 9.8
Shares in a trading company are inherited and business relief is claimed. The beneficiary ceases the trading activity without selling the shares. This will result in a loss of business relief. The withdrawal takes effect by recalculating the CAT which would have been due at the time the beneficiary originally took the benefit on the basis that no business relief was available.

The clawback can be avoided if the property sold is, within one year, replaced by another qualifying business property. If there is not a full reinvestment of the sale proceeds within the one year, the original relief must be recalculated using similar principles as for agricultural relief (as discussed in the next section).

The clawback does not operate where the individual who originally claimed the relief gifts on the property or dies and leaves an inheritance of the property to another recipient.

If development land, which has qualified for business relief, is disposed of in the period commencing six years after the date of the gift or inheritance and ending 10 years after that date, business relief granted will be clawed back in relation to the development value of the land at the original date of the gift or inheritance, i.e. the original valuation date.

"Development land" is defined as meaning "land in the State, the market value of which at the date of a gift or inheritance exceeds the current use value of that land at that date, and includes shares deriving their value in whole or in part from such land".

The current use value in relation to land at a particular time is defined as meaning:

"the amount which would be the market value of the land at that time if the market value were calculated on the assumption that it was at that time and would remain unlawful to carry out any development in relation to the land other than development of a minor nature."

9.4.10 Agricultural Relief

Agricultural relief under section 89 CATCA 2003 is designed to reduce the impact of CAT on the passing of agricultural property from one generation to the next. Similar to business relief, agricultural relief takes the form of reducing the market value of qualifying agricultural property by 90%.

9.4.11 Conditions for Agricultural Relief

A number of conditions must be satisfied before agricultural relief is granted on the transfer of agricultural property. The conditions relate to the type of property and to the donee or successor.

In order for agricultural relief to apply, the following conditions must be satisfied:

- the land must be "agricultural property";
- the donee or successor must be a "farmer"; and
- the donee or successor must be an "active farmer".

Agricultural Property

Agricultural property is defined as:

1. agricultural land, pasture and woodland situated in the EU;
2. crops and trees growing on the land at 1. above;
3. farm buildings and the farm houses or mansion houses as are of a character appropriate to the property;
4. farm machinery, livestock and bloodstock on the land; or
5. a payment entitlement under the EU single farm payment scheme.

Land held in a company is not agricultural land for the purposes of agricultural relief. Therefore, a gift or inheritance of shares in a farming company will not attract agricultural relief. However, as discussed previously, such shares may attract business property relief.

"Farmer" Test

At the valuation date, at least 80% of the market value of the assets of the donee or the successor must be represented by agricultural property, as defined above. Five important points should be noted:

1. The test is applied at the valuation date. As the valuation date can be planned in most circumstances, planning opportunities may be available, i.e. take active planning measures to ensure that the recipient qualifies as a "farmer".
2. The 80% test is applied after receiving the property.
3. The test is applied to the gross value of assets. The gross value of the assets can be reduced by a loan that is secured on an off-farm dwelling. This loan must, however, be used for the purchase, improvement or repair of that house.
4. Anti-avoidance rules provide that the assets which must be included in the farmer test are extended to include:

   (a) the current value of a future interest in expectancy, e.g. a remainderman interest in an asset is taken into account for the purposes of the 80% test; or
   (b) the current value of the reversionary interest where the recipient, prior to taking a gift of farmland, transferred a nine-month limited interest in a private asset to a third party with a view to reducing non-agricultural assets; or
   (c) the full value of property in a discretionary trust where the individual trying to claim agricultural relief is the settlor of the trust and is also a possible beneficiary under the terms of the trust.

Example 9.9

A beneficiary is about to receive a gift of farmland worth €900,000. His only current asset is a home worth €400,000 (€100,000 mortgage outstanding). On receipt of the farmland, his total assets will amount to €1.2 million after deducting the mortgage from the value of the home. However, only 75% of his assets represent agricultural property and therefore he will not qualify for the 90% agricultural relief.

---

5. The farmer test is not applied to gifts/inheritances of standing timber. In other words, any person, regardless of the mix of assets held, is entitled to agricultural relief on growing trees. This exception does not apply to the land on which the trees are growing, and the recipient must qualify as a farmer for the value of the land on which the trees are growing to qualify for agricultural relief. Note, the "active farmer" test (see **Section 9.4.14**) is not applicable to forestry.

Example 9.10

George took an inheritance from his uncle on 1 October 2022. The inheritance comprised the following:

	€
Farmhouse	60,000
Farmland	200,000
Crops	20,000
Land on which timber is growing	50,000
Standing timber	20,000
Livestock	30,000
Farm machinery	20,000
Car	10,000
Cash	40,000
Total	**450,000**

Prior to the receipt of the inheritance, George owned the following assets:

		€
Dwelling house	(Note 1)	290,000
Car		5,000
Cash		5,000
Total		**300,000**

Note 1: the outstanding mortgage on the house at 1 October 2022 was €200,000.

The value of George's entire assets at 1 October 2022, after deducting the mortgage, is €550,000. If his agricultural property is valued at €440,000 (80%) or more, at that date, George would be deemed a farmer for agricultural relief. It is being assumed that George satisfies the "active farmer" test (see **Section 9.4.14**). His agricultural property is as follows:

	€
Farmhouse	60,000
Farmland	200,000
Crops	20,000
Land on which timber is growing	50,000
Standing timber	20,000
Livestock	30,000
Farm machinery	20,000
Total	**400,000**

As the value of the agricultural property owned by George at the valuation date was less than 80% of his gross assets, George is not a farmer for the purposes of agricultural relief. However, agricultural relief is available on the standing timber as the farmer test is not applicable to such property.

As George did not qualify as a "farmer" for agricultural relief purposes, the possibility of claiming business property relief should be investigated. However, a claim for this relief will only be possible if George carries on the farming business as a self-employed individual.

"Active Farmer" Test

The "active farmer" test also applies in establishing if agricultural relief is available. Where a gift or inheritance is taken on or after 1 January 2015, as well as the existing 80% asset test (i.e. the "farmer test"), the recipient must either:

1. farm the agricultural property for a period of not less than six years commencing from the valuation date; or
2. lease the agricultural property for a period of not less than six years commencing from the valuation date. (The agricultural property may be leased to a number of lessees, as long as each lessee satisfies the conditions of the relief.)

In addition, the beneficiary (or the lessee, where relevant) must either:

■ have an agricultural qualification, or achieve such a qualification within four years of the date of the gift/inheritance; or
■ farm the agricultural property for not less than 50% of their "normal working time".

"Normal working time" (including on-farm and off-farm working time) is considered by Revenue to approximate 40 hours per week. Therefore farmers will qualify for the relief provided they spend a minimum of 20 hours working per week, averaged over a year, on the farm. If a farmer can show that their "normal working time" is less than 40 hours a week, then the 50% requirement will be applied to the actual hours worked, subject to being able to show that the farm is farmed on a commercial basis and with a view to the realisation of profits.

Where an individual initially qualifies as an "active farmer" but ceases to qualify within the subsequent six-year period, any agricultural relief previously claimed will be clawed back. The clawback does not apply in the case of crops, trees or under-wood comprised in the gift or inheritance.

9.4.12 Liabilities/Consideration and Other Property

If an individual receives a gift or an inheritance of agricultural property subject to a liability, such as a bank loan or a liability to make a payment to the disponer or a third party, the deduction from the taxable value of the property for the liability or consideration paid must also be reduced by 90%. In addition, if the gift/inheritance comprises both agricultural and non-agricultural property, then the taxable value of each must be computed separately.

Example 9.11

Sean inherits the following assets from his cousin, Michael, in February 2022:

Market value	€
Agricultural land	360,000
Quoted shares	20,000
	380,000

The land is mortgaged for €25,000. Sean, in consideration of the inheritance of all the assets, has paid €20,000 to Michael's nephew, Jim. Sean's only asset is his private residence, which has a market value of €660,000 (mortgage outstanding €600,000). Legal fees and other costs of the inheritance of all the assets amount to €5,000 and are payable out of the estate. Sean has always had an interest in farming. He intends to leave his current job and work full time on the land.

Is Sean a farmer?

Yes – after taking Michael's inheritance, at least 80% of his gross assets comprise agricultural property, livestock, bloodstock and farm machinery.

Is Sean an active farmer?

Yes – Sean should be considered an "active farmer" on the basis that he intends spending all of his normal working time on the farm.

---

1. Computation of taxable value of agricultural property

	€
Market value	360,000
Deduct: agricultural relief @ 90%	(324,000)
"Agricultural value"	36,000

    Less: Liabilities, costs, etc.

    Portion applicable to agricultural property only:

$$€5,000 \times \frac{€360,000}{€380,000} = €4,737$$

Restriction for agricultural value:

€4,737 @ 10%	(474)
Mortgage of €25,000 relates to agricultural property – allowable portion = €25,000 @ 10%	(2,500)
	33,026

Incumbrance-free value:

    Less: Consideration (relates to total property)
    Portion applicable to agricultural property

$$€20,000 \times \frac{€360,000}{€380,000} = €18,947$$

Allowable portion = €18,947 @ 10%	(1,895)
Total value of agricultural property	31,131

2   Computation of taxable value of non-agricultural property

	€
Market value	20,000
Less: Liabilities, costs, etc.	
Legal (balance €5,000 – €4,737)	(263)
Incumbrance-free value	19,737
Less: Consideration:	
Balance €20,000 – €18,947	(1,053)
Taxable value of non-agricultural property	18,684

Total taxable value is €49,815 (€31,131 + €18,684) subject to Group C threshold of €16,250 as the inheritance is taken from his cousin.

9.4.13 Conditional Investment in Agricultural Property

A gift or inheritance of any property will qualify for agricultural relief (provided the beneficiary is a qualifying farmer) if it is given with the express condition, stated in a will or deed, that the gift or inheritance will be invested in agricultural property. Such a benefit will be deemed to have consisted of agricultural property both at the date of the gift or inheritance and at the valuation date if the investment in agricultural property takes place within two years of the date of the gift or inheritance.

9.4.14 Clawback of Agricultural Relief

If property that has qualified for agricultural relief is disposed of or compulsorily acquired within six years of the date of the gift or inheritance, there may be a clawback of relief.

Where a gift or inheritance is taken on or after 1 January 2015, the "active farmer" test provisions must be considered. In such instances, there are separate clawback provisions to be considered.

Agricultural relief is clawed back if:

- any element of the agricultural property is not farmed by an active farmer, or by a lessee who is an active farmer, for at least 50% of the person's normal working time; or
- is not farmed on a commercial basis throughout the six-year qualifying period from the valuation date or, if earlier, the date the activity started.

Where the relief was originally granted because the beneficiary had a relevant farming qualification, a clawback of relief occurs where the agricultural property is not farmed on a commercial basis throughout the six-year qualifying period.

Agricultural relief is clawed back where there is a disposal or compulsory acquisition of the agricultural property (with the exception of crops, trees and underwood) within six years of the date of the gift or inheritance. This can be avoided if the proceeds of the disposal or compulsory acquisition are reinvested in other agricultural property within one year of the sale or within six years of the compulsory purchase.

Where the proceeds of disposal are not reinvested and a clawback arises, the extent of the clawback depends on the amount of the proceeds that are not reinvested. If the full proceeds are reinvested there is no clawback of relief. However, if only parts of the proceeds are reinvested there is a partial clawback of relief.

If development land, which has qualified for agricultural relief, is disposed of in the period commencing six years after the date of the gift of inheritance and ending 10 years after that date, the agricultural relief granted will be clawed back in relation to the development value of the land at the original date of the gift or inheritance, i.e. re-compute the value of the gift as at the original valuation date.

Example 9.12

An inheritance of land is taken from a parent in November 2022.

	€
Open market value of land in November 2022	3,000,000
Current use value of land in November 2022	650,000

Computation of CAT payable:

	€
Open market value of land	3,000,000
Agricultural relief @ 90%	(2,700,000)
Value after agricultural relief	300,000
Group threshold	(335,000)
Taxable value	NIL

Daughter sells land in December 2028 for €9,000,000.

	€
Recalculation of November 2022 liability	
Open market value of land	3,000,000
Agricultural relief (restricted to 90% of €650,000*)	(585,000)
Value after agricultural relief	2,415,000
Deduct: Group A tax-free threshold	(335,000)
Taxable value	2,080,000
CAT payable @ 33%	686,400

* If the disposal is after six years but before the end of the 10th year, agricultural relief is still available but only in respect of the agricultural value (i.e. the current use value) and not the development value.

9.4.15 Agricultural Relief Planning Points

There are significant planning opportunities associated with agricultural relief both in terms of ensuring that the relief applies and in avoiding a clawback of agricultural relief on disposal.

Obtaining agricultural relief:

1. If a beneficiary inherits a mixture of assets, comprising qualifying agricultural property and non-qualifying property, the latter may mean that the beneficiary is not able to satisfy the 80% test. There is likely to be a time gap between the date of death and the valuation date for CAT purposes. If so, this may allow time for the beneficiary to alter the mix of his/her assets so that, when the valuation date arises, they will be able to satisfy the 80% test. This may be achieved in a number of ways, all to be effected before the valuation date:
    - Sell non-agricultural property and invest proceeds in agricultural property.
    - Dispose of non-agricultural property by way of a gift to spouse or civil partner as no CAT, CGT or stamp duty will arise.
    - Purchase additional agricultural property with surplus cash.
    - Purchase livestock on a short-term basis. The livestock could be sold immediately after the valuation date with no adverse tax consequences for the relief claimed.
2. Where the existing level of non-agricultural property is such that it would not be possible to meet the 80% test, arrange to take a gift or inheritance of standing timber, as the 80% test does not apply to standing timber.
3. In the case of an inheritance, consider arranging the will to establish a discretionary trust into which the estate of the deceased will be transferred on his/her death. This would allow the trustees to appoint agricultural property to the beneficiaries before appointing non-agricultural property (see **Chapter 11**).
4. Where the disponer does not own agricultural property, make the gift or inheritance subject to investment in agricultural property within two years of the date of the gift or inheritance. It may be necessary to use the planning techniques outlined above to ensure that the 80% test is met in taking such a conditional gift or inheritance.

All of the above considerations are subject to the claimant being able to demonstrate that they are an "active farmer".

9.4.16 Filing of Returns

When business relief or agricultural relief are claimed, a CAT return will have to be filed with Revenue. The return must be filed by the person in receipt of the gift or inheritance and claiming the relevant relief.

9.4.17 Distinctions between Agricultural Relief and Business Relief

The distinctions between agricultural relief and business relief are as follows:

1. Agricultural relief applies to a farmhouse transferred with a farm. However, a residence transferred with a business does not qualify for business relief. For example, a pub may be a qualifying business asset for the purposes of business relief, but an apartment or living quarters upstairs in the pub will not qualify for the relief.
2. There is no minimum period of ownership for agricultural relief, while there is a minimum ownership test for business relief, i.e. a two-year period in the case of inheritances or five years in the case of gifts.
3. Non-agricultural assets can be used to purchase agricultural assets to plan for the farmer test. There is no such provision for business relief unless the minimum two-year/five-year periods of ownership are satisfied.

4. Unsecured liabilities are apportioned *pro rata* between agricultural and non-agricultural assets, as outlined in the example in **Section 9.4.14**. However, for business relief only liabilities applicable to the business are deductible from the business assets and all other liabilities are deductible from the non-business assets.
5. A beneficiary does not have the option of claiming either agricultural or business relief. If the beneficiary qualifies for agricultural relief, then agricultural relief must be claimed. It is only in the event of a failure to qualify for agricultural relief that business relief can be claimed on agricultural property.
6. In order to avoid a clawback of business relief, the business property must be retained in ownership for at least six years and used for the purposes of carrying on a business. In the case of agricultural relief, a clawback is avoided if that the qualifying "farmer" retains ownership of the property for at least six years (or 10 years in the case of development land), and continues to qualify as an "active farmer" for six years.

9.5   Young Trained Farmer Relief

The young trained farmer relief (YTFR) provides for a full exemption from stamp duty on transfers of farmland and buildings to qualifying young trained farmers. The relief is available until 31 December 2022. To be eligible for this relief, the farmer must be under the age of 35 on the date of the deed of transfer and must have attained one of the necessary agricultural qualifications within a four-year period from the date of the transfer. The young trained farmer must also, for a period of five years from the date on which a repayment claim is made:

■ retain ownership of the land transferred; and
■ spend not less than 50% of their normal working time farming this land.

Generally, the YTFR is claimed at the time of the transfer of a farm. However, a transferee may claim a refund of stamp duty already paid if they failed to claim YTFR when making the return. Such a claim must be made within four years of the date on which the deed of transfer was stamped. A transferee may also claim a refund of stamp duty already paid where they did not hold the relevant agricultural qualification on the date on which the deed of transfer was executed but obtains the qualification within four years of this date.

The YTFR is clawed back if the land is disposed of within a five-year period of:

■ the date on which the deed of transfer was executed, or
■ in the case of the delayed achievement of the relevant agricultural qualification, the date on which the claim for a refund was made, and is not replaced by other land within 12 months of the date of disposal.

9.5.1   Restrictions to the YTFR

The YTFR is restricted to micro- and small enterprises. A micro-enterprise is an enterprise that has fewer than 10 employees, with an annual turnover and/or balance sheet total of not more than €2 million; a small enterprise has fewer than 50 employees and an annual turnover and/or balance sheet total that does not exceed €10 million.

A cumulative lifetime cap of €70,000 also applies to the amount of tax relief that can be availed of by a farmer under the YTFR (for stamp duty) and under the stock relief for young trained farmers and the succession farm partnerships tax credit (both of which are income tax measures).

For the purposes of the calculation of the lifetime cap of €70,000, the value of YTFR is 7.5% of the consideration or the value of the land transferred. However, this amount is reduced where the transfer also qualifies for consanguinity relief (see **Section 9.6.1**). In relation to stock relief, the value of tax relief is the reduction in income tax payable as a result of the allowable expense deduction. In relation to a succession farm partnership, the value of the tax reliefs is the tax credit allowed. The values of all three tax reliefs must be aggregated on claims since 1 July 2014. Where the €70,000 ceiling is exceeded, the restriction on relief is applied on a self-assessment basis as part of the filing of a tax return (whether stamp duty or income tax) to whichever of the reliefs brings the aggregate YTFR and income tax reliefs above the ceiling.

9.6 Stamp Duty Issues on the Transfer of a Family Business

The transfer of assets such as goodwill and property will give rise to stamp duty. Stamp duty only applies to transactions involving the execution of written documents; it does not apply to transactions executed by delivery or oral agreements. However, in order to be legally binding, all conveyances and transfers of land and buildings must be in writing and are, therefore, subject to stamp duty. Land and goodwill will, in general, be the most valuable assets passing with a business and, therefore, will attract significant stamp duty liabilities.

Transfers between married couples and civil partners are completely exempt from stamp duty and as such do not qualify for consanguinity relief.

9.6.1 Transfers of Farmland between Relations (Consanguinity Relief)

Consanguinity relief applies to transfers between close relatives of **farmland only**, subject to certain conditions. Farmland includes buildings on farmland used for farming purposes, but not to a farmhouse as this is considered a residential property. The relief applies to transfers by way of sale or gift.

A fixed 1% rate of stamp duty applies to instruments executed on or after 25 December 2017, subject to the conditions:

1. The individual to whom the land is transferred/conveyed must either:
   (a) farm the land for a period of not less than six years, or else
   (b) lease it for a period of not less than six years to someone who farms the land.
2. The person who farms the land must:
   (a) be the holder of (or, within a period of four years from the date of the conveyance or transfer, become the holder of) a qualification as set out in legislation (i.e. third level qualification in agricultural related topics, veterinary, farm management, etc.); or
   (b) spend not less than 50% of the individual's normal working time farming land (including the land conveyed or transferred).
3. Where the land is leased, the person to whom the land is leased must:
   (a) be the holder of, or within a period of four years from the date of the conveyance or transfer become the holder of a qualification as set out in legislation; or
   (b) spend not less than 50% of the individual's normal working time farming land (including the land conveyed or transferred).

Revenue allows the relief where the land is leased to a partnership or to a company whose main shareholder and working director farms the land on behalf of the company, and to a company that is owned equally by an individual and that individual's spouse or civil partner, and at least one of them satisfies the working director and the farming requirements.

Where the person who farms the land or the person to whom the land is leased is not the holder of a qualification as prescribed under stamp duty legislation at the date of the conveyance or transfer but is going to become the holder of such a qualification within a period of four years from that date, the relief may be claimed on the stamp duty return. However, if that person does not become the holder of a qualification within a period of four years from the date of the conveyance or transfer, the relief no longer applies and interest is due from the date of the conveyance or transfer.

As with the YTFR, consanguinity relief may also be claimed as a refund of stamp duty already paid where the claimant did not hold the relevant qualifications at the time that stamp duty was originally paid, subject to conditions 2 and 3 above being met.

Revenue accepts for the purpose of the relief that "normal working time", including on-farm and off-farm working time, approximates to 40 hours per week. This enables farmers with off-farm employment to qualify for the relief provided they spend a minimum average of 20 hours per week working on the farm. Where the individual can show that his or her normal working time is somewhat less than 40 hours a week, then the 50% requirement will be applied to the actual hours worked, subject to the overriding requirement that the land is farmed on a commercial basis and with a view to the realisation of profits.

For the purposes of consanguinity relief, related persons are:

- lineal descendants (child, grandchild, etc.)
- parent/s
- grandparent/s
- step-parent/s
- uncle, aunt, brother or sister
- lineal descendent of a parent (step-brother or step- sister)
- lineal descendent of a husband (step-child)
- lineal descendent of a wife (step-child)
- lineal descendent of a brother (nephew or niece)
- lineal descendent of a sister (nephew or niece).

9.6.2 Interaction of Consanguinity Relief and Young Trained Farmer Relief

As noted in **Section 9.5.1**, there is a lifetime limit of €70,000 that can be claimed under the YTFR, stock relief and the succession farm partnership tax credit. The YTFR element is valued at 7.5% of the consideration/value of the land transferred but this can be reduced if the transferee also qualifies for consanguinity relief. The consanguinity relief is applied before the YTFR.

Example 9.13

In January 2022, a young trained farmer receives a gift of farmland valued at €1 million from his father. Both consanguinity relief and YTFR apply.

Applying consanguinity relief first, the stamp duty liability would be €10,000 (€1 million @ 1%). The full exemption provided by YTFR then reduces the stamp duty liability to nil, the YTFR claim being for €10,000.

Without consanguinity relief, the YTFR claim would have been for €70,000 (€75,000 capped at €70,000).

9.7 CGT/CAT Offset

Under section 104 CATCA 2003, where the same event gives rise to CGT and CAT, then CGT paid may be credited against any CAT due. It is important to ensure that it is the same event which gives rise to the charge to both taxes. The CGT credit will cease to apply if the asset is disposed of within two years after the date of the gift or inheritance. As both CGT and CAT are currently charged at the rate of 33%, this can be a very valuable relief which, if properly utilised, can effectively eliminate a charge to CAT.

The offset of CGT against CAT arising on the same transaction will likely be used in cases where retirement relief or business relief/agricultural relief is not available, such as on the gift of investment assets from parent to child. Section 104 is also used on the transfer of assets out of a trust where a CGT and CAT liability is triggered on the same event. This is discussed in detail in **Chapter 11**.

The relief operates by allowing for an offset of the CGT paid by the disponer against the CAT liability arising on the recipient where both taxes are triggered on the same event. Therefore, CGT must always be paid while the CAT liability may be sheltered up to the amount of the CGT paid. If the CGT exceeds the CAT liability, no CAT will be payable but there is no refund of the excess CGT.

Example 9.14

Emily took a gift of shares from her cousin, Anne, on 1 September 2022. Anne had already given Emily a €3,000 cash gift on 1 July 2022. Anne had purchased the shares on 1 February 1983 for €15,000 and the shares were worth €190,000 on 1 September 2022.

	€
CGT payable by Anne	
Proceeds	190,000
Cost €15,000 @ 2.253	(33,795)
Gain	156,205
Annual exemption	(1,270)
	154,935
CGT @ 33%	51,129
Gift tax payable by Emily	
Market value of gift (€3,000 exemption already used)	190,000
Threshold amount (Group C)	(16,250)
	173,750
€173,750 @ 33%	57,338
Deduct: CGT "same event" credit	(51,129)
Net gift tax payable	6,209

Anne must pay the CGT of €51,129, while Emily must pay the CAT of €6,209. Emily's base cost for CGT purposes in respect of any subsequent disposal of the shares is €190,000. The credit for the CGT will be clawed back if Emily disposes of the shares before 1 September 2024.

If the CGT liability had been, say, €60,000, Anne would have paid the full amount of CGT and Emily would have had to pay no CAT as the CGT on the same event was greater. However, there would be no refund of the excess capital gains tax that was not utilised for credit.

If Anne had first sold the shares and subsequently given proceeds to Emily, then no "same event transaction" would have taken place and no "same event" credit would have been available.

Stamp duty at 1% per share will also arise on the acquisition of the shares by Emily, provided the shares do not derive value from non-residential land or property in the state (in which case the 7.5% rate applies). Stamp duty payable by Emily is deductible in calculating her CAT liability.

The order of the gifts transferred can have an affect on the efficiencies of the CGT credit against CAT. Where possible, gifts should be structured to ensure that assets with low CGT liabilities or cash are gifted first to the recipient, followed by gifts which give rise to a large CGT liability. The assets with the low gain will use up part or all of the CAT tax-free group threshold, thus maximising the CAT arising on the later gift carrying the large CGT credit.

Example 9.15
A father wishes to gift his daughter a cash gift of €250,000 and an investment property worth €600,000. The CGT exposure on transfer of the investment property is assumed at €130,000. Assume the small gift exemption is already utilised.

Situation 1 – Father gifts property first and cash at a later date
Stamp duty on the transfer of the property is €600,000 × 7.5% = €45,000. If the daughter discharges this liability a deduction for it can be made against her CAT liability.

		€
CGT on gift of property payable by father	(a)	130,000
Daughter's CAT liability: Value of property		600,000
Less: stamp duty liability	(b)	(45,000)
Less: Group A Threshold		(335,000)
Taxable		220,000
Tax @ 33%		72,600
Less: CGT credit (max.)		(72,600)
CAT payable	(c)	0
Father later gifts cash of €250,000 – CGT	(d)	0
Daughter pays 33% CAT (threshold fully utilised)	(e)	82,500
Total taxes (a + b + c + d + e)		**257,500**

Situation 2 – Reverse order of gifts (i.e. cash first and property at a later date)

		€
CGT on gift of €250,000 cash	(a)	**0**
CAT on gift of cash	(b)	**0**
CGT on subsequent gift of property	(c)	130,000
Stamp duty on gift of property	(d)	45,000
CAT on gift of property		600,000
Less: stamp duty		(45,000)
Previous gift of cash		250,000
		805,000
Less: Group A threshold		(335,000)
Taxable		470,000
CAT @ 33%		155,100
Less: CGT same event credit		(130,000)
CAT payable	(e)	25,100
Total taxes (a + b + c + d + e)		**200,100**
Total saving over Situation 1		**57,400**

9.7.1 Negligible Value Claim

In general, CGT loss relief is only available when an asset has been disposed of and the loss has been realised. However, section 538 TCA 1997 provides that the owner of an asset which has become negligible in value may make a claim to have the 'paper' loss treated as realised for CGT purposes. If the Inspector is satisfied that the asset is of negligible value, the asset will be deemed to have been sold for a negligible amount and immediately reacquired for its market value. This has the impact of creating a loss available for use and the asset having a rebased cost of nil (in the event of a future disposal).

The deemed sale of an asset results in the creation of an allowable loss, which may be utilised in the year of assessment in which the claim was submitted. Any excess loss may be carried forward and utilised in subsequent periods. Revenue's *Tax and Duty Manual*, Part 19-01-09, provides guidance on Revenue's position with regard to negligible value. The following is an extract from the manual in relation to Anglo Irish Bank.

"Where, resulting from the provisions of the Anglo Irish Bank Corporation Act 2009, shares in Anglo Irish Bank are transferred to the Minister for Finance, there will be a disposal to which Section 538 TCA 1997 applies. Where a claim is made, the shares will be treated as of negligible value and a loss for 2009 may be calculated. If it later transpires that compensation is received, under the terms of the Act, in respect of the transferred shares, this will be treated, under section 535 TCA 1997, as consideration for a disposal at time of receipt. In such a case, if a negligible value claim was made earlier, there will be no base cost and any chargeable gain arising shall be computed accordingly."

In the event that the asset recovers value in future years and is disposed of, the base cost at the date of disposal will be negligible. This has the effect of ensuring that any chargeable gain arising on the disposal will be preserved and the appropriate amount of tax will be paid.

Example 9.16

Joe Murphy purchased 1,000 shares in Hope Limited in 2007 at a cost of €150,000. Revenue accepts that the shares now have a value of 5 cent each and have become negligible in value. A claim has been accepted under section 538 TCA 1997 in the 2022 tax year.

Joe will be deemed to have disposed of the 1,000 shares and to have reacquired them for €50 (1,000 × 0.05). The position for 2022 is:

	€
Deemed sales proceeds	50
Less: Cost of acquisition	(150,000)
Allowable loss	(149,950)

If the shares subsequently recover in value and are disposed of at a future date, the allowable base cost will be €50.

9.8   Other Useful Capital Tax Reliefs and Exemptions

The capital tax reliefs reviewed above centre around tax-efficient retirement and succession planning both within and outside the family. There are other capital tax reliefs which aid tax efficiencies in their own right, which we will now review.

9.8.1   Favourite Nephew/Niece Relief

Under paragraph 7 of Part One Second Schedule CATCA 2003, a nephew or niece may be deemed to be the child of a disponer and therefore qualify for the CAT Group A tax-free threshold of €335,000 rather than the Group B tax-free threshold of €32,500. The circumstances in which the relief is available are:

1. The nephew/niece, who is a child of a brother or sister of the disponer, or a child of the civil partner of the disponer's brother or sister, has worked substantially on a full-time basis for the period of five years

ending on the date of the disposal of the disposer's beneficial interest in the business, in carrying on, or assisting in the carrying on, of the trade, business, profession or employment of the disposer, and

2. the gift/inheritance consists of:

   (a) property which was used in connection with such trade, business, profession or employment, carried on by the disposer, i.e. the relief only applies to assets used directly in carrying on the business, or

   (b) shares in a trading/professional company owning such property which is under the control of the disposer and of which he is a director.

The question of whether the nephew/niece has worked "substantially on a full-time basis for five years in carrying on the trade, etc." is a question of fact which has to be established in each case. In practice, the individual's record of employment in the previous five years is looked at closely, and effectively the burden of proof rests with the nephew or niece to show that he/she comes within the relieving provision. The two tests are to be applied as follows:

1. the recipient must have worked for more than 24 hours a week for the disponer, or the company in which the disponer held shares, at a place where the business, trade or profession of the disponer or his company was carried on; or

2. the recipient must have worked for more than 15 hours a week for the disponer or the company in which the disponer held shares, at a place where the business of the disponer or the company was carried on provided such business was carried on exclusively by the disponer, his/her spouse or civil partner and the recipient.

This treatment also applies to gifts and inheritances taken by a nephew or niece on the expiration of a limited interest in a trust created by the disponer, but it will not apply to limited interests taken under a discretionary trust. (See **Chapter 11** for further discussion on trusts.)

Example 9.17

An uncle dies and leaves his wife a life interest in the business with remainder to his nephew who has worked on a full-time basis for the business for six years prior to his uncle's death.

On the death of the wife, the nephew (who is the remainderman) will take the business, subject to the benefit of this relief as it is not a discretionary trust. If, on the other hand, the trust that was established on death was a discretionary trust and the business was subsequently appointed to the nephew, then the relief would not be available.

9.8.2 Surviving Child of a Deceased Child

The parent to child threshold of €335,000 also applies to the minor child of a deceased child, i.e. the disponer's grandchild where the disponer's child is deceased.

9.8.3 Surviving Spouse Relief

Schedule 2 CATCA 2003 provides for a specialised CAT relief which permits the surviving spouse/civil partner of a deceased person to "stand in the shoes of the deceased person" and take on the group threshold that the deceased spouse/civil partner would have in relation to the disponer.

The relief applies where, at the date of the gift or inheritance, the donee/successor is the surviving spouse/civil partner of a deceased person who, at the time of his/her death, was of a closer blood relationship to the disponer than the donee/successor.

In these circumstances, for the purposes of computation of the liability, the donee/successor is deemed to have the same relationship to the disponer as the deceased spouse had at the time of death. This can result in the use of a more favourable tax-free threshold for the computation of any liability due.

Example 9.18

Jim dies and leaves €200.000 to his son-in-law, James. James' wife and Jim's daughter, Ann, had died some years previously. In these circumstances, James is deemed to stand in Ann's shoes, vis-àà-vis her blood relationship with her father and, accordingly, the €335,000 tax-free threshold applies. If this relief did not apply, James would be treated as a stranger and a threshold of only €16,250 would apply, resulting in a substantial CAT liability.

9.8.4 Payment of CAT by Surrender of Government Securities

Certain qualifying government securities may be surrendered at par in settlement of CAT liability arising on an inheritance. This provision does not apply to the payment of CAT on a gift or discretionary trust tax liabilities.

Certain government securities are issued on the basis that they will be accepted at par value in payment of an equivalent amount of CAT on an inheritance and interest thereon. The ability to surrender such securities at par effectively results in a discount to the person liable for the CAT.

The conditions that must be satisfied are as follows:

1. Where the liability is inheritance CAT on and in respect of property taken under the will or the intestacy of a deceased person, that person must have owned the Government stock for a continuous period of at least three months immediately prior to death.
2. If the CAT liability arises as a result of property taken "on a death" in any circumstances other than 1., then the stock must have formed part of the relevant property taken by the successor for a continuous period of three months immediately preceding the death. This would cover, for example, a benefit taken on a death from a trust, or by survivorship of property owned as joint tenants.

9.8.5 Transfer of a Site to a Child Relief

CGT Relief on a Disposal of a Site to a Child

A CGT relief is available under section 603A TCA 1997 where a parent or an individual's civil partner transfers land to a child, the spouse/civil partner of a child or a qualifying foster child to enable that child to build a principal private residence. A qualifying foster child is a child who was under the care of the individual making the disposal, and was maintained at the expense of the individual throughout a period of five years prior to the child reaching 18 years of age.

If the value of the land does not exceed €500,000, there will be no CGT payable by the parent on the transfer of the land not exceeding one acre, exclusive of the area on which the house is to be built, to the child. If the value of the land exceeds €500,000, no relief is available.

The purpose for which the land is transferred to the child must be to enable the child to construct a dwelling on the land which will be occupied by the child as their principal private residence. A child who receives such a transfer must construct a residence on the land and occupy it as their principal private residence for a period of three years if they are to avoid a clawback of the relief on a subsequent disposal. The property may not be disposed of by the child, other than to a spouse/civil partner of the child, within the three-year period from commencement of occupation of the principal private residence. If the child breaches the conditions of the relief, then the capital gain which was not charged on the parents or on the individual's civil partner on the original transfer of the land to the child will be deemed to accrue to the child at the time of disposal of the property.

If relief under section 603A is withdrawn from the child for breaching the conditions of the relief, then the relief can be claimed again on a second transfer of a qualifying site from a parent or an individual's civil partner to a child.

Example 9.19

Alison gifts a one-acre site worth €500,000 to her daughter, Chloe, for the purpose of building a principal private residence in October 2022. Chloe has not previously taken a gift from her parents. Planning permission for the site is not currently in place.

The transfer of the site has the following tax consequences:

1. CGT on Alison on the deemed disposal of the site.
2. CAT on Chloe on receiving a gift of the site.
3. Stamp duty on Chloe on taking a transfer of property.

Stamp duty of €37,500 (€500,000 × 7.5%) will arise on the transfer of the property to Chloe. CGT relief under section 603A is available to Alison and she will not pay any CGT.

CAT is payable on receipt of the gift, as follows:

	€
Market value of gift	500,000
Less: Group A threshold	(335,000)
	165,000
Less: small gift exemption	(3,000)
Less: stamp duty	(37,500)
Taxable gift	124,500
Taxed @ 33%	41,085

The net tax cost of the transfer is €41,085 CAT and €37,500 stamp duty payable by Chloe.

If at the time Alison gifted the site to Chloe a connected agreement to build a residential property on it was in place, the 1% stamp duty rate for residential property would have applied.

If Chloe meets the relevant conditions, as she is building a residential property on the site she may be entitled to a refund of 11/15ths of the stamp duty paid at the commercial property rate of 7.5%.

Note that the CGT relief only applies to a gift of a site as a charge to CGT and does not arise on a transfer by will, or any transfer "on a death".

Chapter 9 Summary

Purposes of reliefs for capital taxes

- Encourage the succession of family businesses/farms to the next generation
- Recognise that tax has already been paid on the development of a business, i.e. income tax/corporation tax
- Stimulate and encourage entrepreneurship

Key CGT relief	• Retirement relief – for individuals over 55 years disposal of shares/assets subject to a lifetime threshold of proceeds depending on the disponer's age and the relationship with the donee
	• Revised entrepreneur relief – reduced CGT rate of 10% on disposals of gains up to a lifetime limit of €1 million
	• CGT/CAT offset – if CGT and CAT both apply on the same transaction, CGT liability of the disponer can be offset against the CAT liability of the beneficiary

Key CAT reliefs	• Business relief – facilitates the tax-efficient transfer of a business or company under a gift/inheritance by reducing the value of relevant business property by 90%
	• Agricultural relief – 90% reduction in the market value of agricultural property for CAT, subject to financial farmer and active farmer tests. A farm may also qualify for business relief
	• Dwelling house relief – generally restricted to inheritance of property

| Key stamp duty reliefs | • Farmland transfers between relatives – subject to conditions, stamp duty arising on the transfer of farmland fixed rat 1%. |
| | • YTFR provides full exemption from stamp duty on transfers of farmland and buildings to qualifying young trained farmers |

Questions

Review Questions
(See Suggested Solutions to Review Questions at the end of this textbook.)

Question 9.1

Liquid Ltd is a trading company owned equally by Harry and Hilary Harper, who are aged 56 and 60 respectively. The Harpers are full-time working directors of Liquid Ltd for over 20 years. The assets of Liquid Ltd are as follows:

	€
Property	1,000,000 (cost €400,000 in 2006)
Creditors	120,000
Debtors	40,000
Cash	50,000
Stock	50,000
Plant and equipment	5,000 (cost €80,000 in 2004)
Goodwill	60,000 (no base cost)

Harry and Hilary would like to retire from the business. They have an interested buyer for the business and the property.

Requirement

You have been asked to advise Harry and Hilary on how to tax-efficiently extract funds out of the company.

Question 9.2

In October 2018 Tom gifts a farm worth €1 million to his cousin, Mary. Mary qualifies as a farmer and claims agricultural relief to reduce the taxable value by 90% to €100,000, which is her taxable benefit (subject to annual gift exemption of €3,000 and tax-free Group B threshold in place at the time).

In 2022 Mary sells the property for €1.6 million and reinvests €1 million in other agricultural property, which she actively farms.

Requirement
(a) Calculate the clawback.
(b) Outline the circumstances where the clawback would not occur.

Challenging Question
(Suggested Solutions to Challenging Questions are available through your lecturer.)

Question 9.1

It is November 2022. Your client, Dan Summers, is 56 years old. He has one daughter, Angela, who is 25 years old. Dan wishes to retire and gift his shares in his trading company, Sofa Ltd, to Angela along with the business premises and his 15% shareholding in Investments plc.

Dan originally set up Sofa Ltd as a sole trade in 1981. He then incorporated the business in 2012 and subscribed for 100 shares at €1,000 per share. He has owned 100% of the share capital and has worked full-time for the company since its incorporation. He was a full-time sole trader before incorporation in 2012. Dan did not claim relief under section 600 TCA 1997 on incorporation. The premises from which the business is run is owned personally by Dan. It is valued at €1 million and originally cost him €100,000 in 1981. The company has recently been valued at €6 million.

Dan bought shares in Investments plc, a company quoted on the Irish Stock Exchange, in December 1993 for €100. The shares have recently been valued at €150,000. He would like to gift these shares to Angela.

Angela previously took a gift of cash of €400,000 from her mother in 2000.

Requirement

Dan has asked you, as his Chartered Accountant, to provide tax advice on how he can tax-efficiently gift the shares in Sofa Ltd and Investments plc to Angela.

Impact of Estate Law on Tax Issues

Learning Objective

By the end of this chapter, you should be able to explain how estate law can impact on capital tax planning.

10.1 Introduction to Estate Law

An understanding of estate law is vital for the purposes of providing inheritance and gift tax advice. It would be a waste of the client's money and time if tax planning advice is provided that efficiently utilises tax reliefs and minimises tax arising on an estate but cannot be implemented because of some estate law difficulty, e.g. a spouse's legal right share to the estate is overlooked. We will, therefore, review the basic concepts of estate law and the rights afforded to a spouse and child under the Succession Act 1965 as a first step in the process of inheritance and gift tax planning.

10.1.1 Making a Will and Planning for Tax

Making a will is an essential part of planning for CAT purposes. By making a will an individual can, for example, make maximum use of the CAT thresholds available for his or her children and inter-spouse/civil partner tax exemptions.

If a person wishes his or her assets to be distributed in a certain way after his or her death, this can normally only be achieved by leaving a will. Where an individual dies leaving a valid will, they are said to have died testate; if a valid will has not been made they have died intestate. The term "estate" refers to the total of a person's property on his or her death.

10.2 Succession Act Rights

Succession law is concerned with the distribution of an individual's property on death. The 1965 Succession Act gives the spouse and children of a deceased person certain minimum rights to part of the deceased's estate depending on whether the deceased dies testate or intestate. The Civil Partnership and Certain Legal Rights and Obligations of Cohabitants Act 2010 amends the Succession Act 1965. The amendments provide for the rights of a surviving civil partner.

The following is a summary of rights in an estate provided for under the Succession Act 1965.

10.2.1 Individual Dies without Making a Valid Will

Where a person dies intestate, i.e. without making a valid will, the position is as outlined in the table below.

Individual leaves surviving:	Succession Act dictates:
A spouse/civil partner and no children.	Surviving spouse/civil partner is entitled to 100% of estate.
A spouse/civil partner and children.	The spouse/civil partner is entitled to two-thirds and the children are entitled to one-third divided equally among them.
Children only.	The children share the estate equally.
No spouse/civil partner or children.	Parents/parent share in the estate.
No spouse/civil partner or children or parents.	Equally divided between the brothers or sisters. The surviving children of any brothers or sisters who have already died take their parent's share equally.
No spouse/civil partner or children or parents or siblings.	Equally divided between the nephews and nieces.
None of the above.	Nearest blood relative.

10.2.2 Individual Dies Leaving a Valid Will

An individual may draft their will in any manner they want, but should bear in mind that the Succession Act gives certain minimum rights to the individual's spouse/civil partner and children in certain circumstances outlined in the table below.

Individual leaves surviving:	Minimum legal rights under a will
A spouse/civil partner and no children.	Spouse/civil partner is entitled to a minimum of half of the estate inclusive of the family home.
A spouse/civil partner and children.	Spouse/civil partner is entitled to a minimum of one-third of the estate inclusive of the family home.
	Children do not have a right to a specific percentage of their parent's estate under a will. Section 117 Succession Act 1965 gives a surviving child the right to apply to the courts for a share of their deceased parent's estate under a will on the grounds *that the parent has failed in his moral duty to make proper provision for the child in accordance with his means*. If the court agrees with the claim, then it may order that provision be made for the child out of the estate as the court thinks fit.
Children only.	Children do not have a right to a specific percentage of their parent's estate under a will. Section 117 Succession Act 1965 gives a surviving child the right to apply to the courts for a share of their deceased parent's estate under a will on the grounds *that the parent has failed in his moral duty to make proper provision for the child in accordance with his means*. If the court agrees with the claim, then it may order that provision be made for the child out of the estate as the court thinks fit.

It should be pointed out that the term "spouse" in all cases refers to a person recognised under the law as the spouse of the deceased at the date of death.

Succession rights must always be considered when providing tax advice on estate planning issues. Ensuring that succession rights and co-ownership rights are satisfied is the basis upon which tax advice and tax efficiencies can be developed. If succession rights are breached there is a danger that the associated tax planning will also be defunct.

Example 10.1

Seamus Quinn owns and runs a very successful business. The business is in his name and his daughter, Simone, works with him. Seamus is married to Dearbhla and they live in a house owned in joint names. Seamus goes about making his will in a tax-efficient manner. He decides to leave the business to Simone. His accountant advises Seamus how to structure the passing of the business to Simone so that she qualifies for business relief such that she will pay no tax on her eventual inheritance. Seamus provides in his will that Dearbhla should inherit his share of the house.

At the time of making the will and tax planning for the purpose of claiming business relief, the house has a value of €1 million and the business has a value of €5 million. Under the terms of the will, Dearbhla will receive only approximately 9% of her husband's estate inclusive of the family home (i.e. €500,000 of €5.5 million).

Problems arise when Seamus dies in 2022. Values in 2022 are in line with the values under which the original tax planning was carried out and Dearbhla inherits approximately 9% of Seamus's estate. She is very disappointed with this inheritance and seeks independent legal advice where she discovers that she is entitled to a minimum share of one-third of Seamus's estate including the family home. Dearbhla takes legal action and secures her legal share by taking a share in the business with Simone.

Impact on tax planning

Simone and her mother fight constantly on how best to run the business and within a year Simone sells some of the business assets to buy out her mother's share. A portion of business relief claimed by Simone on her share of the business is now clawed back as she has sold these assets within six years of claiming the relief, thereby breaking a key condition of the relief. Simone is very angry that her father was not advised of Dearbhla's legal right entitlement as she feels he would have structured his will differently. She takes legal action against her late father's professional advisors.

CAT planning for inheritance and gift purposes must always make sense from a tax law perspective and from a succession law perspective.

A basic knowledge of the succession rights of children and a spouse is imperative for anyone offering professional tax advice on estate planning issues and the advisor should actively ensure that all succession law requirements are satisfied before putting the tax plan in place.

10.3 Property Held in Joint Names

Property can be jointly owned as tenants in common or as joint tenants. It is important to distinguish between the two types of ownership, as the death of one owner has very different consequences depending on which type of ownership structure is in place.

10.3.1 Joint Tenants

Where property is co-owned as joint tenants, in the event of the death of one co-owner, the surviving co-owner automatically becomes entitled to the full legal and beneficial ownership of the asset. An asset held in a joint tenancy does not form part of the estate of the deceased as the share passes automatically to the surviving co-owner.

Example 10.2

Background Ken co-owns investment property with his brother, Daniel. Ken does not understand the difference between a joint tenancy and a tenants in common co-ownership arrangement, and assumes that he is free to deal with his property in whatever way he chooses in his will. Ken therefore lists his share of the property as an asset he would like his son to inherit under the terms of his will. Ken's professional advisors do not ask Ken to confirm what type of co- ownership structure is in place and draft the will as per Ken's instructions.

Problems arise when Ken dies and his share of the co-owned property is named as an asset passing to his son. At that stage, Daniel comes forward with a copy of the co-ownership agreement, which clearly states that a joint tenancy exists.

Impact on Estate Planning Ken's share in the property should never have been included in his will as an asset passing to his son and Daniel exercises his automatic inheritance rights to his late brother's share. Ken's son is very annoyed that his father's advisors did not consider what kind of ownership structure was in place, and feels that his father would have provided other assets in place of the share in the investment property, if he had been properly advised. Ken's son takes legal action against his father's advisors on the grounds of negligence.

Section 13(1) CATCA 2003 provides that, on the death of a joint tenant, the remaining joint tenant is deemed to take an inheritance from the deceased joint tenant.

In the above example, on Ken's death, Daniel succeeds to his brother's share and is deemed to take an inheritance from Ken. A Group B threshold is therefore used in the calculation of CAT arising on this inheritance.

10.3.2 Tenants in Common

Tenants in common arise where each owner's share of the asset is separate and distinct from the other's share. The separate and distinct share will form part of the estate on the death of the joint owner, and does not pass automatically to the other joint owner. Property and assets will normally be held as tenants in common where the parties involved are not married and/or where each has contributed separately to the capital invested in or cost of acquiring the asset. In general, each will be a tenant in common to the extent to which they have contributed to the funds to acquire the asset.

Example 10.3

Mr Murphy and Mr Smith purchased an investment property in Dublin. They own the property equally as tenants in common. Mr Murphy recently died unexpectedly. The interest previously owned by Mr Murphy is distinct from that of Mr Smith's. Mr Murphy's interest will form part of his estate and will be allocated in accordance with the terms ofthis will or in accordance with the Succession Act. Mr Smith"s interest in the property will not be affected by the death of Mr Murphy.

10.4   Disclaimers of Benefits

Section 12 CATCA 2003 deals with the effect and consequences of disclaimers of benefits. The section **only applies where the person who disclaims a benefit does not name another person who is to benefit**. Where there is a pure disclaimer the general rules of law (Succession Act 1965) establish who is to benefit. The following points should be remembered:

- Where a person disclaims a benefit they no longer have a liability to CAT in respect of that benefit.
- A disclaimer is not itself a disposition for CAT purposes.
- A person can disclaim for consideration. Any consideration is a benefit moving from the original disponer to the person disclaiming (i.e. a substituted gift or inheritance).
- A **disclaimer in favour of a named person** is considered as an **acquisition and a subsequent disposal** and therefore there is a **double charge to CAT**.

- ▦ A disclaimed legacy falls into the residue. If a residuary legatee disclaims, the residue is distributed as if there was an intestacy as regards the residue.
- ▦ A person cannot partially disclaim the residue or partially disclaim a share of the residue.
- ▦ If a life interest or other limited interest is disclaimed the remainder interest falls in immediately.

Example 10.4

John dies testate on 10 January 2022. He leaves a pecuniary legacy of €60,000 to his brother, Michael, and the residue of his estate to his daughter, Mary. Michael, who is financially well-off, decides to disclaim the legacy to him of €60,000. The legacy falls into the residue of the estate and as such is inherited by Mary. Michael has no liability to CAT as he has disclaimed the benefit to him.

Mary has inherited the entire estate from her father, John, and has taken no benefit from Michael.

Example 10.5

Maureen, a widow, dies testate in March 2022 and leaves the residue of her estate equally to her three children, Noel, John and Mary. Noel, who is living abroad, disclaims his one-third share of the residue under the will, which one-third share then passes equally to the three children as to a one-ninth share each. If Noel also disclaims his one-ninth share of the residue, this one-ninth share then passes equally to John and Mary, who each end up inheriting a half-share of the estate from Maureen.

Example 10.6

Paula inherits a house under her Aunt Nora's will, but disclaims the inheritance of the house in favour of her brother, Tom. As it is not possible to disclaim a benefit in favour of somebody else, this is an inheritance taken by Paula from Nora and then a separate gift of the house by Paula to Tom. Separate claims for CAT on both the inheritance and the gift accordingly arise in this situation.

Example 10.7

Patrick dies and leaves his farm, valued at €350,000, to his son, Robert, and the residue of his estate to his daughter Sheila. Robert, who has no interest in farming, decides to disclaim the bequest of the farm to him in consideration of a payment to him of €250,000 from the estate.

Robert is treated as taking an inheritance of €250,000 from his father, Patrick. Sheila is treated as taking an inheritance from her father, Patrick, of the farm and the residue of the estate, less the €250,000 passing to Robert.

Chapter 10 Summary

Relevance of Succession Act 1965 on tax planning

- Surviving spouse's share of family assets under the Succession Act 1965 must be properly considered – tax planning will be invalid otherwise

Disclaimer of benefits

- No person can be compelled to take an inheritance and a disclaimer is the refusal of an inheritance
- A disclaimer will follow the rules of succession
- Ensure disclaimer will have the desired effect both from a legal and a tax perspective before a deed of disclaimer is executed
- In the case of a pure disclaimer, no CAT will apply to the beneficiary making the disclaimer

Questions

Challenging Question
(Suggested Solutions to Challenging Questions are available through your lecturer.)

Question 10.1

Noel O'Mara has a complicated family life. He is married to Bridget and they have two sons. Noel also has a daughter named Emma, aged 18, from an extra-marital relationship. Bridget does not know about Emma, and Noel wants to keep it that way. Noel has paid modest maintenance for Emma over the years and only sees her on the odd occasion. He now wants to get his affairs in order and provide for his wife and children in the event of his death, but he also wants to protect Bridget from finding out about Emma.

Noel's assets are as follows:

	€
Commercial property recently purchased worth (November 2022)	1,000,000
Property in Spain valued at	2,000,000
Family home valued at	1,500,000
Portfolio of shares and investments	500,000
Total net worth	5,000,000

Requirement
You are Noel's accountant. He asks you for advice on how he should structure his affairs in a tax-efficient manner to provide for each of his children and keep Bridget from finding out about Emma.

Trust and Estate Planning

Learning Objectives

By the end of this chapter, you should have an understanding of trust law for capital tax purposes and be able to:

■ Provide tax advice on:
  ● the application of 6% and 1% charges on trusts;
  ● tax anti-avoidance provisions relating to trusts;
  ● the territoriality provisions of trusts; and
  ● the use of tax exemptions under a trust.

11.1 Introduction to Trusts

The role of a trust is often multi-faceted and has numerous diverse uses, including the control of assets and wealth, the protection of children and incapacitated persons, and complex tax planning structures.

Trust law in Ireland dates back to the Trustee Act 1893, and has more or less remained unchanged since then. Tax law relating to trusts, however, has been updated regularly and, as a result, there are wide-ranging tax consequences to transferring assets to a trust, on running the trust and on the eventual extraction of income and capital out of a trust.

11.1.1 What is a Trust?

A trust is a relationship that exists between the settlor (who transfers assets to the trust) and the trustee for the benefit of the beneficiaries of the trust. The core obligation of a trustee is to act in a fiduciary capacity for the benefit of the beneficiaries.

The specific legal terminology associated with trusts is as follows:

■ **Settlor** The person who transfers assets into a trust is referred to as the settlor. This individual is treated as the source of any benefits received by beneficiaries from the trust.
■ **Trustee** A trustee is an individual appointed by the settlor to ensure that the terms of the trust are carried out. Two trustees are normally appointed, one of whom is usually a professional trustee, such as a solicitor, an accountant or a banker (generally chosen for their impartiality); the other is usually a trusted personal friend or relative of the settlor.
■ **Beneficiary** A beneficiary is an individual who is, or may be, entitled to a benefit under the trust.
■ **Absolute ownership interest** If an individual holds an absolute interest in any property, he is free to deal in that property in any way he wishes.

▪ **Limited interest** A limited interest is effectively the opposite of an absolute interest. There are different types of limited interest, summarised as follows:

- ● **Life interest** An individual holds a life interest in a property if he has the use of the property for the duration of his life. For example, an individual may hold a life interest in a house. He can either live in the house or let it, but he cannot sell it.
- ● **Interest for period certain** If a person holds an interest in property for a fixed period of time, e.g. for 10 years, he is said to hold an interest for a period certain.
- ● **Remainder interest** Refers to the person who is entitled to the absolute interest in property after all limited interests have expired holds the remainder interest and is called the remainderman.

11.2 Types of Trust

There are a number of different types of trusts, which go by a variety of names. The following is an outline of the more common types used today for estate and tax planning purposes.

11.2.1 Simple or Bare Trusts

A simple or bare trust arises where property is held by trustees as nominees. The trustees merely hold the legal title to the trust fund/assets and are not required to perform any duties in respect of the assets held in trust. A bare trust is commonly used where assets are acquired on behalf of minor children (children under the age of 18) who, because of their minority, may not hold an interest directly in the asset.

A bare trust may also be used where an individual purchases assets, such as shares, but does not wish his or her interest to become a matter of public record. The true owner will have the shares registered in the name of a nominee, whose only function is to hold the legal title to the shares for the benefit of the true owner. In a bare trust, the beneficiary has the exclusive right (or would have but for being a minor or a person with a disability) to direct how the asset is dealt with.

Example 11.1: Use of a bare trust for minor children
John and Mary's will provides that all of their assets pass to their three children, Amy, Jean and David, in the event of their deaths. Both John and Mary are killed in a car accident and their assets pass to their children according to their will. Amy is only 10, Jean is 15 and David is 19 at the time of their parents' death.

As Amy and Jean are minors (under the age of 18), under the law they cannot hold title to property. Trustees are appointed for the purpose of legally holding the property for the benefit of Amy and Jean until they each turn 18. As David is aged 19 at the date of his parents' death, he can take direct legal ownership of his share of the inheritance.

Example 11.2: Use of a bare trust to protect privacy
John King is a high-profile businessman who, much to his annoyance, is frequently featured in "Ireland's wealthiest lists" in the Sunday newspapers. For the purposes of protecting his privacy, he sets up a bare trust when buying a substantial shareholding in a company. The nominee's name appears on the share certificate and share register, but the bare trust agreement behind the share purchase ensures that John King retains full control of his investment.

11.2.2 Interest in Possession Trust

The most common form of an interest in possession trust is a life interest trust. A life interest gives the beneficiary, known as the "life tenant", a right to income of the trust fund for a certain period. A life interest in real property will entitle the life tenant to live in the property or receive the rental income, if any, from the property. An interest in possession trust could also entail entitlement to the trust's income or property for a period certain, e.g. Jack has an interest in possession to an asset for 10 years.

In the case of a life tenant, their interest is limited and is not absolute. The person who takes an absolute interest in the income or asset on the expiration of the life tenant's interest is known as the "remainderman". A life interest trust may be wound up with the consent of all the beneficiaries, i.e. the life tenant and remainderman agree to break the trust.

Example 11.3

Paddy Kennedy is a farmer with a large farm. Paddy is very anxious that his son, Pat, inherits the farm and carries on the family tradition. Pat is married to Helen and she does not like the idea of her husband working as an employee on the farm, so they tell Paddy that they want the farm now. While Paddy understands the young couple's need for independence, he is only 60 years old and does not have any investments or income outside of the farm.

Use of Life Interest Trust

Paddy decides to gift the farm to Pat, but to retain a life interest in the farmhouse and also take a life interest in 50% of the farm. This means that Paddy has a legal interest in the house for his lifetime and a legal interest in 50% of the farm until his death, at which stage, Pat, as the named remainderman, succeeds to this life interest. Pat takes a 50% direct ownership of the farm now and has a 50% remainder interest in the farm on his father's death.

Commercial Consequences of the Trust

A few years later, Helen and Pat want to sell the farm but cannot find a buyer on the open market for their 50% share because, commercially, no one wants a property with a life interest (Paddy's 50% life interest) attached to it. Paddy is still determined to keep the farm in the family and refuses to consent to wind up the trust to facilitate Pat and Helen's plans.

11.2.3 Discretionary Trust

A discretionary trust arises where the trust property is held by the trustees to apply the income or capital or both for the benefit of the beneficiaries as the trustees think fit. It is usual for the settlor or the testator to write a letter of wishes to the trustees providing the trustees with guidelines as to how he or she would like the trust fund to be distributed.

However, a letter of wishes is an expression of wishes only and is not legally binding on the trustees. The trustees may well take the wishes of the settlor or testator into account, and usually do, but are not obliged to do so. A beneficiary under a discretionary trust has a right to be considered a potential beneficiary and to have this right protected by a court, although no beneficiary can force the trustees to exercise their discretionary powers in the beneficiary's favour.

Example 11.4

James Darcy has a son named Adam with his former partner, Kim. James and Kim were never married and tensions between them are high since the breakdown of their relationship, which James attributes mainly to Kim's reckless behaviour with money. As Adam is his only child, James wants his wealth to pass to Adam on his death.

Use of Discretionary Trust

However, James does not want Kim to get a chance to blow Adam's inheritance and sets up a discretionary trust under the terms of his will with Adam as beneficiary. James's solicitor and brother are appointed trustees with instructions in a letter of wishes from James, which asks them to ensure that Adam is well provided for but that he does not succeed to the assets of the trust until he is at least 30 years old, and only then if there is no possibility Adam will be influenced by his mother's squandering ways.

continued overleaf

> **Trustees' Discretion**
> James dies when Adam is aged 15 and his assets pass to a discretionary trust as prescribed in the will, with Adam as the named beneficiary. The trustees distribute funds for Adam's maintenance and education. When he is 21, the trustees consider him to be a very responsible young man. They are also sure that Kim is not a bad influence and decide to distribute the full assets of the trust to Adam. As the trust is a discretionary trust, the trustees are not bound by James's letter of wishes and exercise their own discretion in reaching the decision to wind down the trust and distribute the assets in full to Adam.

11.3 Taxation of Trusts

When considering trusts, it is important to bear in mind that a number of taxes, such as CGT, CAT, stamp duty and income tax, can all arise on the trust and the settlor and/or beneficiary at various stages in the trust's life.

For example, a payment out of a discretionary trust could be liable to CAT and income tax. It is therefore important to consider all the tax consequences arising on all trust transactions when advising a client on a particular course of action. For the purposes of this textbook, our primary focus is on how CAT and CGT impact on trust transactions. However, we will also briefly outline the stamp duty and income tax issues surrounding a trust transaction.

The tax issues surrounding trusts can best be analysed by reviewing the life cycle of a trust, summarised as follows:

- the creation of a trust;
- dealing with capital and income of the trust; and
- the appointment of trust assets/funds to beneficiaries.

11.4 Creation of a Trust

The creation of a trust involves the transfer of assets or funds from the settlor to the trust for the benefit of the beneficiaries. The trust can take effect during the lifetime of the settlor, in which case it is known as an "*inter vivos* trust;" or it can take effect under the will of the settlor on his or her death, which is known as a "will trust". The creation of a trust involves the transfer of ownership of assets and will give rise to a tax event under a number of tax heads, which we will now review.

11.4.1 CGT

When a settlor creates a trust during his or her lifetime, the transfer of assets into the trust is a disposal for CGT purposes. The CGT arising (if any) is on the difference between the base cost of the assets and the market value of the assets on the date of the transfer. The settlor could also sell assets to the trust for market value but, generally, the settlor makes a gift of the assets to the trust. The market value at the date the asset is transferred into the trust forms the base cost for the trustees on future disposals made by the trust.

> **Key Issue**
> It is common for a settlor to transfer a cash sum to a trust – this will not carry a CGT implication as cash is not a chargeable asset for CGT purposes.

If the trust is established on the death of the settlor, i.e. comes into effect under the will of the settlor, then the normal CGT exemption set out in section 573 TCA 1997 in relation to assets passing on death applies.

Example 11.5

George purchased land in July 1985 for €50,000. On 1 July 2022, he settled the land on trust for the benefit of his daughter, Anna, when she reaches age 25. The market value of the land in July 2022 is €900,000.

George is deemed to dispose of the property at market value to the trust on 1 July 2022.

	€
Proceeds	900,000
Cost: €50,000 indexed @ 1.713	(85,650)
Gain	814,350
Annual exemption	(1,270)
	813,080
CGT @ 33%	268,316

The base cost of the land for the purposes of any subsequent disposal by the trustees is €900,000.

Stamp duty will also be payable by the trustees on the transfer from George (see **Section 11.4.2**) and will be a deductible expense for CGT purposes on a future sale of the land by the trust.

The CGT considerations on the creation of a trust are the same irrespective of the type of trust, as outlined in **Section 11.2**. Therefore, a disposal is deemed to take place and accordingly CGT may arise on the transfer of assets *inter vivos* to a bare trust, a limited interest in possession trust or a discretionary trust.

11.4.2 Stamp Duty

Where property is settled on trust by way of an instrument, such as a trust deed, the normal result is a charge to stamp duty at:

- 1% on the value of stocks and shares (the 7.5% rate will apply if the shares derive their value from non-residential land and/or buildings in the State);
- 1% on the transfer of the residential property up to €1 million and 2% on any excess over €1 million; or
- 7.5% on the transfer of non-residential property, to the trust.

The charge is enforced by section 30 SDCA 1999, which states that any transfer that operates under a voluntary disposition *inter vivos* is to be charged with the same duty as if it were a transfer on sale. A "voluntary disposition *inter vivos*" relates to a transaction for no consideration or at less than the market value which does not arise on a death. Stamp duty is charged on the market value of the property, rather than on the amount or value of any consideration passing.

Following on from **Example 11.5**, the trust is liable to stamp duty at 7.5% on the transfer of the property by George on 1 July 2022. The trust will therefore need funds of €67,500 to discharge this liability. This represents a significant cost for the trust and must be funded by George transferring cash into the trust or by the trust selling assets to raise the funds.

If the transfer of the assets/property to the trust does not take place *inter vivos* but arises on the death of George, then, as per section 113(c) SDCA 1999, stamp duty rules will exempt the transfer and stamp duty will not arise.

Stamp duty may be triggered on the transfer of assets *inter vivos* to a bare trust, a limited interest in possession trust and on the *inter vivos* transfer of assets to a discretionary trust.

11.4.3 CAT

As the creation of a trust involves the transfer of assets from the settlor to the trust for the benefit of the beneficiary, the CAT implications for the beneficiary on receiving such a benefit must be analysed.

It is possible to take either a gift or an inheritance from a trust. The rules for establishing whether an appointment from a trust is a gift or an inheritance are similar to the general rules governing the receipt of gifts and inheritances.

In general, an appointment will be treated as a gift if the settlor survives the setting up of the trust by at least two years.

As per section 5 CATCA 2003 for gifts and section 10 CATCA 2003 for inheritances, a CAT liability can only arise when a person takes a **beneficial interest in possession over property**. Therefore, the question of whether CAT arises on the creation of a trust does very much depend on the type of trust involved.

Bare Trusts

The beneficiary of a bare trust is beneficially entitled in possession to the assets of the trust. The trustees merely hold the legal title to the trust assets for the absolute benefit of the beneficiary. Therefore, a CAT event is triggered on the transfer of assets to a bare trust and the beneficiary may have a CAT liability depending on his or her relationship to the settlor.

Using the examples set out for bare trusts in **Section 11.2.1,** John and Mary's children **(Example 11.1)** will all be treated as receiving an immediate inheritance from their parents, even if Amy and Jean's benefits are held in a bare trust. CAT will be calculated using the Group A tax-free threshold of €335,000 on the benefits taken from their parents.

In **Example 11.2** John created a bare trust for his own benefit. As a person cannot be taxed on a gift to himself, CAT does not arise when an individual settles property on trust for himself.

Limited Interest in Possession Trusts

In the case of a limited interest in possession trust, benefits taken by the limited interest beneficiary and the remainderman must be each reviewed to establish the CAT consequences of creating such a trust.

The creation of a limited interest in possession trust gives rise to an immediate CAT event on the limited interest holder because he or she has a current interest in possession to the assets of the trust. The valuation of a limited interest in possession is subject to special rules detailed in CATCA 2003 under Table A of Schedule 1 for a life interest, and under Table B of Schedule 1 for the fixed period interest.

The remainderman will only be subject to CAT when the limited interest comes to an end and he or she takes an **absolute interest in possession**.

Example 11.6

We will follow **Example 11.3**, where Paddy established a limited interest in possession trust for his own benefit of 50% of his farm and transferred the balance absolutely to his son, Pat.

As outlined above, an individual cannot be taxed on the settlement of property for his or her own benefit. Therefore, CAT does not apply to Paddy on the creation of the trust. Pat has received an absolute interest in 50% of the farm and a remainder interest in the 50% his father holds as a life tenant.

Pat qualified as a farmer for agricultural relief purposes and did not have a CAT liability on the transfer of 50% of the farm to him absolutely. CAT will not arise in respect of his remainder interest until his father's death.

Paddy lives for 20 years after creating the trust. On Paddy's death, Pat's remainder interest falls into possession and a CAT event is triggered. Pat has non-agricultural assets worth more than his share of the farm, so he fails the farmer test and a CAT liability arises. Pat's CAT is calculated on the market value of the trust assets at the date of Paddy's death.

Discretionary Trusts

CAT will not arise on the creation of a discretionary trust on the basis that the beneficiary does not hold an interest in possession in the settled property.

In the case of a discretionary trust, a beneficial interest in possession only arises when trust property and/or income is appointed to a beneficiary of the trust.

Example 11.7

In **Example 11.4**, Adam is the beneficiary of a discretionary trust under the terms of his late father's will. Therefore, Adam does not have an interest in possession on the creation of the will trust at the date of James's death and CAT does not arise at that point in time.

The trustees are very mindful of the tax costs of the discretionary trust as there is an erosion of Adam's CAT tax-free Group A threshold each time they distribute funds towards his education and upkeep. In addition, the assets in the trust are rising in value every year and a potentially large CAT liability will be triggered if they wait until Adam is 30 years old. Taking into consideration Adam's maturity and the tax costs of holding the assets in the trust, the trustees decide to distribute the assets when Adam is 21. Adam is liable to CAT based on the market value of the assets on the date he takes an interest in possession in the assets of the trust, i.e. the date the trustees distribute the assets out of the trust to him.

Key Issue

Avoid settling assets which generally rise in value in a discretionary trust because CAT is calculated on the market value of the assets on the date the assets are appointed to a beneficiary, not the date the trust is created.

11.5 Dealing with the Capital and Income of the Trust

The trustees are responsible for dealing with the income and capital of the trust. As part of their responsibilities, the trustees must also ensure that all tax liabilities arising on income or gains of the trust are correctly dealt with.

11.5.1 CGT

Generally, trustees have authority to sell trust property in the prudent management of the affairs of the trust. If the trustees make a gain on the disposal of any trust assets, such a gain is taxable under normal CGT rules. However, certain reliefs and exemptions available only to individuals are not available to trustees, such as an annual exemption. Any capital losses incurred by trustees on the disposal of trust property may be set against gains arising on the disposal of other trust property. Such losses may also be carried forward.

Example 11.8

A trust was set up with a share portfolio worth €1 million in 2006.

By 2022, the trustees are very concerned about the fall in value of the shares held by the trust. In an attempt to stem the erosion of the trust fund any further, the trustees sell the shares for €500,000.

CGT arises as follows:	€
Sale proceeds on share disposal	500,000
Base cost of the shares	(1,000,000)
Capital loss	500,000

The base cost for CGT purposes is the value of the shares on the date the assets were settled on the trust. A significant loss arises on this disposal. This loss is available for carrying forward for offset against future capital gains the trust may make.

For CGT purposes, section 567 TCA 1997 distinguishes between assets held by trustees as bare trustees and settled property held in trusts, such as interest in possession trusts and discretionary trusts. If assets are held by a bare trustee for another person who is absolutely entitled to those assets, then all CGT arising on any disposals made by the bare trustee are assessed directly on the beneficiary and he or she is directly liable to any CGT arising. Referring back to **Example 11.2,** any disposal of the shares held by a nominee for John King will be a CGT event taxable directly on John King.

11.5.2 Income Tax

Income of a trust is liable to the standard rate of income tax, which is currently 20%. The income of a trust is generally assessable on the trustees as the persons in receipt of income. Thus, it is necessary for the trustees to make annual returns of income on which they will be charged income tax at the standard rate.

Trustees are not entitled to claim the personal credit, allowances, exemptions or reliefs from income tax that are available to individuals. This is because a trustee is not regarded as "an individual" for income tax purposes.

Trustees are not entitled to an income tax deduction in respect of their annual trust expenses, such as management expenses, in the calculation of taxable trust income.

In contrast with individual taxpayers, trustees are not subject to PRSI or USC in relation to trust income, or the restriction of specified reliefs for high-income earners.

If a beneficiary has an absolute right to trust income (e.g. as a life tenant) or if the trustees mandate income directly to a beneficiary, Revenue may assess that beneficiary to income tax directly instead of the trustees.

11.5.3 Discretionary Trust Tax

As noted in **Section 11.4.3**, a liability to CAT only arises if a person is beneficially entitled in possession to property. As potential beneficiaries of a discretionary trust do not become beneficially entitled in possession to trust property until property is appointed to them, a charge to CAT can be deferred indefinitely.

CATCA 2003 contains anti-avoidance measures to charge "discretionary trust taxes", to allow the Exchequer to raise tax on assets that might otherwise be deferred for a number of years.

A once-off discretionary trust tax of 6% arises on the value of the trust property held in a discretionary trust. Thereafter, an annual 1% charge is levied on all property in the trust on 31 December each year.

The 6% and 1% charges are only intended to penalise trusts designed to defer the payment of **inheritance tax** on an ongoing basis. Where the settlor is still alive, inheritance tax could not arise if the assets were still held personally by the settlor; therefore, the earliest date on which the 6% charge should arise is on the death of the settlor.

Even if the settlor has died, there may be a further deferral of the discretionary trust tax charges if the youngest of the settlor's children, who are potential beneficiaries under the trust, has not reached the age of 21. This is in recognition of the fact that it is generally prudent to defer appointing capital to children under the age of 21. Therefore, the 6% discretionary trust tax charge arises on the latest of the following dates:

1. the date the trust is set up;
2. the date the settlor dies; or
3. the date the youngest of the settlor's children (who are potential beneficiaries under the trust or children of a child of the disponer where such child predeceased the disponer) reaches 21 years of age.

Half of the initial 6% charge will be refunded if all of the property of the discretionary trust is appointed within five years from the date on which the original 6% charge was triggered. This provides a tax planning opportunity to recover half of the initial 6% tax charge. The 6% charge is payable within four months of the valuation date of the inheritance deemed to be taken by the trustees.

The annual 1% charge is payable if there is property in the discretionary trust on 31 December each year. It is payable on the value of the property in the trust on that date. The 1% annual charge is not payable on the first 31 December immediately following the date on which the initial 6% charge is payable.

A discretionary trust, created under a will becomes subject to discretionary trust tax from the date of death of the settlor. Where the discretionary trust is set up for public or charitable purposes, an exemption from the discretionary trust tax may be available. This exemption is subject to anti-avoidance provisions.

Key Issue

Establish a discretionary trust just after 31 December to ensure the maximum deferral of the first annual 1% tax charge.

Example 11.9

Assets of €1 million were transferred to a discretionary trust on 20 January 2022. The valuation date of the assets settled in the discretionary trust is 5 January 2022. The settlor is deceased and the children of the settlor, who are the potential beneficiaries of the trust, are all aged over 21.

The 6% charge (€60,000) is payable within four months of the valuation date of the inheritance deemed to be taken by the trustees, i.e. the 6% charge is payable on or before 20 May 2022.

The 1% annual charge will not arise on 31 December 2022 as the same trust property was subject to the 6% charge in 2022. The first annual charge payment of €10,000 falls due on 31 December 2023.

Surcharge Income

As outlined in **Section 11.5.2**, trustees pay income tax at the standard rate of 20% on the trust income and are not entitled to claim any of the personal allowances or reliefs which are normally available to individuals. However, to the extent that income is accumulated in a trust or funds are held in a discretionary trust, there is provision for a surcharge on undistributed income of such a trust. If the income has not been distributed within 18 months of the end of the year of assessment in which it arises, it will be subject to a surcharge of 20%. The income must be grossed-up at 20% and the surcharge is applied to the gross figure. Effectively this means that the surcharge is imposed on income that has already suffered tax at 20%, but no deduction is given for that income tax paid.

Expenses of management of the trust are not deductible in computing the income tax liability but are deductible in computing the 20% surcharge.

Example 11.10

	€
Gross income of a discretionary trust for 2022	12,000
Deduct: Income tax @ 20% payable by trustees	(2,400)
	9,600
Deduct: Management expenses	
Legal/accountancy/trustee expenses	(1,400)
	8,200
Deduct: Income distributed to beneficiary	(200)
Undistributed income	8,000
Re-gross at standard rate €8,000 × $\frac{100}{80}$	
	10,000
Surcharge @ 20%	2,000

In addition to the income tax liability of €2,400, the trustees must also pay a surcharge of €2,000 if the distributable income of €8,000 is not paid out to the beneficiaries by 30 June 2024 (18 months from the end of 2022). The liability is regarded as part of the income tax liability of the tax year in which the end of the 18-month period falls. In the above example, a surcharge in respect of undistributed income of the tax year 2022 will be regarded as income tax of the year 2024 because the end of the 18-month period after 31 December 2022 falls in 2024.

11.6 Appointment of Trust Assets or Funds to Beneficiaries

Assets and/or funds of the trust can be appointed to the beneficiaries either during the life of the trust or on the winding up of the trust. As an "appointment" is equivalent to a transfer of an asset, a tax event is triggered.

11.6.1 CGT

In addition to being liable to CGT on the actual disposal of trust assets, trustees are deemed to dispose of assets for CGT purposes in the following circumstances:

1. When a person becomes absolutely entitled as against the trustees in relation to settled property except where it occurs on the death of a person with a life interest in the property (section 577(2) TCA 1997).
2. Where, on the termination of a life interest in trust property, the property continues to be settled property (section 577(3) TCA 1997).
3. Where the trustees cease to be resident and ordinarily resident in Ireland (section 579B TCA 1997).

Where any of the above three circumstances arises, the trustees are deemed to dispose of the property at that time and immediately reacquire it at its market value. The trustees must pay CGT on any increase in value between the acquisition cost and the deemed market value.

Example 11.11: CGT under section 577(2)

Michael settled property valued at €700,000 in 2022 in a limited interest trust for his daughter, Mairead, for 10 years and, thereafter, the property is to go to Mairead's son, Milo, absolutely, i.e. event 1 above.

CGT arises on the expiration of Mairead's 10-year limited interest in 2032, when the assets are valued at €1,200,000, because Milo has become absolutely entitled to the trust assets. The trustees must pay a deemed CGT liability calculated as the difference between the value of the assets on the date Michael settled the property on trust and the value of the assets on the date Milo absolutely becomes entitled to the assets.

CGT Computation	€
Market value of assets 2032	1,200,000
Market value of assets 2022	(700,000)
Deduction for stamp duty @ 7.5% paid on transfer of assets to trust	(52,500)
Taxable gain	447,500
Taxed @ 33%	147,675

This will represent a significant cost to the trust, and cash funds in the trust will have to be used to pay the liability or assets will actually have to be sold to pay off the deemed CGT liability. Stamp duty will also arise on the transfer of the property to the trust by Michael.

If Michael had settled property on trust for Mairead for her lifetime, and then to her son absolutely on her death, then CGT would not arise as Milo becomes absolutely entitled to the assets on the death of the life tenant, Mairead.

Example 11.12: CGT under section 577(3)

Angela settles property in a life interest trust for her son, Billy, and thereafter to his son, Raymond, absolutely. However, the trust deed stipulates that if Raymond is under 21 years of age on the death of the life tenant (Billy) then Raymond's benefit will first pass to a trust until he is aged 21, i.e. event 2 above.

Billy dies when Raymond is 15 years old and, as per the terms of the trust, Raymond cannot take an absolute interest in the assets of the trust. These are passed into a trust until he is aged 21. The trustees are treated as making a deemed disposal of the trust assets at the date of Billy's death thus triggering a CGT liability based on the market value of the assets at the date of Billy's death as the property continues to be held on trust for Raymond until he is 21. If there was no stipulation creating a trust until Raymond is 21, then he would have taken an absolute interest in the trust assets on the death of the life tenant, Billy.

Stamp duty will also arise on the transfer of the property to the trust by Angela.

11.6.2 Capital Losses

If a capital loss arises on the appointment of assets from a trust, and the trustees cannot use the capital loss to shelter other gains arising in that tax year on a date before the date of appointment, then the benefit of the unused capital loss is transferred to the beneficiary who took the appointment of the assets, i.e. the unused loss "travels" with the assets to the beneficiary.

11.6.3 CGT/CAT Offset

Under section 104 CATCA 2003, where the same event gives rise to CGT and CAT, then CGT paid may be credited against any CAT due. It is important to ensure that it is the same event which gives rise to the charge to both taxes.

As both CGT and CAT are currently charged at the rate of 33%, this can be a very valuable relief which, if properly utilised, can effectively eliminate a charge to CAT. The relief will be clawed back if the beneficiary disposes of the assets within two years of the date of the gift or inheritance.

Example 11.13

It is 1 October 2022. Joe wants to gift commercial property valued at €800,000 to his nephew, Leo. As Leo is only 12 years old, a bare trust must be established, the trustees of which will hold the legal title to the property.

Joe originally inherited the property himself in February 1975, when it was valued at IR£20,000.

The establishment of the bare trust has the following tax consequences:

1.	**CGT on Joe on gifting property to a bare trust for Leo**	€
	Market value	800,000
	Base cost IR£20,000/0.787564 = €25,395	
	Indexation relief 1975 to 2003 = 7.528	(191,172)
	Gain	608,828
	Less: annual exemption	(1,270)
	Taxable gain	607,558
	Taxed @ 33%	**200,494**
2.	**Stamp duty arising on the trust**	€
	Market value	800,000
	Stamp duty @ 7.5%	**60,000**
3.	**Capital acquisition tax arising on Leo**	€
	Market value of gift	800,000
	Less: small exemption	(3,000)
	Less: stamp duty cost	(60,000)
	Taxable value of gift	737,000
	Group B tax-free threshold	(32,500)
	Net taxable value of gift	704,500
	Taxed @ 33%	232,485
	Less: CGT "same event" credit	(200,494)
	Net CAT payable by Leo	**31,991**
	Total tax cost	
	CGT payable by Joe	200,494
	Stamp duty payable by Leo	60,000
	Net CAT payable by Leo	31,991
	Total tax	**292,485**

Leo will have to be put in funds to meet his tax liabilities. The trustees may consider borrowing money on his behalf to fund the CAT and stamp duty costs or Joe may gift him cash, which would also trigger a CAT liability.

Example 11.14

The details are similar to **Example 11.13**, but in this scenario Joe establishes a discretionary trust and names Leo as a possible beneficiary. On transferring assets to the trust, Joe triggers a CGT liability of €200,494 and the trust incurs a stamp duty liability of €60,000. No CAT arises on the transfer of the assets to the discretionary trust as Leo, or none of the other potential beneficiaries, are beneficially entitled in possession to the assets of the trust (see **Section 11.6.4**).

A number of years later when Leo is 18 years of age, the trustees decide to appoint all of the assets of the trust to him. The assets are now valued at €1,500,000. The following CGT liability arises to the trust:

		€
1.	**CGT payable by the trust**	
	Market value of assets	1,500,000
	Base cost	(800,000)
	Stamp duty paid on original transfer to trust	(60,000)
	Taxable gain	640,000
	Taxed @ 33%	211,200
2.	**CAT payable by Leo**	€
	Market value of gift (Joe is not deceased)	1,500,000
	Less: small gift exemption	(3,000)
	Less: Group B threshold	(32,500)
	Taxable gift	1,464,500
	Taxed @ 33%	483,285
	Less: Credit for CGT arising on same event	(211,200)
	Net CAT payable	272,085

The same event for the purposes of the CAT/CGT offset is the appointment of assets from the trust to Leo when he is aged 18. No credit is available for the CGT incurred by Joe on the establishment of the trust.

In general, stamp duty does not arise on the appointment of assets out of a trust to a beneficiary (see **Section 11.6.5**).

11.6.4 CAT

CAT can only arise when a person takes a beneficial interest in possession over property. In **Section 11.4.3** we discussed how the transfer of assets to an interest in possession trust or a bare trust triggers an immediate CAT event. In the case of a discretionary trust, a CAT event will arise each time the trustees appoint funds out of the trust to the beneficiary for the beneficiaries' upkeep/maintenance and a CAT liability will also arise when the assets of the trust are appointed from the trust to the beneficiary (i.e. the beneficiary takes a beneficial interest in possession to the assets of the trust).

Example 11.15

If we revisit Example 11.4 in **Section 11.2.3** above, we know that Adam is the beneficiary of a discretionary will trust established by his late father. The trust is to provide for Adam's upkeep and education. The trustees decided to distribute the assets of the trust to Adam when he is 21 years old. The assets at the date of James's death were valued at €2,500,000.

The CAT consequences of the above trust are as follows:

Assume Adam receives €30,000 each year since the death of his father from the age of 15 to 20. He then takes a beneficial interest in possession of the assets of the trust, with a market value of €3 million in 2022 when Adam is aged 21. The following CAT will arise:

	€
Current benefit	3,000,0000
Previous benefits (€30,000 × 6)	180,000
Aggregated benefits	3,180,000
Less: Group A tax-free threshold	(335,000)
Net taxable benefit	2,845,000
Taxed @ 33%	938,850

continued overleaf

If Adam had taken an absolute interest under a bare trust when he was aged 15 and the Group A threshold was €280,000, his CAT liability would have been as follows:

	€
Current benefit	2,500,000
Less: Group A threshold when aged 15	(280,000)
Net taxable benefit	2,220,000
Taxed @ 33%	732,600
CAT cost of the discretionary trust	**206,250**

11.6.5 Stamp Duty on Appointment of Trust Funds/Assets

The appointment by the trustees of assets out of the settlement on its termination is not a voluntary disposition or a transfer on sale but is simply an appointment out to the beneficiaries of their beneficial entitlement. By transferring legal ownership of the assets to the beneficiary the trustees have completed title to the property. Therefore, stamp duty does not arise on the appointment of assets to a beneficiary.

11.7 Tax and Estate Planning Using Trusts

Trusts can be effective structures for estate planning purposes. In the context of family estate planning, it may not be appropriate to give certain individuals full control over property and wealth and a trust can be an appropriate method of providing such individuals with benefits, while at the same time protecting the assets.

The following section examines the circumstances where it might be appropriate to consider the use of a trust structure in the context of tax and estate planning.

11.7.1 Discretionary Will Trust for Minor Beneficiaries

Where children are very young and it is difficult to ascertain at the time of making a will what their individual needs might be in the future, a "discretionary trust" might often be the solution. This will allow the trustees flexibility in making provision for the children and, where necessary, if one child has greater needs than another, the trustees can make greater provision for that child.

While discretionary trust tax may arise in the future, it will not arise until the youngest child of the settlor reaches the age of 21 years. It may be possible to appoint the trust assets in advance of the youngest child's 21st birthday to avoid the charge arising.

The key tax consideration in using a discretionary trust is that, while the trust offers protection and control of the assets of the trust, it may give rise to a greater CAT liability in the long-term. This is because the beneficiaries are liable to CAT on becoming beneficially entitled in possession to the trust assets based on the value of the assets on the date of appointment to the beneficiary. If the assets have increased in value since the date the trust was established, then the uplift in value will give rise to a larger CAT tax liability.

If control and asset protection are not at issue, then, for tax purposes, it is generally more tax-efficient for beneficiaries to take a gift or inherit assets directly from a settlor or, if young children are involved, to take a gift or inherit the assets under a bare trust structure as the CAT charge arises immediately and any future uplift in the value of the assets accrues directly to the beneficiary.

Trusts established for the benefit of a permanently incapacitated individual are exempt from income tax, subject to certain conditions. The exemption applies if, at the date of the death of the permanently incapacitated individual, the funds remaining in the trust are applied for charitable purposes. If the deceased permanently incapacitated individual is survived by a child, spouse or civil partner, the trust funds remaining may be applied for their benefit. This exemption came into effect from 1 January 2015 for newly created trusts and for existing trusts that amend their trust deeds to provide for the distribution of the funds to the estate of the permanently incapacitated individual.

11.7.2 Agricultural Relief

Agricultural relief under section 89 CATCA 2003 is available to beneficiaries who qualify as farmers and receive gifts/inheritance of agricultural property provided certain conditions are satisfied. If one of the beneficiaries to an estate has an interest in farming, the trustees could acquire agricultural property using the trust funds and transfer the agricultural property to the beneficiary at such time when the beneficiary qualifies as a farmer and agricultural relief will apply.

If a beneficiary inherits a mixture of assets, comprising qualifying agricultural property and non-qualifying property, the inclusion of non-agricultural property may mean that the beneficiary is not able to satisfy the 80% "farmer" test on the valuation date.

Finance Act 2014 introduced the "active farmer" test for agricultural relief to apply for CAT purposes. The active farmer test comprises three conditions, in addition to the "farmer" test, to qualify for relief where a gift or inheritance is taken on or after 1 January 2015 (see **Section 9.4.14**).

There is likely to be a time gap between the date of death and the valuation date for CAT purposes. If so, this may allow time for the beneficiary to alter the mix of his or her assets, so that when the valuation date arises they will be able to satisfy the 80% test and the active farmer test.

A discretionary trust could be established under a will into which the estate of the deceased is transferred on his/her death. This would allow the trustees to appoint agricultural property to the beneficiaries before appointing non-agricultural property and the beneficiary may qualify as a farmer (if the active farmer test is also satisfied) before taking an interest in possession in the non-agricultural property.

Chapter 11 Summary

When is tax triggered?	<ul><li>On the creation of a trust – CGT, CAT and stamp duty on assets transferred to the trust</li><li>On the appointment of assets/funds to the beneficiaries – CAT on the benefit passing</li><li>On disposals by the trustees – CGT on the disposal of assets</li><li>On income earned by the trust – income tax on dividend income earned</li></ul>
Discretionary trust tax	<ul><li>Anti-avoidance measures to discourage the deferral of CAT</li><li>Applies on later of the date the trust is set up, the date the settlor dies, or the date the youngest of the settlor's children who are potential beneficiaries under the trust reaches 21 years of age</li><li>Use of discretionary trusts as a tax planning vehicle is restricted with anti-avoidance rules under the various tax reliefs</li></ul>

Questions

Review Questions
(See Suggested Solutions to Review Questions at the end of this textbook.)

Question 11.1

Alex Kenny has a successful property rental business, owning 20 houses for residential letting. Keen to make provision for her children, she is considering settling two of these properties and a sum of cash on a trust for the benefit of her twin sons, Luke and Mark, aged 22.

She does not wish her sons to know of the trust and only wants them to benefit from the trust assets or income when and if the need should arise. She will prepare a letter of wishes on how she would like the trustees to deal with the trust assets if one or both of the boys should need financial support over their life; but, ultimately, the trustees will have discretion on how to deal with the trust and for who's benefit.

Requirement
Advise Alex of the tax implications of establishing and operating the trust.

Question 11.2

Jack Murphy is a widower with a farm worth €1.5 million. He has a daughter, Margaret, aged 25, who owns a successful IT company with her husband. They plan to sell the business to an interested buyer in the next year or so for a projected €2 million.

Jack has been given six months to live and wants to get his affairs in order. He has come to you for advice on how best to structure his will in a tax-efficient manner such that Margaret qualifies for the maximum available tax reliefs.

Requirement
Assuming Margaret has not previously received any gifts or inheritances from Jack or his late wife, advise Jack how a trust could be used to tax-efficiently transfer the farm.

Challenging Question
(Suggested Solutions to Challenging Questions are available through your lecturer.)

Question 11.1

Marion is a wealthy widow and mother to Mark, aged 19. Her husband died in 2005 and left commercial property to Marion. The property was originally purchased in 1985 for IR£45,000 and was valued at €1,000,000 at the date of his death. It was his wish that Marion should pass on this property to Mark as soon as he reached a responsible age.

It is now November 2022. Marion is very worried that Mark is not capable of making sound financial decisions should she pass any wealth to him now or in the near future and is strongly thinking about setting up a discretionary trust to control the property, now worth €2,000,000. However Marion is also very tax conscious and has heard that a trust can have considerable tax consequences, especially in a rising property market with values predicted to increase by 14% in the next 10 years.

Requirement
You are Marion's accountant and she has come to you for advice on what to do.

Territorial Provisions for Direct Taxes

Learning Objectives

By the end of this chapter, you should be able to:

- Identify and apply the territorial provisions for income tax, corporation tax, capital gains tax (CGT), capital acquisitions tax (CAT) and stamp duty.
- Provide tax advice on
  - the tax consequences of the territorial provisions in terms of where assets are located;
  - the administrative issues associated with transactions; and
  - foreign domiciled individuals in terms of withholding tax obligations.

12.1 Introduction

The charging section of tax legislation is the legal statement that a tax arises under a particular tax head. It is the first step in setting the basis for how tax is to be calculated, assessed and paid.

The scope of the charge to tax in the legislation states who comes within the charge under the particular tax head. The scope is dependent on factors such as residence, ordinary residence and domicile, and the location of the assets involved in a particular transaction. The impact of residence status and the location of assets on those chargeable to tax are generally known as the territorial provisions. Therefore, as a first step to examining how a business decision triggers a potential charge to tax under a particular tax head from a business and individual perspective, you will need to understand the territorial provisions of the charge to tax in order to advise clients on how best to comply with, and minimise, tax in Ireland.

12.2 Territorial Provisions for Income Tax

The extent of an individual's liability to Irish income tax depends on each of the following three key components:

1. residence;
2. ordinary residence; and
3. domicile.

You should be familiar with the meaning of the terms "resident", "ordinarily resident" and "domicile" from your previous studies but, as a brief reminder, these terms are reviewed again below.

12.2.1 Tax Residence

Tax residence is determined by the number of days an individual is present in Ireland during a given tax year, which runs from 1 January to 31 December. An individual will, therefore, be resident in Ireland in either of the following circumstances:

- if he or she spends 183 days or more in the State for any purpose in the tax year in question; or
- if he or she spends 280 days or more in the State for any purpose over a period of two consecutive tax years, that individual will be regarded as resident in Ireland for the second tax year. However, if an individual spends 30 days or less in either tax year, those days will not be reckoned for the purposes of applying this test.

Example 12.1

Dev Patel spends 140 days in Ireland in year 1 and 150 days in year 2, and will therefore be tax resident in Ireland in year 2. But if he spends 250 days here in year 1 and only 30 days in year 2, then he will be tax resident in year 1 (as he has exceeded the 183-day test), but he will not be treated as tax resident here in year 2 as the 280-day rule is not applicable when the number of days in question are 30 days or less in either tax year.

If an individual intends to be resident in Ireland for the next calendar year, they can request **split-year treatment** in the year of arrival. Split-year treatment means that an individual is treated as resident in Ireland from the date of arrival and their employment income from that date is taxed in Ireland with full tax credits allowed on a cumulative basis. Split-year treatment applies to employment income only.

Split-year treatment can also be claimed in the year an individual leaves Ireland with the intention of not being resident the following year. In this case, the individual's employment income from the date of departure will not be subject to Irish income tax.

12.2.2 Ordinary Residence

The term "ordinary residence", as distinct from residence, refers to an individual's pattern of residence over a number of tax years. If an individual has been a resident in Ireland for three consecutive tax years, then he or she will be regarded as being ordinarily resident from the beginning of the fourth tax year. Conversely, an individual will cease to be ordinarily resident in Ireland having been non-resident for three consecutive tax years.

Example 12.2

Dev Patel has spent the following number of days in Ireland:

Year	No of days	Residency Status	Ordinarily Resident?
2015	140	not resident	n/a
2016	150	tax resident	no
2017	130	tax resident	no
2018	183	tax resident	no
2019	100	tax resident	ordinarily resident
2020	50	not resident	ordinarily resident
2021	0	not resident	ordinarily resident
2022	0	not resident	ordinarily resident
2023	0	not resident	not ordinarily resident

12.2.3 Domicile

Domicile is a concept of general law which applies to individuals only. In general terms, it means residence in a particular country with the intention of residing permanently in that country. Every individual acquires a domicile of origin at birth. An Irish domicile of origin will remain with an individual until a new domicile of choice is acquired. However, before that domicile of origin can be shed, there has to be clear evidence that the individual has demonstrated an active intention to acquire permanent residence in the new country and has abandoned the idea of ever returning to live in Ireland. An individual's domicile status can influence the extent to which foreign-sourced gains are taxable in Ireland.

12.2.4 Day of Presence

A "day" is defined in section 819(4)(b) TCA 1997 as presence in the State at any time during that day.

> **Example 12.3**
> Ken Rivers is a US-domiciled executive working in Ireland. Ken works from Monday to Thursday in Ireland for 40 weeks a year during 2022. Ken catches a flight out of Ireland on a Thursday night. On that basis, he was not resident under either the 280-day test or the 183-day test during 2022. Ken will be tax resident under the 280-day rule if he continues working from Monday to Thursday in Ireland in 2023 onwards.

12.2.5 Effect of Residence and Domicile on an Individual's Charge to Irish Income Tax

The key tax implications of being Irish tax resident and/or non-Irish domiciled on an individual's charge to Irish income tax are:

- An Irish resident individual is assessed to income tax on worldwide income.
- Under the split-year treatment, an individual resident in Ireland in the year of arrival who can show that they intend to remain resident in the following tax year, is not taxable on earnings from an employment exercised outside Ireland in the part of the year before the date of arrival, notwithstanding that they are resident for the full tax year. A similar treatment may apply in a year of departure.
- A non-resident is, in general, only charged to income tax on their Irish-sourced income.
- A non-domiciled individual can avail of the remittance basis of assessment.
- Under the remittance basis of assessment, foreign-sourced income is taxed only to the extent it is remitted by the individual to Ireland in a tax year. The remittance basis of assessment does not apply to foreign employments exercised in Ireland.

Refer to the CA Proficiency 2 course for a more detailed discussion of the impact of residence and domicile status on an individual's charge to Irish income tax.

12.3 Territorial Provisions for CGT – Individuals

Capital gains tax arises for a year of assessment on gains that accrue to an individual during that year on the disposal of chargeable assets. The charge to CGT depends on the residence, ordinary residence and domicile (see above) of the individual making the disposal, and the location of the assets in question.

12.3.1 Effect of Residence and Domicile on an Individual's Charge to CGT

Broadly speaking, the TCA 1997 provides three separate bases for a liability to CGT:

1. Irish resident/ordinarily resident and Irish domiciled individuals;
2. non-domiciled tax residents/ordinarily resident; and
3. non-resident/non-domiciled

Irish Resident/Ordinarily Resident and Irish Domiciled Individuals

Under section 29(2) TCA 1997, a person who is Irish resident or ordinarily resident and domiciled in Ireland is liable to be charged on gains on disposals of both Irish and worldwide assets accruing in the year of assessment regardless of whether the gains from the sale are remitted into the State or not.

Example 12.4

Mary Kelly has lived in Ireland all her life. She is fed up with the bad weather and decides to move to Barbados on 10 January 2021. In 2022, Mary sells all her Irish assets, making a gain of €1.5 million, and an investment property in Hungary, making a gain of €50,000, and puts all of the proceeds directly into her Barbadian bank account.

Mary has the following Irish CGT liability:

Gain arising on the disposal of the Irish assets	€1,500,000
Gain arising on the disposal of the Hungarian property	€50,000
Total gain	€1,550,000
Less: personal exemption	(€1,270)
Taxable gain	€1,548,730
Taxed @ 33%	€511,081

Therefore, CGT is payable in Ireland on all of the gains realised by Mary even though she is no longer Irish tax resident and did not bring the proceeds from the Hungarian disposal into Ireland. Mary is still ordinarily tax resident and Irish domiciled and will remain within the charge to Irish CGT on her worldwide assets until 2024, assuming she remains non-resident for the three consecutive tax years following 2020.

Temporary Non-residence

The territorial provisions for CGT outlined above are subject to an exception that applies to what are known as "temporary non-residents" who dispose of certain assets. This anti-avoidance measure was introduced to counter tax-planning structures whereby individuals went temporarily offshore to avoid large CGT liabilities arising on the disposal of company shares.

Under section 29A TCA 1997, Irish domiciled individuals who try to avoid CGT on the disposal of certain assets by temporarily leaving the State to take up tax residence elsewhere are still liable to Irish CGT if they do not remain outside of Ireland for a period of more than five intervening years from the date of departure to the date of return.

The assets concerned, known as "relevant assets" in the legislation, are a holding in a company the value of which is either 5% or more of the value of all that company's issued share capital or is worth €500,000 or more.

If an individual disposes of all or part of such assets during a period of **not more than five intervening years** from the date of his or her departure from the State, then that individual may be liable to CGT on this disposal.

The CGT charge arises by deeming the relevant assets to be disposed of at their market value on the last day of the year of departure. If there is an increase or decrease in the market value of the assets between the last day of the year of departure and the date they were disposed of, then the market value of the assets on the date they were disposed of will be used for the purposes of the CGT charge. The CGT charge should be included in the individual's return and the tax arising thereon must be accounted for in the year in which the individual is again taxable in the State.

Example 12.5

Kenny McNamara has lived in Ireland all his life and is Irish domiciled.

In 1996 he set up a successful telecommunications company of which he beneficially owns 99% and his wife holds 1%. He received an offer of €50 million for the company from a multinational telecommunications firm in November 2016. He decided to defer the sale for a period so he could move abroad on 20 November 2016 and lose his Irish tax residence and ordinary residence status in the hope of saving €16.4 million in Irish CGT. He located to a tax jurisdiction where he will not be liable to tax on the gains under the local tax law.

If he sells the shares while he is neither resident nor ordinarily resident in Ireland, he will avoid the charge to CGT under section 29 TCA 1997.

If Kenny becomes a tax resident in Ireland again in 2022, then section 29A TCA 1997 applies because he is only a non-resident for the tax years 2017–2021 inclusive, totalling five years, which comes within the "intervening period of not more than five years" and thus fails the test.

If Kenny returns to take up tax residency in Ireland in 2023, there will be six intervening years between the date of departure and return. This is more than "an intervening period of not more than five years", so he would not be within the charge of section 29A.

2016 – resident and ordinarily resident (year of departure);
2017 – not resident – but ordinarily resident;
2018 – not resident – but ordinarily resident;
2019 – not resident – but ordinarily resident;
2020 – not resident – not ordinarily resident;
2021 – not resident – not ordinarily resident;
2022 – not resident – not ordinarily resident;
2023 – resident – not ordinarily resident (year of return).

The anti-avoidance rule under section 29A is a strong deterrent to tax planning that tries to avoid Irish CGT through using non-residency. It imposes a very long period of exile from Ireland, which may not be practical for the very type of person who would like to use that form of planning in the first place.

Non-domiciled Tax Resident/Ordinarily Resident

Under section 29(4) TCA 1997, a person who is an Irish resident (and/or is ordinarily resident) but is not Irish domiciled is chargeable on:

1. gains from the disposal of Irish assets in the year of assessment; and
2. gains remitted into the State in the year of assessment on the disposal of foreign assets.

Section 29(4) TCA 1997 only taxes remittances of gains and, therefore, proceeds arising from the disposal of loss-making assets can be remitted tax free. However, the loss cannot be used in the computation of taxable gains under normal rules, i.e. such losses cannot be offset against other taxable gains arising in the year of assessment and cannot be carried forward for offset in a subsequent year of assessment.

The remitted gains are assessable to Irish CGT in the year the gains are remitted rather than in the year the disposal giving rise to the gain takes place. This treatment only applies where the individual was an Irish resident at the time of the disposal. If a non-domiciled individual remits capital from gains or earnings that arose before he or she took up residency, then such remittances are not taxable under section 29(4) TCA 1997.

> **Example 12.6**
>
> Matti Ludwick is German domiciled and has lived in Ireland on a full-time basis since 2007. Matti is very proud of his German origins and plans to retire to Germany, and would not necessarily be living here if it were not for the fact that he has an Irish wife.
>
> In order to fund the purchase of a home in Ireland in 2007, Matti remitted proceeds arising from the profitable disposal of US property in 2004. The gain arose on a disposal realised by Matti before he became Irish tax resident. Therefore, no CGT was payable on the remittance of the gain in 2007.
>
> Matti disposes of UK property, making a gain of €200,000, and of German property, making a loss of €100,000, in the tax year 2022. He would like to tax-efficiently remit some of the proceeds into Ireland.
>
> On consultation with his Chartered Accountant, Matti remits the proceeds arising from the loss-making German property into Ireland in 2022 and no CGT is payable. In 2023, Matti remits the full proceeds arising from the sale of the profit-making UK property and becomes liable to Irish CGT in 2023 on the gain underlying this remittance.

An anti-avoidance provision in section 29(5A) TCA 1997 applies where a non-domiciled individual makes a transfer of chargeable gains outside the State that would otherwise be subject to the remittance basis. It applies where a non-Irish domiciled individual makes a transfer outside the State of the proceeds of gains to a spouse located offshore with that spouse then bringing the funds into Ireland. The amount brought or received in the State will be deemed to be a remittance by the individual who made the transfer to their spouse or civil partner.

> **Key Issue**
>
> Non-domiciled individuals should always keep profits and gains from transactions which arise before they become Irish tax resident in a separate bank account so that they can clearly identify and remit such funds tax free into Ireland.

Non-resident/Non-domiciled

A person who is neither resident nor ordinarily resident nor domiciled in Ireland may still be within the charge to Irish CGT on the disposal of Irish specified assets under section 29(3) TCA 1997.

Therefore, irrespective of the residence, ordinary residence or domicile of the person making the disposal, Irish CGT may arise on the disposal of the following:

1. Land in the State, including buildings on the land. This is the most common situation whereby a non-resident, non-domiciled individual or entity could come within the charge to Irish CGT. For example, if a French resident pension fund disposes of an office block in Limerick held as an investment asset, then the French pension fund will be liable to Irish CGT as the asset in question is an Irish specified asset under section 29(3) TCA 1997.
2. Minerals in the State, including rights and interests in minerals and other assets relating to mining or minerals, or searching for minerals.
3. Assets associated with a trade carried on in the State by the non-resident through a branch or agency.
4. A non-resident company carrying on a trade in Ireland through a branch is subject to corporation tax on gains arising from the disposal of assets used for the trade, including land and buildings.
5. If a non-resident company disposes of specified assets which are not used for the purpose of its trade or if it disposes of development land, then the non-resident company will be liable to CGT on gains arising on such disposals.
6. Assets situated outside the State of an overseas life assurance company that are used to back its Irish branch's liabilities.
7. Unquoted shares in a company, which derives the greater part of its value from assets outlined in 1. and 2. above, i.e. Irish land and minerals by virtue of section 29(1).

On the sale of shares in an unquoted company by a non-resident/non-domiciled individual or entity, the underlying value of the shares must be examined to establish if the shares derive the greater part of their value from Irish land, buildings or mineral assets. Therefore, commercial share valuation tests must be applied to establish if 50% or more of the value of shares is derived from Irish land/buildings and/or Irish mineral assets in order to assess if the shares qualify as specified assets. Anti-avoidance provisions apply to counter 'cash swamping' transactions, whereby cash and/or other assets are transferred to a company so that its shares do not derive their value from Irish land and buildings.

Key Issue

A non-resident/ordinarily resident, non-domiciled individual or entity can dispose of shares in an Irish quoted company or in an unquoted company which does not derive the greater part of its value from Irish land, building and/or mineral assets, free of Irish CGT. This makes Ireland a good location for international holding companies and investors who can also sell subsidiaries tax free in certain circumstances (see **Section 12.4**).

12.4 Territorial Provisions for Corporation Tax

The liability to corporation tax is primarily based on the concept of residence, which means that resident companies are taxable on their worldwide income. Non-resident companies may be subject to corporation tax if they have Irish-source trading income. Non-resident companies that do not trade in Ireland are not subject to corporation tax, although they may be subject to Irish income tax on Irish-source income (such as rental income from Irish property). The tax residency rules for companies are discussed in detail in CA Proficiency 2 and a brief reminder of these rules is set out below.

12.4.1 Company Residence

The process for determining a company's residence requires consideration of case law, Irish tax law and the provisions of relevant double taxation agreements. In this section we will take a brief look at how to determine a company's residence under tax legislation and case law (refer to CA Proficiency 2 for a detailed discussion of residency rules); double tax treaties will be discussed in **Chapter 13.**

The general rule, as provided for under **section 23A(2)** TCA 1997, is that all companies incorporated in Ireland on or after 1 January 2015 are resident in Ireland. An exception to the rule of incorporation applies if the company is considered to be tax resident in another jurisdiction under a double tax treaty, in which case, the company will not be Irish resident.

If the company was incorporated before 1 January 2015, then until 31 December 2020 the 'old rules' are used to determine whether the company is Irish tax resident, i.e. a company's tax residency is determined by central management and control tests as set out below.

However, even if the company was incorporated before 1 January 2015, if there is a change in ownership and a major change in the nature or conduct of the business of the company, it will be Irish tax resident from the date of the change in ownership.

Residence: Central Management and Control Test

According to established case law, the Irish tax-residence of a company is determined on the grounds of central management and control. The courts, by examining all of the evidence, attempted to ascertain where the central management and control actually abides and laid down the following tests to establish this:

1. location of directors' meetings;
2. location of shareholders' meetings;

3. location of statutory books and company seal; and
4. location where major contracts are negotiated and policy determined.

The test of central management remains a basis upon which a company may be regarded as being resident in Ireland.

12.4.2 Resident Company Charge to Corporation Tax or CGT?

A resident company's taxable gains (other than gains from development land) are computed in accordance with CGT principles but are chargeable to corporation tax.

   Such gains are included in a company's profits for corporation tax purposes and are charged to tax under a formula that ensures that the rate payable on the gain is equivalent to the CGT rate, which is currently 33%.

Example 12.7

Regular Trading Co. disposed of a rental property for €500,000 and incurred legal costs on the disposal of €5,000 in the accounting year ended 31 December 2022.

It originally purchased the property on 22 December 2009 for €120,000. The acquisition was exempt from stamp duty. It incurred professional fees incidental to the purchase of the property of €2,500.

The tax arising on the disposal is calculated as follows:

	€
Proceeds on disposal	500,000
Less: cost of disposal	(5,000)
	495,000
Less: original acquisition cost	(120,000)
Less: costs of acquisition	(2,500)
Taxable gain	372,500
Taxed @ 33%	122,925
Recalculated for corporation tax purposes:	
Rebased chargeable gain (€122,925/12.5%)	983,400
Corporation tax @ 12.5%	122,925

The tax liability should be paid as part of the company's corporate tax liability under the corporation tax payment rules.

Gains realised by companies from disposals of development land are chargeable to CGT and are not included in profits chargeable to corporation tax. Development land is land that has a market value in excess of its current use value.

Example 12.8

Tarento Ltd prepares annual accounts to 30 September. On 1 December 2022 it sells a development site and incurs a CGT liability of €50,000 on the gain. This CGT liability is assessable in the tax year 2022 in accordance with CGT payment rules and the CGT liability must be paid in full by 31 January 2023, i.e. the disposal took place in the "later payment period of CGT" for 2022.

12.4.3 Non-resident Company Charge to Corporation Tax or CGT?

Non-resident companies are chargeable to corporation tax in respect of gains on specified assets, i.e. Irish land, minerals, etc. if:

1. the company carries on, or had carried on, a trade in Ireland through a branch or agency; and
2. the assets were used "in or for the purposes of the trade" or "used or held or acquired for the purposes of the branch or agency"; and
3. the assets are located in the State at the date of disposal.

Non-resident companies are liable to CGT in respect of chargeable gains arising on the disposal of specified assets where such gains are not within the charge to corporation tax, i.e. where the assets disposed of are not assets of an Irish trading branch even if the non-resident company has a branch in Ireland.

Chargeable gains arising on the disposal of development land are liable to CGT and not corporation tax irrespective of the residence of the company.

Example 12.9

A Dutch company carries on a trade of software development through an Irish branch. The branch has a 31 December year end. The Dutch company is forced to rationalise the Irish operation and sells a portion of the plant and equipment realising a gain of €100,000 and a site (not a branch asset), with planning permission for the construction of an industrial unit and offices, realising a gain of €1,100,000.

Both disposals take place on 20 June 2022.

The following Irish tax liabilities will arise:

Corporation Tax

Gain	€100,000
Taxed @ 33%	€33,000
Rebased for corporation tax	€264,000
Taxed at corporation tax	€33,000

This gain must be paid as part of the company's corporation tax liability for the year ending 31 December 2022.

CGT

Gain	€1,100,000
Taxed @ 33%	€363,000

This gain must be paid in accordance with the CGT deadline dates, i.e. it should be paid by 15 December 2022.

Anti-tax avoidance provisions are in place to counteract schemes whereby cash is transferred to a company prior to a disposal of shares in that company. This is to prevent the possibility of the shares then being disposed of at a time when the value of those shares is derived mainly from cash, rather than from Irish land and buildings or Irish mineral rights.

12.4.4 Exit Tax

Section 627 TCA 1997 contains provisions to counteract the potential benefits for companies exiting tax residence in Ireland before disposing of their assets and thereby avoiding a charge to Irish CGT. With effect from 10 October 2018, an 'exit tax' (or 'exit charge') compliant with the EU's Anti-Tax Avoidance Directive (ATAD) (see **Chapter 13**) took effect. The ATAD version of the exit tax is broader than the version in place up to that date, but the rate of the exit tax reduced from 33% to 12.5%. The exit tax applies where:

- a company transfers assets from its permanent establishment in Ireland to its head office or permanent establishment in another country; or

- a company transfers the business carried on by its permanent establishment in Ireland to another country; or
- an Irish resident company transfers its residence to another country.

In the case of a company ceasing to be Irish resident, no exit tax arises where the assets of the migrating company continue to be used as part of a trade in Ireland. The exit tax will also not apply to temporary transfers of assets for specific purposes, such as:

- assets relating to the financing of securities;
- assets given as security for a debt; or
- where the transfer takes place in order to meet prudential capital requirements or for liquidity purposes.

For these exemptions to apply, the asset must be due to revert to the permanent establishment of the company within 12 months of the transfer.

The exit tax rules do not apply to:

- relevant assets within meaning of section 29(1A)(a) TCA 1997 (being land in the State, minerals and mining rights in the State, exploration or exploitation rights of the continental shelf);
- unquoted shares deriving their value directly or indirectly from relevant assets; or
- assets situated outside the State of an overseas life assurance company held in connection with the life business carried on by the company, which at or before the time the chargeable gains accrued were used or held by or for the purposes of that company's branch or agency in the State.

The above assets are not subject to the 12.5% exit tax because such assets are already within the charge to Irish tax, irrespective of the tax-residence of the person who owns them.

The rate of tax on the deemed gain is 12.5%. However, an anti-avoidance provision applies to impose the 33% rate rather than the 12.5% rate if the event that gives rise to the exit tax charge forms part of a transaction to dispose of the assets and the purposes of the transaction is to ensure that the gain is charged at the lower rate – in other words that the transaction is an artificial transaction set up to access the 12.5% rate of tax.

Deferral of Exit Tax

Where the assets are transferred to an EU/EEA country, a company may opt to pay the exit tax over six instalment payments. The first payment is due on the 23rd of month nine after the event which triggered the exit tax where the company is liable to corporation tax.

Where the company is liable to CGT, rather than corporation tax, on the disposal, then the first instalment is due on 31 October in the tax year following the event which triggered the exit tax. The remaining instalments are due on each of the next five anniversaries by reference to the first instalment payment due date. In order to qualify for the instalment arrangement, the company must file a return of specific information with Revenue within 21 days of the event which triggers the exit tax.

An immediate payment of outstanding exit tax and interest (at 0.0219% per day on the full outstanding balance) is triggered when any of the following events occur:

- the assets are sold or otherwise disposed of;
- the assets are transferred to country outside the EU/EEA;
- the company ceases to be resident in the EU/EEA;
- the business carried on by a permanent establishment of the company is transferred to a country outside the EU/EEA;
- the company becomes insolvent or a liquidator is appointed to the company; or
- the company fails to pay the instalments on the due date and this failure has not been rectified within 12 months of that date.

Example 12.10

Euro Ltd is a trading company which operates in Kildare. The company was originally incorporated in Ireland in 2018 and its shareholders were all Irish tax resident. On 1 January 2022, Euro Ltd was taken over by Italia Co. an Italian resident company controlled by individuals resident in Italy. Since the takeover in 2022, the directors' and shareholders' meetings have taken place in Italy. The majority of business is also carried out in Italy. At the time of the takeover in January 2022, Euro Ltd had the following assets:

- Industrial unit in Kildare used for the purpose of its trade
- Commercial building in Germany
- Shares in a Spanish company

In order to determine whether an exit charge is deemed to arise under section 627 TCA 1997, it is necessary to establish if Euro Ltd "exited" Ireland, i.e. ceased to be Irish tax resident, in 2022.

Incorporation Test

Euro Ltd was incorporated in 2018 and is treated as Irish tax resident under the general incorporation rule.

Managed and Controlled in the State

Following the takeover in 2022, the company is likely to be considered to be managed and controlled in Italy as that is the place where the directors' and shareholders' meetings are held, and the majority of the business takes place in Italy.

On the basis that Euro Ltd is managed and controlled in Italy since 1 January 2022, it will be treated as Italian resident from that date. Therefore, it ceased to be Irish tax resident from 1 January 2022.

Exit Charge

Italia Co holds 100% of Euro Ltd's issued share capital. An exit tax is potentially triggered on the chargeable assets held by Euro Ltd when it ceased to be Irish tax resident from 1 January 2022.

Euro Ltd will be treated as operating in Ireland as a branch. As the industrial building is located in the State and is also used for the purpose of Euro Ltd's trade, then an immediate exit tax is not triggered on this asset.

Gains arising on the disposal of the office block in Germany and the shares in the Spanish company are subject to the exit tax on the gain arising on their deemed disposal.

12.5 Tax Clearance and Withholding Tax Obligations

Irish tax on gains can arise on the disposal of Irish assets in circumstances whereby the **vendor** (who is generally the taxpayer) is non-resident in Ireland. So how does the Irish Revenue ensure that taxpayers located overseas actually fulfil their Irish tax obligations on such gains?

This problem is overcome by putting a tax obligation on the **purchaser** of such assets. Under section 980 TCA 1997, a purchaser is obliged to withhold 15% of the total sale proceeds on the sale of certain assets and pay it over to Revenue within 30 days of payment of the consideration for the asset. Interest will run and be charged on the purchaser if the tax is not paid by the due date.

12.5.1 Assets to which Section 980 TCA 1997 Applies

The requirement to deduct tax from the sale proceeds applies only to particular assets, as outlined under section 980(2), where the consideration for the disposal exceeds a specified amount. The withholding tax provisions will only apply to disposals of residential property with consideration in excess of €1 million.

The provisions will apply to other assets, i.e. non-residential property assets, where the consideration exceeds €500,000. The assets to which section 980 applies are:

1. Irish land and buildings;
2. minerals in Ireland or any rights, interests or other assets in relation to mining or minerals or the searching for minerals;
3. exploration or exploitation rights within the limits of the Irish Continental Shelf;
4. unquoted shares in a company deriving their value or the greater part of their value directly or indirectly from 1., 2. or 3. above;
5. unquoted shares, accepted in exchange for shares deriving their value from assets outlined in 1., 2. or 3.; or
6. the goodwill of a trade carried on in Ireland.

The assets detailed under points 1.–4. above should by now be recognisable to you as specified assets under section 29(3) TCA 1997, with the exception of assets associated with a trade carried on in the State by a non-resident through a branch or agency. However, goodwill is noted in the legislation as an asset to which section 980 applies and so comes within the ambit of the legislation by special mention.

Anti-avoidance provisions apply to counter 'cash swamping' transactions, whereby cash and/or other assets are transferred to a company so that its shares do not derive their value from Irish land and buildings. Section 980(2A) applies when there is:

- a transfer of money or other assets from a person connected with the company in which those shares are held,
- which is made before a disposal of relevant assets, and
- the main purpose, or one of the main purposes, of which is the avoidance of tax.

While the rules under section 980 are designed to collect tax in the case of a non-resident where later collection may be impossible, the rules, however, apply to all disposals of the assets outlined above whether by a non-resident taxpayer **or by an Irish resident taxpayer**.

12.5.2 Circumstances where Withholding Tax is Not Applied

Tax does not have to be withheld by the purchaser of an asset in certain circumstances where the vendor is able to produce a tax clearance certificate, known as a CG50 clearance, from Revenue authorising the payments to be made in full. An Irish resident taxpayer making a disposal is entitled to such a clearance certificate as of right, provided he/she applies for it in time, i.e. before the transfer/conveyance of the asset in exchange for consideration, and provided Revenue is satisfied with all of the information contained in the CG50 clearance application form.

A non-resident person will receive such a certificate only where:

1. he/she has satisfied Revenue that he/she has no liability; or
2. he/she has actually calculated, agreed and discharged the CGT liability arising to Revenue.

If the vendor does not have sufficient funds to pay the tax at 2. in advance of the disposal, Revenue will, in certain circumstances, accept a written undertaking from the vendor's solicitor.

The rate of withholding tax is 15% and is chargeable on the full consideration irrespective of the gain or loss arising on the disposal. Where the consideration exceeds the relevant limit (€1 million for residential property and €500,000 in all other cases), the full proceeds are chargeable at 15% and not just the excess over the relevant limit.

Where VAT arises on a transaction, the VAT-inclusive price should be used to determine if the consideration passing exceeds the appropriate limit and to calculate the amount which must be withheld or accounted for on the CG50 clearance application.

Example 12.11

Evita Gonzalla is an Argentine citizen and resident who owns a 50% share in an Irish trading partnership. The remaining 50% of the partnership is held by Evita's former husband, John O'Malley. John is Irish tax resident and domiciled. The partnership's main assets consist of goodwill valued at €510,000 and a commercial unit valued at €1.5 million. The property was originally purchased for €500,000 in July 1991. The business was built up from scratch so the goodwill does not have a base cost.

Evita and John agree to sell the business and property and split the net cash proceeds 50:50, and enter into a contract for sale with an arm's length third-party purchaser on 21 February 2022.

The goodwill and buildings located in Ireland are assets to which section 980 applies. With total proceeds in excess of €500,000, the purchaser will be required to withhold 15% of the total proceeds if John and Evita do not provide a CG50 clearance certificate.

John, as an Irish tax resident individual, can apply for CG50 clearance on his 50% share of the building and goodwill. If the application is made before the closing of the sale and all of the required information is provided with the application, then Revenue will issue a CG50 clearance to John.

CGT on the sale of the property:

		€
Proceeds		1,500,000
Original cost	€500,000	
Indexation	@1.406	(703,000)
Net gain		797,000
John's 50% share		398,500
Less: personal exemption		(1,270)
Taxable gain		397,230
Taxed @ 33%		131,086

John will receive 50% of the gain and must pay CGT of €131,086 on the sale of the building on or before 15 December 2022.

CGT on the sale of the goodwill:

	€
Total proceeds	510,000
Original cost	Nil
Taxable gains	510,000
Taxed @ 33%	168,300

John must pay CGT of €84,150 (i.e. 50% of the tax) in respect of his share of the gain arising on the sale of the goodwill on or before 15 December 2022.

Evita as a non-resident individual will not get a CG50 clearance unless she can establish that no amount of CGT is payable on the disposal or that the CGT arising on the gain is fully discharged and paid to Revenue.

As the goodwill is an asset used for the purposes of a trade carried on in Ireland, it is a specified asset for the purposes of section 29(3)(c) and the building is also a specified asset under section 29(3)(a). Evita is therefore within the charge to Irish CGT, so she cannot get a CG50 clearance on the grounds that she is not liable to CGT. The other option open to her is to provide a calculation and a payment of €131,086 on the sale of the property and €84,150 on the sale of the goodwill to Revenue on applying for a CG50 clearance.

If Evita does not get a CG50 clearance certificate, then the purchaser must withhold €150,750 from the proceeds (15% of Evita's €1,005,000 share). Of course, Evita is obliged to pay the full liability arising on the gain by 15 December 2022 and will be entitled to a credit for the 15% tax withheld at source if she decides not to apply for CG50 clearance.

Please note, for the purposes of this example it has been assumed that John does not satisfy the conditions necessary to avail of the 10% CGT rate for entrepreneurs.

12.6 Capital Acquisitions Tax

Capital acquisitions tax (CAT) is payable by a beneficiary on the receipt of a gift or inheritance. Prior to 1 December 1999, the charge to CAT was based on the domicile of the person making the gift/inheritance or whether the assets were situated in Ireland at the date of the gift/inheritance.

Section 6 CATCA 2003 in the case of gifts and section 11 CATCA 2003 in the case of inheritances provide that an individual who takes a gift or inheritance on or after 1 December 1999 is now generally within the charge to Irish CAT if:

1. the disponer (the person making the gift or inheritance) is resident or ordinarily resident in Ireland at the date of the disposition; or
2. the beneficiary is resident or ordinarily resident in Ireland at the date of the gift or inheritance; or
3. the assets which are the subject of the gift or the inheritance are Irish assets.

The date of the disposition for gift purposes generally means the date that the gift is made. For an inheritance, the date of the disposition generally means the date of the disponer's death.

Special rules apply to non-domiciled persons who, because of taking residency in Ireland, might otherwise have a liability to Irish CAT on worldwide gifts/inheritances made or received by them.

The special rules, which took effect from 1 December 2004, provide that a non-domiciled person is only treated as being resident or ordinarily resident for CAT purposes if the individual has been resident in the State for five consecutive tax years preceding the year of assessment in which the gift/inheritance falls, and the individual must be resident or ordinarily resident in the State on the date of the gift/inheritance. This special rule gives a non-domiciled person the opportunity to plan their stays in Ireland to ensure that they do not come within the ambit of Irish CAT.

Example 12.12

Brigitte has lived full-time in Ireland since 1 January 2009. She is originally from France and has retained a French domicile. Brigitte receives a gift of French property from her French resident father in March 2022. This gift is liable to Irish gift tax in Brigitte's hands because she is tax resident **and** has lived in Ireland for five consecutive tax years preceding the year of assessment in which the gift is made.

If Brigitte had broken her residency in Ireland in any year in the five years before she took the gift, then she would have avoided the charge to Irish CAT on the gift.

12.6.1 Shares in Foreign Incorporated Family-owned Companies

Anti-avoidance measures are in place to ensure that Irish domiciled non-resident individuals cannot avoid Irish CAT on Irish property by artificially changing the locality of Irish situated assets by transferring the assets into a foreign incorporated, family-controlled private company. Shares in a foreign incorporated company would be non-Irish assets. Accordingly, a gift of shares in a foreign incorporated company by a non-resident Irish domiciled person would be outside the charge to Irish CAT.

Where the beneficiary, after taking the gift or inheritance, controls a private company incorporated outside the State, the beneficiary is liable to Irish CAT to the extent that the assets of the foreign company are Irish assets.

This anti-avoidance measure is not applicable if the disponer is not Irish domiciled.

12.6.2 Non-resident Beneficiary

Where a non-resident inherits a benefit with a market value in excess of €20,000 and the personal representative is also non-resident, an Irish-resident solicitor must be appointed to act in connection with the administration of the deceased's estate. This solicitor may be assessed and charged in respect of any CAT due by such a non-resident.

Where a non-resident receives an inheritance and the personal representative is resident in the State, and if the beneficiary is required to and does not file a return and pay the CAT due in respect of the inheritance, then the personal representative may be assessed and charged with the payment of the CAT due by the beneficiary.

The personal representative/solicitor will not be liable for CAT due by the beneficiary where the liability arose due to the fact that the beneficiary had previously received a taxable gift or inheritance and the personal representative had made reasonable enquiries regarding such gifts or inheritances and has acted in good faith.

The personal representative/solicitor will only be held liable to the extent that they have control of the property which is the subject of the inheritance and is entitled to retain funds to cover the CAT liability from the property over which they have control. The personal representative/solicitor is also entitled to raise the funds required to pay any CAT by the sale or mortgaging of any property due to the beneficiary.

12.7 Stamp Duty

Stamp duty is chargeable on instruments, i.e. written documents such as contracts, leases, mortgages, covenants, etc. The instruments are categorised under "heads of charge" in SDCA 1999 and the rate of stamp duty is determined accordingly. The main heads of charge are:

1. conveyance or transfer on sale;
2. a lease;
3. a mortgage; and
4. a bond, covenant or instrument of any kind whatsoever.

The rules for determining a charge to stamp duty are unlike the rules for CAT, CGT, income tax and corporation tax, which have residence and domicile as the basis on which a taxpayer is chargeable to tax in Ireland. For stamp duty purposes, an instrument which falls within a particular category of legal instrument, known as heads of charge, is chargeable to Irish stamp duty if:

1. it is executed in the State; or
2. wherever executed, it relates to any property situated in the State, or any matter or thing done or to be done in the State.

12.7.1 Execution in the State

An instrument executed within the State is chargeable wherever the property, which is the subject matter of the instrument, is located. Accordingly, in the absence of an available relief or exemption, documents affecting the transfer of non-Irish property should be executed abroad.

Example 12.13
An instrument transferring property in the United Kingdom executed in Ireland would be liable to Irish stamp duty even where the vendor or purchaser are non-Irish residents.

12.7.2 Property Situated in the State or any Matter or Thing to be Carried out in the State

A transfer of Irish property no matter where the instrument is executed will fall within the charge of Irish stamp duty.

> **Example 12.14**
> A German citizen purchases a farm in Co. Kerry from a Dutch citizen. Neither the vendor nor the purchaser is tax resident in Ireland and the sale contract is executed in Germany. However, the sale is still liable to Irish stamp duty as the contract relates to property located in Ireland.

Questions frequently arise regarding the words "any matter or thing to be done in the State". The typical example used to illustrate this point, based on relevant case law, arises where consideration for a foreign property consists of the transfer of shares in an Irish company. The share transfer of Irish registered shares (which is a stampable document) will be stampable in Ireland regardless of whether the deed of transfer is executed abroad. Thus the overall transaction is subject to Irish stamp duty.

Revenue has confirmed that the words "any matter or thing" relate to circumstances where an instrument involves a substantive action or obligation to be carried out in Ireland. Where the only link to Ireland is the fact that one or both of the parties to the instrument is resident in Ireland, this will not be considered enough to bring the document into charge.

> **Example 12.15**
> If an Irish person buys an apartment in Florida from another Irish person and the deed of transfer is executed in Florida, a charge to Irish stamp duty will not arise.

Chapter 12 Summary

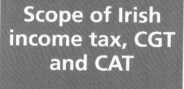

Scope of Irish income tax, CGT and CAT

- Residency – 183-day/280-day tests
- Ordinary/non-ordinary residency – resident/non-resident for three consecutive years
- Domicile – legal concept, generally an an individual takes on the domicile of their father
  - Disposals of Irish specified assets are always liable to Irish CGT
  - Gifts/inheritances of Irish assets are always liable to Irish CAT
  - Irish source income is generally liable to Irish income tax regardless of the residency status of the individual

Scope of Irish corporation tax	• Charged on worldwide profits of companies tax resident in Ireland and profits of Irish branches of non-resident companies • Company is generally regarded as Irish tax-resident if it is managed and controlled in Ireland • Irish incorporated company is Irish tax resident unless the company is treated as tax resident in a state with which Ireland has a double tax agreement (for companies incorporated after 1 January 2015) • Companies incorporated before 1 January 2015 – transitional period up to 1 January 2021
Scope of Irish stamp duty	• Any instrument executed in the State or, wherever executed that relates to any property situated in the State, or any matter or thing to be done in the State, is liable to Irish stamp duty

Questions

Review Question
(See Suggested Solutions to Review Questions at the end of this textbook.)

Question 12.1

Brittas Ltd is a Northern Irish tax-resident company located in Belfast. The company is run by John and Angela Edwards, who are the company directors and 100% shareholders. They are winding down their involvement in the business of the company and moved their home residence to Donegal in 2017, travelling as required to Belfast to deal with company business. The periods of time the Edwards have spent in their Donegal home have resulted in both becoming Irish tax resident from 1 January 2019 to the present date, but they have retained their UK domicile.

They want to retire from the business and gift their 100% shareholding equally to their two sons, Alastair and Josh, in 2022. Alastair and Josh have continued living in Belfast after their parents moved.

The Edwards have asked you, as their Chartered Accountant, to outline the Irish capital tax implications of the proposed gift of the shares in the NI company to Alastair and Josh as a starting point to tax plan the transfer.

Requirement

(a) Outline the Irish CGT implications of the proposed transfer.

(b) Outline the Irish CAT and stamp duty implications of the proposed transfer.

Challenging Question

(Suggested Solutions to Challenging Questions are available through your lecturer.)

Question 12.1

Your client, International Ltd, is faced with substantial trading losses for 2022 and projections for the next few years are also negative. Head office has the challenge of rationalising its assets in an effort to save costs and secure the future of the group.

The following is a list of assets and interests under consideration for disposal:

Asset/Interest	Market Value	Original Cost
80% shareholding in French Co. Ltd	€1,500,000	€500,000
Office block in Germany	€3,000,000	€1,500,000
Industrial unit in Dublin used for trade	€2,000,000	€1,000,000

International Ltd is a trading company, originally incorporated in Ireland in 2010. The chartered accountancy firm you work for acted for the original shareholders of the company, who were bought out in 2013. Your firm continued acting for the new owners of the company. However, not a lot is known about the new owners as the original financial controller continued working for the company after the change of ownership and continued to be the main point of contact with your firm.

You have established the following details about the current owners of International Ltd:

1. Italina Hold Co. is 100% owner of International Ltd.
2. Italina Hold Co. is 100% owned by Luigi and Alba Botticelli, who are Italian citizens.

Luigi and Alba also act as company directors of International Ltd.

You have reviewed the company secretarial file and note that the directors' and shareholders' meetings have taken place in Italy in the last two years and there is also a note on the file to say that the minute books, company seal and share register were sent to Luigi Botticelli in Italy in 2014.

Requirement

You have spoken with the partner in charge of International Ltd, and she has requested that you write a letter to the directors and the financial controller outlining the impact of the company's tax residence status on the charge to Irish tax on gains it will make from the proposed asset disposals.

International Tax Issues

13.1 Double Tax and Relief of Double Tax

13.1.1 How Double Tax Arises

Irish corporation tax is imposed on the worldwide profits, wherever arising, of companies defined as tax resident in Ireland. Therefore, profits arising on a foreign branch of an Irish resident company are taxable in Ireland. In general, the profits of foreign subsidiaries of Irish companies are subject to Irish tax when the profits are distributed to the Irish parent company.

International double taxation issues arise because of overlaps in taxation concepts of the different taxing jurisdictions concerned. Some jurisdictions will tax income or gains because the source of the income or gain, e.g. land, is located in that jurisdiction, while another jurisdiction may seek to tax the same income or gain because the owner of the income or gain is tax resident in its jurisdiction.

Individuals moving from one country to another or spending time in a number of countries may also be taxable in each country on the same income – so double taxation can arise on the same income or gain.

Double taxation relief is concerned with the processes by which countries recognise these multiple tax claims on individuals and companies.

13.1.2 Status of Tax Treaties under Irish Law

Section 826 TCA 1997 gives legal effect to double taxation agreements negotiated by the Irish government with other jurisdictions. These are bilateral treaties and so involve Ireland and one other country. The procedure to enter into a tax treaty involves the negotiation of the terms between the tax authorities, signing of the treaty by each country and ratification by each country's parliament. The terms of any tax treaty will become law in Ireland from the date of insertion of the treaty in the list in Schedule 24A TCA 1997.

For Irish tax purposes, the provisions of Ireland's tax treaties take precedence over national law by virtue of section 826 TCA 1997. The mechanism to give relief from double taxation is set out in Schedule 24 TCA 1997, which provides that articles in a tax treaty can override any provision of the Irish Tax Acts for residents of the other contracting state. Tax treaties do not operate to impose tax, as this is the function of national laws, rather the objective of a tax treaty is to **mitigate double taxation** either by eliminating or relieving it for the residents of either of the contracting states.

At the time of writing, Ireland has concluded tax treaties with 76 countries, 73 of which are in effect.

13.2   The OECD Model Tax Treaty

13.2.1 The Organisation for Economic Co-operation and Development (OECD)

The Organisation for Economic Co-operation and Development (OECD) provides a setting in which governments can compare policy experiences, seek answers to common problems, identify good practices and co-ordinate domestic and international policies. For example, collaboration at the OECD regarding taxation has fostered the growth of a global web of bilateral tax treaties.

In 1963 the OECD introduced the text of a Draft Double Taxation Convention on Income and Capital. Variations of this 'Model Convention' have been subsequently adopted, and it is under constant revision to ensure it reflects the views of member countries on the principles for the relief of double taxation. The most recent update to the Model Convention took place in 2017 and reflected action plans agreed under the BEPS project (see **Section 13.6.1**). These principles have a reasonably wide international acceptance.

Not every country is a member of the OECD and some may seek to adopt the model treaty of the United Nations rather than that of the OECD. The list of OECD member countries is set out in **Appendix 13.1**.

13.2.2 The Model Convention

The purpose of the Model Convention is to give two countries a 'belt and braces' example of a treaty from which they can negotiate their tax treaty. Each article of the Model Convention contains a detailed commentary to expand upon and explain the intention behind each article. Member countries (and, in certain cases, non-member countries) can include comments on the approach they would seek to adopt on that article.

The format of the Model Convention is as follows:

Chapter I – **Scope of the Convention**
>   Article 1 Persons Covered
>   Article 2 Taxes Covered

Chapter II – **Definitions**
>   Article 3 General Definitions
>   Article 4 Resident
>   Article 5 Permanent Establishment

Chapter III – **Taxation of Income**
>   Articles 6–21 Various, covering differing sources of income

Chapter IV – **Taxation of Capital**
>   Article 22 Capital

Chapter V – **Methods for Elimination of Double Taxation**
>   Article 23A Exemption Method
>   Article 23B Credit Method

Chapter VI – **Special Provisions**
> Articles 24–30 Various, including non-discrimination, mutual assistance, territorial scope

Chapter VII – **Final Provisions**
> Article 31 Entry into Force
> Article 32 Termination

Significant articles are discussed in **Section 13.3** in the context of the Ireland/UK tax treaty.

13.2.3 Multilateral Instrument to Amend Double Tax Agreements for BEPS Initiative

The OECD's Multilateral Instrument (MLI) provides a mechanism to allow countries to transpose recommendations from its Base Erosion Profit Shifting (BEPS) initiative (see **Section 13.6.1**) into existing double tax treaties while providing for options in certain areas. The MLI enables Ireland to simultaneously update multiple tax treaties to ensure they comply with certain BEPS recommendations without the need for separate bilateral negotiations.

The MLI took effect in respect of Ireland's bilateral tax treaties from 1 May 2019 and covers 71 out of Ireland's 76 double tax treaties. For a MLI measure to take effect it is necessary that the counter-party treaty jurisdiction has also ratified the MLI.

13.3 The Ireland/UK Tax Treaty: Some Key Aspects

The Ireland/UK tax treaty, based on the OECD Model Convention, was ratified in 1976 and has been amended by Protocols in 1976, 1994 and 1998. It defines whether each state may tax income and capital gains arising to a resident of the other state. Article 21 Elimination of Double Taxation, requires the country of residence to provide relief for double taxation by the credit method for the foreign tax suffered where that income or gains can be taxed in the state where it arises.

13.3.1 Article 1: Personal Scope

Article 1 of the Ireland/UK tax treaty states that it applies to persons who are resident in either, or both, Ireland or the UK, i.e. the "contracting states". Article 4 defines a "resident" of a state as one that "is liable to taxation therein" and it applies to natural persons, companies or any other body that is normally viewed as resident. There is also a negative statement that says that the term would not include those liable to tax only if they derive income from sources in the state.

The Ireland/UK tax treaty does not allow for the concept of dual residence, but it does contain a 'tie-breaker clause' (Article 4) for both natural persons and companies based on their place of effective management (see **Section 13.3.4**).

13.3.2 Article 2: Taxes Covered

The Ireland/UK tax treaty covers the following taxes:

- Ireland: income tax, corporation tax and capital gains tax.
- UK: income tax, corporation tax, petroleum revenue tax, and capital gains tax.

13.3.3 Article 3: General Definitions

This article follows the list of definitions as set out in the Model Convention. As the treaty is agreed law between the states to be used by taxpayers to give clarity on their position, it is vital that there can be no misunderstanding of its provisions. It therefore defines what is meant by the terms "Republic of Ireland", "UK", "nationals", "tax", "contracting state", "person", "company", "enterprise" and "competent authority" in the context of the treaty.

There is a catch-all definition in the last paragraph to say that, in relation to the application of the treaty to a contracting state, unless a term is specifically defined in the treaty, it shall have its normal meaning under the tax laws of that state.

13.3.4 Article 4: Fiscal Domicile

Article 4 provides a mechanism for deciding which state is treated as the state of residence in cases where an individual is dual resident in accordance with the domestic rules of both Ireland and the UK. The 'tie-breaker' provisions are used to establish residency and involve the successive application of a number of objective tests:

1. Where is the individual's permanent home or centre of vital interest? The OECD Model Convention asks a series of questions about where the individual's "centre of vital interest" are, i.e.:
   (a) location of family and social relations;
   (b) location of occupations;
   (c) location of political, cultural or other activities;
   (d) place of business; and
   (e) the place from which property is administered.
2. Where is the individual's habitual abode?
3. Of which state is the individual a national?

If the individual is a national of both states, or of neither, their residence will be determined by mutual agreement of the Irish and UK tax authorities.

Example 13.1

Maeve Longwitch has called you as she wishes to understand her tax position. She considers that she is fundamentally Irish, but she has also spent considerable time in the UK visiting relatives from late September 2021 to April 2022. Maeve has been filing Irish income tax returns since she published her first book of poems in 2007, but she has now received a demand from HMRC in respect of the year ended 5 April 2022 and is quite upset. She asks if she can be tax resident in both Ireland and the UK at the same time.

You explain that, while Ireland's tax year corresponds to the calendar year, the UK's year runs from 6 April. Thus, she would have spent more than 183 days in the UK in tax year 2021/22 and would be considered tax resident in that year under UK tax rules. At the same time, Maeve would have spent sufficient days in Ireland in the tax years 2021 and 2022 to be tax resident there too. Technically Maeve is tax resident in two countries. You hasten to add that the tax treaty between Ireland and UK contains a provision to deal with such cases. You go through the questions with her:

1. Permanent home? Maeve, potentially, has a house in each country available to her in Ireland and in the UK.
2. Habitual abode? It is likely that as, on average, Maeve spends a greater amount of time in Ireland, she would be considered Irish tax resident.
3. Nationality? Maeve is a UK citizen and has a UK passport but, thanks to her Irish grandmother she also holds an Irish passport.

The question of Maeve's tax residency will have to be resolved by mutual agreement between HMRC and Revenue as per Article 4. You volunteer to write to HMRC setting out the facts of the matter, stressing that she has been residing in Ireland for 20 years.

A company may also be deemed tax resident under the domestic laws of both Ireland and the UK. Under Article 4, the tax authorities of Ireland and the UK must endeavour to determine the place of residence of a dual resident company by mutual agreement. The Irish/UK tax authorities will consider factors including the company's place of effective management and the place where it was incorporated.

13.3.5   Article 5: Permanent Establishment

This is an important article and begins with a definition of a permanent establishment (PE) as "a fixed place of business in which the business of the enterprise is wholly or partly carried on". This implies three conditions for a permanent establishment to exist:

1.   there must be a place of business or facility;
2.   the place of business must be "fixed", i.e. must be a distinct place with a degree of permanence; and
3.   the business of the enterprise must be undertaken through this fixed place of business.

Article 5 provides examples of a PE, which include a place of management, a branch office, a factory or workshop. Examples of what does not constitute a PE include the use of facilities solely for the purpose of storage, display or delivery of goods, or for the maintenance of a stock of goods solely for processing by another enterprise, or any combination of the foregoing if the overall activity is of a preparatory or auxiliary nature.

Article 5(4) of the Ireland/UK tax treaty deals with dependent agents. A dependent agent of a UK enterprise who has, and habitually exercises, authority in Ireland to conclude contracts in the name of the enterprise will constitute a PE in Ireland. The agent must be dependent on the enterprise they represent, i.e. be bound to follow instructions as an employee. In addition, the agent must have the authority to bind or conclude contracts regularly on behalf of the enterprise.

A key area to consider is sales. Where sales are concluded in the other state by independent agents of the enterprise, the treaty is clear: there is no taxable presence for it in the other state. However, if the enterprise employs salespersons travelling to, or based in, the other state, it is necessary to examine where the sales contracts are concluded. If the sale is agreed in the other state by the salesperson and they do this on a regular basis, there is a taxable presence there; if not, then there is no taxable presence. In practice it can be difficult to prove where decisions are effectively taken. Good documentation, i.e. contracts, minutes of meetings, etc. is essential. Thus, care should be taken when advising clients on this area.

Clients will often ask about what profits are taxable in the other state (see **Section 13.3.7**), but this question can only be dealt with after you have identified if they have a PE or not.

13.3.6   Article 7: Income from Immovable Property

The Ireland/UK tax treaty provides that rents from property situated in the other state are taxable in the other state (i.e. the UK), but with a right to offset the tax payable against the home state (i.e. Irish) tax on the same income. This allows double taxing, but gives access to relief by way of credit.

13.3.7   Article 8: Business Profits

Article 8 taxes an enterprise in its home state only and exempts it from (double) tax in the other state unless it has a PE in that other state. Where there is a PE, only the profits attributable to that PE, as if it were run as a separate enterprise, can be taxed in the other state. Thus, the PE is allowed deductions from gross income when taxed in the other state and the enterprise is allowed credit relief against the home state taxes arising on the same profits. The process of calculating the profits of the PE can be complex, especially for Irish businesses facing higher UK taxes. In such cases, it is good to document exactly the activities of the PE so that the business can fairly attribute profits to those activities.

13.3.8 Article 11: Dividends

Dividends from an Irish company to a UK resident are exempted from Irish dividend withholding tax (subject to completing the correct forms). Where a UK company pays a dividend to an Irish resident, it will not carry a tax credit against any Irish tax payable.

The Irish tax resident recipient is subject to Irish income tax on the net dividend received.

13.3.9 Article 12: Interest

In broad terms, Article 12 of the Ireland/UK tax treaty taxes a resident on interest in their home state only and exempts them from (double) tax in the other state.

13.3.10 Article 13: Royalties

Again, in broad terms, this type of income is taxable only in the state of residence.

13.3.11 Article 14: Capital Gains

The following gains can be taxed in the other state as well as the home state, with appropriate credit relief for the other state's taxes, i.e.:

- gains on immoveable property in the other state;
- gains on shares deriving their value from immoveable property (other than quoted shares and also partnership or trust asset that derive from such shares); or
- gains on business property of a PE in the other state;
- otherwise, gains are only taxable in the state of residence. The article does not override any domestic provisions relating to capital gains for ordinarily resident individuals. The entire article should be read in full.

13.3.12 Article 15: Employments and Similar

Employment income is taxable in the state of residence of the employee, but it may also be taxable in the source state (where the employer is located). The following three-part test is used to assess if the employment income is taxable in the source state:

1. the employment is exercised in the source state; **and**
2. the employee is present for more than 183 days in the source state; **and**
3. the remuneration is paid by or on behalf of an employer in the source state or the remuneration is borne by a permanent establishment in the source state.

Where this test is 'passed', the income attributable to the source state is taxable based on the period of time spent there by the employee. A double tax credit for tax paid in the source state is allowed against the tax liability of the employee in their home state.

While a UK assignee working temporarily in Ireland may be exempt from the charge to Irish income tax under the terms of the DTA, this does not necessarily preclude the operation of PAYE on their earnings relating to Irish-performed employment duties. The individual may still have to submit a tax return to claim a refund of PAYE operated on their salary.

Income from pensions is treated differently from employment income. Taxing rights on pension income from private-sector pensions (Article 17) is solely given to the recipient's state of residence, notwithstanding that the entire pension fund could have been built up by reference to an employment exercised in the source state. For example, if an Irish individual spends more than 183 days working full-time in the UK, then the UK has the taxing rights on the employment income. If the employee retires and moves back to live in Ireland on a permanent basis, any pension paid by the UK employer is taxable only in Ireland. **Pensions for government services**, however, are normally taxable only in the source state, i.e the paying State (Article 18), and where the individual is a national of the same State paying the government services pension.

Example 13.2
Elizabeth Griffin, a UK citizen, worked in the UK for many years in the House of Lords. She retired to Killarney in January 2022 and is in receipt of a pension from the UK Government. As a consequence of her reloca-tion to Ireland, for the 2022 tax year she is considered to be Irish tax resident and has ceased to be UK tax resident.

The pension received by Elizabeth is only taxable in the UK and is not subject to tax in Ireland under the terms of the Ireland/UK DTA.

13.3.13   Article 21: Elimination of Double Taxation

Article 21 allows for the offset of the other state's taxes against the taxes payable in the state of residence. Only income or gains that arise in the other state, where allowed by the treaty, can be taxed in that other state. The last paragraph of the article sets out that the allocation of profits between the enterprise and its PE should be done on an arm's length basis.

13.3.14   Ireland/UK Double Tax Convention on Estates, Inheritances and Gifts

The Ireland/UK tax treaty applies only to income and capital and does not cover inheritance and gift tax. A similar convention, therefore, has been entered into on estates, inheritances and gifts: the Ireland/UK Double Tax Convention on Estates, Inheritances and Gifts. This too is based on a 'model' OECD Convention.

13.3.15   Trans-border Worker Tax Relief

Trans-border worker tax relief is available where Irish resident individuals are employed in treaty countries for a continuous period of not less than 13 weeks (as per section 825A(1)(a) TCA 1997). It is claimed primarily by cross-border workers who live in the border areas and work in Northern Ireland. As they exercise their employment in the UK for a period of more than 183 days, such employees are normally taxable in the UK in accordance with Article 15 of the treaty.

To be eligible for the relief, the employment must be exercised in a treaty country, the employment income must be taxable in the country where the duties are performed and any foreign tax due on the income must be paid and must not be eligible for repayment. The individual claiming the relief must spend at least one day a week in Ireland and work in the foreign jurisdiction. In this regard, a day is measured by reference to presence at any time during the day. This provision confines the relief to cases where the employee commutes on a weekly or more frequent basis.

Irish public sector employment (in the treaty country) is excluded from the relief. In addition, employment eligible for the remittance basis of taxation is excluded from the relief. Company directors may qualify in respect of their remuneration, but only where the company is trading and not if they are proprietary directors. Income arising in a split year of residence before an employee takes up residence in Ireland is not eligible for the relief. Relief is also not available where seafarer allowance has been claimed.

The relief operates by reducing the individual's Irish tax liability to the "specified amount", calculated by the following formula:

$$\frac{A \times B}{C}$$

where:

A is the individual's total tax liability before any foreign tax credit;
B is the individual's total income excluding the foreign employment; and
C is the individual's total income.

The relief therefore excludes foreign income from Irish tax, but the level of foreign income has an impact on the Irish tax payable by effectively reducing tax credits and bands proportionately. If there is no income other than the foreign employment, Irish tax is eliminated.

Example 13.3

John is a single man who lives in Dundalk but travels on a daily basis to work in Newry. He has employment with a Newry-based company and earns a salary of €30,000 per annum and pays UK tax on this salary of €4,500 per annum. In addition to his employment income, he has net rental income of €4,000 from a rental property in Limerick.

What is John's Irish income tax position for the 2022 tax year?

Prior to section 825A relief

		€
NI employment income		30,000
Irish rental income (B)		4,000
Total income (C)		34,000
Taxable @ 20%		6,800
Tax credits:		
Personal	€1,650	
PAYE	€1,650	(3,300)
Irish tax liability (A)		3,500
Credit for UK tax paid (Note 1)		(2,925)
Tax liability on claiming double tax relief		575

continued overleaf

Note:

1. Calculate tax credit for UK tax – lower of Irish effective rate or UK effective rate:

Irish effective rate = $\dfrac{€3,500}{€34,000} \times 100 = 10.29\%$

UK effective rate = $\dfrac{€4,500}{€30,000} \times 100 = 15\%$

Computation of the amount of UK income chargeable to Irish tax is the income (net of UK tax) grossed-up at the lower of the Irish or UK effective rates, i.e. the Irish effective rate:

$\dfrac{€25,500}{(100 - 10.29\%)} \times 100 = €28,425$

Credit relief is the adjusted UK income at the Irish effective rate: €28,425 × 10.29% = €2,925

Income tax computation with double tax relief:	€
NI employment income adjusted for DTR	28,425
Irish rental income	4,000
Taxable income	32,425
Taxed @ 20%	6,485
Less: tax credits	(3,300)
Tax liability	3,185
Less: credit for UK tax	(2,925)
Tax liability on claiming double tax relief	260

With section 825A relief

The specified amount is:

$$\frac{\text{Irish tax liability} \times \text{Income other than NI employment income}}{\text{Total income}} = \frac{€3,500 \times €4,000}{€34,000} = €412$$

As €412 is higher than the liability after double tax relief of €260, double tax relief should be claimed and cross-border relief under section 825A should not be claimed.

13.4 Taxation of Foreign Income for Irish Resident Individuals and Companies

The main Irish tax issue associated with the taxation of foreign income and gains is whether tax relief is available for foreign tax incurred on income or gains against Irish tax arising on the same income or gains, and the amount of the tax relief available. Double tax relief can take a number of different forms:

- Double-taxation relief can be provided under the terms of a tax treaty, which can:
    - allocate taxing rights between the countries. For example, a treaty may provide that interest income arising in one country is taxable only in the country of residence of the recipient;
    - limit the taxation rights in the source country, for example to 10%;
    - allow a credit for tax incurred in the source country against the tax liability in the country of residence. In this way, the taxpayer pays only a net taxation liability which limits any double taxation;

- provide that income that has been taxed in the source country is exempt from taxation in the residence country. Countries using the exemption method for some income sources include France, Germany, Italy and the Netherlands.
- Double taxation relief can be provided in the domestic law of the country of residence or source. This is known as **unilateral double taxation relief** and generally takes the form of permitting credit relief for foreign tax (as explained in the rest of this section).
- Double taxation relief is also provided for in EU Directives, such as the Parent–Subsidiary Directive, which allocate taxing rights between EU Member States and provide rules for eliminating or mitigating double taxation.

13.4.1 Double Tax Relief Methods

There are three methods of relief to ensure an individual or company does not suffer double tax:

1. by deduction;
2. by exempting the income from the charge to tax in one country; or
3. as a credit.

Deduction Method

The deduction method of double tax relief provides for the deduction of the foreign tax against the income taxable in the residence country. This method is of much less benefit to the taxpayer compared to either the exemption method or the credit method, and does not fully relieve the foreign tax. The overall tax rate will generally be higher when the deduction method is used.

Exemption Method

The exemption method of double taxation exempts income that has borne tax in the other country in accordance with the terms of a double taxation agreement. Under this method, the total tax payable is the tax paid in the residence country. There are various treaty examples of this exemption, such as Article 12 of the Ireland/UK treaty whereby interest derived and beneficially owned by a resident of a contracting state is taxable only in that state. Another example is Article 8 of the Ireland/Germany treaty whereby royalties derived by a resident of one state from a source within the other state are taxable only in the first-mentioned state. Provided the income in the examples outlined does not arise from property or rights used by a branch or agency carrying on a trade in the other contracting state, then the income is simply ignored in the computation of assessable profits in the country from which the income is derived.

Credit Method

The credit method is used to calculate double tax relief in the following circumstances:

1. when a double tax treaty is in place between Ireland and a country that applies foreign tax on income also taxable in Ireland;
2. when foreign tax applies on dividends and branch income received by an Irish resident company and no tax treaty is in place between Ireland and the country which applies the foreign tax. This is unilateral relief under the terms of Irish domestic law, but it follows the credit method for the purposes of calculating the tax relief due in the case of dividend and branch income;
3. when foreign tax arises on the income of subsidiaries of Irish companies that qualify for tax relief under the EU Parent–Subsidiary Directive. (The EU Parent–Subsidiary Directive is beyond the scope of this textbook but it is important to be aware of its existence as another means of facilitating double tax relief.)

A taxpayer can elect not to claim a tax credit for foreign tax, but this is unlikely to be beneficial for the taxpayer.

The foreign taxes for which tax relief can be claimed are limited to taxes charged on income or capital gains that correspond to Irish corporation tax or CGT, but include withholding taxes payable on dividends and underlying taxes paid on profits by the paying company. The underlying taxes can include federal or national taxes and other state, city, canton or provincial taxes. The foreign effective tax rate must be calculated on the profits out of which the dividend is paid and that rate is then used in the unilateral credit relief calculation.

Basic Credit Method Computation for Corporation Tax Purposes

The computation method for calculating a credit for foreign tax is complex and depends on the type of income on which the foreign tax is applied, e.g. branch profits, dividends and interest in the case of companies, and foreign rents or dividends in the case of individuals. While the complex calculations are beyond the scope of this textbook, it is necessary to have a basic understanding of how the credit method of calculating foreign tax relief operates.

To calculate a credit for foreign tax, the following steps apply:

Step 1: Establish the amount of foreign income. Follow the rules applicable under domestic tax law to establish the assessable amount of foreign income.

Step 2: Establish the amount of foreign tax paid on the foreign income

Step 3: Compute the foreign effective rate of tax:

$$\frac{\text{Foreign tax}}{\text{Gross foreign income assessable under Irish domestic tax law}}$$

Step 4: Identify the Irish effective rate, either 12.5% or 25%.

Step 5: Gross-up the net foreign income at the lower of the foreign effective rate of tax or the Irish effective rate of tax.

Step 6: The amount of the credit is:

- the re-grossed amount minus the net foreign income, or
- the amount by which the net foreign income has been re-grossed.

Example 13.4

Step 1:	Foreign income under Irish law		€200,000
Step 2:	Foreign tax		€40,000
Step 3:	Foreign effective rate	20%	
Step 4:	Irish effective rate	12.5%	
Step 5:	Gross-up net foreign income @ 12.5%		€182,857
Step 6:	Credit		€22,857
	Irish tax on foreign income €182,857 @ 12.5%		€22,857
	Less: tax credit		(€22,857)
	Balance of Irish tax due		Nil

The credit for foreign tax in respect of any income cannot exceed the amount of Irish corporation tax attributable to that same income. This is achieved by calculating the "effective rate" of Irish tax on the income and the effective rate of foreign tax. Then the net foreign income is re-grossed at the lower of the Irish effective rate or the foreign effective rate.

Example 13.5

Step 1:	Foreign income under Irish law		€200,000
Step 2:	Foreign tax		€20,000
Step 3:	Foreign effective rate	10%	
Step 4:	Irish effective rate	12.5%	
Step 5:	Gross-up net foreign income @ 10%		€200,000
Step 6:	Credit (amount by which net foreign income is re-grossed)		€20,000
	Irish tax on foreign income €200,000 @ 12.5%		€25,000
	Less: tax credit		(€20,000)
	Balance of Irish tax due		€5,000

Credit relief is more beneficial than relief under the deduction method – the deduction method is essentially an additional trade deduction, whereas the credit method provides a credit against the tax liability that can potentially reduce the Irish tax bill to nil.

Double tax can arise on a number of income sources such as trading royalties, trading interest payments, lease payments, etc. Due to the complexities particular to each income source, this textbook will focus on the two most common income sources on which double tax relief is available, that is branch profits and foreign dividends.

13.4.2 Double Tax Relief for Foreign Branch Profits

An Irish tax resident company operating a cross-border business through a branch or permanent establishment will generally be subject to tax in Ireland at 12.5% on the profits of the foreign branch (because Irish resident companies are taxable on worldwide profits). However, it is also likely that foreign tax will be applied by the jurisdiction in which the foreign branch is trading and so double tax will arise on the same income.

Double tax treaties concluded by Ireland generally provide that tax payable under the domestic laws of the foreign territory on profits is allowed as a credit against Irish tax, computed by reference to the same profits. Where the foreign branch is in a country with which Ireland does not have a double tax treaty, unilateral relief is provided for under Schedule 24, paragraph 9DA TCA 1997. Broadly, the rules for computing relief for branches in treaty and non-treaty states are the same.

Example 13.6

Beta Ltd has a branch in Germany, a tax treaty partner of Ireland. In the year ended 31 December 2022, the branch had trading profits of €150,000. German tax paid amounted to €20,000 (this tax is also the same as tax computed under Irish tax rules). What is the net Irish tax liability on the Germany branch profits?

Double tax relief computation

Step 1:	Foreign income under Irish law		€150,000
Step 2:	Foreign tax		€20,000
Step 3:	Foreign effective rate	13.33%	
Step 4:	Irish effective rate	12.5%	
Step 5:	Gross up net foreign income at 12.5%		€148,571
Step 6:	Credit (amount by which net foreign income is re-grossed)		€18,571
	Irish tax on foreign income €148,571 @ 12.5%		€18,571
	Less: tax credit		(€18,571)
	Balance of Irish tax due		Nil

The foreign tax pooling provisions of Schedule 24, paragraph 9FA TCA 1997 cater for the situation where a company has branches in a number of countries and, in some countries, the foreign tax exceeds the Irish tax on the branch in question, while in others there is no foreign tax on the branch or it is less than the Irish tax on that branch. The amount of foreign tax on each branch that has not qualified for credit relief can be pooled as a credit against the aggregate Irish tax payable on foreign branches.

Example 13.7

Uisce Ltd is an Irish manufacturing company with trading branches located in Germany and Brazil. For the accounting year ended 2022, adjusted trading profits for Irish tax purposes and before foreign tax deduction for the German and Brazilian branches are €150,000 and €500,000, respectively. The German branch profits were subject to German tax of €60,000, while the Brazilian branch profits were subject to Brazilian tax of €10,000. The Irish tax treatment of these foreign branch profits is as follows:

Branch foreign tax credit relief and pooling relief		Germany	Brazil
Step 1	Foreign branch income under Irish tax law	€150,000	€500,000
Step 2	Foreign tax	€60,000	€10,000
Step 3	Foreign effective rate	40%	2%
Step 4	Irish effective rate	12.5%	12.5%
Step 5	Gross-up net foreign income at lower rate (Note 1)	€102,857	€500,000
Step 6	Credit (amount by which net foreign income is re-grossed)	€12,857	€0
	Irish tax on foreign income (Note 2)	€12,857	€62,500
	Less: tax credit	(€12,857)	(€10,000)
	Balance of Irish tax due	Nil	(€52,500)

Notes:

1. German branch income grossed up: (€150,000 – €60,000 = €90,000/87.5%).
2. Irish tax on foreign income

    Germany: €102,857 @ 12.5% = €12,857
    Brazil: €500,000 @ 12.5% = €62,500

Pooling computation

Deductible foreign tax (€60,000 – €12,857)	€47,143	
Less: 12.5% deduction	(€5,893)	
Unrelieved foreign tax for pooling	€41,250	
Allocate against tax on other branch income		€41,250
Irish tax payable		€11,250

Unused credits must be reduced by 12.5% to arrive at the credit available for pooling relief. This deduction takes account of the fact that the Irish company is effectively getting a tax credit based on foreign income of €150,000, while the foreign income liable to Irish tax is the net income re-grossed at the lower Irish tax rate (€102,857 in this example).

Any unused credits can be carried forward for offset against tax on foreign branches in subsequent accounting years.

A foreign branch/permanent establishment can be loss-making, particularly in the start-up years of a trade. The losses of an overseas branch are available for offset against the taxable profits attributable to the Irish company. This would generally not be the case if the foreign business operated through a subsidiary and such losses could only be used against the taxable profits of a related Irish entity, if it can be demonstrated that the losses are 'trapped losses' under section 420C TCA 1997 (which is based on the ruling of the Court of Justice of the European Union in the case of *Marks & Spencer plc v. Halsey* (2005)).

The non-trading profits of an overseas branch of an Irish company are generally taxable at 25% rate of tax rather than the 12.5% rate of tax.

13.4.3 Double Tax Relief for Foreign Dividends

Tax Rate Applied to Foreign Dividends

Foreign income, including foreign dividends, is liable to tax under Schedule D, Case III and the corporation tax rate applicable in the hands of a company receiving the dividend is 25%.

Section 21B TCA 1997 provides for the application of the 12.5% corporation tax rate to dividends paid out of trading profits received from certain non-resident trading entities. These include entities resident:

- in an EU Member State;
- in a country with which Ireland has a double tax treaty in force;
- in a country with which Ireland has signed a double tax treaty that has yet to come into force;
- in a country that has ratified the Joint Council of Europe/OECD Convention on Mutual Assistance in Tax Matters; or
- in a non-treaty country where the company is owned directly or indirectly by a quoted company.

For example, if the dividend is paid out of a foreign subsidiary's trading profits, the 12.5% rate of tax can be applied in the recipient's hands in Ireland (i.e. the parent company). The 12.5% rate will also apply where the dividend is paid through the tiers of foreign trading subsidiaries.

This 12.5% rate will not apply to dividends paid out of excepted trades, typically trades dealing in development property or minerals.

Calculating the Tax Credit

Credit relief is normally available not only for any foreign withholding tax applied on a foreign dividend, but also for tax paid on the profits out of which the dividend has been paid.

Example 13.8

In the year ended 31 December 2022, Ireland Co. received a net dividend of €30,000 from a trading subsidiary company resident in a tax treaty partner state. The dividend was also subject to withholding tax of 10% by the foreign tax authorities. The rate of tax suffered by the foreign subsidiary on its underlying trading profits was 28%.

What is the Irish tax liability arising on the dividend?

Double tax relief computation

Step 1	Gross foreign income (Note 1)		€46,296
Step 2:	Foreign tax (Note 2)	€3,333 + €12,963	€16,296
Step 3:	Foreign effective rate	35.19%	
Step 4:	Irish effective rate	12.5%	
Step 5:	Gross up net foreign income at 12.5% (Note 3)		€34,286
Step 6:	Credit (amount by which net foreign income is re-grossed) (Note 4)		€4,286
	Irish tax on foreign income €34,286 @ 12.5%		€4,286
	Less: tax credit (Note 5)		(€4,286)
	Balance of Irish tax due		Nil

continued overleaf

Notes:

1. Establish withholding tax by re-grossing the net dividend, i.e. €30,000/(1 − 10%) = €33,333. Establish total profits by re-grossing the gross dividend, i.e. €33,333/(1 − 28%) = €46,296.
2. Withholding tax is €3,333 plus underlying tax €46,296 @ 28% = €12,963.
3. Net income €30,000/(1 − 12.5%) = €34,286.
4. Credit = €34,286 − €30,000.

5. Unused credit:

		€
	Total foreign tax	16,296
	Credit claimed	(4,286)
		12,010
	Deduction @ 12.5%	(1,501)
	Unused credit	10,509

The unused credit of €10,509 can be carried forward for offset against foreign dividend income in subsequent accounting periods. Unused credits must be reduced by 12.5% to arrive at the credit available for carry forward. This deduction takes account of the fact that the Irish company is effectively getting a tax credit based on foreign income of €46,296, while the foreign income liable to Irish tax is the net income re-grossed at the lower Irish tax rate, €34,286 in this example.

Onshore Pooling

Onshore pooling allows foreign withholding taxes and underlying taxes (taxes on the profits out of which the dividend has been paid) to be pooled together and used to offset Irish tax on the dividends. However, excess tax on foreign dividends liable at a rate of 12.5% cannot be used against those liable at the 25% rate. Care should therefore be taken when deciding to elect under Section 21B to a have foreign dividend taxed at 12.5% or 25% in terms of onshore pooling relief as excess credits on dividends taxed at 12.5% cannot be offset against tax arising on dividends taxed at 25%. The tax credits do not need to be utilised in the year in which the dividend is received. They can be carried forward indefinitely for offset against Irish tax on future foreign dividends.

Example 13.9

In the year ended 31 December 2022, Ireland Co. received a net dividend of €380,000 from its trading subsidiary resident in France and a net dividend of €360,000 from its trading subsidiary resident in Malta. The rate of tax applied by the French tax authorities was 24% while the rate applied by the Maltese tax authorities 10%. An election was made under Section 21B to have both dividends subject to tax at 12.5%. What is the Irish tax liability arising on the dividend?

Double tax relief computation

		France €		Malta €
Step 1: Gross foreign income		500,000		400,000
Step 2: Foreign tax		120,000		40,000
Step 3: Foreign effective rate	24%		10%	
Step 4: Irish effective rate	12.50%		12.50%	
Step 5: Gross up net foreign income at lower rate		434,286		400,000
Step 6: Credit (amount by which net foreign income is re-grossed)		54,286		40,000
Irish tax on foreign income @ 12.50%		54,286		50,000
Less: tax credit		(54,286)		(40,000)

Tax	(0)	10,000
Less: pooled credit		(10,000)
Net tax due		Nil
Onshore Pooling Workings	**France**	
Total foreign tax	120,000	
Less: credit claimed	(54,286)	
Unused credit	65,714	
Less 12.5% deduction	(8,214)	
Available for pooling	57,500	
Pooled against tax payable	(10,000)	
Excess credit for carry forward	47,500	

Example 13.10

In the year ended 31 December 2022, Eire Co. received a net dividend of €250,000 from its trading subsidiary resident in South Africa and a net dividend of €450,000 from its trading subsidiary resident in Libya. The rate of tax applied by the South African tax authorities was 50%, while the rate applied by the Libyan tax authorities was 10%. As no election is made under section 21B, the dividend from South Africa is subject to tax in Ireland at 25%. As Libya does not have a double tax treaty with Ireland (nor is it a member of the OECD Convention on Mutual Assistance in Tax Matters), the dividend must be taxed at 25%. What is the Irish tax liability arising on the dividend?

Double tax relief computation		**South Africa**	**Libya**
Step 1	Gross foreign income	€500,000	€500,000
Step 2	Foreign tax	€250,000	€50,000
Step 3	Foreign effective rate	50%	10%
Step 4	Irish effective rate	25%	25%
Step 5	Gross-up net foreign income at lower rate (Note 1)	€333,333	€500,000
Step 6	Credit (amount by which net foreign income is re-grossed)	€83,333	€50,000
Irish tax on foreign income @ 25%		€83,333	€125,000
Less: tax credit		(€83,333)	(€50,000)
Tax		(€0)	€75,000
Less: pooled credit			(€75,000)
Net tax due		Nil	Nil

Onshore pooling workings

	South Africa
	€
Total foreign tax	250,000
Less: credit claimed	(83,333)
Unused credit	166,667
Less: 25% deduction	(41,667)
Available for pooling	125,000
Pooled against tax payable	(75,000)
Excess credit for carry forward	50,000

If Eire Co. had elected to have the South African dividend liable to tax at 12.5% under section 21B, then the pooled credit which eliminated the tax on the dividend from the Libyan company would not have been available, because excess credits from dividends taxed at 12.5% cannot be offset against tax arising on dividends taxed at 25%.

Additional Foreign Tax Credit

The additional foreign tax credit (AFTC) is essentially a 'top up' to the 12.5% rate already claimed. It applies to dividends received from companies resident in "a relevant Member State" (i.e. EU, Norway and Iceland) and which are taxable in Ireland at 12.5%. Dividends that are taxable at the 25% rate will have any existing tax credit topped up to 25%.

The formula used to calculate the AFTC is:

$$(A \times B) - C$$

where:

A = the amount of the relevant dividend chargeable to Irish corporation tax;

B = the lower of the Irish corporation tax rate (i.e. 12.5% or 25%) or the "rate per cent of tax, which corresponds, in the relevant Member State in which the source company is resident for tax, to corporation tax in the State, applicable to the relevant profits in relation to the relevant dividend"; and

C = the credit already allowable under Schedule 24 TCA 1997.

Not all dividends will qualify for the above treatment. At a high level, dividends paid out of profits that have not been taxed and have been received directly or indirectly from a company that is not resident in a relevant Member State will be excluded.

Excess AFTC cannot be pooled against tax arising on group foreign dividends.

Example 13.11

Ireland Co. receives a dividend of €70,000 from a Dutch resident trading subsidiary. No withholding tax applied and no tax at source applied either due to loss relief. The Dutch corporation tax of 15% would have applied if loss relief was not available.

AFTC available to Ireland Co. is:

$$(A \times B) - C = €70,000 \times 12.5\% - 0 = €8,750$$

13.4.4 Capital Gains on Foreign Assets

Older Treaties

A number of older double taxation agreements concluded between Ireland and other jurisdictions do not have articles providing for double taxation relief in respect of CGT. Such treaties were negotiated prior to the introduction of CGT in Ireland and, from an Irish perspective, the taxes covered do not include CGT or a similar tax. The treaties in question are with Belgium, Cyprus, France, Italy, Japan, Luxembourg, the Netherlands, Pakistan and Zambia.

Paragraph 9FB, Schedule 24 TCA 1997, grants Irish residents a credit in respect of foreign tax paid on capital gains arising in countries with which Ireland has a tax treaty. This provision applies in respect of accounting periods beginning on or after 1 January 2007.

Disposal of Subsidiaries

Section 626B TCA 1997 provides an exemption from CGT for companies on the disposal of shares in a trading subsidiary company resident in an EU or Irish tax treaty country (see **Chapter 5, Section 5.8**). The relief is unilateral as the other states may or may not allow their residents the same relief.

13.4.5 Trading Losses of Foreign Trades, Branches and Subsidiaries

Losses in Foreign Trades

A foreign trade is one carried on wholly outside of the State by a company resident in the State. For example, an Irish resident company, resident in Ireland because it is incorporated here, but exercising a trade wholly in Germany would be regarded as carrying on a foreign trade. It is taxable under Case III.

A loss on a foreign trade is only available for carry forward against future profits from the same trade. There is no right to offset losses in foreign trades against other profits.

Losses on a Foreign Branch

A trading loss incurred by a branch of an Irish tax resident company should be available for immediate offset against the taxable trading profits of the company for the accounting period in question.

Losses in a Foreign Subsidiary

Where companies are members of a losses group they can surrender losses to each other. However the surrender of losses is only allowed between Irish resident companies, or branches that are within the charge to corporation tax in Ireland. Losses that arise to a non-resident company that is not within the charge to Irish corporation tax cannot be surrendered to an Irish parent company unless the loss is 'trapped', as provided for under section 420C TCA 1997.

Where the surrendering company is not resident in Ireland but is resident in a EEA Member State or a country with which Ireland has a double taxation agreement then section 420C TCA 97, which deals with trapped losses, may apply.

A trapped loss is a loss which cannot be used by the company to which it arose, or any other company in the surrendering EU State or other party to the double taxation agreement, in the current, previous or future accounting period.

A trapped loss can occur where the surrendering company is going into liquidation, or the loss cannot be used due to some other legal provision in the jurisdiction in which the loss arose. A claim for the surrender of a trapped loss must be made within two years of the point in time where it is established that the surrendering company cannot use the loss in any later accounting period.

13.5 Ireland's Incentives as a Location of Choice for Corporates

Ireland actively pursues a tax policy to encourage foreign direct investment (FDI). The key tax benefits offered in Ireland are:

- Ireland has successfully negotiated 76 treaties, which provide for the elimination of double taxation on income such as dividends, interest and branch profits. Where a double taxation agreement is not in place with a jurisdiction, unilateral relief is available which allows credit relief against Irish tax for foreign tax paid in respect of certain types of income.
- The introduction of a Knowledge Development Box (see **Chapter 3, Section 3.8**) and the associated 6.25% rate to qualifying trading income, makes Ireland attractive to knowledge companies (e.g. technology companies).
- The Irish tax of 12.5% applies on certain dividends received by Irish resident companies. Credit is also available in Ireland for foreign tax suffered on the underlying profits.
- Under domestic legislation, there are no dividend withholding tax requirements where the dividend is paid to treaty countries (or intermediary subsidiaries).
- A tax exemption on gains from disposals of qualifying shareholdings (section 626B TCA 1997) (see **Chapter 5, Section 5.8**).
- Ireland grants a 25% credit to companies carrying out qualifying R&D activities in the country. Similar credit relief is also available for expenditure on buildings or structures used for R&D activities (see **Chapter 3, Section 3.7**). This is in addition to the normal tax deduction as a trading expense, which means a potential tax saving of 37.5%.
- Ireland offers an attractive relief for expenditure incurred by companies on certain intangible assets.
- There is no Irish tax cost for companies capitalising an Irish subsidiary.

13.6 Ireland and Global Tax Reform

The early sections to this chapter have set out the reliefs available through the double taxation network and through tax relief provision in domestic legislation for income and gains subject to double taxation. In recent years, however, **non-taxation** of income and gains has become a major policy focus of governments and tax authorities around the world amid allegation of large multinational corporates paying low levels of tax in jurisdictions due to successful international tax structuring. This has led to international initiatives to counter harmful tax practices on a global level and at an EU level.

13.6.1 The BEPS Initiative

In response to weakness to the international tax framework and public controversy regarding the taxation of the profits of multinational enterprises (MNEs), in September 2013 the leaders of the G20 endorsed the OECD Action Plan to address "base erosion and profit shifting" or BEPS for short. The OECD describes the BEPS project in the following terms:

> "BEPS refers to tax planning strategies that exploit gaps and mismatches in tax rules to artificially shift profits to low or no-tax locations where there is little or no economic activity. Although some of the schemes used are illegal, most are not. This undermines the fairness and integrity of tax systems because businesses that operate across borders can use BEPS to gain a competitive advantage over enterprises that operate at a domestic level. Moreover, when taxpayers see multinational corporations legally avoiding income tax, it undermines voluntary compliance by all taxpayers."

The BEPS package provides 15 Actions designed to equip governments with the domestic and international instruments needed to tackle BEPS. Ireland has taken a number of steps towards implementing the BEPS recommendations and was one of the first jurisdictions to implement country-by-country (CbC) reporting.

13.6.2 The Anti-Tax Avoidance Directive (ATAD)

The European Union is also concerned about international tax avoidance and evasion and has responded with the introduction of the Anti-Tax Avoidance Directive (ATAD).

The ATAD is designed to target corporate taxpayers in the EU with cross-border operations. The stated objective of the ATAD is to provide for the effective and swift coordinated implementation of anti-base erosion and profit shifting measures at EU level. The ATAD is binding as to the results it aims to achieve while Member States are free to choose the form and method of achieving those results.

Controlled Foreign Company Rules

Controlled foreign company (CFC) rules are an anti-tax abuse measure, designed to prevent the diversion of profits to offshore entities in low- or no-tax jurisdictions and are required under the ATAD. In Ireland, the CFC rules take effect for accounting periods beginning on or after 1 January 2019. The rules operate by attributing undistributed income of the CFC to the controlling company in Ireland for taxation purposes.

In broad terms, an entity will be considered a CFC under ATAD rules where it is subject to more than 50% control by a parent company and its associated enterprises, and the tax paid on its profits is less than half the tax that would have been paid had the income been subject to tax in the hands of the parent company.

Where an Irish controlling company has been carrying out "significant people functions'" (SPFs) in Ireland, i.e. the Irish company bears the risks and economic ownership of the assets, any undistributed income of the CFC arising from non-genuine arrangements put in place for the purpose of avoiding tax in Ireland is attributed to the Irish controlling company and becomes liable to Irish tax.

> **Key Issue**
> If an Irish company carrying on SPFs in Ireland artificially diverts income to a non-resident company under its control (a CFC) then the Irish company will be subject to Irish tax on the CFC's undistributed artificial profits.

For CFC purposes, a company is considered to have control of a subsidiary where it has direct or indirect ownership of, or entitlement to, more than 50% of the share capital, voting power or distributions.

A number of exemptions apply to operating the CFC rules, including:

- CFCs with low profits (less than €75,000) or a low profit margin (where the arm's-length margin on operating costs is less than 10%).
- The CFC pays a comparatively higher amount of tax in its territory than it would have paid in Ireland.

For accounting periods beginning on or after 1 January 2021, many of the exemptions do not apply to subsidiaries resident in territories which are on the EU's list of non-cooperative jurisdictions for tax purposes. Newly acquired CFCs are allowed a one-year grace period where certain conditions apply.

Where arrangements under which SPFs performed have been entered into on an arm's-length basis, a credit is available against the CFC charge for foreign tax paid on the same income.

13.6.3 Country-by-Country Reporting

Country-by-country (CbC) reporting is part of Action 13 of the BEPS Action Plan and the ATAD. It was introduced in Ireland in 2015 and operates for fiscal years beginning on or after 1 January 2016. CbC reporting is an obligation on an Irish "ultimate parent" of a multinational group, where the group's consolidated revenue (i.e. sales or turnover) exceeded €750 million in the previous fiscal year. The report must be submitted within 12 months of the financial year end and must contain information in respect each jurisdiction in which the MNE group operates.

The information categories are extensive and include: unrelated party revenue, number of employees and the tax identifier number of each constituent entity carrying on a business or tax resident in each jurisdiction. The tax authority of the report remitter can exchange the information with other relevant tax authorities.

13.6.4 Transfer Pricing

Formal transfer pricing provisions were introduced in Ireland in 2010 and were recently amended under Finance Act 2019 to give effect to the OECD's 2017 *Transfer Pricing Guidelines.*

Transfer pricing is the practice used by associated companies to set a price for transactions carried out between their associated business entities. Transfer prices are significant for the taxpayer and tax authorities because the transfer price determines, to a large extent, the income and expenses – and therefore the taxable profits – of associated enterprises in different jurisdictions. In compliance with OECD's *Transfer Pricing Guidelines*, Irish tax law provides that transfer prices must be in accordance with the arm's length principle, in other words the prices charged must be in line with what a unrelated third party would charge on the open market. Ireland also follows OECD guidelines to the effect that transfer prices applied by an enterprise must be supported by documentation and such documentation is subject to compliance obligations and may be audited by Revenue.

Transfer pricing rules apply to trading, non-trading and capital transactions. The rules currently apply to large companies. Small and medium-sized enterprises (SMEs), defined as companies with less than 250 employees and either turnover of less than €50 million or assets less than €43 million, are excluded from the scope of transfer pricing rules for the tax years up to and including 2022. However, this exclusion may be reversed in the future if the government signs a Ministerial Order to give effect to the extension of transfer pricing obligations to SMEs under Finance Act 2019. Revenue's *Tax and Duty Manual*, Part 35A-01-01 provides guidance on the operation of transfer pricing rules and the updates made in Finance Act 2019.

The implications of transfer pricing can be summarised as follows:

1. If Revenue finds that the transfer prices applied by associated companies differ from arm's-length prices, the profits/losses of the associated companies must be recomputed and an adjustment to profits is necessary for one or both associated companies.
2. Companies must maintain documentation in a prescribed format as part of its transfer pricing compliance obligations.
   - Groups with consolidated revenues in excess of €250 million must prepare a 'master file' of transfer pricing documentation of associated companies for inspection by tax authorities. Broadly, a master file provides a high level overview of the groups business.
   - Groups with consolidated revenues in excess of €50 million must prepare a 'local file', a country-specific document detailing information relating to group transactions in the taxpayer's local jurisdiction.

Transfer pricing documentation must be available by the due date of the filing of the tax return to which the document relates. This information must be provided to Revenue within 30 days from the date of a request. Failure to provide the information within 30 days of the request will trigger a penalty of €4,000 or a penalty of €25,000 plus a penalty of €100 per day for taxpayers obliged to maintain a local file. A Revenue transfer pricing audit may also result in tax-geared penalties if there is insufficient documentation to support a transfer pricing arrangement. However, if a taxpayer files the tax return on time and provides Revenue with requested information within 30 days, tax-geared penalties will not apply.

13.6.5 Interest Limitation Rules

Finance Act 2021 includes legislation to enact the interest limitation rule (ILR) mandated by the EU Anti-Tax Avoidance Directive (ATAD) which sets out rules to combat tax avoidance. The ILR requires EU Member States to restrict interest deductibility of companies up to 30% of taxable earnings before interest, tax, depreciation, and amortisation (EBITDA). For accounting periods commencing on or after 1 January 2022, companies are required to apply the ILR unless they qualify for an exemption or a relief (the exemptions and reliefs are discussed below).

The ILR applies to companies which are liable to corporation tax in Ireland and which claim interest relief on their debt funding. It applies to SMEs as well as large multinationals. Companies falling within the ILR will only be able to deduct a maximum of 30% of their taxable EBITDA of the interest payment in any one accounting period.

Where the deductible borrowing costs of a company are restricted in an accounting period, a claim can be made for the restricted amount to be carried forward and deducted from the total profits or chargeable gains of future accounting periods. The disallowed interest can be carried forward for up to five years. In future periods, where the ILR calculation has been applied and the 30% limit has not been reached, the carried-forward amount can also be claimed.

Meaning of Interest

The legislation underpinning the ILR introduces a new definition of 'interest'. For the purposes of the ILR, 'interest' is not limited to its traditional meaning of interest on a loan but has a much wider meaning. Section 835AY(1) TCA 1997 includes a non-exhaustive list of "interest equivalents", including:

- interest;
- foreign exchange gains or losses on interest;
- profit or loss on financial assets or liabilities;
- 'swaps' and other hedging instruments;

- debt arrangement fees;
- discounts on securities;
- the finance element of finance leases;
- the finance element of operating lease income; and
- other amounts economically equivalent to interest.

The ILR also includes the term "net interest equivalent". Companies that have debt will usually have an interest expense in their P&L and will often also earn interest income. The net interest equivalent is the interest expense less the interest income. For example if the interest expense is €10 million and interest income is €2 million the net interest equivalent is €8 million.

Operation of the ILR

The purpose of the ILR is to limit the maximum tax deduction for interest expense by companies to 30% of taxable EBITDA. Taxable EBITDA uses the taxable profits (not the accounting profit) and is calculated using the following formula:

$$\text{Taxable EBITDA} = \text{Relevant profit/loss} + \text{Interest} + \text{Foreign tax deductions} + \text{Capital allowances/charges} + \text{Interest on legacy debt}$$

"Relevant" profit or loss is the profit or loss subject to corporation tax, plus development land gains, less current-year charges and losses but before carried-forward/carried-back losses and group relief. The relevant profit or loss is the starting point of the ILR calculation, from which the taxable EBITDA is determined.

Example 13.12

A company has tax-adjusted profits of €30 million (as taken from its corporation tax return), taxable EBITDA of €15 million (as calculated from the formula) and net interest equivalent of €8 million.

Under the ILR, the interest amount that can be deducted in the corporation tax computation is restricted to 30% of taxable EBITDA, i.e. €15 million × 30% = €4.5 million. The tax-adjusted profits can be reduced by this amount in the current year, and the excess can be carried forward. The current-year corporation tax liability is therefore:

	€m
Tax-adjusted profits	30
Deductible interest under the ILR	(4.5)
Net tax-adjusted profits	25.5
Corporation tax @ 12.5%	3.19

The amount that can be carried forward is the difference between the net interest equivalent and the amount deducted in the current year, i.e. €8 million – €4.5 = €3.5 million.

Interest Groups

The legislation sets out that the ILR applies to a "relevant entity", which can be a single entity or an "interest group". An interest group is made up of either companies that are consolidated for accounting purposes or companies that are in a tax loss group, and which have elected to be in the interest group. A company is not automatically in an interest group, it must elect to be in it. Once elected in, the company must remain in it for three years.

Exemptions

Exemptions that exclude a company from the ILR are available in the following cases:

- where a company or interest group's net borrowing costs is less than €3 million for an accounting period of 12 months there is no restriction of interest deduction (although once this amount is exceeded the entire amount of the exceeding borrowing costs is subject to the restriction);

- where a company is a standalone company, i.e. one that has no associated enterprises or permanent establishments and is not part of a worldwide group;
- for long-term EU public infrastructure projects (a project to provide, upgrade, operate or maintain a large-scale asset with a minimum expected lifespan of 10 years e.g. railways); and
- where the interest is on legacy debt the terms of which were agreed prior to 17 June 2016.

Relief

Where the exemptions outlined above do not apply, the ILR has two reliefs available – the group ratio or the equity ratio – which can apply subject to the relevant conditions being met. Revenue guidance states:

"The group ratio operates to increase the threshold for the allowable amount of exceeding borrowing costs in certain circumstances. The equity ratio operates to exempt a relevant entity from the interest limitation in certain circumstances."

The group ratio is calculated as:

$$\frac{\text{Group } \textbf{net} \text{ borrowing costs}}{\text{Group EBITDA}}$$

If a worldwide group's net borrowing costs as a proportion of EBITDA are greater than 30%, companies in that group can use this higher proportion to calculate its ILR.

The equity ratio is:

$$\frac{\text{Equity}}{\text{Total assets}}$$

If the company's ratio of equity to assets exceeds 98% of the worldwide group's ratio, the ILR does not apply and 100% of interest can be deducted.

Chapter 13 Summary

Double taxation and taxation of foreign income

- Relief available through tax treaties (based on OECD Model Treaty)
- Credit method to calculate double taxation relief
- Trans-border worker tax relief

Global tax reform

- OECD's BEPS initiative
- EU's Anti-Tax Avoidance Directive (ATAD), including CFC rules and interest limitation rules
- Transfer pricing rules
- Country-by-country (CbC) reporting

Questions

Review Questions
(See Suggested Solutions to Review Questions at the end of this textbook.)

Question 13.1

Mr Benn is currently resident in, and is also a national of, Monrovia. He wishes to become tax resident in Utopia due to the lower rates of income and CGT. He is single and owns an apartment in Monrovia. He is a pilot on international routes for the Monrovian national airline. He is a keen showjumper and owns two horses, which are stabled near his home. He is reluctant to sell his Monrovian apartment due to the depressed condition of the housing market in Monrovia. The double tax treaty between Monrovia and Utopia is based on the OECD Model Treaty.

Requirement
What advice would you give Mr Benn to ensure that he is considered to be tax resident in Utopia under Article 4(2) of the Monrovia/Utopia DTT?

Question 13.2

Trainco Limited is an Irish resident company which provides training courses to third parties. It has offices in Belfast and Dublin. The Belfast office provides training courses in Northern Ireland and the Dublin office provides courses throughout the Republic of Ireland. The company maintains separate accounting records for each office. For the year ended 30 June 2022, the Belfast office made a profit of €350,000 and the Dublin office made a profit of €200,000. The accounting profit for each office is equal to the taxable profit.

Requirement
What profits are taxable in the RoI and the UK?

Challenging Question
(Suggested Solutions to Challenging Solutions are available through your lecturer.)

Question 13.1

Ireland Only Ltd operates solely from its office in Dublin and all business decisions have been made there since its original Irish incorporation. However, it recently attended a trade fair and has received several orders from UK-based customers, indicating that a significant portion of business could be generated from UK customers. As the managing director is a very careful but ambitious person, the financial controller has been sent to talk with their accountants before the company embarks on this route. The financial controller has drawn up a number of options on how they could develop a UK business and wants advice on whether or not the company will become taxable in the UK. In addition, the financial controller wants an indication of the levels of profits taxable in the UK. The options are as follows:

1. Attend UK-based trade fairs – take initial enquiries or orders for products, all shipped from Ireland – no UK base.

2. Attend UK-based trade fairs, taking initial enquiries/order and shipping from Ireland, but either:
    (a) employ a UK-based salesperson to follow up with enquiries made at trade fairs; or
    (b) use a UK warehouse to store marketing materials (rather than having to shipping goods back to Ireland after each trade fair); or
    (c) open an office in the UK.
3. Form a UK subsidiary to run all UK-based operations.

Requirement

As you have just qualified as a Chartered Accountant and completed the tax elective, the partner asks you to prepare a note on the corporation tax exposures of each option for the client (but to ignore any VAT implications), which he will review with you.

Appendix 13.1: OECD Member Countries

There are currently 38 full members of the OECD.

Founding members (1961):

Austria	Netherlands
Belgium	Norway
Canada	Portugal
Denmark	Spain
France	Sweden
Germany	Switzerland
Greece	Turkey
Iceland	United Kingdom
Republic of Ireland	United States of America
Luxembourg	

Admitted later (listed chronologically by year of admission):

Italy (1962)	Slovak Republic (2000)
Japan (1964)	Chile (2010)
Finland (1969)	Estonia (2010)
Australia (1971)	Israel (2010)
New Zealand (1973)	Slovenia (2010)
Mexico (1994)	Latvia (2016)
Czech Republic (1995)	Lithuania (2018)
Korea (1996)	Colombia (2020)
Hungary (1996)	Costa Rica (2021)
Poland (1996)	

The OECD's focus has broadened over time to include extensive contacts with non-member economies and it now maintains co-operative relations with more than 70 of them.

General VAT Issues

Learning Objectives

By the end of this chapter, you should have a detailed knowledge of transactions or events which trigger a charge to VAT. In particular, students should be familiar with the VAT issues that arise when a person disposes of a business (whether through sale of assets or shares).

14.1 The Charge to VAT and Some Basic Terms

Section 3 Value-Added Tax Consolidation Act 2010 (VATCA 2010) is the "charging section" within Irish VAT legislation. This section imposes a VAT charge on the following:

1. the supply for consideration of goods by a taxable person acting in that capacity when the place of supply is the State;
2. the importation of goods into the State from outside the EU;
3. the supply for consideration of services by a taxable person acting in that capacity when the place of supply is the State;
4. the intra-Community acquisition for consideration by an accountable person of goods (other than new means of transport) when the acquisition is made within the State; and
5. the intra-Community acquisition for consideration of a new means of transport when the acquisition is made within the State.

To fully understand when the charge to VAT arises, it is important to be familiar with the basic terms referred to above and which are defined within the legislation:

- "taxable person" – section 2(1) VATCA 2010 states that a taxable person "means a person who independently carries on a business in the community or elsewhere";
- "accountable person" – section 5 VATCA 2010 defines an accountable person as "a taxable person who engages in the supply, within the State, of taxable goods or services". Accountable persons are obliged to register for VAT in Ireland;
- "State" – the 26 counties of the Republic of Ireland.

14.2   The Conditions for an Irish VAT Charge to Arise

It is worth taking a closer look at the charging section. Each of the following needs to be present for the transaction in question to be subject to VAT:

1. A supply of goods or services…
2. for consideration…
3. where the place of supply is in the State…
4. by a taxable person (i.e. a person liable to VAT)…
5. acting as such.

1. Supply of Goods or Services

In general, a supply of goods is the transfer of ownership of tangible goods. This is a straightforward concept. Examples of supplies of goods include sales of clothing, cars, computers, etc. In each case, the recipient of the supply has taken the ownership of tangible property.

A supply of goods is also deemed to take place if a person transfers goods from a taxable (i.e. liable to VAT) use to an exempt use. The most common example of this is where an individual takes goods from a business for personal use. Another example is where a person provides both taxable and exempt supplies and transfers goods (e.g. a computer) used in the taxable business to the exempt business, such as a bank carrying on both normal banking services (exempt) and leasing services (taxable). Such a supply is generally referred to as a "self-supply". No input credit is allowed for VAT charged on a self-supply (see **Section 14.4**). Therefore, such VAT represents a cost to the trader who has made the self-supply.

A supply of a service, on the other hand, is the provision of an intangible benefit, such as tax advice, legal advice, repair services, the leasing of tangible moveable property and hotel accommodation. Examples like tax and legal advice are readily understood. However, examples such as the leasing of tangible moveable property, e.g. computers, are a little more obscure in that the recipient benefits from the use of tangible property but does not, in fact, receive ownership of that property.

Goods and services can be classified as either taxable (i.e. liable to VAT) or exempt. Supplies that are exempt from VAT are mainly listed in Schedule 1 VATCA 2010. If a good or service is not listed in that Schedule, then they are generally taxable, i.e. VAT should be charged on a supply of such a good or service. If the supply is exempt, no VAT is chargeable on a supply of goods/services and no input credits can be claimed by the supplier.

Examples of exempt services are education, medical, banking, insurance, bookmaking, etc.

An example of an exempt supply of goods arises where the person making the supply was not entitled to an input credit on the acquisition of the goods. This could arise in two distinct situations:

■   First, a VAT input credit is not available on certain goods regardless of whether the person is a taxable person or not. In Ireland, no input credit is available on the purchase of passenger cars with the exception of those in emission bands A, B or C (see **Section 14.4**). If a VAT-registered person (other than a motor dealer) sells such a car, no VAT is chargeable and the supply is exempt. That person would not have been entitled to recover any of the VAT when the car was acquired by them.

■   Secondly, persons making exempt supplies, e.g. insurance companies, are not entitled to claim an input credit on acquisition of any goods or services. Therefore, if such a person sells any goods that were used for the purposes of their exempt services, the supply is exempt.

2.   For Consideration

Although there are certain exceptions, VAT generally does not arise where no consideration is received by a supplier for goods or services. For example, a street busker would usually not be required to account for VAT on monies received from the public as the payments made are usually accepted as donations from the public (as opposed to consideration for a service provided).

3. Within the State (i.e. 26 counties)

This would appear to be a very straightforward concept. However, there are separate place of supply rules for goods and services and these rules determine whether or not a particular supply has taken place within Ireland. (These rules are considered later in this chapter.)

4. By a Taxable Person

A person could satisfy all of the other conditions within the charging section but a supply may still not be subject to VAT if the person is not a taxable person. For example, a person below the VAT registration threshold (€75,000 for goods and €37,500 for services) would not be an accountable person, although they could elect to register for VAT. If a person below the threshold does elect to register, they must then account for VAT on their supplies.

Special rules exist for farmers and fishermen. Even where their farming activities are in excess of the relevant thresholds, they are not obliged to register for VAT. However, they may elect to register. Farmers who are not registered for VAT are entitled to receive an additional 5.4% of their sales from their purchasers (who in turn can recover this amount from the Revenue Commissioners). This is known as the "flat-rate addition" for the farmer. Such farmers are known as "flat-rate farmers".

A nil threshold applies in respect of the supply of property. A person must register and operate VAT on such supplies (see **Chapter 15**).

5. Acting as Such

A person who is a taxable person (in relation to certain supplies) may make other supplies effectively in a private capacity. For example, a person carrying on a furniture retail business may sell his private house. The fact that the person is a taxable person does not oblige him to charge VAT on the disposal of his private house, as the disposal is not in the course of his business.

In general, these five conditions need to be satisfied or a transaction will not be subject to VAT. (Note, however, that other parts of the legislation may bring a transaction within the charge even where some of the conditions above are not satisfied.)

14.3   Accounting for VAT

Accountable persons are generally obliged to account for VAT on the "invoice basis". This means that VAT becomes due when they raise an invoice (or when the invoice should have been raised). For example, invoices raised in January and February should be included in the January–February VAT return and submitted by 23 March via ROS (see **Section 14.14**).

Certain persons may qualify to account for VAT on the "cash-receipts basis". There are two ways to qualify. First, where the annual turnover does not exceed €2,000,000 and, secondly, where greater than 90% of turnover is to unregistered persons. There can be significant cash flow advantages for persons operating on this system, particularly where customers are slow to pay.

14.4   VAT Recovery and Non-deductible Expenses

In general, a person who charges VAT on all of his or her supplies is entitled to reclaim VAT on expenses incurred in running the business. Conversely, a person who only makes VAT-exempt supplies is not entitled to recover any VAT incurred by them.

It is important to note that supplies subject to VAT at 0% rate will give a trader a right to recover VAT on their inputs, while supplies that are exempt will deny the trader that recovery. Thus, care should be taken to use the 0% or exempt rates correctly on sales invoices as they impact on the trader's recovery of VAT suffered.

14.4.1 VAT Input Credit Position for Partially Liable/Partially Exempt VAT-registered Businesses

A VAT-registered business may be engaged in a variety of activities, some of which are liable to VAT and some of which are VAT exempt. In such circumstances, the VAT input credits that such a business can claim will be restricted. The following rules are applied:

■ VAT on purchases that are used **solely** for the VAT-registered business are available for full input credit.

■ No VAT credit is available in respect of VAT on purchases used solely for exempt activities.

■ For purchases relating to the general operation of the business, known as dual-use inputs, the taxpayer's turnover is used in the first instance to establish the VAT-apportionment rate. Where this method does not accurately reflect the use of the inputs, the taxpayer may use another apportionment method.

Example 14.1

X Limited	€ million
Annual turnover	10
Sale of taxable goods	7
Sale of exempt goods	3
	10

1st: Full input credit for VAT on purchases used **solely** for taxable activities.
2nd: No input credit for VAT on purchases used **solely** for exempt activities.
3rd: Apportionment (on turnover basis) for VAT on general purchases used for the entire business.

A typical dual-use input would be the annual audit fee:	€
Audit fee	10,000
Plus 23% VAT	2,300

Input credit for 70%   × €2,300 = €1,610
No input credit for 30% × €2,300 = €690

As X Ltd has 70% recovery in relation to dual-use inputs, it can recover €1,610 of VAT in relation to the annual audit fee. The same would apply to general overheads, such as rent, heat, phone, etc.

14.4.2 VAT Charges on which Input Credit is not Allowed

There are certain categories of expenses in Ireland for which VAT cannot be reclaimed, even where the business is involved in making supplies that are 100% subject to VAT. A deduction is not allowed in respect of VAT incurred by a **VAT-registered** business on any of the following:

■ The provision of food, drink, residential accommodation or other personal services supplied to the taxable person, his agents or his employees. (**Note:** a certain element of VAT paid on hotel accommodation for attendance at qualifying conferences is allowed.)

■ Entertainment expenses incurred by the taxable person, his agents or his employees.

■ The acquisition, hiring or leasing of **passenger** motor vehicles other than as stock-in-trade or for the purpose of a business which consists in whole or in part of the hiring of motor vehicles or for use in a driving school business for giving driving instruction. This restriction does not apply to commercial vehicles. A small concession was introduced in this area for certain low-emission cars whereby 20% of the VAT incurred on the cost of a new passenger vehicle registered after 1 January 2009 can be reclaimed as long as the vehicle is used for at least 60% business purposes and the vehicle falls within categories A, B or C for VRT purposes.

- The purchase of petrol otherwise than as stock-in-trade. VAT can, however, be reclaimed in respect of motor diesel or liquid petroleum gas used for business purposes.
- VAT in respect of goods or services used by the taxable person for the purposes of an exempt activity or for the purposes of an activity not related to his business, e.g. a personal purpose.
- VAT in respect of goods or services for which the registered trader does not have a valid VAT invoice.

Subject to the above exceptions, VAT is deductible against a taxable person's liability in the following situations:

- VAT charged to a taxable person by other taxable persons on supplies of goods (including fixed assets) and services to him which are used for the purposes of the taxable business, whether for resale or not.
- VAT paid by the taxable person on goods or services imported into the State for the use of the business, whether for resale or not.

In general, an input credit can be availed of in the period the invoice is issued and not necessarily the period in which it is paid. However, where the consideration due has not been paid before the last day of the third taxable period following the initial period, it will be necessary to reduce the input credit entitlement. The legislation contains a formula, the effect of which is to pro-rate the amount of VAT repayable with the amount of consideration remaining unpaid. When the consideration is subsequently paid, the taxpayer can subsequently adjust their input VAT for the period in which payment is made to account for the input VAT recoverable.

Example 14.2: Recovery of VAT on unpaid invoices
An invoice is received dated 10 January 2022. VAT on this was recovered in the January/February 2022 period. The invoice was only paid in November 2022. An adjustment should have been made in the July/August 2022 VAT return for the VAT recovered on the January 2022 invoice. The November/December 2022 VAT return should account for an additional input of VAT in respect of the January 2022 invoice.

14.5 Group Registration for VAT Purposes

Two or more persons can apply to Revenue to be included in a VAT group. It is important to note that granting such an application is at the discretion of the Revenue Commissioners. Revenue will generally seek to ensure that the following conditions are satisfied before permitting VAT group registration:

- two or more persons established in the Republic of Ireland and at least one of them is an accountable person (registered or required to register and account for VAT);
- are closely bound by financial, economic and organisational links; and
- it is necessary or appropriate for the purposes of efficient and effective administration, including the collection of VAT.

The following should be noted in relation to VAT groups:

- A VAT group can contain individuals, as well as body corporates.
- A VAT group may also include a person involved in VAT exempt activities.
- Companies do not necessarily need to be in a legal group or corporation tax group to qualify.
- Revenue is entitled to oblige persons to form a VAT group (this is rare).

Any persons wishing to form a VAT group must jointly apply in writing to the VAT section of their local Revenue District to secure approval for group registration. This must be formally granted by Revenue and will generally only apply from the taxable period (where notifications have been issued from Revenue to the various parties). VAT group registrations cannot be backdated, but Revenue does have the power to backdate a VAT group cancellation.

14.5.1 Impact of Group Registration

The following points should be borne in mind when considering group VAT registration as all are automatic once Revenue allows the group registration:

- The group will nominate a single group remitter for VAT purposes, who will be responsible for VAT compliance for the entire group. The remitter will be the only entity in the group to file a VAT return. The other members of the group are known as non-remitters.
- The group remitter must, therefore, lodge all VAT returns and make all payments for the entire group with the Collector-General.
- VAT invoices are not necessary in respect of transactions between the individual group members. This facilitates cash flow within the group as it allows one company to pay another company without VAT arising. It should be noted that there is an exception in respect of issuing of VAT invoices as regards certain property transactions (see below).
- Each person in the group is jointly and severally liable in the event that timely payment of appropriate VAT is not made. (Note: this is a significant disadvantage to joining a VAT group and should not be underestimated.)
- All VAT invoices issued by group members to third parties will show the VAT number of the individual company making the supply.

Example 14.3: Benefit of creating a VAT group

X Ltd and Y Ltd are both owned by Peter Jones. X Ltd is involved in VAT-exempt training, while Y Ltd is involved in providing consultancy services (which are subject to VAT). Both companies employ several members of staff. Some of the marketing and administration work for X Ltd is carried out by the employees of Y Ltd and an invoice is raised for €10,000 at the end of every month to X Ltd for the provision of these services.

If X Ltd and Y Ltd are not in a VAT group, 23% VAT will arise on top of the monthly invoice. X Ltd will not be able to recover this VAT as it is engaged in VAT-exempt activities. However, if both companies are in a VAT group, there should be no obligation for a VAT invoice to be raised. This should result in a substantial saving for X Ltd of €2,300 per month or €27,600 per annum.

However, VAT group registration will reduce VAT recovery for the group as a whole. The members of the VAT group are deemed to be a single taxable person, therefore, as X Ltd is VAT-exempt, Y Ltd's input VAT recovery will be diluted.

14.5.2 Sale of Property within a VAT Group

The sale of property from one entity to another within a VAT group is excluded from the usual VAT group relief provisions. VAT must be charged on the intragroup sale of a property (assuming VAT arises on the sale).

The company making the sale will issue a VAT invoice and the company purchasing the property will secure an input credit, assuming it is entitled to 100% VAT recovery. As the output VAT and input VAT will be recorded on the same VAT return, no payment to Revenue should actually be required. If the acquirer of the property was only entitled to 80% input credit, then only 80% of the VAT charged by the other VAT group member could be recovered by it and a payment to Revenue would be required.

14.6 Transfer of Business Relief

When a person decides to sell a business, it can generally be done in one of two ways. If the person is a sole trader, they can only choose to dispose of the assets of the business. However, if the person operates through a company, then they are more likely to dispose of their shareholding in the company, rather than just selling off the assets of the company. The VAT issues which arise under both scenarios are very different.

14.6.1 Disposal of Business Assets

Usually, when a VAT-registered business disposes of assets on which it has claimed a VAT input credit, then it must charge VAT to the purchaser. The VAT charge is based on the price plus VAT (at the same class of rate as the VAT-registered business incurred on the acquisition of the asset). Normally, therefore, if a VAT-registered business disposes of a building on which VAT was incurred on acquisition, then VAT at 13.5% would have to be charged on the sales price. If equipment, furniture, etc. is sold, VAT at 23% would be chargeable. The same is true for intangible assets such as goodwill, intellectual property, etc.

However, where the following conditions are met, the transfer of assets in connection with the transfer of a business is deemed not to be a supply for VAT purposes and VAT should not be charged to the purchaser:

1. the purchaser is an accountable person. Section 5(1) VATCA 2010 states that all taxable persons (i.e. businesses) who make taxable (i.e. VATable) supplies of goods or services in the State are "accountable persons"; and
2. the transfer **must** constitute an undertaking or part of an undertaking capable of being operated on an independent basis.

This is commonly referred to as "transfer of business relief". The sections of the VATCA 2010 concerned are section 20(2)(c) and section 26. These sections effectively deem such a transaction not to be a supply of goods or services and to be outside the scope of VAT. In order for the relief to apply, the seller must transfer a mixture of assets which would be capable of assisting in the operation of a business. In a typical sale of a business, a vendor is likely to be disposing of some or all of the following assets – stock, premises, staff, cash/bank, contracts, goodwill, debtors, plant and equipment, etc. It is not necessary for **all** of these items to be disposed of for the relief to apply, but it is likely that at least several of them should be present.

For example, a retailer selling a business premises should also sell the stock, debtors, creditors, etc. which would assist in the operation of a business entity. However, the relief is unlikely to apply in the case of a sale of fixtures of a retail operation without the corresponding sale of the business entity.

It is not a requirement that the supplier must transfer a going concern, i.e. legislation permits the sale of a business or part of a business. This could be the transfer after the business has ceased trading.

If all these conditions are satisfied, the transaction is **not liable to VAT** (i.e. outside the VAT net) and the vendor is not entitled to charge the purchaser VAT. This relief is not optional; once the conditions are satisfied, it is automatically applied.

This can be a useful relief on the transfer of an unincorporated business to a company, on the transfer of trades between members of a group of companies, on the sale of a business by a company to an individual, or on the sale of a business by a company to another company.

If the above conditions are satisfied, the seller of the asset is not entitled to charge VAT. If, however, he incorrectly does so and the purchaser pays the VAT, Revenue is entitled to refuse to give an input credit in respect of such VAT payment, which was effectively incorrectly charged. Accordingly, it is vital that the purchaser of an asset (where a business or part of a business is being taken over) resists any attempt by the vendor to charge VAT on the transaction. If any doubt exists, the purchaser should request the vendor to seek clarification of the VAT position from the vendor's Inspector of Taxes. Equally, if a vendor does not charge VAT when it should have been charged, then they will remain liable for the VAT. Consequently, prior to completing the transaction, it is often in both parties' interest to seek clarification from Revenue whether the relief does in fact apply. It should be noted that this relief will not apply to non-established persons (i.e. persons who are outside the State).

14.6.2 VAT Recovery for Vendor and Purchaser: Disposal of Business Assets

Both parties to a transaction involving the disposal of a business are likely to incur significant fees from advisors (e.g. legal and accounting). The question arises as to whether or not the VAT on such fees can be recovered. Although the vendor has made a supply which is outside the scope of VAT, section 59(2)(m) VATCA 2010 allows the vendor to recover VAT on costs associated with such a transaction where the supply would otherwise have been taxable.

Assuming the purchaser of the business is going to carry on a vatable trade, he or she should be entitled to recover VAT on the costs in the usual manner.

14.6.3 Disposal of Shares

The transfer of business relief does not apply where a company (which owns a business) is sold, as this will involve a sale of the shares. Transactions involving the sale of shares are exempt from VAT. Therefore, no VAT arises on the consideration received for the shares from the purchaser. As the vendor has made an exempt supply, the vendor cannot recover the VAT on costs associated with the transaction. However, as an exception, the vendor can recover VAT on costs incurred relating to the sale of shares to parties outside of the EU. Note the difference between this and the position where the business is sold by way of an asset sale.

The purchaser is also unlikely to be able to recover VAT on the costs, as they have merely acquired shares in a company. In general, this is not an activity that entitles the purchaser to recovery of VAT.

It is vital that you, as a student of tax planning, understand the difference between the two scenarios and recognise when transfer of business relief applies.

14.6.4 Reorganisations

Transfer of business relief can also be used when companies are involved in reorganisations. In a classic company reorganisation, a new company (NewCo) will be established and all of the assets of the trade (sometimes with the exception of the property) will be transferred to NewCo. This transaction may be done with a future sale in mind, or it may simply be done to arrange the affairs of the group more efficiently.

The consideration for the trade will generally be the issue of shares in NewCo to either the old trading company or to the shareholders of the company. With regard to the transfer of assets to NewCo, transfer of business relief should apply, meaning VAT does not arise on that transfer (see **Chapter 7**).

14.7 VAT Implications of Liquidations

VATCA 2010 imposes certain obligations on liquidators who are appointed to companies in Ireland. Where a liquidator disposes of the tangible assets of a company, then the liquidator must register for VAT and account for VAT. While the company is still considered to be the person who made the supply, VAT must be returned on the liquidator's VAT return (and not on the company's VAT return). This assumes that the assets in question are subject to VAT in the first place. For example, if the only asset of the company was a passenger car and the disposal of that asset would not give rise to a VAT charge, then the liquidator would not be required or entitled to register for VAT in respect of the particular liquidation. Assuming the liquidator disposes of goods giving rise to a VAT liability, he must register for VAT within 14 days of disposing of the assets.

A liquidator is obliged to file a VAT return and remit the tax due on the supply.

It is important to note that supplies of services (e.g. intangible assets such as intellectual property) are not covered by the relevant section. Therefore, VAT on the disposal of such items should be included in the VAT return of the company in question.

Liquidators are generally entitled to reclaim VAT incurred on costs associated with the liquidation. Such costs would include the liquidator's fees. The entitlement to VAT recovery assumes that the liquidator disposes of assets that will give rise to a VAT liability. It is generally recommended that such refund claims are submitted in the same return as the disposal of the assets of the company.

It is important to remember that transfer of business relief may apply to a disposal of the business by the liquidator and the comments made above regarding VAT recovery in **Section 14.6.2** should also apply.

14.8 Place of Supply Rules

You will recall that Irish VAT only applies to transactions that take place (or are deemed to take place) in the Republic of Ireland. In most situations, it will be clear where a transaction has occurred but this is not always the case. VAT legislation, therefore, contains rules that determine where the relevant supply has occurred. There are two sets of rules: one for supplies of goods and one for supplies of services. As you will see below, these rules are very different.

14.8.1 Place of Supply of Goods

The place of supply of goods is deemed to be as follows:

- If the goods are to be transported, then the place where the transportation begins is deemed to be the place of supply. For example, if X Ltd (based in Dublin) sells goods from its warehouse to Y Ltd in London and despatches the goods to Y Ltd, the place of supply is Ireland as that is where the transportation of the goods commenced.
- Goods that are supplied and installed are deemed to be supplied at the location where the installation takes place. For example, if an Irish company wins a contract to supply and install goods at a UK manufacturing plant, the place of supply would be the UK and not Ireland.
- In all other cases, the location of the goods at the time of supply determines the place of supply. It is important to note that it is the location of the goods that is relevant and not the parties to the transaction. For example, X Ltd (based in Dublin) owns goods which it has stored in a warehouse in Munich, Germany. It sells the goods to Z Ltd (another Dublin company), which also has a warehouse in Germany. The place of supply for this transaction is Germany. Similarly, if a US person sold goods to an Australian person (where those goods were in Ireland at the time of supply), the place of supply would be Ireland.

14.8.2 Place of Supply of Services

The rules in relation to the place of supply of services are much more complicated than those which determine the place of supply of goods. There are two general rules for the supply of services, concerning:

1. supply to non-taxable persons, or
2. supply to business customers.

Supply to Consumers

The first general rule concerns supplies made to consumers (i.e. customers who are not taxable persons; this could include private individuals but also other entities that are not involved in any economic activities). These are often called B2C services.

The basic rule here is that the supply of services is deemed to take place where the place of business of the supplier is located (i.e. where the supplier is established). If the supplier has more than one establishment, the establishment most closely associated with the supply should determine the VAT treatment. If the supplier has no establishment, the place of supply is its place of residence.

Example 14.4

An Irish accountant provides general advisory services to a private individual in Germany. The place of supply is Ireland (section 34(b) VATCA 2010) and therefore Irish VAT must be included on the invoice to the consumer in Germany.

Supply to Business Customers

The second general rule concerns supplies made to business customers. These are often called B2B services. The basic rule here is that the place of supply is deemed to be where the customer is established. If the customer has several establishments, then the place of supply will typically be where the establishment most closely associated with the supply is located.

> **Example 14.5**
> An Irish accountant provides general advisory services to a business in Germany. The place of supply is where the German customer is located (section 34(a) VATCA 2010). However, the German recipient is deemed to be the accountable person in respect of this supply and is therefore liable to account for VAT on the reverse charge basis in Germany on the value of the services supplied.

While Irish VAT will not apply on a service supplied by an Irish business to an EU business, the Irish supplier may be responsible for operating VAT in the location of the business customer. It is therefore necessary to determine who is responsible for accounting for the VAT in the Member State in question. In most cases, the Irish supplier can quote the customer's VAT number on the invoice and include a line stating, "The recipient is obliged to self-account for VAT in accordance with Article 56(1) Council Directive (2006/112/EC)". In some cases, however, it may be necessary for the Irish supplier to register for VAT in the other Member State and to account for VAT there.

Supply to Non-EU Business Customers

Where an Irish business provides services to business customers located outside the EU, the place of supply is where the business customer is located and is therefore outside the scope of Irish VAT.

> **Example 14.6**
> An Irish accountant provides general advisory services to a business in Norway. The place of supply is where the customer is located, i.e. Norway, and is therefore outside the scope of VAT.

Supply to Non-EU Customers

VAT is generally not chargeable on the following services supplied to non-business customers established outside the EU:

- transfers and assignments of copyrights, patents, licences, trademarks and similar rights;
- advertising services;
- the services of consultants, engineers, consultancy firms, lawyers, accountants and other similar services, as well as data processing and the provision of information;
- obligations to refrain from pursuing or exercising, in whole or in part, a business activity or a right;
- banking, financial and insurance transactions, including reinsurance, with the exception of the hire of safes;
- the supply of staff;
- the hiring out of movable tangible property, with the exception of all means of transport;
- the provision of access to, and of transport or transmission through, natural gas and electricity distribution systems and the provision of other services directly linked thereto;
- telecommunications services;
- radio and television broadcasting services;
- electronically supplied services.

Services not included in this list that are supplied to a non-business customer outside the EU are subject to Irish VAT at the appropriate rate.

> **Example 14.7**
> An Irish accountant provides general advisory services to a private individual in Norway. The place of supply is where the Norwegian customer is located, i.e. outside the EU and therefore the scope of VAT.

Exceptions to the General Rules

There are a number of exceptions to the above general rules that apply to a range of services. For example, in the case of services relating to property (immovable goods), the place of supply is where the property is located.

Another exception is the supply of digital services to a non-taxable person (e.g. a private individual). In such cases the place of supply is where the customer is established, has a permanent address or usually resides (B2C). This rule applies regardless of whether or not the supplier is located in or outside the EU.

The place of supply of certain services can also be subject to special rules known as "use and enjoyment provisions", i.e. VAT is applied where the service is used and enjoyed (these rules are beyond the scope of this textbook).

VAT E-commerce Rules Post-1 July 2021

New VAT rules for e-commerce came into effect in the EU from 1 July 2021. These rules will be particularly significant for anyone selling goods online or running an online marketplace.

The aim of the new rules is to:

- ensure that VAT is paid where goods are consumed or the services paid for are provided;
- create a uniform VAT regime for cross-border supplies of goods and services;
- offer businesses a simple system to declare and pay their VAT in the EU, using the (Import) One Stop Shop portal;
- introduce a level playing field between EU businesses and non-EU sellers.

The EU has developed new online tools where businesses can register and take care of their VAT obligations for all their sales in the EU. This replaces the previous system whereby online companies were obliged to register for VAT in each EU country before they could sell to consumers there.

The new system, called the One Stop Shop (OSS), comprises a single, quarterly EU VAT return for e-commerce cross-border distance selling of goods. OSS replaces the Mini One Stop Shop (MOSS) which covered only the supply of electronic, broadcasting and telecommunications services to consumers (B2C).

From 1 July 2021, B2C sellers dispatching their goods from a single country will no longer be required to register for foreign VAT and complete multiple VAT filings in countries where they are selling. Instead, they can opt to complete and file a OSS filing alongside their regular domestic VAT return that will list all their EU sales. The seller will then remit the VAT due to their home VAT authority, which then forwards the taxes to the appropriate countries.

Non-EU sellers may also apply to use the OSS regime, and need only nominate any single EU Member State to register and file in.

Returns are on a calendar-quarter basis and must be submitted along with the relevant payment within 20 days of the end of the calendar-quarter return period. For example, the return, for the calendar quarter ending on 31 March 2021, must be submitted by 20 April 2021. The VAT due in respect of supplies in all EU Member States must be paid in euros, at the same time as the return, into a bank account designated by the relevant tax authority. Nil returns must also be submitted. The VAT rate used is that of each Member State of consumption at the time the service was supplied. Therefore, assuming a business is charging uniform gross amounts for the same service to consumers throughout the EU there will be a loss of margin on sales in Member States with higher VAT rates (for example, Sweden at 25%), but an increased margin on sales in Member States with lower VAT rates (for example, Luxembourg at 17%).

> **Example 14.8**
> Digi Ltd is a US company that supplies e-commerce services to private customers located across the EU. Digi Ltd registers for the VAT OSS online service in Ireland, and accounts for the VAT due on its B2C e-commerce service sales in other Member States where it does not have an establishment, by submitting a single VAT OSS return and any related payment to the Irish Revenue.
>
> The Irish Revenue then sends an electronic copy of the appropriate part of the OSS return, and the related VAT payment, to each relevant Member State's tax authority on its behalf.

Import One Stop Shop

The Import One Stop Shop (IOSS) came into effect in the EU in from 1 July 2021 and the VAT exemption for the importation of goods into the EU with a value of €22 or below was removed. As a result, all goods imported into the EU are now subject to VAT. If the sale of goods to buyers in the EU is facilitated through an electronic interface, the electronic interface is considered to have made the sale and is, in principle, liable for the payment of VAT.

The IOSS was created to facilitate and simplify the declaration and payment of VAT for distance sales of imported goods with a value of €150 or below. It facilitates the collection, declaration and payment of VAT for sellers that are supplying goods from outside the EU to customers in the EU. In practice this means that these suppliers and electronic interfaces can collect, declare and directly pay the VAT to the tax authorities of their choice, rather than having the customer pay the import VAT at the time the goods are delivered.

Receipt of Services from Abroad

In the case of an Irish business receiving a service in Ireland from a non-Irish supplier that falls under the general B2B rule, the Irish recipient of the service must self-account for VAT on the services under the reverse charge mechanism. The Irish business customer records the receipt of the services by including a liability for sales VAT at the appropriate Irish rate in Box T1 of the relevant VAT return (as if it had supplied the service to itself) and may take a simultaneous input VAT deduction in Box T2 of the same VAT return to the extent that the Irish trader receives the service for the purposes of a VATable business.

If the purchaser, i.e. the Irish business, is entitled to full VAT recovery, then the purchase is VAT-neutral. However, if it is not receiving the services for a VATable (deductible) business, then the output VAT accounted for under the reverse charge mechanism is payable to Revenue and is a real cost to the purchaser. The VAT-exclusive value of the service must also be reported in Box ES2 of the Irish business's VAT return.

Supply of Services: Basic Rules – Summary of Irish VAT Position

Supplier of Service	Recipient of Service	Irish VAT charged?	Irish VAT charged by
Irish	Non-EU business	No	N/A
Irish	EU business person	No	N/A
Irish	Irish business	Yes	Supplier
Irish	Non-EU private (general)	Depends on nature of the service	Supplier (if VAT applies)
Irish	EU private	Yes	Supplier
Irish	Irish private	Yes	Supplier

14.9 VAT on International Transactions

This section outlines the VAT treatment associated with typical transactions involving Irish companies which bring goods into the State or despatch goods out of the State.

14.9.1 Imports from Non-EU Member States

VAT is payable at the point of entry on the importation of taxable goods into the State (i.e. goods brought into the Republic of Ireland directly from **outside** the EU). The important provisions relating to imports can be summarised as follows:

- VAT at the same rate as applies to the sale of the particular goods within the State is charged at the point of importation. Zero-rated/exempt goods therefore attract no liability on importation.
- VAT is payable before the imported goods are released by the Customs Authorities unless the importer is approved for the Deferred Payments Scheme (see below).
- Eligibility under the Deferred Payments Scheme will permit payment of the VAT liability in respect of the goods on the 15th day of the month following the month in which the goods are released from Customs and the VAT becomes due. Importers wishing to participate in the Deferred Payments Scheme must make an application to the appropriate Collector of Customs and Excise. Under the scheme, the Customs and Excise Authorities are authorised by the importer to secure payment of the VAT by the issue of a direct debit voucher drawn on the trader's bank. To qualify for this scheme, the importer must be able to obtain a guarantee from his bank that the VAT liability demanded for imports will be paid to the Customs Collector.
- The value of imported goods for the purposes of assessment to VAT is their value for Customs' purposes, determined on a delivery to State basis, together with any taxes, duties and other charges levied inside the State on the goods.
- A VAT-registered person who imports goods during a taxable period is entitled to claim an input credit in his VAT return for that period for the VAT paid or payable in respect of the goods imported. VAT-registered persons who are in a permanent repayment position as a result of VAT paid at the point of importation are permitted to make monthly returns.
- Goods imported into the Shannon Customs Free Airport Zone from outside the State are not liable to VAT.

14.9.2 Acquisitions from EU Member States

General Rule
The rules relating to the VAT treatment of acquisitions from EU countries to the State vary according to the VAT status of the purchaser. These are dealt with below.

Acquisition by Irish VAT-registered Traders
When an Irish VAT-registered trader is purchasing goods from a supplier in another EU country, the following procedures need to to be followed:

1. The Irish purchaser must provide the foreign supplier with their Irish VAT number.
2. The foreign supplier will check that this VAT number is valid (this is done through the European Commission's Taxation and Customs Union website).
3. The supplier then supplies the goods at the zero rate.
4. The Irish purchaser will self-account on the reverse charge basis for Irish VAT on the goods at the rate that would apply to the goods if they had been purchased in the State.
5. Although the Irish purchaser is registered for Irish VAT, he or she will only receive a corresponding credit for the Irish VAT liability in the same two-month VAT period in which the liability on importation arose where he or she is entitled to fully recover the VAT on inputs. Accordingly, the transaction should be cash-neutral. An Irish VAT liability will subsequently arise when the Irish trader sells the goods.

Example 14.9

In July 2022, an Irish-registered trader imports goods from the UK costing €40,000 exclusive of VAT and a large new car costing €30,000 exclusive of VAT. In the same period, the VAT on its sales amounted to €60,000 while its deductible input VAT (ignoring imports) amounted to €38,000.

The July–August 2022 VAT return details are as follows:

	€
VAT on sales (output VAT)	60,000
Add: VAT on imports of goods (€40,000 @ 23%)	9,200
VAT on imported car (€30,000 @ 23%)	6,900
Total output VAT	**76,100**
VAT on purchases (input VAT)	38,000
Add: VAT on imports (€40,000 @ 23%)	9,200
VAT on imported car **(Note)**	N/A
Total input VAT	**47,200**
Net VAT payable	**28,900**

Note: this example assumes no recovery is available on the car.

Acquisitions by Unregistered Traders, Exempt Businesses and Government Departments

Any imports of **goods** by such bodies are not subject to Irish VAT. Instead, foreign VAT will be payable in the Member State of the supplier at the VAT rate applicable there. If the annual value of such an entity's intra-community acquisitions exceeds or is likely to exceed €41,000 in any continuous period of 12 months, then it must register for Irish VAT in the State. It will then provide its supplier with a VAT number in order not to pay "foreign" VAT to its supplier, i.e. the goods will be zero-rated coming into Ireland. However, the purchaser will have to account for Irish VAT, at the appropriate rate applicable in the State, on the goods purchased. No Irish VAT is charged on a subsequent sale as the registration is applied to imports only and does not affect the exempt status of the entity generally. Therefore, the entity continues to be treated as exempt for all other purposes and hence is not entitled to an input credit in respect of the Irish VAT liability arising on importation.

If such entities receive **services** from a non-EU supplier, they are obliged to register for VAT in respect of the "importation" of such services, regardless of the value of the services received. Such a VAT registration is to ensure that Irish VAT is paid on the importation of the service under the "reverse charge" rule.

Example 14.10

The details are the same as in the previous example except that the trader carries on an exempt business activity, e.g. banking, insurance, etc. Due to the level of acquisitions (assume for the purposes of this example that they exceed €41,000 per annum), the trader is obliged to register for VAT in respect of such acquisitions.

The July–August 2022 VAT return details are as follows:

	€
VAT on sales (exempt)	N/A
Add: VAT on imports of goods (€40,000 @ 23%)	9,200
VAT on imported car (€30,000 @ 23%)	6,900
	16,100

As this is an exempt business, there is no question of VAT input credits arising. Thus, the net VAT payable is €16,100.

Acquisitions by Private Individuals

Goods purchased by Irish resident individuals from other Member States are subject to a foreign VAT charge in the other State only. Therefore, an Irish individual who orders goods from Germany will probably purchase those goods at the German VAT-inclusive price, and no additional Irish VAT will be payable provided the goods purchased are for private and not business use.

These provisions do not apply to purchases of new means of transport (i.e. motor cars, boats and aircraft). Such purchases are always subject to VAT in the Member State of the purchaser.

Distance Selling Purchases by Private Individuals

Distance selling occurs when a supplier in one EU Member State sells goods to an individual in another Member State. The purchaser will not be registered for VAT and the supplier is responsible for delivery. Examples of distance selling include mail-order sales, internet shopping and telesales.

Where such businesses supply goods in Ireland in excess of €10,000 in any 12-month period, then it is obliged to register for VAT in Ireland. In such circumstances, Irish VAT only would be charged to the purchaser. To alleviate the administrative burden on the seller they would register for the One Stop Shop system (see **Section 14.8.2**).

14.9.3 Exports to Non-EU Member States

Broadly speaking, goods which are exported outside of the EU are not liable to VAT in Ireland and the zero rate is applied. It does not matter whether the purchaser is a business or private customer. However, it is important that the Irish supplier is satisfied that the goods have indeed left the EU. If the supplier cannot demonstrate to the Revenue Commissioners that the goods have left the EU, then the supplier will remain liable for the VAT arising on the transfer.

14.9.4 Despatches to Other EU Member States

Where a VAT-registered trader in Ireland supplies goods to a VAT-registered trader in another Member State, the transaction will be zero-rated in Ireland and will be liable to VAT in the Member State of the purchaser. This treatment only applies if the foreign customer is registered for VAT in his home country and supplies his foreign VAT number to the Irish exporter. Additionally, the seller must quote the foreign buyer's VAT number on his sales invoice and, as outlined above, the vendor must be able to demonstrate that the goods were physically despatched from the State (e.g. copies of freight documentation, etc.). In the event that no foreign VAT number is provided by the customer, then the Irish supplier should charge Irish VAT at the appropriate Irish VAT rate (i.e. the same rate that would apply if the customer were based in Ireland).

14.9.5 Despatch/Export Businesses

An Irish trader who incurs VAT on purchases or imports for the purposes of a business, and who despatches/ exports goods manufactured in the State, is entitled to the usual input credits (subject only to the normal restrictions). As the sales for such a trader will be zero rated, this usually results in a constant VAT repayment situation. Such persons may be permitted to submit monthly VAT returns to facilitate earlier repayment of input tax.

Additionally, provided a trader can demonstrate that at least 75% of their turnover is derived from despatches/exports out of the State, they are entitled to apply to the Revenue Commissioners to have *all* goods/services acquired by them in the State or imported from abroad to be treated as zero-rated supplies. The relevant details are contained in section 56 VATCA 2010. Once a trader receives the relevant authorisation, they can then provide the details to their suppliers. All of the suppliers are then obliged to zero-rate all sales, of both goods and services, to that trader until such time as the authorisation expires or is withdrawn. This zero-rating does not extend to supplies of passenger motor vehicles, petrol, entertainment, etc., and other items where the trader would not be entitled to recover VAT in the normal course of trading.

To apply for a 'VAT 56' authorisation, the trader must demonstrate that the turnover requirements have been met for the 12-month period before the application is lodged. Therefore, start-up businesses will need to wait 12 months before they can apply for this authorisation.

14.10   VAT Under the Protocol on Ireland/Northern Ireland

From 1 January 2021, a new VAT regime exists in Northern Ireland which affects how Irish businesses trade with Northern Ireland and with Great Britain. Broadly, under the Protocol on Ireland/Northern Ireland, the UK (i.e. Northern Ireland and Great Britain) will have three different VAT regimes:

Northern Ireland	EU VAT law applies for trade in **goods**
Northern Ireland	UK VAT law applies for trade in **services**
Great Britain	UK VAT law applies for trade in **goods and services**

14.10.1 Trade in Goods: Ireland/Northern Ireland

Northern Ireland will remain part of the UK VAT regime but EU VAT rules for goods will continue to apply. Therefore, from 1 January 2021, the current VAT treatment should continue to apply to trade in goods between Ireland and Northern Ireland. This means that:

1. Supplies of goods from Ireland to Northern Ireland businesses (i.e. B2B sales) should be treated as zero-rated intra-EU dispatches.
2. For B2C sales from Ireland to Northern Ireland, the distance sale rules will apply.

Trade in Goods: Ireland/Great Britain

Sales of goods from Great Britain to Ireland will be treated as imports into Ireland. Import VAT will be due by the importer in Ireland.

B2B sales of goods from Ireland to Great Britain will be treated as exports from Ireland. No Irish VAT will be charged on these goods, i.e. they will be zero-rated supplies. The responsibility for VAT will fall to the importer in Great Britain. Irish businesses should retain evidence that the goods have been exported from Ireland.

For B2C sales of goods from Ireland to Great Britain, the Irish seller will be liable to charge UK VAT on goods shipped from Ireland to consumers in Great Britain.

14.10.2 Supply of Services

While the Northern Ireland Protocol means Northern Ireland will remain aligned with EU rules for trade in goods, Northern Ireland will continue to follow UK rules for services.

B2B Services

The VAT treatment applicable to the supply of most B2B services between Ireland and the UK will largely remain the same (i.e. the place of supply is the place where the business receiving the services is established). If an Irish business **receives** services from a company based in the UK, Irish VAT will be due on those services. If an Irish business **supplies** services to a company based in the UK, UK VAT will be due on those services.

B2C Services

In general, for B2C services the place of supply is the place where the supplier is established. However, many services supplied from Ireland to non-business customers outside the EU will not be subject to Irish VAT. Subject to the "use and enjoyment provisions", VAT will not be due on the following services supplied to non-business customers established outside the EU:

- Transfers and assignments of copyrights, patents, licences, trademarks and similar rights.
- Advertising services.
- The services of consultants, engineers, consultancy firms, lawyers, accountants and other similar services, as well as data processing and the provision of information.
- Obligations to refrain from pursuing or exercising, in whole or in part, a business activity or a right.
- Banking, financial and insurance transactions including reinsurance, except for the hire of safes.
- The supply of staff.
- The hiring out of movable tangible property, with the exception of all means of transport.
- The provision of access to, and of transport or transmission through, natural gas and electricity distribution systems. This includes the provision of other services directly linked thereto.
- Telecommunications services.
- Radio and television broadcasting services.
- Electronically supplied services.
- Services not included in the list above, supplied to a non-business customer outside the EU are subject to Irish VAT at the appropriate rate.

Services supplied to a non-business customer outside the EU that are not included in the list above will be subject to Irish VAT at the appropriate rate.

14.11   Requirement to Retain Records

All records pertaining to VAT transactions must be retained for six years from the date of the latest transaction to which they refer unless the special written permission of the Inspector of Taxes has been obtained for their retention for a shorter period. Generally, this permission is only given subject to certain conditions. The six-year VAT record-keeping period also applies to liquidated companies.

This requirement applies to all books, records and documents relevant to a taxable person's business, including invoices, credit notes, receipts, accounts vouchers, import documentation, bank statements, cash till rolls, etc. There is an extended time period in respect of both records and linking documents that relate to certain transactions, such as a Revenue investigation, any claim made by the taxpayer and any appeal. Such documents must be retained until such time that the relevant proceedings have been determined or expired.

14.12   Inspection of Records

Authorised Revenue officials have the power to enter any premises in which they have reason to believe a business is being carried on and to require production of or search for business records, to remove them, etc.

In practice, VAT-registered businesses are visited by Revenue on a periodic basis to ensure that the system is operating correctly. Visits can also take place **before** VAT registration is initially granted or, for example, where the VAT return for a VAT period shows a substantial refund.

Revenue has the power to inspect and remove records. This provision enables Revenue to serve a notice on a company requiring them to provide "information, explanations or particulars" in relation to books and records or any other documents held by the company that may be of assistance to Revenue in identifying taxpayers who are suppressing the level of their sales by attempting to conceal the true quantum of their purchases. Failure to comply with the requirements of the Revenue request can result in the imposition of a €4,000 fine.

14.13   Expression of Doubt

If a trader has any difficulty as to the treatment of a transaction for VAT, then he should set out details of the transaction together with an explanation of why the VAT treatment of same is in doubt in a letter which must be lodged with the relevant VAT 3 return. The letter must identify the amount of VAT which is in doubt. Also, the VAT 3 return must be submitted by the 23rd day following the end of the VAT period (see **Section 14.14**). While this facility is important, the time frame (i.e. 23 days from the end of the VAT period) in which the expression of doubt claim has to be prepared is extremely tight (compared with 10 months for income tax returns), especially if relevant transaction documents and detailed legislative/ case law arguments are to be submitted in support of the claim. Section 81 VATCA 2010 provides that in the case of a genuine expression of doubt, interest will not be payable on any additional amount.

Where Revenue finds that tax on the doubtful transaction is correctly due but the trader had a genuine case for making an expression of doubt claim, then no interest or penalties will apply to the additional VAT liability provided it is paid no later than the due date for payment of VAT for the period in which the trader is advised of Revenue's decision.

14.14 Compliance Matters

VAT returns are generally submitted for two-month periods. The due date for VAT returns and payments is the 23rd of the following month, e.g. the VAT return for January–February 2022 is required to be filed on or before 23 March 2022. VAT returns are required to be submitted electronically together with payment of any VAT liability.

In certain circumstances, it may be possible to submit returns monthly (e.g. where the trader is in a constant refund position). It is also possible to submit returns and pay VAT due less frequently (every four months or every six months). These less frequent filing periods are generally available to traders with small annual VAT liabilities. Finally, Revenue may allow a trader to submit returns annually. However, it will generally insist on monthly direct debits being paid during the course of the year which should more or less match the ultimate liability. A balancing payment/refund can be made once the return has been filed.

Chapter 14 Summary

VAT on supplies of goods and services

- VAT arises on a supply for consideration by a taxable person acting as such where the place of supply is the State
- If the place of supply is outside of Ireland, Irish VAT does not arise
- Accountable persons must register for VAT, submit VAT returns and VAT payments, provide invoices and keep records

Cross-border transactions

- Imports/exports are goods arriving from/dispatched to non-EU Member States
- Intra-Community supply and acquisition of goods – goods dispatched between businesses in other EU Member States
- Distance sales – goods dispatched to a private consumer (not VAT-registered) in another EU Member State
- A charge to Irish VAT on services supplied by Irish businesses cross-border depends on if the supply is to an EU business/non-business customer or to a non-EU customer
- Zero-rating of supplies of goods and services to, and intra-Community acquisitions and imports from outside the EU, by certain accountable persons (section 56 VATCA 2010)

Other key concepts

- Transfer of business relief – when a supply of a business undertaking (or part of) to a VAT-registered purchaser it is outside the scope of VAT
- VAT grouping – allows a number of persons to be treated as a single person for VAT purposes. Benefits are reduced administrative burden and improved cash flow

Questions

Review Questions
(See Suggested Solutions to Review Questions at the end of this textbook.)

Question 14.1

Peter Jones owns 100% of the shares in Jones Plumbing Ltd. Peter is considering selling his business and two potential purchasers have made significant offers. Simon Smith has offered to buy Peter's shares in the business. Tony Taylor has offered to buy the assets in the company.

Requirement
Comment on the VAT issues arising under both scenarios.

Question 14.2

Kevin Kelly transferred a freehold property to his trading company. Both Kevin and the company were included in a VAT group at the time.

Requirement
Comment on the VAT treatment.

VAT and Property

Learning Objective

By the end of this chapter, you should be familiar with the VAT issues which arise in relation to property transactions after 1 July 2008.

15.1 Introduction

This chapter deals with transactions involving properties in Ireland. In this context, property includes all land and buildings in the State. The term used in the legislation is "immovable goods". Any transaction involving property outside the State will not be subject to Irish VAT but may be subject to VAT in the country where the property is located.

There is a wide variety of transactions which involve property. A person could buy or sell a freehold interest in a property or could assign a 999-year lease to someone. Alternatively, a person could create a lease to someone for 20 years or for a much shorter period (e.g. four years, nine months).

15.2 Post-1 July 2008 Rules: Current Rules

A significant reform of the VAT on property legislation was introduced with effect from 1 July 2008. Prior to 1 July 2008, separate VAT rules applied to sales of property and to leases of property. These 'old' VAT rules are outside the scope of this textbook, but be aware that such rules existed when dealing with VAT on property transactions in practice.

15.2.1 Sale of Freeholds

For VAT to arise on the disposal of a property, there are generally three conditions that must be satisfied:

1. it must be supplied for consideration in the course of business;
2. the property must have been developed in the 20-year period prior to the supply; and
3. it must be considered "new".

The concept of "in the course of business" is very broad. In general, a taxpayer is considered to be in business if they are engaged in an economic activity. This is irrespective of the financial results of the activity or whether the activity is within the scope of VAT. A transaction entered into in a private capacity is not done in the course of business (e.g. an individual who purchases a house to live in for the rest of their life). The position can differ, however, when the motive of the taxpayer is to realise a gain, e.g. an investor sells a property that was intended for letting. Where the motive for the realisation is the generation of profit, typically the transaction will be considered to be a trading transaction. In determining whether a transaction is trading in nature, consideration should be given to the badges of trade.

15.2.2 Definitions

"Developed"

A property is regarded as being "developed" when:

- a new building is constructed; or
- an existing building is extended, altered or reconstructed; or
- an existing building is demolished; or
- some engineering or other operation or work is carried out that adapts the building for materially altered use. (Work that is not designed to make a material alteration in the use to which a building is put is not development. Thus, no account is taken of fencing, land drainage, laying of roads for agricultural purposes and so on.)

Development, other than "minor development", essentially makes a property "new" for VAT purposes. For example, where an undeveloped property or an "old" property is developed, the properties are considered "new" for VAT purposes following the completion of that development.

Work on maintaining or repairing a property generally does not constitute development, although the facts of the case would need to be considered. The fact that planning permission had been obtained for development does not, of itself, constitute development for VAT purposes.

Example 15.1: Agricultural work

Eoin (a farmer) owns a 20-acre undeveloped field. In 2017, he spends €150,000 on agricultural works adding an access road to get to the field, fencing the entire field and adding a drainage system. He uses the field for agricultural purposes.

In 2022, he sells the field to Vincent. Even though Eoin has spent substantial money and has carried out engineering works on the land, the work did not "materially alter" the land (since it was a farm before and is still a farm after). The sale is not liable to VAT as the field is not developed.

"Minor Development"

"Minor development" is a level of development that does not make a property "new". It can be described as development that does not (and is not intended to) adapt the property for a materially altered use, provided that the cost of such development does not exceed 25% of the consideration for the (subsequent) supply of the property. To determine if a property has been materially altered, it is necessary to establish what the property was capable of being used for before and after the work is carried out.

Example 15.2

Peter acquired a property in 2015 for €15 million plus VAT. In 2022, he added a small extension for €400,000. He then sold the property for €20 million. The development work carried out by Peter would be considered minor as the cost of the works is clearly less than 25% of the selling price of the property and the works done did not materially alter the use of the property.

> **Example 15.3**
> James owns a warehouse and in 2022 work is carried out that is completed at a cost equal to less than 25% of its sale price. The work upgrades the warehouse to a standard required for modern warehouses. After the work is completed, James sells the warehouse. The sale is exempt from VAT as the work is considered "minor development". If, however, the warehouse is turned into an apartment block and is then sold to a property developer, the sale is taxable as the work has "materially altered" the building. The building is developed and has been made "new".

"New"

The supply of a property is taxable only if the property is considered new. The test for whether a property is considered new depends on whether the transaction is the first-ever sale of the property "on completion" (see below), or a second or subsequent sale since the time that the most recent development of the property was completed. The supply of a developed property will be liable to VAT if either of the following rules applies:

1. The five-year rule – a property is considered new for a maximum period of five years from the date on which the property itself or a development of the property (other than a minor development) is completed. It does not matter if the property has been occupied or not.
2. The two-year rule – where a completed property has been supplied at least once (to someone other than a connected party), the period for which the property is considered new is limited to a period of two years following the occupation of the property.

"Completion"

"Completion" in the context of property means that the development of the property has reached the state where the property can effectively be used for the purposes for which it was designed. The physical state that the property is in when completed (i.e. the degree of finishing and fitting that will have been carried out) will depend on its intended use and may vary from one type of building to another.

Finishing and fitting work that is normally carried out by the person who will use the property, whether as owner or tenant, does not itself have to be completed for the property to have reached the point of being "completed". In all cases, one essential requirement for completion is the connection of all of the utility services that will enable the property to be used for the purposes for which it was designed. The five-year rule for taxable supplies of completed property begins from the date of completion.

Note: the supply of an uncompleted property that is made in the course of business is always taxable (e.g. a half-constructed building). The two- and five-year rules only apply once the property has been completed.

"Occupied"

A property is "occupied" when it is fully in use, the use being one for which planning permission for the development of the goods had been granted. It is essential to note that this use is a physical, practical use and not a purely economic or legal occupation. The two-year rule for second and subsequent supplies of a property begins on the date of occupation following completion. The two-year rule is an aggregate occupation of all tenants.

Example 15.4

A property developer acquires a site in 2012. He constructs an industrial building and it is completed in 2022. The following situations can then arise:

- If he disposes of the building immediately, he will be required to charge VAT as the property is clearly new.
- If he cannot find a buyer and is unable to sell the building until 2028, he is not obliged to charge VAT as the property is no longer new (it is completed more than five years).
- If he lets the property for three years and then sells it in 2026, he will be obliged to charge VAT. This is because, even though the property has been occupied for more than two years, the sale by the developer is the first supply since completion.
- However, assume he sells the building to an unconnected party (X Ltd) in 2022 and charges VAT @ 13.5%. X Ltd then occupies the building for three years and disposes of it. X Ltd is not obliged to charge VAT on the disposal. This is because the building has been occupied for more than two years **and** the sale by X Ltd is not the first supply of the building since it was completed. Therefore, the property is no longer considered "new".
- If X Ltd had developed the property during its ownership and then sold it, the property may then be considered "new" and again, this will depend on whether the work done by X Ltd would or would not be considered minor development.

15.2.3 Residential Property Developers

Where the property is residential property, the supply by the person who developed it in the course of business (i.e. a property developer) or by a person connected with the property developer is always taxable. The two- and five-year rules do not apply to supplies of residential property by a property developer/builder.

Example 15.5

Joe the builder constructs 20 apartments in 2022. He sells 15 of them but, due to a downturn in the market, he is unable to sell the remaining five. He is able to let three of the apartments and they remain let for 10 years. In 2032, he sells the five apartments. He must charge VAT on the sale even though they have all been completed for more than five years and three of them have been occupied for the entire 10 years.

15.2.4 Undeveloped Property Sold with Connected Building Agreement

The rules contain a "connected building agreement" provision. Where an undeveloped property (or otherwise exempt property) is disposed of in connection with a building or development agreement, the disposal of the property is always subject to VAT. This is an anti-avoidance measure which was introduced to prevent the loss of VAT to the Exchequer.

15.2.5 Option to Tax

Where a property is supplied when it is no longer considered "new", the supply is exempt from VAT. The vendor is therefore not obliged to charge VAT. However, the seller and the purchaser may jointly opt to tax the supply if they are both carrying on businesses in the State. Where the option to tax is exercised, the **purchaser must account for the VAT** on the supply on the reverse charge basis. We will see when we look at the Capital Goods Scheme (**Section 15.4**), that a vendor may have a very good reason to want to charge VAT on the sale of a property.

> **Example 15.6**
> ABC Ltd acquired a property in 2018 for €10 million plus VAT. ABC Ltd recovered all of the VAT as the property was to be used for the purposes of ABC Ltd's taxable trade. In 2026, ABC Ltd decides to dispose of the property. Assuming ABC Ltd has not carried out any development work since it acquired the property, the property is no longer considered "new" for VAT purposes. Therefore, the sale of the property is exempt from VAT and ABC Ltd does not need to charge VAT. However, if the purchaser (XYZ Ltd) agrees, ABC Ltd can opt to tax the disposal and VAT then arises on the transaction.
>
> Unlike the sale of a "new" property, the VAT is dealt with by reverse-charge and XYZ Ltd will self-account for the VAT in its VAT return. If the property is sold for €12m plus VAT of €1.62 million, then XYZ Ltd will include €1.62 million of VAT in the output (sales) section of its VAT return, but will also include €1.62 million of VAT in its input (purchases) section of its VAT return (this assumes it is entitled to 100% VAT recovery).

15.2.6   Letting of Property

Lettings of property are exempt from VAT but the landlord may, with some exceptions, exercise an option to apply VAT to a letting. The legislation does not draw a distinction between leases of 10 years or more, and leases of less than 10 years. Certain very long leases are treated as a supply of the property. These are referred to as freehold equivalent leases and are treated as a supply (sale) of the property itself.

> **Example 15.7**
> A grant of a 20-year lease is exempt from VAT with an option to tax the lease. However, the grant of a 999-year lease, where the tenant effectively acquires the property, would not be treated as an exempt letting. It would be treated as the sale of the property and the usual rules for determining whether or not VAT should be charged would apply.

A landlord who makes an exempt letting is not entitled to deduct VAT incurred on the acquisition or development of a property, which is subject to the letting. Where a landlord opts to tax a letting, that service becomes subject to VAT at the standard rate (currently 23%). The landlord is entitled to deduct VAT incurred on the acquisition or development of a property that is to be used for the purposes of making taxable lettings.

> **Example 15.8**
> Peter and Paul both acquire commercial properties in Dublin for €500,000 each plus VAT of €67,500. Peter grants a lease to a tenant and opts to tax the lease. He therefore is entitled to recover the €67,500 of VAT he incurred on acquisition of the property. He is then obliged to charge VAT at 23% on top of the rent. Paul also grants a lease to a tenant but decides not to opt to tax the lease. Paul does not charge VAT on the rents received but he is not entitled to recover the VAT on acquisition of the property and, if he has already recovered it, he must repay the €67,500 to Revenue.

The option to tax applies to individual lettings of properties. Under the 'old' rules, i.e. pre-1 July 2008, a waiver applied to all short-term lettings (lettings of less than 10 years) granted by the landlord. That is not the case with the option to tax rules. Indeed, it may well be that a landlord may opt to tax a letting of part of a building while making an exempt letting of the rest of the building.

The landlord must either confirm in writing with the tenant that the letting will be taxable or issue a document to the tenant stating that the letting will be taxable. In practice, it should be made clear in the lease agreement that the landlord has decided to opt to tax a particular letting.

There are restrictions on the option to tax rents. The option to tax cannot apply in the following circumstances:

- Where the property is occupied for residential purposes.
- Where the letting is between connected persons (unless the tenant is entitled to deduct at least 90% VAT recovery).
- Where the property is occupied by a person who is connected with the landlord (unless that person has at least 90% VAT recovery).

Note: "connected" is very widely defined.

These restrictions are mainly designed to prevent persons acquiring properties for an exempt purpose and recovering the VAT on the acquisition.

Example 15.9

John is a doctor and is exempt from VAT. He wishes to acquire a new property to trade from. He has identified a property and the vendor has told him that VAT will be charged on the sale. Without the restrictions referred to above, John's wife Sarah could acquire the property, reclaim the VAT from Revenue and then opt to tax a letting to John.

In such a position, Revenue may ultimately receive as much VAT in the long-term (remember Sarah would need to charge VAT on the rent which John could not recover). However, the restriction will not allow Sarah to opt to tax the letting, which means she would be unable to reclaim the VAT if she acquires the property.

15.2.7 Termination of an Option to Tax

A landlord can terminate an option to tax rents by either entering an agreement in writing with the tenant that the rents will no longer be taxable or by issuing a notice in writing to that effect.

An option to tax rents will be terminated automatically:

- if the landlord becomes "connected" with the tenant (unless the tenant has 90% VAT recovery);
- if the property becomes occupied by a person connected with the landlord (unless he/she has 90% VAT recovery); or
- if the property is used for residential purposes.

Terminating an option to tax may have consequences for the landlord under the Capital Goods Scheme (see **Section 15.4**).

15.3 Transitional Measures

Transitional measures bridge the gap between the current and old rules. These measures determine the VAT treatment of a disposal of a property that is held by a taxable person on 1 July 2008, until that person disposes of the interest in the property.

These transitional measures can be particularly relevant today where it is becoming common for landlords and tenants to agree to a surrender of an old lease (i.e. a lease dated pre-1 July 2008). This may happen so as to enable the landlord to 'take back' the building in order to redevelop it.

15.3.1 Supply of Freeholds: Transitional Measures

The VAT treatment on the supply of a "transitional property" (i.e. the sale of a property completed prior to and held as at 1 July 2008) depends on whether or not the vendor had VAT recovery when the interest was acquired or developed pre-1 July 2008. Where the vendor was entitled to deduct any of the VAT incurred on the acquisition or development of the property, the VAT treatment of the supply of the property is the same as the treatment that applies to properties completed on or after 1 July 2008 (see **Section 15.2**).

Where the property is considered new (under the two- and five-year rules), the supply of the property is taxable. The taxable amount is the full consideration for the supply.

Where the person making the supply was not entitled to deduct any of the VAT incurred on the acquisition or development of the property, the supply of the property on or after 1 July 2008 is exempt from VAT.

However, the seller and the purchaser may jointly opt to tax the supply, if they are both engaged in business. Where the option to tax is exercised, the purchaser must account for the VAT on the supply on the reverse-charge basis.

Example 15.10
Big Bank plc acquired a new property in January 2008 but was unable to recover any VAT as it used the property for an exempt purpose. It decides to sell the property in January 2022. Under the transitional rules, the sale of this property is exempt from VAT. However, the vendor and the purchaser may agree to opt to tax (i.e. charge VAT on) the sale.

15.3.2 Assignments or Surrenders of Long Leases: Transitional Measures

These rules broadly follow the transitional rules in relation to freeholds. Where the tenant was not entitled to recover VAT on the acquisition of the lease, a subsequent assignment or surrender of the lease is exempt from VAT. However, the tenant could agree with the assignee or landlord (depending on the circumstances) to opt to tax the transfer of the leasehold interest. In such a case, a formula is provided in the legislation to determine the value of the transfer and also the relevant VAT amount. The formula is complex and is outside the scope of this textbook.

Where the tenant was entitled to recover VAT on the acquisition of their interest, an assignment or surrender after 1 July 2008 will be subject to VAT. Again the formula noted above will determine the value of the transfer and the related VAT.

15.4 The Capital Goods Scheme: Main Provisions

The Capital Goods Scheme (CGS) is a mechanism for regulating deductibility over the "VAT-life" of a capital good. For VAT purposes, a capital good is a developed property. The scheme operates by ensuring that the deductibility for a property reflects the use to which the property is put over the VAT-life (or adjustment period) of the property.

15.4.1 Operation of the CGS

The VAT incurred on the acquisition or development of a property is deductible in accordance with the normal rules relating to deductibility. A person who is engaged in a fully taxable economic activity is entitled to deduct all of the VAT charged on the acquisition or development of a property to be used in the business. A person who is engaged in partly taxable and partly exempt economic activities is only entitled to deduct the percentage of VAT charged that corresponds to the percentage of taxable use.

The first 12 months following completion (or acquisition, where the property is acquired following the completion) is known as the "initial interval", at the end of which the taxpayer must review the amount of VAT deducted on the acquisition or development of the property. If the proportion of taxable use of a property during that 12-month period differs from the proportion of the VAT deducted on the acquisition or the development of that property, then an adjustment is required. If too much has been deducted, the taxpayer must pay back the excess. If too little had been deducted initially, the taxpayer is entitled to claim the deficiency as an input credit.

Example 15.11

ABC Ltd acquires a property in January 2022 and pays VAT of €100,000. The company generally has a 100% VAT recovery and recovers all of the VAT. At the end of 12 months, the company realises that, during the 12-month period, it actually had a 90% VAT recovery. The company must repay 10% of the VAT (€10,000) at that point to Revenue.

This adjusted amount, which is deductible for the first 12 months, is the benchmark figure for comparison purposes under the scheme for the remainder of the VAT-life of the property. Over the VAT-life of the property, the scheme requires the owner to carry out an annual review (i.e. at each "interval") of the use to which a property is put (in terms of taxable or exempt use). Where there is a change in the proportion of use for taxable purposes for any year in comparison with the use during the initial 12 months, an adjustment of a proportion of the VAT deductibility will be required.

The annual adjustments will reflect the difference between the use in the initial 12 months and the use in the year being reviewed. Ultimately, the proportion of VAT deducted following all annual adjustments will reflect the actual use of the property over the adjustment period or VAT-life of the property. The VAT-life of a property is made up of 20 intervals. In the case of a refurbishment, the VAT-life is 10 intervals. Except in relation to the second CGS interval (see **Section 15.4.2**), a CGS interval is 12 months.

Example 15.12

Following on from the last example, ABC Ltd had recovered €90,000 of VAT at the end of the first interval (it initially recovered €100,000 and then repaid €10,000). The annual adjustments will therefore be based on the revised figure of €90,000.

It is important to note that, for the majority of businesses, these CGS reviews will have no effect. For example, if a company deducts all of the VAT charged on acquisition or development and engages in wholly taxable activities during the adjustment period, then no adjustments will arise. The CGS does not apply to any person who acquires a property on which VAT is not chargeable.

15.4.2 "VAT-life" (Adjustment Period) of a Capital Good

As outlined above, the scheme provides that in most cases each capital good will have a VAT-life or adjustment period of 20 intervals. It is during this period that adjustments are required to be made. Once the period has elapsed, there are no further obligations under the scheme.

Certain properties have an adjustment period of 10 intervals. Where development work is carried out on a previously completed building, a new capital good to the value of the cost of the development is "created" by this development work. This is known as a "refurbishment". The adjustment period for a refurbishment is 10 intervals. This means that there can, in some cases, be two or more capital goods in relation to a single property at one time.

As indicated previously, following the first 12 months (known as the "initial period"), the taxpayer must review the amount of VAT deducted and compare it to the actual taxable use.

Example 15.13A

GTC Ltd purchases a property on which VAT is charged on 13 September 2022. The VAT amount is €1,000,000. GTC recovered all of the VAT on the basis that it would be carrying on 100% taxable activities. The "initial interval" begins on that date and ends 12 months later on 12 September 2023. At the end of the first interval, GTC Ltd calculates it is only entitled to 80% recovery. It therefore repays €200,000 to Revenue.

The "second interval" begins on the day after the initial interval ends and ends at the end of the owner's accounting year in which the initial interval ends. The purpose of this interval is to align the adjustments that may be required under the scheme with the owner's accounting year.

Example 15.13B

GTC Ltd's accounting year ends on 31 December. The "initial interval" ends on 12 September 2023 (in the accounting year that ends 31 December 2023).The "second interval" begins on 13 September 2023 (day following end of initial interval) and ends on 31 December 2023, i.e. at the end of the accounting year during which the initial interval ends.

It performs several calculations at this point:

1. The total tax incurred was €1,000,000
2. The total reviewed deductible amount is €800,000
3. The base tax amount is €50,000 (€1,000,000/20 intervals)
4. The reference deduction amount is €40,000 (€800,000/20 intervals)

At the end of the second interval, GTC calculates that it still has an 80% VAT recovery. It, therefore, requires no adjustment under the Capital Goods Scheme. It verifies this by performing the following calculation:

Base tax amount = €50,000
Interval deductible amount €40,000 (Base tax amount × the VAT recovery % in this interval (i.e. 80% in this case)) Reference deduction amount = €40,000
As the interval deductible amount and the reference deduction amount are the same, no adjustment is required.

A "subsequent interval" means each interval after the second interval until the end of the adjustment period. The interval immediately following the second interval begins on the day after the end of the second interval and ends at the end of the owner's accounting year.

Example 15.13C

As the "second interval" ends on 31 December 2023, the third interval will begin on 1 January 2024 and will end on 31 December 2024. Each "subsequent interval" will run from 1 January to 31 December until the end of the 20th interval on 31 December 2041.

Assume that the recovery rate for GTC Ltd stays at 80% for the next four intervals. No adjustments are required. However, in the seventh interval, the recovery rate increases to 90%. At the end of the interval, GTC Ltd performs the following calculation:

Base tax amount = €50,000
Interval deductible amount = €45,000, i.e. €50,000 × 90%
Reference deduction amount = €40,000

As the interval deductible amount is greater than the reference deduction amount, GTC Ltd is entitled to reclaim an extra €5,000 in its VAT return. It makes sense for GTC Ltd to get a refund of VAT as its recovery rate has increased. When it acquired the property and performed the adjustment after the initial interval, it understood that it was going to have 80% VAT recovery for the remainder of the adjustment period for the property. As it is now using the property for 90% taxable purposes, this entitles it to reclaim more of the VAT from Revenue. If the recovery rate stays at 90% for the remainder of the adjustment period, GTC Ltd will be entitled to recoup €5,000 at the end of each period.

However, if the recovery rate drops, GTC Ltd may be required to make a payment to Revenue. Suppose the recovery rate in the tenth interval drops to 75%. At the end of the interval, GTC Ltd performs the following calculation:

Base tax amount = €50,000
Interval deductible amount = €37,500, i.e. €50,000 × 75%
Reference deduction amount = €40,000

As the interval deductible amount is actually less than the reference deduction amount, GTC Ltd must pay €2,500 to Revenue (€2,500 is the difference between the two figures). It does this by including the relevant amount in its VAT return.

> **Example 15.14**
>
> Pearse Ltd acquires a property on 1 August 2022 with a VAT charge of €100,000 for the purposes of its (fully VATable) equipment leasing trade. Therefore, Pearse Ltd takes full VAT recovery of the €100,000 VAT charge in its July/August 2022 VAT return. Pearse Ltd has a 31 December accounting year end.
>
> The initial interval for the property runs from 1 August 2022 until 31 July 2023, after which Pearse Ltd must review its actual usage of the property in the initial interval. It transpires that the company's actual VAT recovery position in relation to the property for the initial interval was in fact 90% rather than 100% (as the company partly used the property for VAT-exempt activities). Therefore 10% of the VAT that was originally recovered (€10,000) must be repaid by Pearse Ltd to Revenue after the end of the initial interval. The adjusted €90,000 of VAT that was actually recoverable by Pearse Ltd is set as the benchmark figure for the purposes of the CGS scheme and is divided into 20 portions for each of the 20 intervals in the VAT life of the property, i.e. €90,000/20 = €4,500.
>
> The second interval for the property runs from 1 August 2023 until Pearse Ltd's year end of 31 December 2023. In the second interval, Pearse Ltd continued to use the property for 90% VATable activities, so no adjustment was required under the CGS.
>
> However, in the third interval (a 12-month period running from 1 January 2024 to 31 December 2024) Pearse Ltd used the property for 95% VATable activities and therefore had 95% VAT recovery entitlement on the property. Pearse Ltd compares this VAT recovery entitlement with the benchmark 90% VAT recovery for the initial interval. As there has been an "increase" in VAT recovery entitlement for that interval, Pearse Ltd is entitled to make a VAT reclaim from Revenue for €250 after the third interval as follows:
>
> Reference deduction amount = €4,500
> Interval deductible amount = €100,000/20 × 95% = €4,750
> Difference = €250 (reclaim in Pearse Ltd's VAT return)
>
> If Pearse Ltd's usage in the following interval remains at 90% VAT recovery entitlement, no adjustment is required for those intervals. However, if the level of VAT recovery falls below 90%, Pearse Ltd would be required to make a repayment to Revenue.
>
> It should also be noted that if there were separate capital goods in the same property (e.g. refurbishment capital goods), Pearse Ltd would need to review the usage of each capital good and separate CGS review calculations would be required for each capital good.

Special rules known as 'big swing' adjustments apply where the taxable use for an interval differs by more than 50% from the taxable use for the initial interval. The big swing rules recognise the fact that there has been a significant change in the taxable activities of the business and that a full adjustment is required. This adjustment is not based on 1/20th of the VAT incurred but is based instead on the full VAT incurred reduced by the number of intervals that have already expired in the adjustment period. The formula for calculating the big swing adjustment is outside the scope of this textbook, however, it is important to be alert to the fact that a major change in the use of a property may necessitate a large CGS adjustment, which will trigger a VAT payment or refund.

Rent-to-Buy Schemes

Rent-to-buy schemes are offered by property developers to attract potential buyers of the property. There are different variations of the scheme (the details of which will affect the VAT treatment), but essentially an individual rents the property under a letting agreement and at some stage within a pre-agreed period is given the option to purchase the property.

As the property will be used for an exempt purpose during the period when it is rented, the developer is obliged to make an adjustment in respect of the VAT claimed on the acquisition and development costs. Given that the property is being rented by the person who developed it, the immediate full VAT clawback provision does not apply. Instead, the developer is liable to repay 1/20th of the VAT deducted on the acquisition and development of the property at the end of the second and each subsequent capital goods scheme interval for as long as the property is rented (subject to a maximum rental period of 20 years). When the property is eventually sold, it will be subject to VAT.

This position also applies where the property developer lets the property because they are unable to sell it, i.e. the treatment is not confined only to rent to buy schemes.

Example 15.15

A developer constructs a house for sale in 2019, with a cost of constructing the house of €1,000,000, plus VAT of €135,000, all of which he deducts. The development of the house is completed on 15 July 2019. He is unable to sell the house and instead rents it out. The letting is for three years and is created on 4 August 2019. His accounting year end is 31 December. There is no immediate clawback of the VAT deducted, although the lease is VAT-exempt.

The CGS initial "interval" in respect of the property begins on 15 July 2019 and ends on 14 July 2020. The second interval ends on 31 December 2020, which is the end of the accounting year. The third interval ends on 31 December 2021. An adjustment arises at this point in accordance with section 64(3) VATCA 2010, which essentially amounts to his paying back 1/20th of the VAT deducted in respect of the acquisition and development of the property. At the end of each subsequent interval in the taxable period following the end of each 31 December financial year, if the taxable property is not used for a taxable purpose, there will be an adjustment.

At the end of the lease in August 2022, he sells the property for €1,200,000 to a third party. The sale includes VAT at 13.5%. There is no VAT credit given for the previous 1/20th clawbacks that arose while the property was used for a VAT exempt lease. No further clawback of inputs arises as the taxable supply of the property in August 2022 constitutes a taxable use for the fourth and all subsequent intervals.

He must account for 13.5% VAT of €142,731 (€1,200,000 × 13.5/113.5) for the July–August 2021 taxable period, being the VAT due on the sale of the property.

15.4.3 Capital Goods Record

Owners of capital goods are required to keep detailed records of the amounts incurred on the relevant properties. They are also obliged to keep a record of the annual adjustments which are made at the end of each interval. The "capital good record" is specific to each capital good. It is important to remember that, each time a property is developed, a new capital good is created. It is also important to remember that a newly acquired property may have an adjustment period of 20 intervals, but an extension to that property (a refurbishment) may only have an adjustment period of 10 intervals. Therefore, a person may have several capital good records for the property in question.

15.4.4 Disposals of Capital Goods

It is quite possible that a person will dispose of a capital good before the end of the adjustment period for that capital good. If the property is "new", then the person will be obliged to charge VAT on the disposal. In such a case, the person will charge VAT at 13.5% on the consideration received. From the perspective of the Capital Goods Scheme (CGS), where a person disposes of a property during the adjustment period (and VAT is charged on the disposal), the person is deemed to have used the property for 100% taxable purposes for the remainder of the adjustment period. Depending on the circumstances, this may result in a repayment of VAT to the vendor if they were not using the property for a fully taxable use.

Example 15.16

Peter bought a newly completed property in 2022 and recovered all of the VAT as he was engaged in fully taxable activities. His adjustment period for the property is 20 intervals. After one year, Peter sells the property. Peter charges VAT on the sale of the property. Peter is deemed to have used the property for 100% taxable activities for the remainder of the adjustment period (19 intervals). As Peter originally recovered 100% of the VAT, no adjustment is required.

> **Example 15.17**
> Paul bought a newly completed property in 2022. However, as Paul is a dentist, he was unable to reclaim any of the VAT on the purchase. After one year, Paul sold the property and charged VAT on the disposal. Paul is deemed to have used the property for 100% taxable activities for the remainder of the adjustment period (19 intervals). As Paul did not recover any VAT when he acquired the property, he is now entitled to reclaim 95% (19/20) of the VAT he originally paid and did not recover.

If the property being disposed of is not new, then the disposal may not be subject to VAT. Where a person disposes of a property and VAT is not charged, the person is deemed to use the property for a fully exempt purpose for the remainder of the adjustment period. Depending on the circumstances, this may lead to a payment of VAT by the vendor to Revenue.

> **Example 15.18**
> Jason bought a property for his fully taxable trade in 2022. He recovered all of the VAT. After five intervals, he disposed of the property. As the property was no longer considered new, he was not obliged to charge VAT and did not opt to do so. However, under the Capital Goods Scheme, Jason is required to repay 75% (15/20) of the VAT he reclaimed when he acquired the property as he is now deemed to use the property for an exempt purpose for the remaining 15 intervals.

> **Example 15.19**
> Mary (a doctor) bought a property in 2022 and was unable to recover any of the VAT. She disposed of the property in 2028 and, as the property was no longer considered new, she did not charge VAT. No adjustment is required for Mary as she did not recover any VAT in the first place.

15.4.5 Interaction of the CGS and Opting to Tax Disposals

It is important to remember that a person disposing of a property that is not considered 'new' may not be obliged to charge VAT on the disposal but may agree with the purchaser to opt to tax the sale. When making this decision, the vendor should consider their own position under the CGS and the VAT status of the purchaser.

Suppose for example, a shop owner buys a new shop in 2022 and recovers all of the VAT. His adjustment period under the CGS is 20 intervals. In 2035 he decides to sell the property. As the property is no longer considered "new" for VAT purposes, he can dispose of it without charging VAT. However, if he does that he will be obliged to repay to Revenue approximately 35% (7/20ths) of the VAT he recovered when he bought the property. This will be a real cost to him. However, if he agrees to opt to tax the sale, he will not be required to make any payment to Revenue. Clearly, from the vendor's position, it is more desirable to opt to tax the disposal.

If the purchaser intends to use the property for a taxable purpose (e.g. as a shop), he will probably not have any objection to the "option to tax" as he will be entitled to reclaim the VAT charged. If, however, he intends to use the property for an exempt purpose (e.g. as a bookmaker), he will not want to pay VAT on the purchase price as he will be unable to recover this VAT.

In such a case, it is possible that the two parties may agree that the option to tax is not utilised and perhaps the purchaser will compensate the vendor for the repayment that will then be required. Each case needs to be considered on its own merits to determine whether or not a vendor should opt to tax a sale. Additionally, the direct tax consequences of any payment of compensation from one party to another would need to be carefully considered before the best course of action is determined.

15.4.6 *Interaction of the CGS and Opting to Tax Lettings*

The same issues arise when a landlord is granting a lease to a tenant. A landlord has the option to tax rents received under a lease, which would clearly constitute using the property for fully taxable purposes; opting to not tax rents would be using the property for fully exempt purposes.

A fully taxable tenant is not likely to have any problems with paying VAT on rent as they can recover this VAT. However, a tenant engaged in VAT-exempt activities will not be able to recover this VAT and will therefore not wish to pay any VAT. Clearly, such a tenant would prefer the landlord not to opt to tax the letting. As with the disposal of freehold, it is possible that the tenant will make a payment to a landlord not to opt to tax a letting. Careful consideration needs to be given to all of the tax consequences which may arise from such a payment. Every case is different and all of the facts would need to be known before a landlord decides whether or not to opt to tax a lease.

15.4.7 *Interaction of the CGS and Transfer of Business Relief*

Where a person acquires a property as part of a transfer of a business, section 20(2)(c) or section 26 VATCA 2010 deems the transfer to be outside the scope of VAT. However, such a person is obliged under the CGS to monitor the use to which the property is put. The exact workings will depend on the circumstances as follows:

- the transfer occurs when the property would have been considered 'new' (i.e. where the supply of the property would have been liable to VAT if transfer of business relief had not applied); or
- the supply of the property would have been VAT exempt in the absence of VAT transfer of business relief (e.g. where the supply takes place when the property would not have been considered 'new').

Where the transfer occurs during the period when the sale of the property would have been taxable but for the transfer of business relief, the following treatment applies:

- The seller is deemed for the purposes of the CGS to have made a VATable supply of the property.
- The purchaser is deemed to have been charged the VAT that would have been charged in the absence of the relief.
- The amount of VAT that would have been charged is treated in the hands of the purchaser as the "total tax incurred" for the purposes of the CGS.
- The purchaser must calculate how much of the "total tax incurred" would have been deductible if they had been charged that VAT.
- The difference between the amount charged and the amount deductible is payable to Revenue.

However, if the supply of the property would have been VAT-exempt in the absence of VAT transfer of business relief (e.g. where the supply takes place when the property would not have been considered "new"), then the following treatment applies:

- No VAT arises on the transferor of the business assets.
- The purchaser essentially "steps into the shoes" of the seller for the purposes of the CGS. The purchaser inherits the adjustment period, i.e. if six intervals have elapsed, then there will be 14 intervals remaining in the adjustment period for the transferee.

Similarly, under section 56 VATCA 2010 (see **Section 14.9.5**) where a holder of a section 56 certificate acquires a property, they will generally not be charged VAT by the vendor. Nonetheless, for the purposes of the CGS, that person will be treated as if they had paid VAT and will be obliged to make the appropriate adjustments, if necessary.

Chapter 15 Summary

VAT on the sale of freehold property

- VAT is charged on a sale where:
  - property was developed 20 years prior to the current sale
  - property is supplied in the course of a business
  - property is 'new' under the 5-year or 2-year rule
- Vendor will face a clawback of VAT previously recovered on the property if the sale is not liable to VAT
- The joint option to tax can be used to avoid a clawback of VAT if the property is not 'new'

VAT on letting property

- Lettings of property on or after 1 July 2008 are exempt from VAT
- Landlord's option to tax may be used to charge VAT on the lease and avoid clawback of VAT recovered by landlord

The Capital Goods Scheme

- A capital good is a developed property
- CGS regulates VAT deductibility over the VAT-life of a capital good
- If the use (taxable or exempt) of the property changes over its VAT-life, a CGS adjustment could give rise to a VAT payment/repayment

Questions

Review Questions
(See Suggested Solutions to Review Questions at the end of this textbook.)

Question 15.1

On 1 September 2009, Meta Ltd acquired a newly developed commercial premises for €900,000 plus VAT and reclaimed all the VAT incurred on the acquisition of the property. The property was immediately put to use for the purposes of its trade. Throughout the period of ownership, Meta Ltd was entitled to a 100% recovery of VAT. Meta Ltd makes its accounts to 31 December each year.

In January 2022, Meta Ltd put this property on the market and in December 2022 an insurance company agrees to buy the premises to use in its VAT-exempt activities.

Requirement
Set out the VAT consequences of the various transactions relating to this property.

Question 15.2

Barry Woods developed 10 residential properties for sale. The units were completed in March 2019. He sold five of the properties immediately and rented the remaining five. He sold three more units in March 2024 and finally sold the remaining two units in March 2034.

Requirement
Comment on the VAT implications.

Challenging Question
(Suggested Solutions to Challenging Questions are available through your lecturer.)

Question 15.1

Oliver O'Tool is a property developer. He plans to undertake the following transaction in 2022:

- In January 2014 he completed the development of Retail Unit A, which cost him €200,000 plus 13.5% VAT. He leases the property to ABC Ltd under a 20-year lease for an annual rent of €120,000. The lease was created in May 2014. ABC Ltd wishes to surrender the lease back to Oliver. Oliver already has another tenant lined up under a 10-year lease.
- In 1994 he purchased a residential property. In June 2018 he carried out substantial redevelopment of the property and changed it into a retail unit (Retail Unit B) at a cost of €121,000 plus 13.5% VAT. He now intends to sell the unit for €600,000 plus VAT (if any).
- In July 2009 he completed the development of Retail Unit C at a cost €400,000 plus 13.5% VAT, which he reclaimed. He now plans to sell the unit to his brother, who will operate a GP clinic from the premises, for €450,000 plus VAT (if any).
- In January 2006 he completed the development of Residential Unit D at a cost of €220,000 plus 13.5% VAT. No further development has been carried out since then. He now plans to sell the unit for €380,000 plus VAT (if any).

Requirement
Explain the VAT consequences for each transaction proposed by Oliver.

Revenue Compliance Interventions and Revenue's Powers

Learning Objectives

By the end of this chapter, you should be able to:

■ Advise a client on Revenue compliance interventions under the *Code of Practice for Revenue Compliance Interventions*, effective from 1 May 2022.
■ Describe the enquiry, request for assistance and seizure powers available to Revenue.

16.1 Introduction

Revenue compliance interventions are a common feature of the self-assessment system. It is therefore essential for a Chartered Accountant to know how to approach them, both from a technical and practical perspective. In this chapter we consider the types of intervention that Revenue can make and how they are conducted (in accordance with the *Code of Practice for Revenue Compliance Interventions*) as well as the legislative powers that Revenue has at its disposal.

16.2 Compliance Interventions and Chargeable Persons

There are two tax systems in operation in Ireland, commonly referred to as self-assessment and PAYE (Pay As You Earn). Under PAYE, income tax on employment income is paid by deduction; with self-assessment, however, tax is paid directly by "chargeable persons", as in the case of trading income, investment income, rental income and capital transactions, etc. Part 41A TCA 1997 is the legislative basis for the self-assessment system of taxation covering persons liable to income tax, corporation tax and CGT. It sets out the rules of the tax system and the obligations on the taxpayer to pay tax and submit returns by specified dates. In essence, the self-assessment system places the onus on the taxpayer to meet their obligations correctly and on time without prompting from Revenue. It therefore allows for taxpayers to voluntarily correct mistakes to a tax return, but also allows Revenue to examine tax returns and to pursue tax fraud or tax evasion.

All companies are chargeable persons, but not all individuals are chargeable persons. The definition of a chargeable person, and therefore who is required to furnish a return to Revenue, is contained in sections 959A and 959B(1) TCA 1997. Insofar as this applies to individuals, chargeable persons are:

■ non-PAYE taxpayers;
■ a company director who is the beneficial owner of or is able to directly or indirectly control more than 15% of the ordinary share capital of the company;

- PAYE taxpayers with gross non-PAYE income of less than €50,000 and a net assessable income thereon of more than €5,000; and
- PAYE taxpayers also in receipt of gross non-PAYE income of €50,000 or more which is covered or largely covered by losses, capital allowances and other reliefs. The €50,000 limit applies to gross income from **all** sources and not from each separate source. An individual becoming a chargeable person under this rule continues to be a chargeable person for future years, as long as the source(s) of the non-PAYE income continues to exist, irrespective of the amount of the annual gross income.

Other provisions also force individuals into chargeable person status:

- Where an Irish resident opens a foreign bank account of which they are the beneficial owner, they are to be regarded as a chargeable person for the years of assessment during which the account is opened.
- Recipients of share options charged to tax under Schedule E become chargeable persons.
- Where a person acquires certain foreign life policies, he or she will be deemed to be a chargeable person for the chargeable period.
- Where a person acquires a material interest in an offshore fund, they are deemed to be chargeable persons.

If an individual is not a chargeable person for any given year of assessment, Revenue still has the right to raise enquiries, but such an enquiry will not take the form of a compliance intervention. Furthermore, a person who does not make a return because they are not a chargeable person for a given year cannot be subject to a surcharge.

Finally, penalties arise in respect of incorrect returns. Where the legislation does not require a return to be provided, a penalty for any given year cannot be applied. There may, however, be tax owing; and interest arising on the tax owing.

Example 16.1

Josephine holds 17% of the ordinary share capital of Josephine Ltd. She is also a director of the company and her only source of income is her salary from Josephine Ltd, upon which PAYE is operated.

Josephine is classed as a proprietary director for tax purposes and is, therefore, obliged to make an annual income tax return under the self-assessment system, even though all of her income is subject to PAYE. Therefore, under sections 959A and 959B(1) TCA 1997, she is a chargeable person and her income tax returns are open to a Revenue compliance intervention.

16.3 Revenue Compliance Interventions

The most recent *Code of Practice for Revenue Compliance Interventions*, which came into effect on 1 May 2022 (and is therefore referred to as the 2022 Code), introduces a new three-tier system of Revenue compliance interventions set out in the Compliance Intervention Framework, the purpose of which is "to provide a consistent graduated response to taxpayer behaviour, ranging from extensive opportunities to voluntarily correct mistakes up to the pursuit of criminal sanctions for cases of serious fraud or evasion".

These graduated compliance interventions are:

- **Level 1** – an intervention to support compliance (e.g. bulk-issue non-filing reminders, profile interviews and self-reviews). The taxpayer retains the right to an unprompted qualifying disclosure (see **Section 16.3.3**).
- **Level 2** – an intervention to challenge non-compliance using risk review or a Revenue audit. The taxpayer retains the right to a prompted qualifying disclosure (see **Section 16.3.3**).
- **Level 3** – an intervention confronting non-compliance by means of an investigation. The taxpayer is no longer entitled to make a qualifying disclosure regarding the matter under investigation.

The three levels are not sequential, i.e. it does not proceed from Level 1 to Level 2 to Level 3. Rather:

> "Revenue may initiate an intervention at any level of the framework in response to a perceived risk. This may arise without any previous intervention at a lower level in relation to the taxpayer concerned. In certain circumstances, however, risks identified during an intervention may lead to the initiation of a higher level intervention."

Generally, taxpayers are selected for compliance intervention based on various "risk driven methodologies", such as REAP (Risk Evaluation, Analysis and Profiling system, which allows for the screening of all tax returns against sectoral and business norms and provides a selection basis for checks or audits) and real-time risk analytics (for VAT and PAYE). However, the 2022 Code adds:

> "While these methods of case selection will continue, Revenue's approach to compliance management is evolving to reflect the increasing incidence of real time tax administration."

The availability of real-time data will allow Revenue to "identify and address non-compliance as it arises", with the result that Level 1 interventions will be initiated more quickly.

In addition to its risk-based selection approach, Revenue will also operate a random audit programme to validate the integrity of the system. **Table 16.1** gives an overview of the levels of intervention.

TABLE 16.1: REVENUE COMPLIANCE INTERVENTIONS

Intervention Level	Type of Intervention	Disclosure Availability	Possible Outcome
Level 1	• Self-reviews • Profile interviews • Filing reminders (bulk issue) • Cooperative Compliance Framework actions	Unprompted qualifying disclosure	• Tax plus statutory interest • Reduced penalties (nil where self-correction remains available) • No publication of details • No prosecution
Level 2	• Risk review • Tax audit	Prompted qualifying disclosure	• Tax plus statutory interest • Reduced penalties • No publication of details • No prosecution
Level 3	Investigations	No qualifying disclosures	• Tax plus statutory interest • Higher penalties • Publication (if threshold conditions met) • Prosecution (in certain cases)

16.3.1 Level 1 Compliance Interventions

The purpose of Level 1 compliance interventions is to support taxpayers (and encourage compliance) by "reminding them of their obligations and providing them with the opportunity to correct errors without the … need for a more in-depth inquiry". Examples of Level 1 interventions include:

- reminders of outstanding returns;
- request to self-review, e.g. in real time during the submission of a review, or by letter if there is a particular issue or notification for taxpayers to be alerted to;
- profile interviews;
- engagement with businesses under a Cooperative Compliance Framework (CCF).

Level 1 interventions only occur where Revenue has not already engaged in any detailed review of the taxpayer's case. This allows the taxpayer to self-correct the error (without penalty) or to make an unprompted disclosure (see **Section 16.3.3** for more detail).

Where a Level 1 intervention gives rise to more serious issues that warrant escalation to Level 2 or Level 3 interventions, the taxpayer will receive appropriate notification; at this point the opportunity to make an unprompted qualifying disclosure ceases.

16.3.2 Level 2 Compliance Interventions

Level 2 compliance interventions comprise risk-based reviews and audits on data provided by taxpayers (from tax returns) ranging from "examination of a single issue within a return to comprehensive tax audits". They may be desk-based, i.e. conducted without a visit to the taxpayer's place of business, or field-based (generally involves a site visit, but may also be 'virtual', e.g. video-conferencing).

There are two types of Level 2 intervention:

1. **Risk Review** – "a focused intervention to examine a risk or a small number of risks on a return". For example, the risk review may focus on a particular aspect of a return.
2. **Revenue Audit** – "an examination of the compliance of a person with tax and duty legislation having particular regard to the accuracy of specific returns, statements, claims or declarations". Unlike a risk review, it is initiated where there is a greater level of perceived risk. It may focus on a single issue or tax head, or it may involve an investigation across multiple taxes and tax periods. It can also be subsequently extended to include additional issues, taxes or years/periods depending on the issues uncovered. An audit will also collect any tax in arrears.

Notification of a Level 2 Compliance Intervention

In all Level 2 interventions, a taxpayer (and their agent) will receive 28 days notification, i.e. the intervention will commence 28 days from the date of the notification letter (unless otherwise agreed between Revenue and the taxpayer). The notification letter will clearly indicate the type of compliance intervention to be undertaken, i.e. risk review or audit, and its scope (e.g. a single issue, a single tax for a specific period/year, or a comprehensive audit for multiple years/periods).

Where a risk review is escalated to an audit, the original review is regarded as ceased (and the opportunity to make a prompted disclosure is no longer available) and the audit is seen as a new intervention. As such, Revenue must issue a new notification letter and the taxpayer has a further 28 days' notice and another opportunity to make a prompted qualifying disclosure, but only in relation to the new notification (i.e. the scope of the audit).

Upon receipt of a notification letter, the taxpayer can "address areas of default or non-compliance" by making a prompted qualifying disclosure. However, once the intervention has commenced (or is deemed to have commenced) this option is no longer available. Additional time to prepare a disclosure (up to 60 days) may be available upon request.

Conduct of a Risk Review

Risk reviews were introduced by the 2022 Code and provide the taxpayer with a further opportunity to make a qualifying disclosure and mitigate penalties or other actions. The risk review is a "focused intervention to examine a risk or a small number of risks". For example, it will specify a single tax head for a specified period and focus on one aspect of that tax (rental income, say). Revenue therefore expect most risk reviews to be desk-based and performed by way of correspondence.

If a risk review has commenced and the taxpayer has not responded within the 28 days, the opportunity to make a prompted qualifying disclosure is lost. The 2022 Code states: "Revenue will make every effort to contact taxpayers and their agents to remind them of the impending commencement". If there is still no response, Revenue may look to visit the taxpayer's premises, or they may simply issue a notice of assessment of the amount of tax due.

If in the course of the review additional information comes to light which requires the widening of the intervention's scope (beyond that specified in the notification letter), the risk review may be escalated to an audit, i.e. to include other tax heads and accounting periods.

Conduct of a Revenue Audit

Once a notification of a Revenue audit has been received, the taxpayer should establish the scope of the audit so as to be properly prepared. The following should be considered when assessing the scope of the audit:

- Is it a single tax head audit, e.g. VAT or CGT, etc.? Or is it a multi-tax head audit combining a number of tax heads, e.g. VAT and relevant contracts tax (RCT)?
- Is it a comprehensive audit covering all tax heads? If yes, establish all tax heads relevant to the client.
- Is it a transaction audit, e.g. CAT business relief claim, purchase of a property? If yes, establish the specific transaction under review.
- What tax period does the audit cover?
- Have tax returns been submitted for the tax head and period under review?

At the commencement of a field audit, the Revenue auditor will identify themselves, explain the purpose of the audit and offer the taxpayer an opportunity to make a prompted qualifying disclosure. After that point the taxpayer can no longer make a qualifying disclosure.

Some of the key points pertaining to the conduct of an audit are:

- Revenue regularly use e-audit techniques to ensure that business tax returns are based on the information contained in the underlying electronic records.
- The taxpayer (or their information technology supplier) will be required to provide the necessary data downloads.
- A receipt is given for any records removed from the premises. The auditor will try not to retain any records for longer than a month. If more time is required, the taxpayer will be advised of this.
- A written record of all requested replies and other requirements, whether raised at the initial interview or subsequently, should be kept by the taxpayer to ensure the audit is conducted in an orderly way.

16.3.3 Level 3 Compliance Interventions

A Revenue investigation is the Level 3 compliance intervention. It "focuses on tackling high risk practices and cases displaying risks of suspected fraud and tax evasion". It is initiated where Revenue has "evidence or concerns of serious tax evasion", and in some cases may lead to criminal prosecution.

If during a Revenue audit serious issues or concerns come to light that warrant an escalation to a Level 3 investigation, the audit can be ceased and an investigation initiated. The taxpayer will be notified by letter, which will include the wording: "Notification of a Level 3 Compliance Intervention – Revenue Investigation". Importantly, once an investigation is initiated, the taxpayer can no longer make **any** type of qualifying disclosure and so cannot avail of any mitigation of penalties, avoid publication of final settlement or avoid possible criminal prosecution.

Revenue auditors engaged in the investigation of serious tax evasion may visit a taxpayer's place of business without advance notice, providing the appropriate notification at the visit.

16.4 Disclosures and Penalties

The legislative provisions dealing with disclosures and penalties for various tax defaults are set out in sections 1077A–1077E TCA 1997 and the 2022 Code (see **Section 16.3**) provides guidance. (The *Code of Practice* is updated regularly so it is important to ensure that the correct version is consulted depending on when the tax default at issue arises.)

16.4.1 Tax-geared Penalties

Tax-geared penalties means that the penalty is expressed as a percentage of the tax (but not the interest) in question. The default tax-geared penalty is 100% of the tax and is provided for in section 1077E TCA 1997. There are three categories of tax default to which penalties will apply. The categories are important because they determine the percentage penalty to be applied to the tax in question.

Deliberate Behaviour Penalties

Deliberate behaviour is not defined in TCA 1997 and is, therefore, given its normal meaning. In general, deliberate behaviour involves either a breach of a tax obligation with indicators consistent with intent on the part of the taxpayer, or a breach that cannot be explained solely by carelessness. The 2022 Code lists a number of indicators for this category:

- Failing to keep proper books and records required by tax law to enable the taxpayer's correct tax liability to be determined.
- Repeated omissions or a large single omission of transactions from the books and records of the business.
- Omissions from tax returns.
- Providing incomplete, false or misleading documents or information.
- Claiming a refund of tax when not lawfully entitled to that refund.
- Failing to operate fiduciary taxes (PAYE, VAT, RCT).
- Concealment of bank accounts or other assets.

The above list should not be considered exhaustive.

Careless Behaviour Penalties

"Careless" is defined in section 1077E TCA 1997 as meaning the "failure to take reasonable care". Where there is careless behaviour, the penalty to apply depends on whether that careless behaviour gave rise to significant consequences. Significant consequences is not defined in TCA 1997, but is the phrase used to describe the statutory penalty applicable where the tax underpaid exceeds 15% of the tax correctly payable.

The test of reasonable care is "whether a taxpayer of ordinary skill and knowledge, properly advised, would have foreseen as a reasonable probability or likelihood the prospect that an act (or omission) would cause a tax underpayment, having regard to all the circumstances". The taxpayer cannot avoid the responsibility of making a correct return by engaging a tax agent. If all relevant matters have not been brought to the attention of the agent, the taxpayer has not taken due care.

The 2022 Code lists a number of indicators consistent with careless behaviour on the part of the taxpayer, which includes the following (non-exhaustive) list of examples:

- estimation of accounts items;
- neglecting to categorise expenditure into allowable and disallowable categories for tax purposes;
- neglecting to take advice on an issue of interpretation where either a tax agent or Revenue should have been approached for guidance;
- whether the taxpayer obtained advice before deciding on action;

- the extent of the tax at risk – the greater the tax at risk, the greater the care required;
- the size and nature of the business;
- the internal controls in place;
- the standard of record keeping in the business;
- any systems failure and the reasons for that failure;
- the frequency of the error made.

A case involving an isolated error with minor tax implications will be viewed in a different light to a case with more frequent errors.

Careless Behaviour With Significant Consequences

Taxpayers must exercise care in fulfilling their tax obligations. Careless behaviour with significant consequences is a lack of due care rendering tax liabilities returned by the taxpayer, or repay-ment claims made, substantially incorrect. Careless behaviour with significant consequences is distinguished from deliberate behaviour by the absence of indicators in the facts and circumstances of the default, which are consistent with intent.

Careless Behaviour Without Significant Consequences

Careless behaviour without significant consequences is intended to cater for defaults of a minor nature that are discovered during many Revenue audits, for example, computational errors and inadequate adjust-ments for personal expenditure in the profit and loss account. Careless behaviour without significant con-sequences is distinguished from careless behaviour with significant consequences by the application of the "15% rule" – that is, for the behaviour to be in the tax default category of careless behaviour without significant consequences, the tax shortfall must not exceed 15% of the total tax liability.

Example 16.2

Careless behaviour	Example A	Example B
Tax payable as per incorrect tax return	€50,000	€100,000
Tax actually due	€80,000	€112,000
Tax underpaid	€30,000	€12,000

In Example A, the "careless behaviour with significant consequences" penalty applies as the tax underpaid exceeds 15% of the €80,000 ultimately due.

In Example B, the "careless behaviour without significant consequences" penalty applies as the tax underpaid does not exceed 15% of the €112,000 ultimately due.

A category of innocent error also exists where Revenue is satisfied that the tax default is not a deliberate tax default, and is not attributable in any way to the failure by the taxpayer to take reasonable care to comply with his/her tax obligations, i.e. the error was neither deliberate nor due to insufficient care on behalf of the taxpayer. Where the category of innocent error applies, no penalty is payable so long as the underpayment is €6,000 or less. Interest will, however, apply from the due date of the liability until the date of payment.

16.4.2 Concept of "Full Cooperation"

The 2022 Code and section 1077E TCA 1997 provide for mitigation of penalties where a taxpayer fully co-operates with Revenue in reaching a settlement. "Full cooperation" is indicated by:

- having all books, records and linking papers available at the commencement of the intervention;
- having appropriate personnel available at the time of the intervention;
- responding promptly to all requests for information and explanations;

- responding promptly to all correspondence; and
- prompt payment of the intervention settlement liability.

Lack of co-operation under the 2022 Code is indicated by:

- refusing reasonable access to the business premises;
- refusing reasonable access to the business records, including linking papers;
- failing to provide information known to the taxpayer which could be used in determining whether an underpayment arises; and
- delays by the taxpayer in the course of the intervention where there was no reasonable excuse for those delays.

16.4.3 Qualifying Disclosure

As set out in the 2022 Code and section 1077E(1) TCA 1997, a taxpayer can make a complete qualifying disclosure of irregular tax issues to Revenue and benefit from the following:

- non-publication of the taxpayer's name and settlement;
- non-prosecution, which is effectively a Revenue assurance that an investigation (level 3 interventon) with a view to prosecution will not be initiated; and
- mitigation of penalties, depending on the category of the tax default and the level of co-operation.

There are two forms of qualifying disclosure: prompted and unprompted.

1. Prompted Qualifying Disclosure
A prompted qualifying disclosure is available to the taxpayer where Revenue has issued a valid Revenue audit notification to the taxpayer. Where a taxpayer makes a full prompted qualifying disclosure, he or she will avail of the benefits of non-publication, Revenue assurances for non-prosecution and penalty mitigation.

In the case of a prompted disclosure, the disclosure must state the amounts of all previously undisclosed liabilities to tax and interest within the scope of the audit or audit enquiry. This may include related liabilities for tax heads or periods which are not within the scope of the intervention (see **Table 16.2** below).

2. Unprompted Qualifying Disclosure
This is an opportunity for a taxpayer to regularise their tax affairs by voluntarily disclosing any errors, omissions or irregularities giving rise to tax underpayments before notification of an audit issue, or before the taxpayer is contacted by Revenue regarding an investigation into their affairs.

Where a taxpayer makes an unprompted qualifying disclosure, they will avail of the benefits of non-publication, Revenue assurances for non-prosecution and a greater degree of penalty mitigation compared to a prompted qualifying disclosure.

In the case of all disclosures, whether prompted or unprompted, the disclosure must state the amounts of all previously undisclosed liabilities to tax, interest and penalties on foot of deliberate behaviour by the taxpayer.

In cases not involving deliberate default and where a notification has issued or a Level 2 compliance intervention is in progress, the taxpayer may still have the benefit of an unprompted qualifying disclosure in respect of tax irregularities not within the initial scope of the level 2 compliance intervention provided Revenue has not formally extended its scope.

Example 16.3

Gregory Norman, a sole trader, has a PAYE underpayment of €35,000 arising from careless internal procedures for making PAYE returns. He was selected for Revenue audit in respect of PAYE in June 2022 and opted to make a prompted qualifying disclosure in respect of the PAYE underpayment. In order to make a full and complete prompted qualifying disclosure, Gregory must ensure that he declares all tax irregularities relating to the PAYE underpayment. All careless behaviour defaults occurring in the period under audit must be disclosed before the audit commences and he must pay the tax and interest at the outset. The question of penalties can be decided later.

In 2023, Gregory finds himself the subject of an audit in respect of a CGT disposal he made in 2019. In preparation for the audit, Gregory's accountants discover that some of the items claimed as capital deductions in calculation of the CGT liability are actually revenue items. Gregory makes a prompted qualifying disclosure under the careless behaviour without significant consequences category of default. His 2022 disclosure will not be revisited as the CGT underpayment is in the category of careless behaviour without significant consequences and does not disturb the disclosure he made in 2022 in respect of the PAYE irregularities of the business under the careless behaviour category of default. The 2022 disclosure, therefore, continues to be treated as a qualifying disclosure.

Example 16.4

Smith Bros Ltd has a PAYE tax underpayment of €2 million in respect of cash payments to 20 employees working for the company for five years. The directors have knowingly omitted these workers from the payroll and have gone to some lengths in hiding all evidence from company records and accounts. The company was selected for audit in June 2022 and the directors decided to make a prompted qualifying disclosure in respect of the underpayment of €2 million. On examination of the facts, the company's accountant advised that it was likely that Revenue would categorise the irregularity as deliberate behaviour category of default and, on that basis, the company should make a full disclosure of all undisclosed liabilities to tax and interest and penalties. The company directors made the qualifying disclosure assuring the accountant that there were no other related or unrelated tax irregularities in the company.

Three years on after making the qualifying disclosure, Smith Bros Ltd comes within the terms of a Revenue investigation into a CGT deferral scheme. The company participated in an aggressive CGT tax planning scheme in 2020, which a recent High Court case has found to be in the nature of tax evasion. As the 2022 disclosure was an incomplete disclosure, Smith Bros Ltd will lose the benefits of a previously availed of qualifying disclosure, such as penalty mitigation, non-publication and non-prosecution.

The requirements for a qualifying disclosure are summarised in **Table 16.2**.

TABLE 16.2: REQUIREMENTS FOR A QUALIFYING DISCLOSURE

Category of Default	Type of Qualifying Disclosure	Requirement for a Qualifying Disclosure (accompanied by payment of tax, duty and interest but not the penalty)
Deliberate behaviour	Prompted and Unprompted	State the amounts of all liabilities to tax and interest, in respect of all tax heads and periods where liabilities arise, as a result of deliberate behaviour.
Careless behaviour	Prompted	State the amounts of all liabilities to tax and interest in respect of the relevant tax head, related liabilities and periods, within the scope of the proposed audit.
Careless behaviour	Unprompted	State the amounts of all liabilities to tax and interest, in respect of the tax head and periods the subject of the qualifying disclosure.

The essential elements of a qualifying disclosure, as set out in section 1077E TCA 1997, are:

- ▥ the disclosure must be in writing and signed by or on behalf of the taxpayer;
- ▥ the tax, duty and interest owed must be paid on submission of the disclosure; and
- ▥ a full explanation and particulars of the chargeable amounts must be included, along with a statement of the amount of tax, duties, PRSI, levies due for each period concerned.

It is important to note that, while the qualifying disclosure need not state the amount of penalties due, penalties must be agreed and subsequently paid to avoid court proceedings being instigated by Revenue.

Whether the disclosure is prompted by an audit notification or otherwise, some taxpayers are precluded from making a qualifying disclosure. Taxpayers precluded from making a qualifying disclosure include holders of accounts, persons investigated by the Moriarty or Mahon Tribunals, taxpayers within the scope of an inquiry carried out wholly or partly in public and a taxpayer with a tax irregularity related to an offshore matter. Offshore matters include accounts held outside the State, income or gains from a source outside the State and property located outside the State. Taxpayers had the opportunity to disclose tax irregularities relating to offshore matters with the full complement of qualifying disclosure benefits until 30 April 2017 under a public Revenue audit campaign. Therefore, if a tax-payer could already have availed of the benefits of penalty mitigation, non-publication and non-prosecution under special public investigations, the taxpayer may not be entitled to avail of the benefits of a qualifying disclosure on subsequent tax irregularities. However, they could still benefit from penalty mitigation by co-operating with Revenue as outlined in **Table 16.3** and from non-publication under the 2022 Code (depending on the amount of the tax default and the nature of the penalties) as discussed in the following section.

An important enhancement to the penalty mitigation arrangement is provided for under section 1077E TCA 1997. It says that, after five years, any further qualifying disclosure will be treated as if it were a first qualifying disclosure with maximum penalty mitigation. Therefore, where a qualifying disclosure is made in respect of a particular tax head and no further disclosure is made in respect of that tax head within five years, the benefits of qualifying disclosure are available to that taxpayer again on tax irregularities arising after the five-year interval.

The categories of default, penalties and mitigation under full cooperation, unprompted disclosure and prompted disclosure under section 1077E TCA 1997 and the 2022 Code are summarised in **Table 16.3**.

TABLE 16.3: PENALTIES FOR TAX DEFAULT – QUALIFYING DISCLOSURES

PENALTY TABLE A	UNPROMPTED QUALIFYING DISCLOSURE MADE		
Disclosure	Category of Behaviour	Penalty %	Full cooperation penalty reduced to
All unprompted qualifying disclosures in this category	Careless behaviour without significant consequences	20%	3% of tax/duty default
First unprompted qualifying disclosure in this category	Careless behaviour with significant consequences	40%	5% of tax/duty default
	Deliberate behaviour	100%	10% of tax/duty default
Second unprompted qualifying disclosure in this category	Careless behaviour with significant consequences	40%	20% of tax/duty default
	Deliberate behaviour	100%	55% of tax/duty default
Third or subsequent unprompted qualifying disclosure in this category	Careless behaviour with significant consequences	40%	40% of tax/duty default
	Deliberate behaviour	100%	100% of tax/duty default

PENALTY TABLE B	PROMPTED QUALIFYING DISCLOSURE MADE		
Disclosure	Category of Behaviour	Penalty %	Full cooperation penalty reduced to
All prompted qualifying disclosures in this category	Careless behaviour without significant consequences	20%	10% of tax/duty default
First prompted qualifying disclosure in this category	Careless behaviour with significant consequences	40%	20% of tax/duty default
	Deliberate behaviour	100%	50% of tax/duty default
Second prompted qualifying disclosure in this category	Careless behaviour with significant consequences	40%	30% of tax/duty default
	Deliberate behaviour	100%	75% of tax/duty default
Third or subsequent prompted qualifying disclosure in this category	Careless behaviour with significant consequences	40%	40% of tax/duty default
	Deliberate behaviour	100%	100% of tax/duty default

The penalties and mitigation where no qualifying disclosure has been made are shown in **Table 16.4**.

TABLE 16.4: PENALTIES FOR TAX DEFAULT – NO QUALIFYING DISCLOSURE

	NO QUALIFYING DISCLOSURE		
	Category of behaviour	Penalty %	Full Cooperation Penalty Reduced To
All defaults where there is no qualifying disclosure	Careless behaviour without significant consequences	20%	15%
	Careless behaviour with significant consequences	40%	30%
	Deliberate behaviour	100%	75%

16.4.4 Disclosures to Avoid Publication

Revenue is empowered to publish names of tax defaulters by reason of section 1086 TCA 1997. However, it cannot publish a taxpayer's name in relation to a default if, before any investigation or enquiry has commenced, the person has voluntarily furnished a complete qualifying disclosure in writing to the Revenue auditor. Therefore, if a disclosure is made either before an audit notification is received or, alternatively, after receipt of an audit notification but before the actual inspection commences, the making of the disclosure avoids publication.

Publication on the tax defaulters list is also avoided in cases where the aggregate of the tax settlement including the underpaid tax, interest and penalties, does not exceed €50,000 (€35,000 in respect of liabilities arising between 1 January 2017 and 1 May 2022 and €33,000 in respect of liabilities arising between 1 January 2010 and 1 January 2017). Publication is also avoided in cases where the penalty does not exceed 15% of the amount of the tax ultimately due, i.e. cases of careless behaviour without significant circumstances.

16.4.5 *If a Settlement cannot be Reached*

The penalty and mitigation provisions are provided for in section 1077E TCA 1997, which essentially puts civil penalties in audit settlements on a statutory footing. A penalty is due under the TCA 1997 if there has been:

- deliberate behaviour;
- careless behaviour with significant consequences; or
- careless behaviour without significant consequences.

A key feature of the legislation is that Revenue can instigate court proceedings where an agreement on penalties cannot be reached and thereby have the court decide on the penalty applicable to each particular case. Under section 1077B TCA 1997, Revenue can notify the taxpayer of its opinion on penalties due and, if the penalty is not agreed and paid by the taxpayer within 30 days, Revenue may refer the matter to a District Court, Circuit Court or High Court depending on the quantum of the penalty.

The benefits of non-publication are also lost if a case that qualifies for non-publication is brought before a court. This penalty determination mechanism, together with the prospect of a court hearing, will in effect provide significant additional leverage to Revenue officers in settling a compliance intervention.

If the penalty is the subject of dispute between the taxpayer and Revenue or remains unpaid, then the following procedure may be applied by Revenue:

Step 1: Based on the evidence available, a Revenue officer may form an opinion that a taxpayer is liable to a penalty.

Step 2: If the penalty is to be pursued, a Notice of Opinion will issue to the taxpayer and a copy will be sent to the taxpayer's agent.
If the taxpayer agrees with the opinion of the Revenue officer and pays the penalty, then that is the end of the matter.

Step 3: If there is no agreement on the amount of the penalty or no payment of an agreed penalty (or no response from the taxpayer) within 30 days, the Revenue officer may make an application to a relevant court for that court to determine that the taxpayer has contravened a relevant statute giving rise to a penalty.

Step 4: Where a court makes a determination that the taxpayer is liable to a penalty and makes an order for the recovery of that penalty, Revenue may collect and recover the amount in the same manner as the collection of tax.

16.5 Self-correction, No Loss of Revenue and Inability to Pay

A number of concepts and procedures are available in the 2022 Code that are very important in agreeing a tax settlement with Revenue. Each of the key concepts is now discussed.

16.5.1 *Self-correction*

The 2022 Code provides a facility for the taxpayer to self-correct for tax adjustments within certain time limits without the imposition of penalties. The conditions for self-correction are as follows:

- the taxpayer must notify Revenue in writing of the adjustments to be made;
- the taxpayer must include a computation of the correct tax and statutory interest payable;

- a payment in settlement must accompany the submission; and
- specific time limits apply for self-correction for income tax, corporation tax, CGT, VAT, PAYE/PRSI and RCT.

While this self-correction facility protects against the imposition of penalties, interest on late payment of the tax will still fall due for payment along with the extra tax payable as a result of the adjustment. Self-correction does not apply in the case of deliberate behaviour.

Income Tax, Corporation Tax and CGT

Self-correction must take place for the above taxes within 12 months of the due date for filing the return. For example, a self-correction for a corporation tax issue arising in the accounting year end of 31 December 2021 can be made within 12 months of the due date for filing the 2021 return. The 2021 return must be filed before 23 September 2022, so it follows that a self-correction can be made before 23 September 2023.

VAT

Self-correction must take place before the due date for filing the income tax or corporation tax return for the chargeable period during which the relevant VAT period is included.

> **Example 16.5**
> A business operating as a sole trader prepares annual accounts to 30 September. If that sole trader wishes to self-correct the VAT return for July–August 2022, then we must establish the accounting period in which that VAT period arises, which is the year ended 30 September 2022. This accounting period is within the tax year 2022, the income tax return for which must be filed before 31 October 2023. Therefore, a self-correction of July–August 2022 VAT return must be made on or before 31 October 2023 or within 12 months of the ROS filing deadline.

It should be noted that for bi-monthly remittances of VAT, if the net underpayment of VAT for the two-month period being corrected is less than €6,000, the amount of the tax can be included (without interest or notification to Revenue) as an adjustment to the next VAT return to be submitted.

PAYE/PRSI

The self-correction of errors or mistakes in PAYE monthly returns (income tax, PRSI and USC) must take place by the due date for filing the annual income tax/corporation tax return within which the relevant PAYE period ends. For example, a company with a 31 December 2022 year end has until 23 September 2023 to make the self-correction of an error to avoid a penalty.

16.5.2 No Loss of Revenue

"No loss of revenue" refers to the situation where, although tax was not properly accounted for by the taxpayer, there is no cost to the Exchequer as a consequence. This expression is not provided for in the legislation, but is covered in the 2022 Code, which lists a number of instances where a "no loss of revenue" claim will not be accepted, such as:

- where the default is in the deliberate behaviour category;
- where there is a general failure to operate the tax system;
- where "no loss of revenue" is not proven to the satisfaction of Revenue;
- where the taxpayer has not co-operated;
- where the "no loss of revenue" claim was not submitted in writing;
- where a "no loss of revenue" tax default penalty is not agreed and paid.

A "no loss of revenue" claim must be made by way of a qualifying disclosure.

16.5.3 Inability to Pay

Revenue acknowledge that there are cases where the financial resources of a taxpayer do not permit payment in full of the tax due. Revenue will consider such claims and will assess the taxpayer's maximum capacity to pay by reference to their assets and the earning potential of the trade, profession or employment. In considering the claim, the health and age of the taxpayer may also be relevant. All evidence that will support the claim of 'inability to pay' must be included in one comprehensive submission to Revenue. In assessing an inability to pay claim, Revenue may look for the following information:

- a signed statement of affairs reflecting the taxpayer's current situation as at the time of the settlement;
- a formal settlement offer document;
- a copy of the last accounts;
- a list of all assets held and the reason for non-disposal of these assets to pay the tax liability;
- an explanation as to why a loan cannot be raised or evidence of loan refusal;
- calculations of projected income and expenditure; and
- a signed statement confirming that the tax default giving rise to the underpaid tax has now been rectified.

Interest will continue to accumulate throughout the period of the instalment arrangement.

One of the conditions of a qualifying disclosure is that the liability due must be paid in full. Therefore, a qualifying disclosure is not accepted in inability to pay situations.

Revenue may accept a phased payment arrangement under a qualifying disclosure. A real, genuine and accepted proposal to pay the agreed liability (involving payment or an agreed phased payment arrangement made in accordance with Revenue's instalment arrangement procedures) will satisfy the payment criteria for a qualifying disclosure. Where the taxpayer fails to honour a phased payment arrangement, and Revenue are satisfied that the disclosure and intention to pay were not bona fide, the disclosure will be deemed not to be a qualifying disclosure.

16.6 Revenue Powers

We will now take a step back from the procedures and tax laws for conducting a Revenue compliance intervention and focus on the scope of Revenue's powers to seek information from the taxpayer and accountant, as well as the scope of Revenue's search and seizure powers.

16.6.1 Categories of Revenue Powers

There are three categories of Revenue powers, namely:

1. audit;
2. investigation; and
3. investigation with a view to criminal prosecution.

16.6.2 Routine Powers

Revenue regards the use of powers in an audit situation as "an exercise of routine powers". The primary legislative basis for seeking information in the course of an audit is set out in section 899 TCA 1997 as the "inspector's right to make enquiries to satisfy himself as to the accuracy of the returns made". Part 41A TCA 1997 also gives a statutory basis to the right of an inspector to make enquiries and amend assessments.

These powers are usually exercised at a pre-arranged meeting to audit the books and records of the relevant taxpayer.

16.6.3 Non-routine Powers

The second category of "non-routine powers" may be used by Revenue in the course of either an investigation or an investigation with a view to criminal prosecution. The legislative basis for these non-routine powers is to be found in sections 900 to 927 TCA 1997.

A key indicator of the type of investigation being conducted is whether or not a search warrant has been obtained. If a search warrant is obtained, then it is clear that Revenue intends to investigate the matter with a view to criminal prosecution.

Revenue also have the power to request information in respect of an unnamed taxpayer, or group or class of unnamed taxpayers. Revenue can apply for a High Court order requiring a third party or financial institution to provide information in relation to an unnamed taxpayer, or group or class of unnamed taxpayers. In certain circumstances, Revenue will be able to request that the High Court order not be disclosed to any person.

16.6.4 Revenue's Search and Seizure Powers

Revenue's search and seizure powers are to be found in the provisions governing non-routine powers.

Access to a Home
Article 40.5 of the Irish Constitution protects the inviolability of the dwelling of the citizen, guaranteeing that it "shall not be forcibly entered save in accordance with law". This provision clearly protects the home of the citizen against unlawful entry.

Revenue's main search and seizure powers broadly provide that:

■ Revenue has the right to enter any premises without a warrant, except premises wholly used as a dwelling house, and to seize documents; and
■ Revenue is also permitted to enter, search, examine and retain documents and other records for the purpose of examination. Clearly, this gives rise to an issue in relation to any premises that are partly used for domestic/business purposes, such as a home or business premises.

In general, no objective criteria need to be satisfied, such as a suspicion that an offence has been committed, before the Revenue's search and seizure powers can be exercised, except in the case of premises used wholly as a dwelling house.

Revenue is required to obtain a warrant to search premises that are "wholly used as a dwelling house". A warrant may be issued by a district judge where he or she is satisfied that it is proper to do so.

In summary, the Revenue Commissioners cannot gain access without a warrant to a taxpayer's home or that of his or her tax advisor. However, this does not preclude Revenue from arriving at a home address and seeking access by consent.

Access to a Business Premises
Revenue's main search and seizure powers are set out in sections 903, 904 and 905 TCA 1997, and broadly provide that Revenue has the right to enter any premises without a warrant, except premises wholly used as a dwelling house, as well as to seize documents. Entry without a search warrant (usually as part of an investigation) is provided for under section 905 TCA 1997.

Section 905 entitles Revenue to enter a business premises, but not a private residence, at all reasonable times:

■ without warrant or notice;
■ to inspect documents or records;

- to remove business records; and
- to require reasonable assistance, including provision of information and explanations or furnishing documents.

Section 905 permits an authorised officer to enter business premises to obtain information from a taxpayer in connection with his own tax liabilities but does not allow Revenue to use this power to seek information regarding a class of unidentified persons, i.e. customers, suppliers, etc.

Under enhanced powers introduced by section 908C TCA 1997, Revenue is entitled to obtain a search warrant which will be specifically used in cases where a criminal prosecution is intended. The person whom this power is most likely to affect is an employee, where ultimately material disclosed by the employee may be used in the criminal prosecution of his or her employer.

Under the search powers, provided a search warrant is obtained in the District Court, Revenue will be entitled to:

- search the premises;
- search any persons who are at the premises;
- search "anything" on the premises;
- require any persons found on the premises to give their name, address, occupation and produce material in their possession when requested;
- have the person explain the value and relevance of material (such as books, records or other things, including a computer) found on the premises;
- examine, seize and retain any material found on the premises and to take any necessary steps to preserve such material and to prevent interference with it; and
- where records are held on computer, request any person to direct and find such information.

16.6.5 Revenue's Information-seeking Powers

As described at **Section 16.6.2**, Revenue has general powers to make enquiries as it may deem necessary.

Additional powers are granted in sections 900, 901, 902 and 902A TCA 1997. These powers were intended for use by Revenue in "non-routine cases" to enable it to work effectively against tax evasion and the commission, or attempted commission, of tax offences. These powers enable Revenue to require books, records or certain other documents to be made available for inspection.

None of these information-seeking powers allows Revenue to carry out a "trawling exercise" in respect of any class of unidentified persons. Therefore, Revenue must have a specific enquiry in respect of a specific person or persons for which information is sought.

16.6.6 Statement of Affairs

Section 960R TCA 1997 empowers Revenue to require a taxpayer to prepare and submit a statement of affairs within 30 days of the date of the notice. A statement of affairs is a statement of the assets and liabilities of a taxpayer. This document must contain details relating to the market value of all assets and liabilities at the specified date, together with details of the taxpayer's income and expenditure. Trustees may be asked to provide a statement of affairs in respect of the assets and liabilities of a trust. The person completing the statement of affairs must also sign it and include a statutory declaration that the statement is correct to the best of that person's knowledge and belief. A statement of affairs can be used by Revenue should it commence legal proceedings against a taxpayer.

16.7 Revenue Powers and the Professional Advisor

16.7.1 Powers to Seek Information

Under Revenue's information-seeking powers, section 905(2)(c) TCA 1997 provides that no person shall be required to disclose to an authorised officer "professional advice of a confidential nature given to a client (other than advice given as part of a dishonest, fraudulent or criminal purpose)". Therefore, under these provisions, a Chartered Accountant properly advising a client would not be required to disclose any information or professional advice of a confidential nature given to a client.

However, section 908D TCA 1997 specifically provides for a District Court order to produce evidential material from third parties when investigating a criminal (Revenue) offence. The only documents that may be excluded from the scope of such an order are those that are subject to legal privilege. In the UK case, *Prudential plc v. Special Commissioner for Income Tax* (2013), the UK Supreme Court determined that legal advice privilege should not extend to communications in connection with advice given by professional people other than lawyers. Professional advice of a confidential nature given to a client by a Chartered Accountant is not protected unless it is also subject to 'legal privilege'. A Chartered Accountant who fails to comply "without reasonable excuse" with an order under section 908D TCA 1997 will be guilty of an offence and liable on summary conviction to a fine not exceeding €5,000 and/or imprisonment for a term of up to six months.

16.7.2 Revenue Powers to Report Professionals to a Professional Body

Under section 851A TCA 1997, where a Revenue officer has formed the view that the work of a tax advisor does not meet professional standards, they may report the matter and provide relevant information to the tax advisor's professional body. Any information provided to a professional body may only be used by that body for the purposes of any investigation of the matter reported.

Revenue's Tax and Duty Manual, *Failure by an Agent to meet the Professional Standards of a Professional Body – Revenue referrals to Professional Bodies under Section 851A TCA 1997* states that the following key points should be noted:

"● Only serious cases will be referred by Revenue to the relevant professional body,
● A section 851A TCA 1997 report will be made **after** the compliance intervention is finalised and closed,
● Revenue's intention to make a section 851A TCA 1997 report to the professional body will not be raised or discussed by the Revenue officer with the agent or taxpayer during the compliance intervention,
● The Accountant General's and Strategic Planning Division (AG&SPD) will issue the section 851A TCA 1997 referral to the professional body based on the information supplied by the Division,
● All referrals will be subject to approval by an Assistant Secretary."

In the context of any review of Revenue powers that may impact directly or indirectly on Chartered Accountants or tax advisors, it is important to be aware of the aiding and abetting provision. Section 1078 TCA 1997 is used against any person (being primarily financial or professional advisors) who knowingly facilitates tax or duty evasion, including attempted evasion. It is an offence if a person is:

"…knowingly concerned in the fraudulent evasion of tax or being knowingly concerned in, or being reckless as to whether or not one is concerned in, facilitating the fraudulent evasion of tax."

A person convicted of an offence under this section will be liable on summary conviction to a fine not exceeding €5,000 and/or a term of imprisonment not exceeding 12 months. On conviction on indictment, the person will be subject to a fine not exceeding €126,970 and/or a term of imprisonment not exceeding five years.

Section 1079 TCA 1997 obliges auditors and tax consultants, who become aware in the course of their normal work of material tax evasion or non-compliance committed by a client company, to report this breach to the company and request the company to either rectify the matter or report it to Revenue.

Section 1079 also provides that if, at the end of six months, it is not established to the satisfaction of the auditor or tax consultant that the matter has been so rectified or reported, the auditor must cease to act as auditor, or cease to advise the company in relation to tax matters, for a period which is the earlier of either three years from the date of the (auditor/consultant's) report to the company, or until the auditor or consultant is satisfied that the matter has been rectified or reported. Where an auditor or tax advisor resigns under this section, this fact must also be reported to Revenue. It should be noted that the section does not prevent assisting or advising a company in preparing for or conducting legal proceedings, which are pending at the end of the six-month period in question.

16.8 General Tax Avoidance Provisions

Section 811 TCA 1997 is a general anti-avoidance provision that deals with transactions that have little or no commercial reality and are primarily intended to avoid, reduce or defer a tax liability. However, where a transaction to avoid tax is undertaken in the way provided for but also **intended** by legislation, then this is not regarded as tax avoidance unless there is misuse or abuse of the legislation. Avoidance should not be confused with evasion; tax evasion is an illegal act, with the intention to not pay tax that is rightfully due.

16.8.1 *Tax Avoidance Surcharge and Interest*

Where a taxpayer is found to have entered into a tax-avoidance transaction which gives rise to a tax advantage, section 811 TCA 1997 may apply a "tax avoidance surcharge" of up to **30% of the tax advantage**. The surcharge may be reduced where a "qualifying avoidance disclosure" is made within a certain timeframe. The level of reduction of the surcharge will depend on whether or not the transaction was a "disclosable transaction" under the mandatory disclosure requirements below.

16.8.2 *Mandatory Disclosure*

The mandatory disclosure regime requires advisors or taxpayers to provide Revenue with specified information about a transaction that has certain characteristics. A taxpayer may need to confirm with their advisor whether or not a transaction is a "disclosable transaction" in order to be in a position to determine whether or not this regime will apply to them. If the transaction is a disclosable transaction, the taxpayer is obliged to include a "transaction number" (or Revenue reference number) in their return. Transaction numbers are issued by Revenue to a promoter following the submission of a valid mandatory disclosure. Where a valid mandatory disclosure submission is not made or is made late, penalties apply (see *Revenue's Guidance Notes on the Mandatory Disclosure Regime* at www.revenue.ie).

Chapter 16 Summary

Revenue compliance interventions

- Level 1 – filing reminders, self-reviews, etc. Taxpayer can make unprompted qualifying disclosures
- Level 2 - risk reviews and audits. Only prompted qualifying disclosures can be made
- Level 3 – investigations. No qualifying disclosures and possible prosecution and publication of details

Revenue audits

- Provided for under sections 1077A-1077E TCA 1997 and *Code of Practice for Revenue Compliance Interventions*
- Potential implications – tax payments, interest, penalties, publication of details and possible prosecution
- Qualifying disclosure gives a taxpayer opportunity to mitigate penalties and avoid publication and prosecution

Revenue powers

- Wide-ranging powers – audit, investigation, seek information from taxpayer and from third parties such as financial institutions
- Power to use confidential taxpayer information to report a Chartered Accountant to Professional Standards
- General tax avoidance legislation to counter tax-avoidance

Questions

Review Questions
(See Suggested Solutions to Review Questions at the end of this textbook.)

Question 16.1

James Jenner had a holiday home in Spain which he rented out from 2015 to 2019. He did not include the net foreign rental income in his yearly income tax returns. He did not make a qualifying disclosure in respect of the rental income prior to 30 April 2020.

In October 2022, James's sole trade business was the subject of a Revenue audit. During the course of preparing for the audit, he advises you that professional fee income of €50,000 was not declared in the relevant tax return.

Requirement
What options are available to James in terms of reducing his exposure to penalties, publication and prosecution?

Question 16.2

It is 26 November 2022. Your client, Dermot O'Neill, has just received notification of a Revenue audit. The audit will be in respect of VAT and income tax for the period 1 January 2021 to 31 December 2021. Dermot has advised you that, for a number of months during the audit period, he did not operate VAT on his sales. He works as a self-employed building contractor. All work undertaken by him was invoiced to corporate customers. As far as he is aware, these customers were all VAT-registered. In addition to the VAT irregularity, Dermot has indicated that it was his practice to do "the odd cash-in-hand job". He did not include these receipts in his 2020 or 2021 income tax returns.

Dermot is eager to regularise his tax affairs and co-operate with Revenue. However, he is concerned that his current inability to pay his tax will have an adverse impact on his position.

Requirement
What options are available to Dermot in terms of reducing his exposure to penalties, publication and prosecution?

Challenging Question
(Suggested Solutions to Challenging Questions are available through your lecturer.)

Question 16.1

You have received a letter of audit notification in respect of your client, Builders & Co. Ltd, on 15 June 2022 stating that an audit is to be carried out on 28 July 2022. The audit notification states that the following tax heads are under review for the purpose of the audit:

- VAT for the six periods up to and including November–December 2020;
- PAYE for the year of assessment 2020; and
- RCT for the period 1 January 2020 to 31 December 2020.

Builders & Co. Ltd is wholly owned by its two directors, Jim and Joe Jones, and has a 31 December year-end.

Following a meeting with the directors, the following information is made available to you:

- Joe and Jim have invested in an apartment in Portugal which you were not previously aware of. The apartment generated net rental income of approximately €5,000 per annum since its purchase in 2019.
- The company paid €50,000 in cash to three staff members in 2020.
- Builders & Co. Ltd took cash for "tarmac" work on a number of sites worth €100,000 in 2020.
- Builders & Co. Ltd contracted a haulage firm, Manix Ltd, for site-clearance work in 2019 and 2020. Payments totalling €200,000 were made by Builders & Co. Ltd for the contract with Manix Ltd. Builders & Co. failed to deduct RCT on payments made to Manix Ltd.

Requirement

Identify the tax issues for consideration for the audit of Builders & Co. Ltd. Outline the Revenue audit implications of the issues identified, and inform the directors of their options for making a disclosure and agreeing penalties.

Appendix 1: Summary of Tax Planning and Other Issues

This Appendix provides a high-level review of key tax issues that may require consideration in the various business circumstances that can arise. It is a summary document to help identify the key tax issues that will require consideration in any practical situation presented. It does not review and summarise the various technical aspects of each tax matter. These should be reviewed separately, either within this textbook or from previous study materials.

Sole Trader: Commencement and Operation of a Sole Trade

- Commencement to trade rules – assessment rules for new trades.
- Liability to income tax as a sole trader – consider the general exposure to income tax and at what rate (i.e. standard rate or higher rate).
- Case I/II sole trade losses – surrender tax losses against other income (aim to maximise loss relief at the highest rate of tax).
- Projected sole trader losses? It may be beneficial to continue to operate as a sole trader if losses are expected in the foreseeable future (i.e. surrender loss relief against other income).
- Computation of taxable profits – disallowed expenditure.
- Pension planning requirements and maximising tax relief.
- Will VAT registration be required?
- What rate of VAT will apply to supplies made in the course of the sole trade?
- What will the rate of VAT recovery be (i.e. 100% recovery or partial recovery)?
- Will staff be required? If so, there will be a need to register for PAYE/PRSI and operate PAYE/PRSI on all payments/benefits to staff.

The Incorporation Decision

- Will the company qualify for the start-up exemption?
- Are significant profits anticipated? The 12.5% rate of corporation tax may be attractive from a business perspective.
- Is limited liability a commercial requirement for the business?
- Transfer of a sole trade business to a limited company – transfer of a business relief is available from a CGT and a VAT perspective.
- Will property used by the business be held by a company or continue to be held personally?
- If funding is required, EIIS relief may be an option.
- Is a holding company structure required? You may wish to consider reorganisation reliefs or group relief if such a structure is required.
- Can it be structured so that the shareholders will be able to avail of entrepreneur relief?
- Company will have to register for VAT, PAYE/PRSI and corporation tax.
- Various rates of corporation tax depending on the source of the company's income.
- Close company legislation must be considered carefully.

- Scope for additional pension planning in a new company – director's pension scheme.
- Loss relief rules in a company.
- Cash extraction.
- Is there a future exit strategy from the business? Consider the implications of an asset sale versus a share sale (on exit from a business).

Funding a New Company

- Could the company qualify for EIIS investment?
- Should the company take a bank loan and repay the bank loan from after-tax profits?
- Should the company seek outside investors?
- Plan for regular tax outflows – VAT, PAYE and corporation tax payment requirements/deadlines.
- R&D tax credits – maximise tax relief and/or seek a cash refund.

Cash Extraction from a Company

- Establish the extent to which shareholders will require cash from the business – if significant cash is not needed by shareholders, the balance of cash can remain within the company.
- Maximise cash extraction at a low rate of tax.
- Salary option.
- Dividends (and deemed dividends to shareholders).
- Redundancy, if certain shareholders/employees leave the business. Termination payments could be relevant.
- Pension planning for key executives/working shareholders.
- Loans to shareholders and close company rules.
- Liquidation of the company.
- Consider the close company legislation when extracting cash/assets from a company.

Close Company Issues

- Establish if a company is a close company.
- Identify any close company surcharge issues (i.e. surcharge arising on undistributed estate and investment income within a close company).
- Election to make a dividend "non-surchargeable".
- Payments made out of the company could be deemed to be distributions in the hands of the recipients.
- Transfer of value out of a close company to its participators could also be deemed to be an income distribution.
- Loans to shareholders/participators – obligation to withhold tax on such loans and pay it over to Revenue.

Buying the Assets of a Business: Purchaser Issues

- Consider an apportionment of the purchase price between various asset classes. It may be possible to maximise the value of assets that will qualify for capital allowances (e.g. plant and machinery). The asset purchase agreement could specify the apportionment of the purchase price.

- It is not possible to purchase tax losses when the assets of a business are being acquired (as opposed to a share purchase).
- Consider the stamp duty that will arise on the purchase of assets. If the value is significant, there could be a significant stamp duty cost (7.5% of asset value).
- Consider the base cost of chargeable assets for future disposal purposes.
- VAT is likely to arise on the purchase of assets (unless transfer of a business as a going concern relief can apply). If a property is being acquired and this relief applies the VAT history of the property will be required as the purchaser will take on the VAT history of the property.

Buying the Shares of a Company: Purchaser Issues

- A due diligence review of the company will be required.
- Warranties should be sought in respect of historical tax issues.
- Is the share purchase of a single company or a holding company with more than one subsidiary?
- Has group relief been claimed in respect of assets transfer inter-group (i.e. CGT and stamp duty relief)?
- Consider the issue of latent gains within the company.
- Is there a future exit strategy from the company (or the company's assets)? Is the purchase of shares the optimal purchase option?
- Does the company have tax losses? Can these losses be claimed by the new company owner following the sale? Consider the "loss-buying" provisions and restrictions thereon.
- The 1% stamp duty rate will apply to the purchase of shares, which is often more attractive to the purchaser than the 7.5% rate on the purchase of a business/assets.
- Has the purchase price been discounted for issues within the company (i.e. tax risks, latent gains, etc.)?

Selling the Assets of a Business: Seller Issues

- Tax implications of making the sale.
- Valuation of the assets/business – how is this to be done?
- Apportionment of total consideration between various asset classifications.
- Balancing charges on the sale of assets that qualified for capital allowances – if a charge arises, this could be a significant tax cost for the seller.
- If the sale is made by a company, does the company have tax loss relief to shelter any profit/gain arising on the disposal of assets?
- Does the sale of assets/business constitute a cessation of the trade in the company?
- If the sale is made by a company, how will cash be extracted from the company?
- Could the purchaser be persuaded to purchase the shares in the company if it were a better option for the seller?

Selling the Shares of a Company: Seller Issues

- Tax implications of making the sale – most likely CGT treatment on the disposal of shares.
- Is the seller a company or an individual?
- Retirement relief might be available if shares are sold by an individual.

- Are all business assets held within the company? Are any assets (e.g. property used by the company) held personally?
- A due diligence review may be undertaken.
- Warranties may be provided in the share purchase agreement or a similar legal document.
- Full exit from the business?
- If a share sale is by a company, participation exemption may be available (section 626B TCA 1997).

Reorganisation of a Business: Company Amalgamations

- Identify situations whereby company amalgamations need to take place.
- Amalgamation could happen when a holding company structure is being put in place (perhaps to replace a cluster of personally held companies).
- Amalgamation could occur on a merger of two third-party companies/groups.
- Amalgamation could be a restructuring opportunity to tidy up a complex corporate group.
- Key CGT issue – the transfer of shares will constitute a disposal of a chargeable asset for CGT purposes – amalgamation relief is available so that the transfer does not trigger CGT on the disposal of the shares.
- Stamp duty should arise on the acquisition of shares – amalgamation relief allows an exemption from stamp duty on foot of a bona fide amalgamation.
- Note that the acquiring company must obtain control of the target company, the restructuring must be undertaken for bona fide commercial reasons and that the stamp duty relief requires that shares being issued in the acquiring company must represent at least 90% of the value of the target company.

Reorganisation of a Business: Transfer of a Business

- Identify situations where a transfer of an undertaking could take place.
- The transfer involves the transfer of a business to a new company in exchange for the issue of shares in the new company to the transferor (or the holder of shares in the transferring company).
- While group relief could be claimed to facilitate the same transfer, there is however a 10-year clawback period. There is no clawback period associated with the transfer of an undertaking relief, provided there is a reorganisation that satisfies the conditions in section 615 TCA 1997. If so, the undertaking can be transferred to the new company (at which time it is not in the group) in return for shares in the new company, and no CGT will arise as the assets transfer at no gain/no loss.

VAT: General Business Issues

- Is VAT registration required?
- What rate of VAT will apply to supplies?
- Does the company/trader have full VAT recovery? If not, are they appropriately computing the level of VAT that is not recoverable?
- Is the company's VAT history in order (e.g. outstanding/late returns, etc.)?
- Does the company incorrectly claim back VAT on non-allowable items (e.g. petrol, hotel costs, entertainment, purchase/hire of passenger cars, etc.)?
- When was the company's last VAT audit? This could be an indicator of possible VAT issues.
- How does the company treat items for which they have to self-account for VAT?

PAYE: General Business Issues

- Is the operation of PAYE by the employer correct?
- Does the company have a good compliance history (e.g. no late returns, etc.)?
- Does the company pay cash to employees?
- Is PAYE operated on all payments to shareholders/directors? If not, are all other payments treated as distributions to shareholders? The close company rules are also relevant here if the company is a close company.
- Does the employer retain all required records in respect of expense payments made to staff?
- Does the employer pay unvouched expenses to staff members?
- Does the employer have payroll/BIK/redundancy policies?
- Have redundancy payments been computed correctly?

Corporation Tax: General Business Issues

- Has the company met its preliminary tax requirements?
- Does the company have expense items which must be added back for computational purposes?
- Does the company intend to sell valuable assets? Exposure to a balancing charge may apply if capital allowances have been claimed.
- Is loss relief available?
- Consider the order of loss relief.
- Is group relief available for surrender/claim?
- Is there a close company surcharge exposure?

Investor Wishing to Enter a Business: Typical Tax Considerations

- How will the investor take a holding in the company?
- Issue of new share capital by company to investor.
- Loan notes (with or without interest applying) and small shareholding.
- Loan notes only (with interest applying).
- Purchase of shares from existing shareholder.
- Repayment of an interest-free loan note can be received tax-free by the investor.
- If shares are purchased, the base cost on a future disposal of shares will be the purchase price.
- If a nominal shareholding is taken (e.g. 100 shares for €100 which will equal a % shareholding in the business), the base cost on the future disposal of shares is nominal (i.e. full exposure to a gain).
- Could the investor use a holding company to purchase shares in a target company? If so, there could be potential to make use of section 626B TCA 1997 participation exemption on a future disposal.
- Will a due diligence review be required?
- Can the shareholder take a small holding now with an option to purchase a further interest at a later date?
- Importance of the investors establishing a future exit strategy from the business (including their intended term of holding the investment).
- Is a restructuring of the business required prior to the investor investing funds? (For example, a holding company may be put in place to take ownership of a group of companies, so that the investor can take an interest in the whole group.)

Investor/Shareholder Wishing to Exit a Business: Typical Tax Considerations

- Are there any loans owing by the company to the shareholder due for repayment? The repayment of these loans is likely to involve a tax-free reimbursement of funds.
- If a share sale is planned, will retirement relief be available?
- Is entrepreneurs' relief available on the sale of shares or assets?
- Is a restructuring or a reorganisation of the business required prior to exit of the shareholder?
- What is the base cost of the shares held for CGT purposes?
- Will the shares be sold to a connected party? If sold at an undervalue, the market value will be deemed to be the sale price.
- Will the timing of the share sale be relevant? It may be required to take into account the CGT payment deadlines prior to completing the share sale.
- If a company is making the share disposal, will the participation exemption be available?
- If a full exit from a business is planned by way of company asset/trade sale, how will the shareholder extract the post-sale funds from the company? An exposure to double taxation must be considered in this scenario.

Appendix 2: Taxation Reference Material for Tax Year 2022

Table of Contents

INCOME TAX, USC & PRSI

Income Tax Rates 2022

Single/Widowed/ Surviving Civil Partner with Qualifying Children	Rate	Single/Widowed/ Surviving Civil Partner without Qualifying Children	Rate	Married Couple/ Civil Partners	Rate
First €40,800	20%	First €36,800	20%	First €45,800/€73,600[1]	20%
Balance	40%	Balance	40%	Balance	40%

[1] Depending on personal circumstances of married couple/civil partners.

Non-refundable Tax Credits 2022

	Tax Credit
	€
Single person	1,700
Married couple/civil partners	3,400
Widowed person/surviving civil partner (year of bereavement)	3,400
Widowed person/surviving civil partner tax credit – no dependent children	2,240
Widowed person/surviving civil partner tax credit – with dependent children	1,700
Single Person Child Carer Credit (additional)	1,650
Widowed parent/surviving civil partner tax credit – with dependent children	
Year 1 after the year of bereavement	3,600
Year 2 after the year of bereavement	3,150
Year 3 after the year of bereavement	2,700
Year 4 after the year of bereavement	2,250
Year 5 after the year of bereavement	1,800
Employee tax credit	1,700
Earned Income Tax Credit	1,700
Sea going naval personnel credit	1,500
Fisher Tax Credit (maximum)	1,270
Age tax credit – single/widowed/surviving civil partner	245
Age tax credit – married/civil partners	490
Incapacitated child tax credit	3,300
Dependent relative – income limit €15,740	245
Home carer's credit – income limit €7,200 (lower)/ €10,400 (upper)	1,600
Blind person	1,650
Both spouses/civil partners blind	3,300
Third-level education fees[1]:	
Full-time course	800
Part-time course	1,100

[1] There is a maximum level of qualifying fees, per academic year, of €7,000 per student, per course, subject to the first €3,000 (full-time) or €1,500 (part-time) being disallowed (per claim, not per course). Relief is at the standard rate of tax on the amount of the qualifying fees.

Income Tax Allowances and Reliefs 2022

Deduction for employed person taking care of incapacitated person (maximum)	€75,000
Provision of childcare services	income limit €15,000
Rent-a-Room relief (maximum)	€14,000

Income Tax Exemption Limits for Persons Aged 65 and Over 2022

	€
Single/widowed/surviving civil partner	18,000[1]
Married/civil partners	36,000[1]

[1] Dependent children: increase exemption by €575 for each of first two, and by €830 for each additional child.

Pension Contributions

The maximum amount on which tax relief may be claimed in 2022 in respect of qualifying premiums is as follows:

Age	% of Net Relevant Earnings[1]
Under 30 years of age	15%
30 to 39 years of age	20%
40 to 49 years of age	25%
50 to 54 years of age	30%
55 to 59 years of age	35%
60 years and over	40%

[1] The earnings cap for 2022 on net relevant earnings is €115,000.

Preferential Loans

The specified rates for 2022 are:

- 4% in respect of qualifying home loans;
- 13.5% in respect of all other loans.

Motor Car Benefit in Kind

Annual Business Kilometres	Cash Equivalent (% of OMV)
24,000 or less	30%
24,001–32,000	24%
32,001–40,000	18%
40,001–48,000	12%
48,001 and over	6%

Motor Vehicle Category Based on CO_2 Emissions

Vehicle Category	CO_2 Emissions (CO_2 g/km)
A/B	0g/km up to and including 140g/km
C	141g/km up to and including 155g/km
D/E/F	156g/km and upwards

Restricted Cost for Motor Lease Expenses

Restricted Cost of Passenger Motor Vehicle for Capital Allowances and Motor Leases Expenses Restriction Purposes

Specified Limit	€
From 1 January 2007	24,000

Restricted Cost for Motor Vehicles bought on/after 1 July 2008

Category	CO_2 Emissions	Restriction
A/B	0–140g/km	Use the specified amount regardless of cost.
C	141–155g/km	Two steps to calculate limit: 1. take the lower of the specified limit or cost; 2. limit is 50% of this amount.
D/E/F	155+g/km	No allowance available.

Capital Allowances

Plant and Machinery

Expenditure incurred on or after 4 December 2002:

Plant and machinery	12.5% straight-line
Cars other than those used as a taxi or in car-hire business	12.5% straight-line

Industrial Buildings

Expenditure incurred on or after 1 April 1992	4% straight-line

Civil Service Mileage and Subsistence Rates

Motor Car Travel Rates (effective from 1 April 2017)

Official Motor Travel in a calendar year	Engine Capacity		
	Up to 1,200cc	1,201cc–1,500cc	1,501cc and over
0–1,500km	37.95 cent per km	39.86 cent per km	44.79 cent per km
1,501–5,500km	70.00 cent per km	73.21 cent per km	83.53 cent per km
5,501–25,000km	27.55 cent per km	29.03 cent per km	32.21 cent per km
Over 25,001km	21.36 cent per km	22.23 cent per km	25.85 cent per km

Motor Cycle Travel Rates

Official Motor Travel in a calendar year	Engine Capacity			
	Up to 150cc	151cc to 250cc	251cc to 600cc	601cc and over
Up to 6,437km	14.48 cent per km	20.10 cent per km	23.72 cent per km	28.59 cent per km
Over 6,437km	9.37 cent per km	13.31 cent per km	15.29 cent per km	17.60 cent per km

Subsistence Rates

Overnight Allowances[1] (from 1 October 2018)			Day Allowances[2] (from 1 December 2021)	
Normal rate (up to 14 nights)	Reduced rate (next 14 nights)	Detention rate (next 28 nights)	10 hours or more	5 hours (but less than 10 hours)
€147.00	€132.30	€73.50	€39.08	€16.29

[1] Night allowance: the employee is at least 100km away from their home or place of work and covers a period of up to 24 hours from the time of departure, and any further period not exceeding five hours.
[2] Day allowance: the employee is at least 8km away from their home or normal place of work.

Universal Social Charge 2022

Employment Income

The rates of USC (where gross income is greater than €13,000 per annum) are:

Rate of USC	Annual Income	Monthly Income	Weekly Income
0.5%	First €12,012	First €1,001	First €231
2.0%	€12,013–€21,295	€1,002–€1,775	€232–€410
4.5%[1,2]	€21,296–€70,044	€1,776–€5,837	€411–€1,347
8.0%[1,2]	Balance	Balance	Balance

[1] Persons aged 70 years and over with income of €60,000 or less are not liable at the 4.5%/8% rates but instead pay at 2.0%.
[2] Persons who hold a full medical card and with income of €60,000 or less are not liable at the 4.5% or 8% rates but instead pay at 2.0%.

Exempt Categories

- Where an individual's total income for a year does not exceed €13,000.
- All Department of Social Protection payments.
- Income already subjected to DIRT.

Self-assessed Individuals

The rates of USC (where gross income is greater than €13,000 per annum) are:

	Aged under 70/Aged 70 and over with income >€60,000/Full medical card holder with income >€60,000	Aged 70 and over with income of €60,000 or less/Full medical card holder with income of €60,000 or less
First €12,012	0.5%	0.5%
Next €9,283	2.0%	2.0%
Next €48,749	4.5%	2.0% (max. €38,705)
Balance[1]	8.0%	N/A

[1] An additional USC charge of 3% is payable by individuals on self-assessed income (excluding employment income) in excess of €100,000 in a year, regardless of age.

Surcharge on Use of Property Incentives

There is also an additional USC surcharge of 5% on investors with gross income greater than €100,000 where certain property tax reliefs have been used to shelter taxable income.

PRSI 2022

Employees' and Employers' Rates

Employee's income	Employee rate	Employers' rate
Income of €38–€352 per week	Nil	8.8%
Income of €352–€410 per week	4%	8.8%
Income greater than €410 per week	4%	11.05%

Employee PRSI Credit

An employee PRSI credit of a maximum of €12 per week is available to Class A employees with gross earnings between €352.01 and €424 per week. The credit is reduced by one-sixth of gross earnings in excess of €352 per week. The reduced credit is then deducted from the employee PRSI liability calculated at 4% of gross weekly earnings.

Self-employed

Individuals in receipt of income of €5,000 or less in 2022 will not be subject to PRSI. Where income is greater than €5,000, PRSI at 4% is payable subject to a minimum contribution of €500. For those with an annual self-employed income of in excess of €5,000 but who have no net liability to tax, the minimum contribution is €300 for 2022 (payable directly to the Department of Social Protection).

LOCAL PROPERTY TAX

Valuation Table 2022

Valuation Band Number	Valuation Band €	Mid-point of Valuation Band €	LPT in 2022 (full-year charge) €
01	0 to 200,000	N/A	90
02	200,001 to 262,500	N/A	225
03	262,501 to 350,000	306,250	315
04	350,001 to 437,500	393,750	405
05	437,501 to 525,000	481,251	495
06	525,001 to 612,500	568,751	585
07	612,501 to 700,000	656,251	675
08	700,001 to 787,500	743,751	765
09	787,501 to 875,000	831,251	855
10	875,001 to 962,500	918,751	945
11	962,501 to 1,050,000	1,006,251	1,035
12	1,050,001 to 1,137,500	1,093,750	1,190

continued overleaf

Valuation Band Number	Valuation Band €	Mid-point of Valuation Band €	LPT in 2022 (full-year charge) €
13	1,137,501 to 1,225,000	1,181,251	1,409
14	1,225,001 to 1,312,500	1,268,751	1,627
15	1,312,501 to 1,400,000	1,356,251	1,846
16	1,400,001 to 1,487,500	1,443,751	2,064
17	1,487,501 to 1,575,000	1,531,251	2,284
18	1,575,001 to 1,662,500	1,618,751	2,502
19	1,662,501 to 1,750,000	1,706,251	2,721
20	1,750,001 +	N/A	2,830 +

Local Adjustment Factors 2022

The local adjustment factor (LAF) increasing or decreasing the basic LPT rate in operation for 2022:

Local Authority	LPT Rate Adjustment
Carlow County Council	5% increase
Cavan County Council	15% increase
Clare County Council	15% increase
Cork City Council	9% increase
Cork County Council	7.5% increase
Donegal County Council	15% increase
Dublin City Council	15% decrease
Dún Laoghaire–Rathdown County Council	15% decrease
Fingal County Council	10% decrease
Kerry County Council	7.5% increase
Kildare County Council	10% increase
Kilkenny County Council	15% increase
Laois County Council	10% increase
Leitrim County Council	15% increase
Limerick City & County Council	15% increase
Longford County Council	15% increase
Mayo County Council	10% increase
Monaghan County Council	15% increase
Offaly County Council	15% increase
Roscommon County Council	15% increase
Sligo County Council	15% increase
South Dublin County Council	15% decrease
Tipperary County Council	10% increase
Waterford City & County Council	10% increase
Wexford County Council	10% increase
Wicklow County Council	6% increase

CORPORATION TAX

Rates of Corporation Tax

Trading Rate of Corporation Tax

The trading rate of corporation tax is **12.5**% and applies to the following income and gains:

- Schedule D, Case I and Case II profits;
- capital gains (as adjusted); and
- certain foreign dividends.

Passive Rate of Corporation Tax

The passive rate of corporation tax is 25% applies to the following sources of income:

- Case III income, i.e. foreign income and untaxed Irish interest (excluding certain foreign dividends taxable at 12.5%);
- Case IV income, i.e. taxed Irish income and miscellaneous income not taxed under any other Case of Schedule D;
- Case V income, i.e. Irish rental income; and
- income from an "excepted trade".

CAPITAL GAINS TAX

Rates and Annual Exemption

	Rate
Disposals on or after 6 December 2012	33%
Disposals on or after 7 December 2011 and before 6 December 2012	30%
Disposals on or after 8 April 2009 and before 7 December 2011	25%
Annual exempt amount for 2022 is €1,270	
Where revised entrepreneur relief applies:	
Disposals on or after 1 January 2017	10%
Disposals on or after 1 January 2016 and before 1 January 2017 20%	20%

Indexation Factors

Year of Assessment in which Expenditure Incurred	5 April 1997	5 April 1998	5 April 1999	5 April 2000	5 April 2001	31 Dec 2001	31 Dec 2002	31 Dec 2003 et seq.
1974/75	6.017	6.112	6.215	6.313	6.582	6.930	7.180	7.528
1975/76	4.860	4.936	5.020	5.099	5.316	5.597	5.799	6.080
1976/77	4.187	4.253	4.325	4.393	4.580	4.822	4.996	5.238
1977/78	3.589	3.646	3.707	3.766	3.926	4.133	4.283	4.490
1978/79	3.316	3.368	3.425	3.479	3.627	3.819	3.956	4.148
1979/80	2.992	3.039	3.090	3.139	3.272	3.445	3.570	3.742
1980/81	2.590	2.631	2.675	2.718	2.833	2.983	3.091	3.240
1981/82	2.141	2.174	2.211	2.246	2.342	2.465	2.554	2.678
1982/83	1.801	1.829	1.860	1.890	1.970	2.074	2.149	2.253
1983/84	1.601	1.627	1.654	1.680	1.752	1.844	1.911	2.003
1984/85	1.454	1.477	1.502	1.525	1.590	1.674	1.735	1.819
1985/86	1.369	1.390	1.414	1.436	1.497	1.577	1.633	1.713
1986/87	1.309	1.330	1.352	1.373	1.432	1.507	1.562	1.637
1987/88	1.266	1.285	1.307	1.328	1.384	1.457	1.510	1.583
1988/89	1.242	1.261	1.282	1.303	1.358	1.430	1.481	1.553
1989/90	1.202	1.221	1.241	1.261	1.314	1.384	1.434	1.503
1990/91	1.153	1.171	1.191	1.210	1.261	1.328	1.376	1.442
1991/92	1.124	1.142	1.161	1.179	1.229	1.294	1.341	1.406
1992/93	1.084	1.101	1.120	1.138	1.186	1.249	1.294	1.356
1993/94	1.064	1.081	1.099	1.117	1.164	1.226	1.270	1.331
1994/95	1.046	1.063	1.081	1.098	1.144	1.205	1.248	1.309
1995/96	1.021	1.037	1.054	1.071	1.116	1.175	1.218	1.277
1996/97	-	1.016	1.033	1.050	1.094	1.152	1.194	1.251
1997/98	-	-	1.017	1.033	1.077	1.134	1.175	1.232
1998/99	-	-	-	1.016	1.059	1.115	1.156	1.212
1999/00	-	-	-	-	1.043	1.098	1.138	1.193
2000/01	-	-	-	-	-	1.053	1.091	1.144
2001	-	-	-	-	-	-	1.037	1.087
2002	-	-	-	-	-	-	-	1.049
2003 et seq.	-	-	-	-	-	-	-	1.000

VAT

VAT Rate	Examples
Exempt	▪ Medical, dental and optical services ▪ Insurance services ▪ Certain banking services ▪ Educational services ▪ Funeral services ▪ Gambling and lotteries ▪ Transport of passengers (and their baggage) ▪ Certain lettings of immovable goods
Zero rate	▪ Supply of most foodstuffs (excluding those specifically liable at the standard rate) ▪ Printed books and booklets (excluding stationery, brochures, etc.) ▪ Most clothing and footwear for children under 11 years of age ▪ Oral medicine (excluding food supplements) ▪ Exported goods (i.e. despatched outside the EU) ▪ Sea-going ships (more than 15 tonnes) ▪ Fertilizer ▪ Animal feed, other than pet food
Standard rate (23%)	All goods and services that are not exempt or zero-rated, or are not liable at the other specific rates. Includes: ▪ Alcohol, soft drinks, bottled drinking water, juices ▪ Chocolate and confectionery, biscuits, crisps, ice cream and similar ▪ Adult clothing and footwear ▪ Office equipment and stationery
Reduced rate (13.5%)	▪ Fuel for power and heating (coal, peat, etc.) ▪ Supply of electricity and gas ▪ Waste disposal services ▪ Non-residential immovable goods, including supply and development ▪ Supply of concrete and concrete goods ▪ Repair and maintenance of movable goods ▪ General agricultural and veterinary services ▪ Short-term hire of cars, boats, caravans, etc. ▪ Food supplements ▪ Driving instruction ▪ Supply and hire of live horses and greyhounds
Second reduced rate (9%)	▪ Subscriptions for certain sporting activities ▪ Hairdressing services ▪ Printed newspapers, e-newspapers, magazines and periodicals and e-books ▪ Supply of hot food, including take-away food ▪ Hotel/holiday accommodation, including caravan parks and camping sites ▪ Admission to cinemas, theatres, certain musical performances, museums and fairground amusements
Farmer flat-rate addition (5.5%)	Supply of agricultural products and services by non-VAT-registered farmers to VAT-registered customers
Livestock rate (4.8%)	▪ Supply of livestock ▪ Supply of horses intended for foodstuffs

STAMP DUTY

Rates 2022

	Rate
Shares	1%
Residential property:	
Consideration up to €1m	1%
Excess over €1m	2%
10 or more houses/duplexes in 12 months*	10%
Non-residential property	7.5%

* With effect from 20 May 2021.

CAPITAL ACQUISITIONS TAX

Rates

	Rate
Benefits taken on or after 6 December 2012	33%
Benefits taken on or after 7 December 2011 and before 6 December 2012	30%
Benefits taken on or after 8 April 2009 and before 7 December 2011	25%

Exemption Thresholds

	Group Threshold		
	A	B	C
Benefits taken on or after 9 October 2019	335,000	32,500	16,250
Benefits taken on or after 10 October 2018	320,000	32,500	16,250
Benefits taken on or after 12 October 2016	310,000	32,500	16,250
Benefits taken on or after 14 October 2015 and before 12 October 2016	280,000	30,150	15,075
Benefits taken on or after 6 December 2012 and before 14 October 2015	225,000	30,150	15,075
Benefits taken on or after 7 December 2011 and before 6 December 2012	250,000	33,500	16,750
Benefits taken on or after 8 December 2010 and before 7 December 2011	332,084	33,208	16,604

Limited Interest Factors

Table A

1	2	3	4 ·
Years of Age	Joint Factor	Value of an interest in a capital of €1 for a **male** life aged as in Column 1	Value of an interest in a capital of €1 for a **female** life aged as in Column 1
0	.99	.9519	.9624
1	.99	.9767	.9817
2	.99	.9767	.9819

continued overleaf

1	2	3	4
Years of Age	Joint Factor	Value of an interest in a capital of €1 for a **male** life aged as in Column 1	Value of an interest in a capital of €1 for a **female** life aged as in Column 1
3	.99	.9762	.9817
4	.99	.9753	.9811
5	.99	.9742	.9805
6	.99	.9730	.9797
7	.99	.9717	.9787
8	.99	.9703	.9777
9	.99	.9688	.9765
10	.99	.9671	.9753
11	.98	.9653	.9740
12	.98	.9634	.9726
13	.98	.9614	.9710
14	.98	.9592	.9693
15	.98	.9569	.9676
16	.98	.9546	.9657
17	.98	.9522	.9638
18	.98	.9497	.9617
19	.98	.9471	.9596
20	.97	.9444	.9572
21	.97	.9416	.9547
22	.97	.9387	.9521
23	.97	.9356	.9493
24	.97	.9323	.9464
25	.97	.9288	.9432
26	.97	.9250	.9399
27	.97	.9209	.9364
28	.97	.9165	.9328
29	.97	.9119	.9289
30	.96	.9068	.9248
31	.96	.9015	.9205
32	.96	.8958	.9159
33	.96	.8899	.9111
34	.96	.8836	.9059

continued overleaf

1	2	3	4
Years of Age	Joint Factor	Value of an interest in a capital of €1 for a **male** life aged as in Column 1	Value of an interest in a capital of €1 for a **female** life aged as in Column 1
35	.96	.8770	.9005
36	.96	.8699	.8947
37	.96	.8626	.8886
38	.95	.8549	.8821
39	.95	.8469	.8753
40	.95	.8384	.8683
41	.95	.8296	.8610
42	.95	.8204	.8534
43	.95	.8107	.8454
44	.94	.8005	.8370
45	.94	.7897	.8283
46	.94	.7783	.8192
47	.94	.7663	.8096
48	.93	.7541	.7997
49	.93	.7415	.7896
50	.92	.7287	.7791
51	.91	.7156	.7683
52	.90	.7024	.7572
53	.89	.6887	.7456
54	.89	.6745	.7335
55	.88	.6598	.7206
56	.88	.6445	.7069
57	.88	.6288	.6926
58	.87	.6129	.6778
59	.86	.5969	.6628
60	.86	.5809	.6475
61	.86	.5650	.6320
62	.86	.5492	.6162
63	.85	.5332	.6000
64	.85	.5171	.5830

continued overleaf

1	2	3	4
Years of Age	Joint Factor	Value of an interest in a capital of €1 for a **male** life aged as in Column 1	Value of an interest in a capital of €1 for a **female** life aged as in Column 1
65	.85	.5007	.5650
66	.85	.4841	.5462
67	.84	.4673	.5266
68	.84	.4506	.5070
69	.84	.4339	.4873
70	.83	.4173	.4679
71	.83	.4009	.4488
72	.82	.3846	.4301
73	.82	.3683	.4114
74	.81	.3519	.3928
75	.80	.3352	.3743
76	.79	.3181	.3559
77	.78	.3009	.3377
78	.76	.2838	.3198
79	.74	.2671	.3023
80	.72	.2509	.2855
81	.71	.2353	.2693
82	.70	.2203	.2538
83	.69	.2057	.2387
84	.68	.1916	.2242
85	.67	.1783	.2104
86	.66	.1657	.1973
87	.65	.1537	.1849
88	.64	.1423	.1730
89	.62	.1315	.1616
90	.60	.1212	.1509
91	.58	.1116	.1407
92	.56	.1025	.1310
93	.54	.0939	.1218
94	.52	.0858	.1132
95	.50	.0781	.1050
96	.49	.0710	.0972

continued overleaf

1	2	3	4
Years of Age	Joint Factor	Value of an interest in a capital of €1 for a **male** life aged as in Column 1	Value of an interest in a capital of €1 for a **female** life aged as in Column 1
97	.48	.0642	.0898
98	.47	.0578	.0828
99	.45	.0517	.0762
100 or over	.43	.0458	.0698

Table B

(Column 2 shows the value of an interest in a capital of €1 for the number of years shown in Column 1.)

1	2	1	2
Number of years	Value	Number of years	Value
1	.0654	26	.8263
2	.1265	27	.8375
3	.1836	28	.8480
4	.2370	29	.8578
5	.2869	30	.8669
6	.3335	31	.8754
7	.3770	32	.8834
8	.4177	33	.8908
9	.4557	34	.8978
10	.4913	35	.9043
11	.5245	36	.9100
12	.5555	37	.9165
13	.5845	38	.9230
14	.6116	39	.9295
15	.6369	40	.9360
16	.6605	41	.9425
17	.6826	42	.9490
18	.7032	43	.9555
19	.7225	44	.9620
20	.7405	45	.9685
21	.7574	46	.9750
22	.7731	47	.9815
23	.7878	48	.9880
24	.8015	49	.9945
25	.8144	50 and over	1.000

Suggested Solutions to Review Questions

Chapter 1

Question 1.1

Terminal loss relief calculation for last 12 months of trading:

	€
Case I loss for 6 m/e 30 June 2023	55,000
Case I loss for 6 m/e 30 June 2022 (€5,000 × 6/12)	2,500
Terminal loss relief available	57,500

Application of terminal loss relief:

	2022	2021	2020
	€	€	€
Case 1	0	25,000	22,000
Sec 385 relief	0	(25,000)	(22,000)
Net assessable Case I	0	0	

Unutilised loss is €10,500 (€57,500 – €25,000 – €22,000).

Chapter 4

Question 4.1

(a) When a liquidator is appointed, they take beneficial ownership of the assets of the company. During the winding up, when the liquidator disposes of the assets legally owned by the company. The liquidator is liable to pay any corporation tax arising on gains (or CGT on disposal of development land) and is required to file the necessary return to Revenue.

(b) When a liquidator is appointed, an accounting period ends. Therefore, corporation tax returns need to be filed for the year ended 30 June 2022 and the period ended 15 September 2022. The return for the period ended 15 September 2022 is due within three months, i.e. by 15 December 2022. The return for the year ended 30 June 2022 is normally due by 23 March 2023. However, due to the commencement of the winding up of the company, the due date is brought forward to three months after the commencement of the winding up of the company, i.e. within three months of 15 September–15 December 2022.

(c) As the shares in Burst Ltd now have no value, John can make a negligible value claim. He can get CGT loss relief for the unrealised capital loss of €50,000 in 2022 by making a claim to Revenue. When the liquidation is complete and the company is dissolved, at that stage the shareholder will have made a disposal of shares for CGT purposes (when an asset ceases to exist this is a disposal for CGT purposes) and could claim relief for the loss on shares without having to make a negligible value claim.

Chapter 5

Question 5.1

(a) OIL Ltd's excess of management expenses over the total profits for the accounting period is €11,800. Management expenses do not include any amounts carried forward from earlier periods. So, in this case, the €2,500 management expenses brought forward from the previous accounting period are disregarded.

Calculation of OIL Ltd's excess management expenses for the purposes of group relief:

	€
Current-year management expenses	15,000
Less: Case III income	(3,200)
Excess management expenses	11,800

GAS Ltd's total profit, as reduced by other reliefs, is €9,400, calculated as follows:

	€
Trading profits	10,000
Less: charges paid	(600)
Total profits as reduced by other reliefs	9,400

The group relief is limited to the smaller of €11,800 and €9,400, i.e. €9,400.

(b) OIL Ltd's corporation tax computation for the accounting period to 31 March 2022 is as follows:

	€
Case III income	3,200
Less: management expenses	(3,200)
Corporation tax profits	Nil

OIL Ltd's carry forward position as at 31 March 2022 is as follows:

	€	€
Management expenses (including amounts brought forward from earlier periods)		17,500
Less: allowed in computation	(3,200)	
Less: Surrendered as group relief	(9,400)	(12,600)
Excess management expenses available to carry forward		4,900

GAS Ltd's revised profits chargeable to corporation tax for the accounting period to 31 March 2022 are as follows:

	€	€
Case I income		10,000
Less: charges	(600)	
Less: group relief claimed	(9,400)	(10,000)
Revised corporation tax profits		Nil

Question 5.2

First, compute Company B's excess charges over the gross profits for the accounting period.

The total profits are calculated without taking into account losses of any other period. However, chargeable gains are calculated according to CGT principles prior to being brought into the company's total profits. Thus, the allowable losses carried forward reduce the current-year gains to give a net figure. This capital gain is recomputed as the chargeable gain for inclusion in the company's total profits, i.e. the capital gain of €3,200 is reduced by the €1,800 capital losses brought forward and then the factor of 33%/12.5% is applied to give a chargeable gain of €3,696.

Calculation of Company B's excess non-trade charges:	€	€
Charges		5,500
Chargeable gain recomputed	3,696	
Case III	1,000	
Less: Management expenses	(2,000)	2,696
Excess charges		2,804

Company A's total profit as reduced by other reliefs is €1,300, calculated as follows:

	€	€
Trading profits		1,000
Case III income	500	
Less: charges paid (used to offset higher rate income first)	(200)	300
Total profits as reduced by other reliefs		1,300

The group relief is limited to the lesser of €2,804 and €1,300. Therefore, Company A can claim a maximum amount of €1,300.

Question 5.3

(a) The maximum amount of losses available for consortium relief for each company is:

  ▨ Tree Ltd has losses of €400,000 available. This must first be offset against other relevant trading income under section 420A TCA 1997 before it can be used in any value-based claim. €90,000 of the losses can be used in a value-based claim under section 420B to offset the Case III income.
  ▨ As Garden Ltd and Tree Ltd have an overlapping period of nine months, the maximum losses available are:
    ● 9 months × €290,000 = €217,500; or
    ● 9 months × €400,000 × 40% = €120,000.
    Maximum loss available under section 420A is €120,000.
  ▨ Park Ltd – €200,000 or €400,000 × 10% = €40,000. Maximum loss available under section 420A is €40,000.
  ▨ Pitch Ltd – €160,000 or €400,000 × 30% = €120,000. Maximum loss is €120,000 under section 420A. A claim under section 420B TCA 1997 is also possible and the maximum loss is the loss available for surrender (i.e. €400k − €120k − €40k − €120k − €90k = €30,000) or

(€40,000 × 30%) @ 25%/12.5% (i.e. the amount of loss which needs to be claimed to reduce corporation tax on 30% of Case III to €Nil) = €24,000. Maximum claim under section 420B is €24,000.

This will ensure all of Tree Ltd's loss is used to the maximum extent possible and €6,000 is available for carry forward:

- under section 396B   €90,000
- under section 420A   €280,000
- under section 420B   €24,000
- carry forward   €6,000

(b)

Corporation Tax Computations

	Tree Ltd	Garden Ltd	Park Ltd	Pitch Ltd
	€	€	€	€
Case I		290,000	200,000	160,000
Less: section 420A claim		(120,000)	(40,000)	(120,000)
Revised Case I @ 12.5%	Nil	170,000	160,000	40,000
Case III @ 25%	45,000	Nil	Nil	40,000
Less: non-trade charge			(75,000)	
Total income	45,000	170,000	85,000	80,000
Corporation tax payable:				
@ 12.5%	Nil	21,250	10,625	5,000
@ 25%	11,250	Nil	Nil	10,000
Less: value-based claim under section 420B				
– Tree €90,000				
– Pitch €24,000	(11,250)			(3,000)
Final liability	Nil	21,250	10,625	12,000

Chapter 6

Question 6.1

The carry forward of trading losses incurred before a substantial change in ownership of a company is not allowed where, in a three-year period, there is:

- a change in ownership and either (b) or (c) occur;
- a major change in the nature or conduct of the company's trade; or
- the activities of the loss-making trade had become small and negligible and there is a change in ownership before any considerable revival of the trade.

A change in the machinery used might appear to be a major change. If McIlroy Ltd closes the Spanish division, this may also be seen as a major change in the services provided.

The opening of a German division might be considered to be a major change in markets and customers, and therefore the losses might be not be available to carry forward against the profits of this division.

Question 6.2

(a) Rover Ltd owns 12% of Ford Ltd, i.e. the 8% direct holding and the 4% indirect holding through Porsche Ltd. As Rover Ltd controls Porsche Ltd, the shares in Ford Ltd are treated as being owned by Rover Ltd because both companies are members of a 51% group. Therefore the sale of the shares would qualify for the participation exemption.

(b) On their own, the remaining shares in Ford Ltd would not qualify for the participation exemption. However, under the group provisions noted above, the exemption is still available for disposals in the 12 months following 1 July 2022. Therefore, any potential sale should be carried out before 1 July 2023.

Chapter 7

Question 7.1

The tax implications for Derry plc on issue of shares in exchange for undertaking would be:

- The issue of shares in Derry plc to Pat Casey in exchange for the undertaking of Casey Ltd will result in the transfer of Casey Ltd's factory and business to Derry plc. If the conditions of section 80 SDCA 1999 are satisfied, Derry plc will avoid a stamp duty liability on the purchase of the factory and business.
- As Derry plc is acquiring the assets of Casey Ltd it will avoid the risk of assuming the history of Casey Ltd as a company. Under section 615 TCA 1997, Derry plc will take on the original base cost of the assets of Casey Ltd as the exchange will be deemed to be carried out for no gain/no loss.

The tax implications for Casey Ltd and Pat Casey would be:

- CGT relief under section 615 TCA 1997 can be claimed by Casey Ltd on the transfer of its assets to Derry plc, which would result in the transfer taking place for no gain/no loss.
- If the conditions of section 587 TCA 1997 are satisfied, then Pat will avoid an upfront CGT liability on the effective disposal of his shares in Casey Ltd and the new holding in Derry plc will be treated as if it were the original holding in Casey Ltd. However, Pat must sell his shares in Derry plc to access the wealth attributable to his Casey Ltd shares.

Chapter 8

Question 8.1

(a) Henry is treated as making a disposal of his business assets for a consideration of natural love and affection. As Ronan is a connected person to Henry under section 549 TCA 1997, the disposal will come within the ambit of section 547 TCA 1997 and, therefore, market value must be used as the consideration paid for the transfer in the calculation of CGT arising on the disposal.

Gina is not a connected person under section 549. However, the disposal still falls within section 547 because the disposal is not an arm's length bargain. Therefore, the market value must be used as consideration paid for the transfer in the calculation of CGT arising on the disposal.

The CGT payable by Henry is as follows:

	€
Goodwill	
Consideration based on market value	150,000
Less: base cost at 6 April 1974	
= €10,000 indexed @ 7.528	(75,280)
Gain	74,720
Less: annual exemption	(1,270)
Taxable gain	73,450
CGT @ 33%	24,239
Premises	
Consideration based on market value	250,000
Less: base cost at 6 April 1974	
= €15,000 indexed @ 7.528	(112,920)
Taxable gain	137,080
CGT @ 33%*	45,236

*CGT at 33% applies on the basis that Henry doesn't satisfy the conditions for retirement relief or entrepreneur relief.

Under the terms of section 547, Ronan and Gina will be deemed to have a base cost each of €75,000 and €125,000 for the goodwill and premises respectively on future disposal of these assets. Ronan and Gina will also have a stamp duty liability on the market value of the goodwill of €11,250 (€150,000 × 7.5%) and on the market value of the premises of €18,750 (€250,000 × 7.5%).

(b) As Ronan and Gina are not legally married, CGT will arise on the transfer of assets as proposed. Gina will incur a CGT liability on any uplift in the value of her 50% share of the business assets between the date of disposal to Ronan and the date of the gift from Henry. Market value rules under section 547 will be applied in the calculation of her CGT as this is not an arm's length bargain. Gina can take a deduction for her share of the stamp duty paid on the gift of the business assets in the calculation of CGT on the current disposal.

Ronan may qualify for principal private residence relief on the disposal of his share of his principal private residence to Gina with the market value used in the calculation of available relief. Again, for the purposes of section 547, Ronan will be treated as having taken Gina's share of the assets for a consideration equal to the market value on the date of transfer.

Question 8.2

(a) The gift of 10% of Mrs Kenny's shares to Aisling gives rise to a charge to CAT and stamp duty.

For CAT purposes, the shares passing must be valued in accordance with section 27 CATCA 2003. This provides that where a beneficiary, together with his relatives, nominees and trustees, controls the company, the value of the shares received by the beneficiary are to be valued as a proportionate part of the value of the company as a whole. Therefore, under section 27, the value of the 10% shareholding is €200,000, which is 10% of the total shareholding held by Aisling and her parents.

For stamp duty purposes, commercial minority valuations are acceptable under section 19 SDCA 1999 as long as this is representative of the open market value. Therefore, for stamp duty purposes, the 10% shareholding can be valued at €125,000, which is the minority valuation provided by the professional valuer.

(b) Aisling, as the beneficiary, will be exposed to any surcharges for providing incorrect valuations to Revenue.

For CAT purposes, the true valuation in accordance with the rules of section 27 CATCA 2003 is €200,000, while the proposed incorrect valuation is €75,000. The market value of the asset in the return as a percentage of the correct market value is therefore 37.5%. This will give rise to a surcharge of 30% of the correct CAT liability and must be paid in addition to the actual CAT liability arising based on a valuation of €200,000.

With regards to CAT, as Aisling has filed an incorrect CAT return, she will be liable to a fixed penalty of €3,000. As an incorrect stamp duty return will also have been filed, a separate fixed penalty of €3,000 will apply. In addition to these fixed penalties, interest will apply on the underpayment at a rate of 0.0219% per day for both CAT and stamp duty. It is assumed that late filing penalties will not arise on the basis that the returns will be filed on a timely basis.

Aside from the penalties referred to above, as an accountable person Aisling will be considered to have acted carelessly or deliberately in relation to the disclosure of information relating to the facts and circumstances affecting the stamp duty liability. Consequently, a fixed penalty of €1,265 will apply. A tax-geared penalty equal to the amount by which the duty is underestimated will apply as a result of non-disclosure of the relevant facts. The quantum of the tax-geared penalty will be influenced by factors such as whether the non-disclosure was deliberate, if the taxpayer was co-operative and if there was an unprompted voluntary disclosure.

Chapter 9

Question 9.1

One option open to the Harpers is to liquidate the company and extract the funds available by way of a capital distribution. The capital distribution may qualify for retirement relief under section 598 TCA 1997. The sale of the property will trigger the following CGT liability in the company:

	€
Proceeds on sale of property	1,000,000
Base cost	(400,000)
Taxable gain	600,000
CGT @ 33%	198,000
Net proceeds after tax	802,000
Proceeds on sale of goodwill	60,000
Base cost	Nil
Taxable gain	60,000
CGT @ 33%	19,800
Net proceeds after tax	40,200

Debtors, cash and the proceeds on the sale of the stock and plant are sufficient to pay the company's creditors and liquidator's fees.

Therefore, net cash available for distribution amounts to €842,200.

A capital distribution will be treated as a CGT event under section 583 TCA 1997. As Harry and Hilary qualify for retirement relief on the disposal of their shares under section 598, by concession, they will qualify for retirement relief on taking the capital distribution provided the liquidation takes place within six months of the sale of the property and goodwill. Assuming the liquidation qualifies under the concession, Harry and Hilary can take a capital distribution of up to €750,000 each and qualify for retirement relief. Therefore, their capital distribution of €421,100 each is within the threshold and retirement relief applies.

Question 9.2

(a) Original market value of property $\times \dfrac{\text{(Amount not reinvested)}}{\text{(Sale proceeds)}} \times 90\%$

$€1,000,000 \times \dfrac{€600,000}{€1,600,000} \times 90\%$

$= €375,000 \times 90\% = €337,500$

CAT on the clawback amount of €337,500 will then be charged at 33%.

(b) The clawback will not apply in the following circumstances:

- if the property disposed is replaced by other agricultural property within one year (or within six years in the case of compulsory acquisition); or
- if the property disposed is growing crops or standing timber; or
- if the donee or successor dies before the land is sold or compulsorily acquired; or
- the property is sold or compulsorily acquired more than six years (10 years for development land) from the date of the (original) gift or inheritance, which is the date the beneficiary had become beneficially entitled in possession to the benefit.

Chapter 11

Question 11.1

CGT on transfer of property into trust
The transfer of the properties to the trust is considered a disposal for CGT purposes. The gain/loss will be calculated as the difference between the market value of the properties at the date of transfer to the trust and Alex's acquisition cost for the properties. No CGT will arise on the transfer of the cash to the trust.

Stamp duty
A stamp duty liability of 1%/2% will arise on the market value of the residential properties at the date of transfer to the trust. No stamp duty liability should arise on the transfer of the cash to the trust.

CAT/Discretionary trust
It appears that the trust is a discretionary trust as the trustees have discretion as to who will benefit from the trust and when. As no beneficiary will be beneficially entitled in possession to the properties or the cash on the transfer to the discretionary trust no CAT liability will arise.

Luke and Mark are over 21 years of age; however, as the settlor, Alex, is still alive, no discretionary trust taxes currently arise.

Taxation of income in the trust

The trust is subject to income tax at 20% on the rental profit. The same rental deductions are available to the trust under Case V as available to an individual. If the income of the trust is not distributed within 18 months of the end of the year of assessment in which it arises, a 20% surcharge is imposed.

Question 11.2

There are two options open to Jack.

1. Direct inheritance option, which would result in the following tax liability:

	€
Market value of estate	1,500,000
Less: Group A tax-free threshold	(335,000)
Taxable inheritance	1,165,000
Taxed @ 33%	384,450

Agricultural relief under section 89 CATCA 2003 is not available as Margaret fails the farmer test due to the value of her shares in her IT company.

2. Trust option – alternatively, a discretionary trust may be used to maximise agricultural relief.

In his will Jack could provide that the farm passes into a discretionary trust, with Margaret named as a beneficiary. The trustees could then wait to appoint the farm to Margaret at a time when she has sold her shares in the IT company and possibly structured her financial affairs such that she fulfils the financial requirements of the "farmers test", i.e. she could settle her share of the proceeds on a trust for her children. Margaret could actively farm the land herself or lease it to an active farmer.

An initial discretionary trust tax liability of 6% on €1.5 million on the creation of the trust would apply. However, 50% of this liability paid will be refunded if the farm is appointed to Margaret within five years from when the 6% liability is triggered. An annual discretionary trust tax of 1% of the value of the trust may also apply, but again, this can be avoided if the farm is appointed to Margaret as soon her financial affairs are arranged to show that 80% or more of her assets are agricultural assets.

Chapter 12

Question 12.1

(a) Capital Gains Tax

A gift of assets/property between connected parties is subject to CGT, calculated on the difference between the original base cost of the asset and the market value of the asset on the date of the gift. Therefore, we must consider if Mr and Mrs Edwards are within the charge to Irish CGT to establish if a CGT liability will be triggered on the proposed gift of the shares to Alastair and Josh.

Mr and Mrs Edwards are Irish tax resident since 1 January 2019 but have remained UK domiciled. Under section 29(4) TCA 1997 persons who are Irish resident (or ordinarily resident) but not Irish domiciled are chargeable to Irish CGT on:

- gains from the disposal of specified assets in the year of assessment; and
- gains remitted into the State in the year of assessment on the disposal of foreign assets.

On the basis that Brittas Ltd is a NI tax resident company and shares in that company are foreign assets, then the transfer of the shares should not give rise to an Irish CGT liability and, as there are no proceeds from which to remit the gains into the State, any gain can never be taxable in Ireland.

However, this opinion is based on the understanding that the company is managed and controlled in Belfast rather than Donegal. Management and control of the company will be dependent on demonstrating that the directors' meetings and the shareholders' meetings are all held in Belfast, and that the statutory books and company seal are held in Belfast. It must also be demonstrated that decision-making and negotiations of major contracts and company policy all take place in Belfast. If it considered that the management and control of the company takes place in Donegal, then Irish CGT must be considered and a review of the Irish/UK double taxation agreement will also be necessary.

(b) **Capital Acquisitions Tax**

As the shares in Brittas Ltd are passing by way of a gift, we must consider if Irish CAT will arise on this transaction. In general, a charge to Irish CAT will arise under section 6 CATCA 2003 if:

1 the disponer (the person making the gift) is resident or ordinarily resident in Ireland at the date of the gift; or
2 the beneficiary is resident or ordinarily resident in Ireland at the date of the gift; or
3 the gift comprises an Irish asset.

Alastair and Josh are UK tax resident individuals, so point 2. is not an issue. The shares are those of a UK registered company and, on the basis that the share register is held in Belfast, the shares will not be treated as Irish assets. Therefore, Mr and Mrs Edwards' Irish tax residency is the key issue to explore to determine if Irish CAT will apply.

Non-domiciled persons will not be considered resident for CAT purposes if the individual has not been resident in the State for five consecutive tax years preceding the year of assessment in which the gift falls. As the Edwards are tax-resident since 1 January 2019, they do not have five consecutive years of residency between 2019 and 2022. Therefore, the gift of the shares should not come within the ambit of Irish CAT as the transfer takes place before the Edwards have five consecutive years of residency in the Republic.

Stamp Duty

The tax residency of the transferor or transferee is not an issue for determining the scope of Irish stamp duty. The charge to stamp duty will be determined by whether the instrument is executed in the State or if the instrument relates to any property situated in the State or any matter or thing done or to be done in the State.

The gift of the shares will have to be legally documented in the company's share register and the share transfer document will be subject to stamp duty accordingly. However, on the basis that the shares in question are not Irish assets and the share register is held outside Ireland (i.e. in NI), then the transfer should not be liable to Irish stamp duty so long as the instrument effecting the transfer is not executed in the Republic.

Summary of Irish Capital Tax Implications of Proposed Gift

Based on the information provided, the conclusion is that the Edwards family should not have Irish CGT, CAT or stamp duty liabilities if the share transfer takes place in 2022, and the company is not managed and controlled in the Republic of Ireland and the transfer document is not executed in the Republic.

Of course, UK tax issues will arise on the proposed gift. It should be recommended that the Edwards seek professional UK tax advice.

Chapter 13

Question 13.1

As a national of Monrovia, Mr Benn will be considered to be tax-resident there under the Model Treaty test (c) if his residence cannot be determined by the tests at (a) and (b). Therefore, in order to be considered tax resident in Utopia and benefit from the lower rates of taxation, he should do as much as possible to ensure that he meets the permanent home, centre of vital interests or habitual abode tests set out at Article 4(2) (a) and (b).

Mr Benn should rent or buy a property in Utopia which can become his permanent home in that State. As he is unwilling to sell his Monrovian apartment, he should consider letting it out so that it is no longer permanently available to him. If this is not feasible, as he may need to use it to be close to the airport for his employment duties, he would then have a permanent home in both States.

If Mr Benn has a permanent home in both States, he will need to ensure that his centre of vital interests is in Utopia, in order that he can be tax resident in that State under the treaty provisions. The OECD Commentary requires regard to be had to his family and social relations, his occupations and his political, cultural or other activities. It can be difficult to demonstrate that a person's centre of vital interests has moved, so Mr Benn should do as much as possible to show that he has moved his centre of vital interests to Utopia, and not retained it in Monrovia.

Mr Benn's employment will continue to be based in Monrovia, as a pilot for the Monrovian national airline. He is single but, as a national of Monrovia, it is likely that he has family connections in that State. One way in which he could demonstrate that his centre of vital interests has moved to Utopia is to move his horses to stables near his new home in Utopia. He could then join a local show-jumping team and take part in competitions in Utopia.

If Mr Benn has a permanent home in both States and it is not possible to demonstrate in which one he has his centre of vital interests, he will be deemed to be resident in the State where he has his habitual abode. This is likely to be the State where he stays more frequently and the OECD Commentary states that regard must be had not only to stays at his permanent home in the State in question but also at any other place in the same State.

Mr Benn should aim to spend as little time as possible in Monrovia. He will clearly be required to stay there, either in his apartment or a hotel, to undertake his pilot duties. He is also likely to wish to spend some time with family and friends. As a pilot on international routes, he will also be spending significant amounts of time staying in neither State. Mr Benn should keep a careful record of the amount of time spent in each State and ensure that a clear majority of his time is spent in Utopia.

Due to the nature of Mr Benn's occupation, he may have difficulty with the centre of vital interests and habitual abode tests. Therefore, the advice should be that he not retain a permanent home in Monrovia and instead stay in hotels when access to the airport is required.

Question 13.2

Under Article 8(1) of the Ireland/UK tax treaty, HMRC can only tax the profits arising in the Northern Ireland PE. Therefore the amount subject to tax in the UK would be €350,000.

Under Irish domestic legislation, an Irish resident company is subject to tax on its profits wherever arising. Article 8(1) does not prevent Revenue from also taxing the profits which arise in the UK. Therefore, the amount subject to tax in Ireland would be €550,000.

Under Article 21, relief may be by way of a credit against the Irish tax liability for the UK tax paid on the €350,000 of profits taxed in the UK.

Chapter 14

Question 14.1

Sale of Shares to Simon Smith

The sale of shares is a VAT-exempt activity. No VAT would therefore arise on the transaction. Peter would be unable to recover any VAT incurred on costs associated with the sale. Assuming Tony is acquiring the shares to hold as an investment, he will also not be entitled to recover any VAT incurred on costs associated with the transaction.

Sale of Assets to Tony Taylor

If the company sells the assets of the business (e.g. stock, goodwill, premises, etc.), then the VAT treatment of each asset will need to be considered. However, the sale of the company's entire assets is likely to qualify for transfer of business relief. The transaction would therefore be outside the scope of Irish VAT. Even though no VAT would arise in relation to the transaction, Jones Plumbing Ltd should be entitled to recover VAT on costs associated with the transaction. Assuming Tony Taylor is acquiring the assets to operate a plumbing business, he should also be entitled to recover VAT on his costs associated with the transaction.

Question 14.2

For VAT purposes, transactions between members of a VAT group are generally ignored (i.e. VAT invoices not required, no VAT paid, etc.). However, this does not apply to the supply of immovable goods. Therefore, Kevin will need to consider whether VAT arises on the sale of the property (i.e. if it is 'new' for VAT purposes) or whether it is an exempt sale on which a joint option to tax can be made.

The key point to remember here is that VAT is not ignored in respect of transactions regarding the supply of immovable goods.

Chapter 15

Question 15.1

On the acquisition of the property in September 2009, Meta Ltd reclaimed VAT of €121,500 (i.e. €900,000 × 13.5%).

As this property is no longer considered new, i.e. it is over five years since its last development and there has been 24 months' occupation, VAT does not apply on the sale.

However, as the property is being sold in its adjustment period of 20 years, a clawback of VAT will arise under the Capital Goods Scheme if the joint option to tax is not made. The insurance company may not wish to exercise the joint option to tax as it intends to use the premises in its VAT-exempt activities. This is likely to be a matter for negotiation between the parties when the pre-contract VAT enquiries are completed by Meta Ltd and provided to the purchaser.

Question 15.2

Barry would have been entitled to recover all of the VAT on developing the units, as he was doing so with a view to their sale. The sale of the five properties would be subject to VAT. As the property is residential, Barry cannot opt to tax the lettings and will suffer an annual Capital Goods Scheme adjustment for each interval the remaining five units are let. The special relief for developers will apply whereby the VAT will be repaid over 20 years. The sale of the three properties in 2024 and the remaining two units in 2034 will all be subject to VAT. This is because the two-year and five-year rules do not apply to developers of residential properties.

Chapter 16

Question 16.1

James should make a disclosure of both sources of income to Revenue in advance of the audit. However, he cannot make a qualifying prompted disclosure because he is specifically precluded under section 1077E (15A) TCA 1997 as the disclosure relates to offshore matters.

James can co-operate fully with Revenue to mitigate his penalties. However, he may face publication on the tax defaulters list if his settlement exceeds €50,000. If James is found to have fraudulently under-declared his tax liability he could face prosecution, which could have been avoided if the option of making a qualifying disclosure was available to him.

Question 16.2

Dermot should make a prompted qualifying disclosure of the VAT irregularity and the underpayment of income tax in advance of the audit. By co-operating fully with Revenue, he should hopefully be able to mitigate his penalties and avoid prosecution.

In relation to the failure to charge VAT on sales, consideration should be given to whether it may be feasible for a "no loss of revenue" claim to be made. The likely success of this claim would be contingent upon the customers being registered for VAT and having full VAT recovery (see **Section 16.4.2** for details).

Despite not currently being in a financial position to discharge his tax liability, the 2022 Code allows for qualifying disclosures to be accepted when accompanied by part-payment and an acceptable schedule of payments. In accessing an ability to pay submission, Revenue may request:

- a signed statement of affairs reflecting the taxpayer's assets, liabilities and income (this would be as at the last day of the month preceding the date of the Revenue audit);
- a formal letter of offer;
- a copy of the latest accounts;
- a list of assets held (if assets are to be retained and not sold, an explanation as to why they will not be sold);
- an explanation as to why a loan cannot be raised;
- a calculation of projected income and expenditure; and
- a signed statement confirming that the tax default giving rise to the underpaid tax has now been rectified.